Understanding China

More information about this series at https://link.springer.com/bookseries/11772

Yan Wang

Chinese Labour Law

Theory and Practice

Springer

Yan Wang
Bondo & Toga Law Firm
Dalian Maritime University
Dalian, Liaoning, China

ISSN 2196-3134 ISSN 2196-3142 (electronic)
Understanding China
ISBN 978-981-16-8100-4 ISBN 978-981-16-8101-1 (eBook)
https://doi.org/10.1007/978-981-16-8101-1

This Springer imprint is published by the registered company Springer Nature Singapore Pte Ltd.
The registered company address is: 152 Beach Road, #21-01/04 Gateway East, Singapore 189721, Singapore

For my beloved wife, Lili Meng and my dearest son, Yuhao Wang

Acknowledgements

As the Chinese old saying goes on, only after the pregnancy of ten months, can a newborn baby be delivered. One year ago, I started to write this book: Chinese Labour Law: Theory and Practice. Obviously, writing the book seems to be more difficult. First and foremost, I am deeply grateful to Springer, the world's well-known publisher, and their excellent staff, especially Ms. Shalini Monica C, Ms. Lydia Wang and Nobuko Hirota.

Additionally, I thank my tutor, Prof. Yuzhuo Si, former president of Dalian Maritime University, for his valuable suggestions and guidance with regard to this book, especially the topic of employment of seafarers in China.

Finally, special thanks are owed to my family and friends for their patience and support. Without their generous support, this book would not be possible.

Dalian, the PRC
September 2021

Yan Wang

Contents

About the Author

Yan Wang Ph.D. in maritime law and an attorney at law, specialises in the field of civil and commercial law, labour law and maritime law. He is also a member of the China Maritime Law Association, the arbitrator of the Dalian International Arbitration Court and Changde Arbitration Commission. He has published the following books: *Shipping Financial Market Policies and Legal Practice* (Liaoning University Press, 2019), *Rotterdam Rules* (Law Press, 2014) and *The Records of the International Military Tribunal for the Far East* (Shanghai Jiaotong University Press, 2015). His articles have appeared in different Chinese legal journals.

Chapter 1
Basic Theory of Labour Law

Sources of Chinese labour law are various and complex and may be easily understood from substantive and procedural perspectives. Understanding the characteristics of Chinese labour law helps to grasp it in an overall way. It is necessary to understand the scope of Chinese labour law from its subject matter's perspective, and its subject matter should be understood in a broad sense, that is, a labour relationship and other social relationships closely related to a labour relationship. Protection of labourers' rights, respect for autonomy in management and construction of harmonious labour relationships are the three fundamental principles that should be followed in understanding and applying Chinese labour law. Chinese labour law is a comparative independent branch of legal science. With the coming into force of the Civil Code of the People's Republic of China (the Civil Code), it is more evident that Chinese labour law overlaps with Chinese civil law.

1.1 Historical Review of Labour Law

The importance of labour cannot be overemphasised. Labour is the source of all wealth and is the prime basic condition for all human existence and, in a sense, labour created man himself. However, it is generally thought that labour and labour law evolved in a different way. Regardless of the origin of labour law, which may be controversial, it is safe to say that labour law developed rapidly with industrial revolutions.

Y. Wang, *Chinese Labour Law*, Understanding China,
https://doi.org/10.1007/978-981-16-8101-1_1

1.1.1 Origin and Development: From the Worldwide Perspective

The origins of labour law can be traced back to the remote past and the most varied parts of the world. At least in Asia, the provisions related to labour can be seen in the Code of Hammurabi, which is considered to be the earliest uniform code of written laws. The Code of Hammurabi established the wages of labourers, that is, six gur of grain per year for a boatman, 8 gur of grain per year for a field-labourer, 6 gur of grain per year for a herdsman, 6 se of sliver per day for a labourer from the beginning of the year to the fifth month and 5 se of silver per day from the sixth month to the end of the year. However, the provisions related to labour in the Code of Hammurabi are few, and they cannot be called labour law, as is known today. The fast development of productive forces emancipated by industrial revolutions from the eighteenth century onward gave rise to labour law. The Factory Act 1802 in the United Kingdom is the first modern labour law. German took the lead in enacting work-related laws in 1884. After the October Revolution of 1917, Bolshevik Russia adopted the first decree of labour and the labourers worked 8 h per day and were entitled to pensions. In 1918, under the leadership of Lenin, the Labour Code was enacted, which is the first socialist labour law and has a great influence on Chinese labour legislation.

1.1.2 Origin and Development: From the Chinese Perspective

In China, labour law can be traced back to the Dynasty of Chou, and according to the Chou Rituals, the official in charge of women needleworkers distributed the materials to women in the palace to weave and appraised their performance. According to the Bamboo Slips of the Dynasty of Qin, which were unearthed in Shuihudi in December 1975, legal provisions existed regarding the management of the handicraft industry and production quotas. In fact, similar provisions are scattered in the legal documents of later dynasties. However, modern labour legislation was not made in China until the beginning of the twentieth century.

1.1.2.1 The Republic of China (1912–1949)

During the Beiyang Warlord Period, the Ministry of Agriculture and Commerce of the Beiyang Government promulgated the Provisional Rules on Factories, which provided for the minimum age for employment, working hours and rest hours, limits on child labourers and women labourers, wages and benefits. In 1922, the Nineteen Guidelines of Labour Law were passed by the Secretary Department of China Labour Union, which was the headquarters of the worker movement led by the Chinese Communist Party, and they set forth the right to assembly, association and strike, the eight-hour workday, the minimum wage, employment insurance and protection of women and children labourers. In 1929, Guomingdang, the Nationalist Party of China promulgated the Trade Union Act. In 1931, the Nanjing Government promulgated the Factory Act, which provided for women and child labour, working hours, rest and holidays, wages, the termination of employment contracts, labourers' benefits, factory security and sanitary equipment, allowances and compensation, and labourers' meetings and apprenticeships. In the same year, the Labour Act was passed by the Chinese Soviet Republic Government, which contained this chapter (General Provisions), Chap. 2 (Procedures of Employment), Chap. 3 (Collective Contract and Employment Contract), Chap. 4 (Working Hours), Chap. 5 (Rest), Chap. 6 (Wages), Chap. 7 (Women, Young and Children Labourers), Chap. 8 (Labour Protection), Chap. 9 (China Federation of Labour Unions), Chap. 10 (Social insurance), Chap. 11 (Labour Disputes) and Chap. 12 (Supplementary Provisions).

Unfortunately, the historical circumstances at that time did not allow such labour legislation to come into play. However, such legislation influenced the development of labour law after the foundation of the People's Republic of China.

1.1.2.2 The People's Republic of China

After the foundation of the People's Republic of China, a series of labour laws and regulations were promulgated. In June 1950, the Central People's Government made the Trade Union Act of the People's Republic of China, and in the same year, the Ministry of Labour promulgated the Regulations on Labour Dispute Solution Proceedings. The Government Administration Council promulgated the Regulations of Employment Insurance of the People's Republic of China in February 1951 and the Resolutions of Employment in August 1952. In 1957, the Labour Law of the People's Republic of China was ready to be drafted. However, the work was interrupted by the Anti-rightist Movement, which lasted from approximately 1957–1959 and consisted of campaigns to crack down the alleged rightists and the Great Leap Forward, which was a five-year plan of forced agricultural collectivisation and rural industrialisation. During the Cultural Revolution, legal nihilism, a trend that denied the social value of law, prevailed, which made it impossible to put the labour law into practice. The rule of law in China encountered a dark period.

From 1977 to 1993, the legal order gradually returned to normal. However, the labour laws and regulations were characteristic of the planned economy. The outdated labour laws and regulations were not adapted to the emerging market economy.

Since 2000, new labour laws, regulations and related juridical interpretations have been springing up like mushrooms. The Labour Law of the People's Republic of China (The Labour Law of 2018) was promulgated in 1994 and revised in August 2009 and December 2018. The Labour Law of 2018 contains 13 chapters: general provisions, employment promotion, labour contract and collective contract, working hours and rest and holidays, wages, labour security and health, special protection of women labourers and young labourers, vocational training, social insurance and benefits, labour disputes, supervision and inspection, legal liabilities and supplementary provisions. The Ministry of Labour and Social Security released the Notice of Establishment of Labour Relationships on 25 May 2005, which is very important for identification of the establishment of labour relationships. In June 2007, the Labour Contract Law of the People's Republic of China (The Labour Contract Law of 2012) was promulgated and revised in December 2012 to improve the labour contract system, and the Regulations on the Implementation of the Labour Contract Law was adopted in September 2008. To regulate the employment models, the Provisional Measures of Labour Dispatch were adopted by the Ministry of Human Resources and Social Security of the People's Republic of China in 2013. To solve the problems with the application of labour laws and regulations, Judicial Interpretations (No. 1) by the Supreme People's Court of Issues Concerning the Application of Law in Hearing the Cases of Labour Disputes were passed by the Supreme People's Court of the PRC, which entered into force as of 1 January 2021, which consolidated and replaced the Interpretations (No. 1) by the Supreme People's Court of Issues Concerning the Application of Law in Hearing the Cases of Labour Disputes released in 2001, the Interpretations (No. 2) by the Supreme People's Court of Issues Concerning the Application of Law in Hearing the Cases of Labour Disputes released in 2006, the Interpretations (No. 3) by the Supreme People's Court of Issues Concerning the Application of Law in Hearing the Cases of Labour Disputes released in 2010 and the Interpretations (No. 4) by the Supreme People's Court of Issues Concerning the Application of Law in Hearing the Cases of Labour Disputes released in 2012.

1.2 Sources of Chinese Labour Law

The meanings of sources of law may vary in different contexts. In accordance with Black's Law Dictionary, source of law, also termed *fons juris*, means something (such as a constitution, treaty, statute, or custom) that provides authority for legislation and for judicial decisions. In the context of legal research, the term "sources of law" can refer to three different concepts that should be distinguished. First, sources of law can refer to the origins of legal concepts and ideas. Second, sources of law can refer to governmental institutions that formulate legal rules. Three sources of law can refer to the published manifestations of the law.[1]

[1] Garner (2014, p. 1610).

1.2.1 Substantive Labour Law

1.2.1.1 The Constitution of the People's Republic of China

The Constitution of the People's Republic of China (The Constitution) plays a fundamental role in the rule of law. The Constitution was promulgated on 4 December 1982 and was revised on 12 April 1988, 29 March 1993, 15 March 1999, 14 March 2004 and 11 March 2018. The Constitution lays down the fundamental principles of the Labour Law of 2018. Article 14 of the Constitution provides that the State continuously raises labour productivity, improves economic results and develops productive forces by enhancing the enthusiasm of the working people, raising the level of their technical skill, disseminating advanced science and technology, improving the systems of economic administration and enterprise operation and management, instituting the socialist system of responsibility in various forms and improving the organisation of work and that the State establishes and improves the social security corresponding to economic development. Article 42 provides that citizens of the PRC have the right as well as the duty to work. Article 43 provides that labourers have the right to rest. Article 48 formulates the principle of equal pay for equal work between men and women.

1.2.1.2 Laws

In accordance with the Legislation Law of 2015, laws are the body of legal rules enacted by the National People's Congress and the Standing Committee of the National People's Congress, which exercise legislative power. The labour-related laws can be divided into three categories. The basic law, the first category, is the Labour Law of 2018, which was formulated in 1994 and revised in 2018. The second category is called the act, which centers on a special topic, such as the Trade Union Law, the Law of Promotion of Employment, the Labour Contract Law of 2012 and the Safety Production Law. The third category is other laws embodying labour-related rules. For example, the Vocational Education Law provides that an enterprise shall bear the expenses of vocation education for its labourers or the applicants to be employed.

It should be noted that the judicial interpretations issued by the Supreme People's Court are not the sources of law, although they play a very important role in juridical practice.

1.2.1.3 Administrative Regulations

Article 65 of the Legislation Law of 2015 provides that with a view to the application of laws, the State Council promulgates administrative regulations in accordance with the Constitution and the laws. The labour-related regulations include the Regulations on the Implementation of the Labour Contract Law, the Regulations on Work-related Injury Insurance and the Regulations on Women Labourer Protection.

1.2.1.4 Local Laws

In accordance with the Legislation Law of 2015, local laws, or provincial laws, are regional laws promulgated by the People's Congress or its Standing Committee in provinces, autonomous regions and province-level municipalities. For example, the Regulations on Liaoning Province Worker Labour Rights and Benefits Protection were promulgated by the second conference of the Standing Committee of the 12th People's Congress of Liaoning Province. The local laws are made to respond to the situations in every province.

1.2.1.5 Ministerial Regulations

In accordance with the Legislation Law of 2015, the ministerial regulations are made by the ministries of the State Council and other organs directly under the State Council. For example, the Measures on Online Recruitment Service Administration were enacted by the Ministry of Human Resources and Social Security of the PRC on 18 December 2020.

1.2.1.6 Local Regulations

In accordance with the Legislation Law of 2015, local regulations are promulgated by local governments at the levels of provinces, autonomous regions, cities where provincial capitals are located, and larger cities. For example, the Provisional Regulations on Liaoning Wage Payment were promulgated by the government of Liaoning Province on 25 August 2006.

1.2.1.7 International Legal Instruments

Apart from the reservations, the international conventions ratified by China are also the sources of Chinese labour laws. To date, 19 international labour-related conventions have been ratified. For example, the Maritime Labour Convention, 2006, was ratified by China in 2015. Most conventions cannot apply directly in China. They always come into play by means of Chinese legislation.

1.2.2 Procedural Labour Law

1.2.2.1 The Labour Dispute Mediation and Arbitration Law

The Labour Dispute Mediation and Arbitration Law was promulgated on December 29, 2007 and contains General Provisions (this chapter), Mediation (Chap. 2), Arbitration (Chap. 3) and Supplementary Provisions (Chap. 4). The general provisions are about the scope of labour application and the fundamental principles to cope with labour disputes. Mediation is not compulsory, but once the mediation agreement is concluded, it is enforceable. Labour arbitration is different from commercial arbitration in that (1) labour arbitration is compulsory, (2) the time limit of labour arbitration is one year, (3) labour arbitration is free of charge, and (4) some labour arbitral awards are not final and if the parties are not satisfied with the arbitral awards, they can lodge a civil lawsuit to settle the labour disputes.

1.2.2.2 The Regulations on Labour Security Supervision and Inspection

The Regulations on Labour Security Supervision and Inspection were promulgated by the State Council in 2004. Article 11 provides items that are subject to labour security supervision and inspection. Such items are labour contracts, working hours and rest, social insurance and so on. Chapter 3 shows how labour security supervision and inspection work. An appeal to labour security supervision and inspection is another expedited channel for labour protection.

1.2.2.3 The Civil Procedure Law

Any party who is not satisfied with the labour arbitral award may lodge a civil suit in court. On the occasion, the Civil Procedure Law comes into play. Civil litigation is totally different from labour arbitration. The Civil Procedure Law provides for jurisdiction, trial organisations, challenges, evidence, mediation, common proceedings of first instance, summary proceedings, common proceedings of second instance, hearing supervision, and enforcement proceedings.

1.3 Concept and Characteristics of Labour Law

1.3.1 Concept of Labour Law

Law is one of social tools to regulate social relationships. Literally, labour law is the law related to labour. Here, labour can be understood as a modifier, meaning labour relationships. According to Black's Law of Dictionary, labour law means the field of law governing the relationship between employers and employees, esp. law governing the dealings of employers and the unions that represent employees, also termed employment law or industrial law.[2] In China, Shi Shangkuan, a famous jurist in China, viewed labour law as the law that was related to labour and, to be specific, the whole body of legal system governing the labour relationships and its correlated relationships.[3] Professor Huang Qinyue defined labour law as the whole body of laws that are directly or indirectly related to labour relationships, and he further believed that labour law was composed of employment law (individual labour relationships), labour relations law (collective labour relationships), labourer social security and welfare law, labour market law and working environment rights law.[4] It is generally accepted that labour law means a branch of the legal system, the body of legal norms regulating the labour relationship and other social relationships that are closely related to the labour relationship. This view is often taken in judicial decisions in China. For example, in the Civil Decision of Second Instance of the Case of Labour Contract between Shanghai Jahwa United Co., Ltd. and Wang Zhuo (2015 Hu SIC CTD CF 747), the Second Intermediate People's Court of Shanghai held that labour law governed the social relationship in the course of employment (the labour relationship) and other social relationships that were closely related to the labour relationship, such as social insurance, trade unions, labour disputes, labour supervision and enforcement and labour law was the unification of labourer protection and labour supervision, mixing public law and private law and the right to terminate a labour contract was restricted by way of government interference.

1.3.2 Characteristics of Labour Law

1.3.2.1 Mixture of Public Law and Private Law

Traditionally, Roman jurists divided law into "*jus publicum*" (public law) and "*jus privatum*" (private law). The complexity of social relationships has made the dichotomy between public and private law outdated. Due to the privatisation of public law and the publicisation of private law, it is proper to view labour law as the mixture of public law and private law, also called social law.

In the Civil Decision of Second Instance of the Case of Labour Dispute between China Rise Financial Holding and Zhang Libu (2020 Jing 03 CF 11108), to distinguish between a labour relationship and a labour service relationship, the Third Intermediate People's Court of Beijing held that labour law was characteristic of social law, mixing the nature of public law and private law, and unlike in contract

[2] Garner (2014, p. 1005).

[3] Shangkuan (1978).

[4] Yueqin (2003).

law and other private laws, the rights and obligations under labour law could not be freely stipulated by the parties to a labour relationship and were compulsory in the sense of social security.

1.3.2.2 Law of Labourers' Rights Protection

One of the legislative aims of the Labour Law of 2018, the mainstay of the field of labour law, is to protect the labourers' legitimate rights and interests. Article 3 of the Labour Law of 2018 provides that labourers shall have equal right to employment and choice of occupation, the right to labour remuneration, rest and vacations, protection of occupational safety and health, training in vocational skills, social insurance and welfare, and submission of labour disputes for settlement and other rights related to labour stipulated by law. As an important part of labour law, the Regulations of Social insurance are typical of the law of rights protection.

In the Administration Decision of Retrial of Administration Confirmation of Labour and Social Security between Wei Limin and Chongqing Nanan District Human Resources and Social Security (2020 Yu AR 1), the Higher Supreme People's Court of Chongqing held that the important aim of labour legislation was to protect the labourers' legitimate rights and interests, the legislative intent of identification of work-related injuries was to protect the rights to medical treatment, economic compensation and vocational rehabilitation in case that an innocent labourer sustained work-related injuries or occupational diseases and labourers' rights protection always took priority. In addition, various forms of civil, administrative and criminal liabilities are prescribed by labour law to protect the rights of labourers.

1.3.2.3 Law of Labour Management

From a micro perspective, labourers are the primary source of productivity, and enterprises organises labourers to work to obtain profits. Labour law provides helpful guidance for enterprises. It covers the whole lifespan of a labour relationship, including the conclusion, performance, modification, revocation and termination of labour contracts. Enterprises shall abide by the provisions of working hours, rest and vocations, wages, labour security and health, and social insurance and keep a balance between labourers' rights protection and self-management of labourers. From a macro perspective, labour law is a tool by which the state can stabilise the labour relationships, regulate the laboour market, and advance economic development and social progress. The Labour Law of 2018, the Social Insurance Law, and the Regulations on Labour Security Supervision empower competent organs to directly or indirectly put state policies into practice and harmonise labour relations.

1.4 Subject Matter of Labour Law

In a narrow sense, the subject matter of labour law is a labour relationship and, in a broad sense, is a labour relationship and other social relationships closely related to a labour relationship. The latter is prevailing.

1.4.1 Labour Relationships

In China, it is generally accepted that the labour (legal) relationship means the reciprocal rights and obligations created between employing units and labourers. The term "labour relationship" is the cornerstone of labour law, and it is relevant to the scope of labour law. To demarcate the boundary of the labour relationship, employing units and labourers should be defined first, which may be found in the Labour Law of 2018 and the Labour Contract Law of 2012. However, it is not easy to exactly tell the labour relationship from the relationship of labour services. In practice, the main differences between the labour relationship and the relationship of labour services are as follows: (1) the labour relationship arises between a legal person or an organisation (collectively referred to as an employing unit) and an individual labourer; in contrast, the relationship of labour services may arise between legal persons or organisations, or between a legal person or organisations and an individual person or between individual persons. (2) There is a mixture of property relationships and personal relationships in the labour relationship, and a labourer provides labour for an employing unit and is personally, economically and organisationally subordinated to his employing unit. In contrast, the parties in the relationship of labour services are on an equal footing. (3) Regarding the labour relationship, a labourer is entitled to wages, social insurance and benefits; however, the parties in the relationship of labour services are entitled only to remuneration. (4) Wages are paid on the basis of labour and performance and in a continuous and regular way, while remuneration for the relationship of labour services is paid on the basis of market principles, and the payment is often one off. (5) Obligations in the labour relationships, such as payment of social insurance, minimum wage standards, and working hours, are often compulsory. However, the obligations in the relationship of labour services may be freely stipulated between the parties. (6) The labour relationship is mainly governed by labour law, and the relationship of labour services is governed by civil law.

The above view is held by the majority of the courts in China, which may be found in the Civil Decision of Second Instance of the Case of Labour Dispute between Beijing Yesway Connect Service Co., Ltd. and Xu Lizhen (2019 Jing 01 CF 4942) made by the First Intermediate People's Court of Beijing, the Civil Decision of Second Instance of the Case of Labour Dispute between Shenzhen Runtong Industrial Development Co., Ltd. and Hong Zhaoji (2019 Yue 03 CF 31) made by the Intermediate People's Court of Shenzhen and the Civil Decision of Second Instance of the Case of Labour Dispute between Ningbo Fenghua Xuedoushan Water Co., Ltd. and Tang Liping (2020 Zhe 02 CF 5167) made by the Intermediate People's Court of Ningbo.

1.4.2 Other Social Relationships Closely Related to a Labour Relationship

1.4.2.1 Labour Administration Relationships

A labour administration relationship arises between labour administration organs and employing units, labourers, and labour service agencies. Labour administration organs include labour administration departments at the national and local levels, that is, the Ministry of Human Resources and Social Security of the PRC, the Department of Human Resources and Social Security at the provincial level, and the Bureau of Human Resources and Social Security at the municipal, county, or district levels. The Ministry of Human Resources and Social Security of the PRC is responsible for national labour policy standards and regulations and managing the national social security system and is thus responsible for labour force management, labour relations and social insurance management.

1.4.2.2 Labour Service Relationships

A labour service relationship arises between a labour service agency and an employing unit or a labourer. The labour service agencies are subject to the Regulations on Employment Services and Employment Administration, promulgated by the Ministry of Labour on 5 May 2007 and recently revised on 14 December 2018. The labour service agencies include public employment service agencies sponsored by labour security administration departments and employment intermediaries approved by labour security administration departments. A labourer may be employed via public employment service agencies or employment intermediaries or by directly contacting potential employing units. An employing unit may directly recruit labourers or entrust public employment service agencies or employment intermediaries to recruit labourers. Public employment service agencies shall provide the following services for labourers for free: (1) employment policy and law consulting, (2) release of job supply and demand information, (3) employment guidance, (4) employment aid, (5) employment and unemployment registration, and (6) other public employment services.[5] Public employment service agencies shall provide the following services for employing units: (1) guidance services for recruitment, (2) recruitment agency, (3) transregional recruitment services, (4) enterprise human

---

[5] The Regulations on Employment Services and Employment Administration, Article 25.

resources management and consultation, and (5) agency services for labour security.[6] Employment intermediaries may (1) match labourers with employing units, (2) recommend labourers to employing units and households, (3) guide employment and provide human resources management and consultation services, (4) collect and release job supply and demand information, and (5) organise job fairs.[7] For online recruitment, the Regulations on Online Recruitment Service Administration will apply, which was promulgated by the Ministry of Human Resources and Social Security and entered into force as of 1 March 2021. In addition, the Regulations on Outbound Labour Service Cooperation Administration, promogulated by the State Council on 16 May 2012, applies to overseas employment.

1.4.2.3 Labour Group Relationships

A trade union is an organised group of labourers. In accordance with the Trade Union Law, promulgated on 3 March 1992 and revised on 27 August 2009, trade unions are mass organisations of the working class formed by labourers and staff members on a voluntary basis.[8] The basic duties and functions of trade unions are to safeguard the legitimate rights and interests of labourers and staff members. While protecting the overall interests of the entire Chinese people, trade unions shall represent and safeguard the legitimate rights and interests of labourers and staff members. Trade unions shall coordinate labour relations and safeguard the rights and interests enjoyed in work by the labourers and staff members of enterprises through consultation at an equal footing and the collective contract system. Trade unions shall, in accordance with the provisions of laws and through the congresses of the labourers and staff members or other forms, organise the labourers and staff members to participate in democratic decision-making and management of and democratic supervision over their own employing units.[9] In practice, the role of the trade union is often underappreciated.

1.4.2.4 Labour Dispute Settlement Relationships

Labour dispute settlement relationships arise between labour settlement organs and employing units, and labourers. Labour settlement organs include labour mediation organs, labour arbitration organs and courts. Accordingly, labour dispute settlement relationships are governed by the Labour Dispute Mediation and Arbitration Law and the Civil Procedure Law.

---

[6] The Regulations on Employment Services and Employment Administration, Article 26.

[7] The Regulations on Employment Services and Employment Administration, Article 52.

[8] The Trade Union Law, Article 2.

[9] The Trade Union Law, Article 6.

1.5 Fundamental Principles of Labour Law

The fundamental principles are understood as basic norms from which other legal norms are derived. They serve as the guidelines of the law and play an important role in lawmaking, legal interpretation and the application of law. Regarding labour law, the fundamental principles are as follows.

1.5.1 Protection of Labourers' Rights

The labourers' rights are the cornerstone of labour law. From the point of view of the legal development, the reason that the branch of labour law took shape is that labourers could not be sufficiently protected by traditional civil law. In the context of the Labour Law of 2018, labourers have a right to equal employment, occupational choice, remuneration, labour security and protection, vocational training, social insurance and welfare and legal remedies.[10] A labourer may have a unilateral right to terminate the labour contract if he gives a 30-day notice or, in the probation period, a 3-day notice.[11] If a labourer is not paid in full or in time, he may terminate the labour contract and be entitled to economic compensation.[12] Accordingly, the protection of labourers' rights shall be taken into consideration when the employing unit's rules are made.

1.5.2 Respect for Autonomy in Management

It is generally thought that the Labour Law of 2018 is slanted in favor of labourers, which is always subject to criticism. However, this does not mean that there is no room for autonomy in management in the Labour Law of 2018. Autonomy in management is a key driver of the development of companies. Without autonomy in management, companies would have no economic vitality, and the protection of the labourers' rights would end in empty talk. Unfortunately, the meaning of autonomy in management is ambiguous. In spite of this, companies are free to determine the form of wage distribution and the wage level on the basis of the characteristics of operation and economic results, which is provided by Article 47 of the Labour Law.

The payment of the year-end bonus is a case in point. Employing units may, at their discretion, determine the amount of the year-end bonus and the conditions of the payment of the year-end bonus. In the Civil Decision of Hearing Supervision of the Case of Recovery of Labour Remuneration between Zhou Jianguo and Shanghai Branch, Du Pont China Holding Co., Ltd. (2019 Hu CA 1837), the Higher People's

[10] The Labour Law, Article 3.

[11] The Labour Law, Article 31.

[12] The Labour Law, Article 32.

Court of Shanghai held (1) that the year-end bonus was different from the wages a labourer was paid in exchange for his or her normal labour; (2) that the year-end bonus, in relation to the wages, was specific, motivating, differential and unstable; and (3) that there were no specific stipulations between the labourer and the employing unit and the employing unit had no rules related to the payment of the year-end bonus, the payment of year-end bonus fell into the scope of the autonomy in management. Similarly, in the Civil Decision of Retrial Review and Hearing Supervision of the Case of Labour Dispute between Wang Wei and Beijing Qiang Hua Printing House (2018 Jing CA 1758), the Higher People's Court of Beijing held that an employing unit might, at its discretion, pay the year-end bonus and the rule that the labourer whose attendance rate was lower than 75% shall not be entitled to the year-end bonus was legal.

1.5.3 Construction of Harmonious Labour Relationships

More often, it is not easy to strike the balance between the protection of labourers' rights and respect for autonomy in management. If too much emphasis is placed on the protection of labourers' rights, employing units will lack initiative and vice versa. On 21 March 2015, the Opinions of the CPC Central Committee and the State Council concerning Construction of Harmonious Labour Relationships were issued. Labour arbitration serves as the tool for the construction of harmonious labour relationships, which can prevent parties in dispute from resorting to fierce litigation in court. Domestic management is also very important, by which labourers have the right to know, participate, express and supervise.

To construct harmonious labour relationships, an employing unit should manage in a fair and proper way. In the Civil Decision of the Second Instance of the Case of Labour Contract between Shanghai Ansheng Property Management Co., Ltd. and Wang Wenzheng (2020 Hu 02 CF 10692), the Second Intermediate People's Court of Shanghai held that (1) an employing unit and a labourer should perform the labour contract fully, sufficiently and properly; (2) a labourer shall observe the rules of an employing unit; and (3) an employing unit shall exercise its management right in good faith and in a tolerate and fair way. In this case, on the night of 5 January 2020, Wang Wenzheng asked for leave because he was told that his father was critically ill, but Shanghai Ansheng Property Management Co. refused. When Wang Wenzheng returned to the company, he was told that his father passed away and decided to go home to deal with the funeral rites. Finally, the company fired him on the grounds that he was absent from work for three days. The Second Intermediate People's Court of Shanghai affirmed the Civil Decision of First Instance that the termination of the labour contract was illegal. To fill in the legal gaps of labour law and reduce its rigidity, the doctrine of public order and good morals are often applied to stabilise labour relationships.

1.6 Legal Status of Labour Law

On the one hand, it is generally thought that labour law is comparatively independent. On the other hand, it is true that labour law interacts with other branches of laws. Evidence of the interaction between labour law and other branches of laws may be seen in the following discussion.

1.6.1 Labour Law and the Constitution

The Constitution was first applied in the case of Qi Yuling v Chen Xiaoqi, which was considered to be the landmark case of China's judicialisation of the Constitution. However, the Judicial Interpretations of the Supreme People's Court concerning whether Civil Liability is applied to Constitutional Right to Education was repealed in 2008. Since then, China's judicialisation of the Constitution has been banned in practice. The reality is that some constitutional rights are often discussed in the civil decisions of labour disputes. The boundaries of freedom of speech were drawn in the Civil Decision of Second Instance of the Case of Labour Dispute between Shen Yuan and Airbus (China) Enterprise Management and Services Co., Ltd. (2019 Jing 03 CF 12053). The court of first instance held: (1) that a labourer had the freedom of speech, which should be protected in the field of employment; and (2) that the freedom of speech should be subject to the general principles of labour relationships and a labourer should not infringe on others' right to reputation and trade secrets. In this case, the reputation of Airbus (China) Enterprise Management and Services Co., Ltd. was damaged by her wordings of *Sting Operation, Cooking up Charges, Bullying,* and *Merciless Exploitation.* A similar view was held by the Intermediate People's Court in the Civil Decision of Second Instance of the Case of Reputation between Tong Jialuo and Tao Bao (China) Soft Co., Ltd. (2017 Yue 03 CF 17033). Freedom and privacy of correspondence were discussed in the Civil Decision of Second Instance of the Case of Labour Dispute between LGESY Electronic Shenyang Co., Ltd. and Gao Fengyun (2016 Liao 01 CF 1192). In this case, Gao Yanfeng defended that (1) according to Article 40 of the Constitution, the freedom of and privacy of correspondence of citizens of the People's Republic of China were protected and the nondisclosure agreement in dispute violated her freedom and privacy of correspondence and (2) it was not constitutional that LGESY Electronic Shenyang Co., Ltd. collected her email without her consent. However, the court held that Gao Yan did infringe upon LGESY's right to trade secrets. In addition, it should be noted that in the civil proceedings of labour disputes, the application to a court for collecting WeChat chat logs will be denied, which was confirmed in the Civil Decision of Second Instance of the Case of Labour Contract between Deli Technology (Zhuhai) Co., Ltd. and Zhou Sufang (2018 Yue 04 CF 3153) on the grounds that no organisation or individual may, on any grounds, infringe upon the freedom and privacy of citizens' correspondence except in cases where to meet the needs of state security or of investigation into criminal offences, public security or procuratorial organs are permitted to censor correspondence in accordance with procedures prescribed by law. For the right to strike, the current laws in China remain silent, and strikes are prohibited in practice despite China ratifying the International Covenant on Economic, Social and Cultural Rights in 2001, of which Subparagraph d of Paragraph 1 of Article 8 provides that the State Parties to the present Covenant undertake to ensure the right to strike, provided that it is exercised in conformity with the laws of the particular country. However, it doesn't mean that there are no strikes. Strikes are often considered to be absenteeism regardless of the nature of the cause of strikes. This view is seen in the Civil Decision of First Instance of the Case of Labour Dispute between Zhang Hui and Hainan Shengsheng Department Store (2013 Long CF 1394) and the Civil Decision of Second Instance of the Case of Labour Contract between Zhang Baoyu and Shanghai Anji Xunda Transportation Co., Ltd. (2018 Hu 02 CF 4635).

1.6.2 Labour Law and Civil Law

The Labour Law of 2018 is closely connected with the Civil Code. Paragraph 2 of Article 464 of the Civil Code provides that an agreement on establishing a marriage, adoption, guardianship, or similar personal relationships shall be governed by the provisions of laws providing for such personal relationships; in the absence of such provisions, the provisions of this Book (Book Three Contracts) may be applied mutatis mutandis according to the nature of such agreements. To some degree, labour contracts are in the nature of personal relationships, which makes it possible for labour relationships to be subject to the Civil Code. For example, the principle of public order and good morals is provided by Article 8 of the Civil Code, on which the Labour Law remains silent. However, it is common that the principle of public order and good morals is quoted in the decisions of labour disputes. In the Civil Decision of First Instance of the Case of Labour Dispute between Zhao Lin and CITIC Securities (2018 Jing 0105 CF 59772), Zhao Lin had a love affair with a woman and had an illegitimate child, which violated the rules of CITIC Securities, and the court of first instance held that it was legal for CITIC Securities to dismiss Zhao Lin according to the principle of public order and good morals.

Storing pornographic videos and pictures in the office computer may also be a convenient excuse for terminating labour contracts. In the Civil Decision of Second Instance of the Case of Labour Contract between Huang Liming and Shanghai R&D Branch, Trane Air Conditioning System (China) Co., Ltd. (2020 Hu 01 CF 5545), the First Intermediate People's Court of Shanghai held that Huang's storing many pornographic videos and pictures in his office computer went against the rules of Trane as well as the principle of public order and good morals and that it was legal for Trane to terminate the labour contract with Huang Liming.

Taking the unilateral termination of labour contracts as another example, when resignation takes effect is not provided in labour law, but this problem can be solved by resorting to the Civil Code. Article 134 of the Civil Code provides that a civil juristic act may be accomplished through unanimous consent of two or more parties, or through one party's unilateral expression of intent. In the Civil Decision of Second Instance of the Case of Labour Contract between Suzhou Branch Standard Chartered China, Fang Zhen and Suzhou New District Branch Standard Chartered China(2020 Su 05 CF 6560), the Intermediate People's Court of Suzhou held: (1) that a person performing a civil juristic act may withdraw an expression of intent and the notice of withdrawal of the expression of intend shall reach the counterparty prior to or at the same time with the counterparty's receipt of the expression of intent; (2)that Fang Zhen sent the resigning report via email on 14 January 2019 and his intent of resignation reached his employing unit; (3) that there was no point recalling his email dated 14 January 2019. A similar view is also seen in the Civil Decision of Second Instance of the Case of Labour Dispute between Beijing Taichengxin Measurement and Control Tech Co., Ltd. and Luo Qiyu (2020 Jing 02 CF 2871), where two notices of termination were sent by Beijing Taichengxin Measurement and Control Tech Co., Ltd. and the Second Intermediate People's Court of Beijing held that the first notice was given to show its intent.

It is noteworthy that the Personal Information Protection Law was passed on 20 August 2021, which will make the interplay between labour law and the Civil Code much closer and more frequent. Article 13 of the Personal Information Protection Law provides the principle of necessity for employing units. Accordingly, employing units should make its rules to handle the personal information of labourers.

1.6.3 Labour Law and Company Law

Corporate organisation and behaviors are governed by company law. Human resource management and democratic management are important aspects of corporate governance. Human resource management includes recruitment, remuneration, rewards and disciplinary sanctions, performance assessment, termination of labour contracts and other things. The status of shareholders, directors, supervisors, the CEO and the legal representative may be controversial in labour law. The labour relationship between top management and an employing unit will be discussed later. Democratic management is related to labourers' congress, labourer representative congress and trade unions. Additionally, Article 4 of the Labour Contract Law of 2012 provides the requirements of labourer representative congress and equal consultation with the trade union or labourer representatives where the corporate rules concerning remuneration, working hours, labour discipline, social insurance and welfare are made.

If the democratic requirements are not met, such rules cannot be used as the tool of human resource management. However, the requirements may vary from one province to another. The courts in Zhejiang Province, Shandong Province, Hebei Province, Hunan Province and Anhui Province stick to the view that the courts may invoke corporate rules that do not meet domestic requirements, provided that such rules comply with laws and regulations and are not unreasonable, while most courts hold the opposite view that domestic requirements are necessary for corporate rules to be valid.

Another problem often arises from the interplay between labour law and company law. Whether the dispute of equity incentives is in the nature of labour disputes remains controversial. In the Civil Decision of Second Instance of the Case of Labour Dispute between Liang Ping and Tianjin Bonna-Agela Technology Co. Ltd. (2021 Jing 03 CF 7026), the Third Intermediate People's Court of Beijing held: (1) that generally the nature of equity incentives should be identified; (2) that the dispute of virtual equities, such as stock appreciation rights and dividend rights was in the nature of labour disputes; and (3) that the dispute of actual equities, such as restricted equities incentive was in the nature of civil disputes.

References

Garner, B. A. (2014). Source of law. In *Black's Law Dictionary* (10th ed., p. 1610). MN: Thomson Reuters.

Shangkuan, S. (1978). *Fundamental Theory of Labour Law*. Chinese Taipei: Zheng Da Publishing House [in Chinese].

Yueqin, H. (2003). *New Essays on Labour Law*. Beijing: China University of Political Science and Law Press [in Chinese].

Chapter 2
Labour Relationships

The concept of a labour relationship is the cornerstone of labour law, which defines the scope of application of labour law. The labour legal relationship is the mixture of equality and subordination and mandatoriness and autonomy and keeping it in mind may help to understand the reasoning behind the civil decisions involving labour disputes. The elements of a labour legal relationship include subjects, the subject matter and contents, that is, the rights and obligations of both parties. Identifying a labour relationship is the starting point of solving a labour dispute, and the establishment of a labour relationship should be judged in accordance with the Notice of Establishment of Labour Relationships, although it may seem insufficient today. Labour relationships in the context of the gig economy are more complex, which poses some challenges to the traditional approach to identifying the establishment of a labour relationship.

2.1 Overview of Labour Relationships

2.1.1 Concept of Labour Relationships

From the perspective of translation, *劳动关系* (Chinese pinyin: lao dong guan xi) is called labour relations or relationships, both of which can be interchangeable in Chinese law. The reason is that it has multiple meanings and can be understood in various ways, which will be discussed later.

Labour relationships are a field of study that can have different meanings depending on the context in which they are used. In China, relationships have different meanings in different scenarios. From the perspective of the social economy, labour relations have the nature of social relationships that involve employing units and labourers. Enterprises for which labourers work play a fundamental role in social production. The society would not exist without production. From the perspective of administration, labour relationships mean the body of all activities related to the

Y. Wang, *Chinese Labour Law*, Understanding China,
https://doi.org/10.1007/978-981-16-8101-1_2

administration of labour relations, involving administrative organs, employing units and labourers. In this sense, the term "employment relations" is often used. From the legal perspective, l relationships mean the labour legal link between employing units and labourers and have the same meaning as labour legal relationships. In the context of legal research as well as court decisions, labour relationships are short for labour legal relationships. The labour legal relationship means the reciprocal rights and obligations created between employing units and labourers. In the legal field, the terms "employment relationship" and "employment relations" are rarely seen in China because "employment" is thought to be tinged with some feudal colour.

2.1.2 Characteristics of Labour Legal Relationships

2.1.2.1 Equality and Subordination

In abstract, a labourer and an employing unit are equal in legal status. Either a labourer or an employing unit has an independent and equal personality. A labourer may apply for a job position on his own. In a labour market, a labourer may select a proper employing unit, and vice versa; a labourer and an employing unit may negotiate with each other on an equal basis. A labourer and an employing unit may modify, terminate or renew a labour contract by consensus. However, in a specific legal relationship, a labourer is subordinate to an employing unit once a labour contract is signed. An employing unit may exercise its power to command or discipline a labourer. Of course, the nature of subordination will be diluted if workplace governance is worker participative.

2.1.2.2 Mandatoriness and Autonomy

The labour legal relationship tends to be mandatory, because it plays a very important role in stabilizing the social economic order and advancing the social progress. Given that labourers are often in a weaker position, the government often intervenes with the labour legal relationships between labourers and employing units and promulgates mandatory laws and regulations with regard to working hours, labour security and protection. Accordingly, autonomy is limited in the labour legal relationships. For example, with regard to the grounds for termination of a labour contract, autonomy is restricted to protect the interests of labourers.

2.1.3 *Elements of Labour Legal Relationships*

2.1.3.1 Subjects

Subjects of a labour legal relationship means the parties to a labour legal relationship. They are primary actors in a labour legal relationship. Without them, a labour legal relationship cannot exist. Generally, subjects of a labour legal relationship refer to an employing unit and labourers. In the case of labour dispatch, a labour dispatch unit (also called a labour dispatching unit), a dispatched labourer and a labour-user unit (also called a labour receiving unit) are the subjects of the atypical labour legal relationship.

2.1.3.2 Subject Matter

The subject matter of a labour legal relationship means the object that the rights and obligations are directed at. In Chinese academia, scholars do not agree on what the subject matter of a labour legal relationship is. Some thinks the subject matter is the behavior of a labourer, while others think the subject matter is the capacity for physical labour.

2.1.3.3 Contents

The contents of a labour legal relationship mean the reciprocal rights and obligations of an employing unit and a labourer. The rights and obligations come from the labour contract between them and from the related laws and regulations. A labourer may be entitled to wages and remuneration, rest and holidays, social insurance and other benefits, labour security and labour protection and is obliged to comply with the related laws and regulations, and the rules made by an employing unit. An employing unit may exercise its power to command and discipline a labourer. Often, such content is stipulated in the labour contract. In case that there is no written labour contract, the related laws and regulations will apply.

2.2 Criteria to Identify Labour Relationships

The operation of labour law is based on the premise that there is establishment of a labour relationship. However, it is not very easy to judge whether there is establishment of a labour relationship. There are different approaches to dealing with the thorny issue in light of legal culture, social security and economic development in different jurisdictions.

According to Employment Relationship Recommendation, 2006 (No. 198), Members should promote clear methods for guiding workers and employers as to the determination of the existence of an employment relationship, may consider clearly defining the conditions applied for determining the existence of an employment relationship, for example, subordination or dependence and should consider the possibility of defining in their laws and regulations, or by other means, specific indicators of the existence of an employment relationship, which might include (1) the fact that the work: is carried out according to the instructions and under the control of another party; involves the integration of the worker in the organisation of the enterprise; is performed solely or mainly for the benefit of another person; must be carried out personally by the worker; is carried out within specific working hours or at a workplace specified or agreed by the party requesting the work; is of a particular duration and has a certain continuity; requires the worker's availability; or involves the provision of tools, machinery by the party requesting the work; (2) periodic payment of remuneration to the worker; the fact that such remuneration constitutes the worker's sole or principal source of income; provision of payment in kind, such as food, lodging or transport; recognition of entitlements such as weekly rest and annual holidays; payment by the party requesting the work for travel undertaken by the worker in order to carry out the work; or absence of financial risk for the worker.[1]

For China, in theory, subordination is a main criterion for establishment of a labour relationship and in practice the Ministry of Labour and Social Security released the Notice of Establishment of Labour Relationships on 25 May 2005, which serves as the benchmark for the identification of the establishment of a labour relationship.

2.2.1 *The General Understanding of Subordination*

Generally, subordination is understood from the following three perspectives in Chinese academia.

2.2.1.1 Personal Subordination

Personal subordination is opposite to personal independency. The phrase of personal subordination means that a labourer is under the control of his employing unit with regard to the type of work, the means of work, working hours, and the place of work. However, the degree of control varies due to the nature of work, the skills, the scale of an enterprise and the corporate culture. It may be questionable whether personal subordination applies to senior managers, top professionals, or in-house contractors.

[1] Employment Relationship Recommendation (2006).

2.2.1.2 Organisational Subordination

Organisational subordination means that the integration of the labour a labourer provides into the production system of an employing unit. Organisational subordination makes a labourer become a member of an employing unit and accordingly he is obliged to comply with the rules made by the employing unit. Regardless of whether the degree of the autonomy of a labourer is high or not, he is organisationally subordinated to his employing unit once he is a member of the employing unit.

2.2.1.3 Economic Subordination

Economic subordination may be understood from the following perspectives: First, the economic subordination is inside the organisation. Within the same organisation, a labourer is in a weaker position in relation to an employing unit and a labourer depends on the production materials and the job provided by his employing unit to work and get paid while the employing unit has the independent right to operation and manages its production system. Second, the economic subordination is outside the organisation. An independent operator may be economically subordinated to another independent operator if the former operator is in a weaker position in relation to the latter. Economic subordination outside the organisation may solve the problems with Internet platform labourers.

2.2.2 Background and Aims of Notice of Establishment of Labour Relationships

Before 2005, some employing units did not sign labour contracts with their labourers, which always made it difficult to protect labourers and adversely affected the harmony and stabilisation of labour relationships. With a view to regulating the employment market, protecting the legitimate interests of labourers, and promoting social stabilisation, the Ministry of Labour and Social Security released the Notice of Establishment of Labour Relationships on 25 May 2005, which provides guidance for labour arbitration commissions and courts on effectively identifying the existence of labour relationships and on distinguishing labour relationships from other forms of contractual arrangements, such as outsourcing. The Notice of Establishment of Labour Relationships is so important that it is repeatedly seen in the civil decisions related to labour disputes.

2.2.3 Conditions for Establishment of Labour Relationships

Although an employing unit fails to sign a labour contract in writing with a labourer, the labour relationship is established where the following conditions are met.

2.2.3.1 An Employing Unit and a Labourer Have the Capacities Specified by Laws and Regulations

The capacities of an employing unit are not clearly set out in the Labour Law of 2018, the Labour Contract Law of 2012 or the Regulations on the Implementation of the Labour Contract Law. Article 2 of the Labour Law of 2018 shows that enterprises and individual economic organisations within the territory of the People's Republic of China are subject to the Labour Law of 2018. Nongovernmental and nonprofit units are introduced by Article 2 of the Labour Contract Law of 2012. Article 3 of the Regulations on the Implementation of the Labour Contract Law provides that the partnerships including accounting firms, law firms and foundations fall within the scope of employing units specified in the Labour Contract Law of 2012. Furthermore, Article 4 of the Regulations on the Implementation of the Labour Contract Law provides that the branch of the employing unit specified in the Labour Contract Law of 2012 may sign a labour contract with its labourer where it gains a business licence or incorporation certificate; the branch may be entrusted by the employing unit to sign a labour contract with its labourer where it does not gain a business licence or incorporation certificate. The capacities of the employing unit shall be further determined with reference to the Companies Law, the Partnership Law, and the Foreign Investment Law of the People's Republic of China.

A person is eligible for the labourer specified in the Labour Law of 2018, the Labour Contract Law of 2012 and the Regulations on the Implementation of the Labour Contract Law if he is not less than 16 years old but does not exceed the statutory age of retirement. The statutory age of retirement for a male labourer is 60 years old, the statutory age of retirement for a female labourer is 50 years old and the statutory age of retirement for a female labourer who takes a management job is 55 years old. It is noteworthy that interns are not within the meanings of the labourer specified in the Labour Law of 2018.

2.2.3.2 All the Rules Duly Made by an Employing Unit Are Applicable to a Labourer, Who is Under the Labour Management of the Employing Unit and Gets Paid for the Work Arranged for by the Employing Unit

A labourer is subordinated to an employing unit in the course of the performance of the labour contract. In theory, subordination of a labourer to an employing unit is understood to mean that the employing unit or its representative directs the performance of the work and the labourer is under the management of the employing unit; and the economic dependency of a labourer on an employing unit means that the wages or remuneration received by the labourer constitute his only or main source of income. Subordination was reflected in many court decisions and orders, such as the Civil Order of Retrial Reviewing and Hearing Supervision of the Case of Labour Dispute between China Financial & Economic Publishing House and Zhao He (2020 Jing CA 4446) made by the Higher People's Court of Beijing.

2.2.3.3 The Work a Labourer Does is Part of the Business of an Employing Unit

What constitutes "part of the business" is controversial. The scope of the business of an employing unit is often determined with reference to the business licence. Sometimes, whether the term of business is long or short is also taken into consideration. In the Civil Order of Retrial Reviewing and Hearing Supervision of the Case of Confirming the Labour Relationship between Deng Guiren and Lechang Ashui Metal and Machinery Processing Factory (2016 Yue CA 8053), Deng Guiren, the applicant for retrial, argued that it was unlawful for the court of second instance to held that the labour relationship was not established on the grounds that the work was not part of the long-term business of Lechang Ashui Metal and Machinery Processing Factory and that the court of second instance raised the threshold for the establishment of a labour relationship, and the Higher People's Court of Guangdong confirmed the establishment of the labour relationship but did not comment on the argument of Deng Guiren. Regardless, the business licence cannot be conclusive for the establishment of a labour relationship. Otherwise, it is hard to explain why there exists a labour relationship between the employing unit whose business is to manufacture and its security guard.

2.2.4 Evidence for Establishment of Labour Relationships

In determining the establishment of labour relationships, courts often take into account the following evidence: (1) a pay statement or record (payroll), and a record of payment of social insurance contributions; (2) a work card or service card provided by an employing unit to a labourer to show his identity; (3) "registration form" "application form" and other recruitment forms filled in by a labourer; (4) a record of work attendance; and (5) testimonies of other labourers. An employing unit bears the burden of proof with regard to items (1), (3) and (4) because it possesses them. If an employing unit denies the establishment of labour relationships, it shall produce the related evidence. In the Civil Order of Appeal and Application for Retrial of Confirmation Labour Relationship between Chongqing Qisen Biomass Fuel Co., Ltd. and X (2018 Yu CA 301), the Higher People's Court of Chongqing held that

Chongqing Qisen Biomass Fuel Co., Ltd. failed to produce the evidence to prove that there was no labour relationship between them and that X was hired by Hu Yinyun and the petition for retiral was rejected. If a labourer fails to produce evidence for the establishment of a labour relationship, the court may deny his claim. In the Civil Order of Retrial Review and Hearing Supervision of the Case of Labour Contract between Yu Yunchu and Zhuhai Norion Technology Co. Ltd. (2017 Yue CA 4171), the Higher People's Court of Guangdong held that the business card, the signed business contracts and the photos of a commodities fair, which were not part of the evidence listed in Article 3 of the Notice of Establishment of Labour Relationships, could not be solely used for the proof of establishment of labour relationships. It is noteworthy that sometimes the evidence is judged from the substantive perspective. In the Civil Decision of Retrial of the Case of Labour Dispute between Cong Mingzi and Weihai Daily (2016 SC CA 148), the Supreme People Court held that there was no establishment of a labour relationship on grounds of the personal nature of labour relationships and the provision of production materials, despite that Cong Mingzi produced the evidence with regard to the work card, working clothes, and the banking card and payment of wages.

2.3 Practical Issues Related to Labour Relationships

2.3.1 Other Conditions for Establishment of Labour Relationships

In some cases, the Notice of Establishment of Labour Relationships may not be enough for courts to identify whether a labour relationship is established, so they have to resort to the following additional factors.

2.3.1.1 Intentions of the Parties to Establish Labour Relationships

No consensus ad idem equals no contract. Consensus ad idem is necessary for the establishment of labour relationships. Some courts hold that in addition to the conditions of establishment of labour relationships stipulated in the Notice of Establishment of Labour Relationships, the intentions of the parties to establish a labour relationship are required.

In the Civil Decision of Second Instance of the Case of Labour Contract between Hu Gaofeng and Tiandu Food (Beijing) Co., Ltd. (2019 Jing 01 CF 4781), the First Intermediate People's Court of Beijing upheld the decision of first instance and held that there was no labour relationship between Hu Gaofeng and Tiandu Food (Beijing) Co., Ltd. on the grounds that (1) participation in the daily management and decision making in accordance with the agreement between the shareholders did not necessarily mean that there was establishment of the labour relationship between them; (2)without the signature of the legal representative or the related resolution of the shareholders, Hu Gaofeng himself affixed the corporate seal on the labour contract did not show the intention of Tiandu Food (Beijing) Co., Ltd. to establish the labour relationship, (3) Hu Gaofeng got the position as the CEO by the agreement of the shareholders instead of by the usual recruitment process; and (4) although there was nothing in law to prevent a shareholder from establishing a labour relationship, it was still relevant to identify whether participation in daily decision making was required by the investment agreement or by the labour relationship.

In the Civil Decision of Second Instance of the Case of Labour Dispute between Zhuanghe Broadcasting and Television Station and Qin Menglai (2019 Liao 02 CF 1004), the Intermediate People's Court of Dalian held that (1) despite that Qin Menglai, the appellee, was eligible for the labourer, the labour relationship was not necessarily established and (2) the true intentions of both parties should be further taken into account; (3) from the two copies of internship certificates, it could be seen that both parties intended that Zhuanghe Broadcasting and Television Station, the appellant, only provided the off-campus internship for the appellee. In this case, the intentions to establish a labour relationship are an independent factor to identify whether a labour relationship is established or not.

Similarly, in the Civil Decision of Second Instance of the Case of Confirmation of Labour Relationship between Guangzhou GZL International Travel Service Ltd. and Chen Li (2019 Yue 01 CF 18698), the Intermediate People's Court of Guangzhou held that the Social Tourist Guide Service Contract was in the nature of a contract for services, from which it could be seen that Guangzhou GZL International Travel Service Ltd. and Chen Li did not intend to establish a labour relationship. In contrast, other courts hold that the intentions to establish a labour relationship are in place once the three conditions specified in the Notice of Establishment of Labour Relationships are met. In other words, the intentions to establish a labour relationship are not an independent factor. The Second Intermediate People's Court of Shanghai held the latter view in the Civil Decision of Second Instance of the Case of Labour Contract between Ge Yuehong and Qiaomami House Service (Shanghai) Co., Ltd. (2020 Hu 02 CF 4695).

2.3.1.2 The Provision of Tools and Production Materials

Clearly, the ownership of tools and production materials by a labourer points in the direction of an independent contractor in that it shows a comparatively high measure of independence. In the Civil Order of Appeal and Application for Retrial of the Case of Labour Dispute between Wang Tao and Danyang Yunda Express Co., Ltd. (2019 Su CA 1728), the Higher People's Court of Jiangsu held that Wang Tao used his own vehicle to collect parcels from shippers and make deliveries to consignees and there was no labour relationship between Wang Tao and Danyang Yunda Express Co., Ltd.

Similarly, in the Civil Decision of Second Instance of the Case of Labour Dispute between Beijing Branch Jiangsu Jieruida Information Technology Co., Ltd. and Liang Zhuqiang (2020 Jing 03 CF 9685), the Third Intermediate People's Court of Beijing held that Liang Zhuqiang was supplied with the working clothes, the tool kit and the cleaning machine by Jiangsu Jieruida Information Technology Co., Ltd. (Beijing Branch), and there was a labour relationship between Jiangsu Jieruida Information Technology Co., Ltd. (Beijing Branch) and Liang Zhuqiang.

2.3.1.3 The Continuity of Business

In the Civil Order of Retrial Reviewing and Hearing Supervision of the Case of Contract for Services between Wu Xiaobin and Guangzhou Niowoo Information Technology Co., Ltd. (2018 Yue CA 8467), the Higher People's Court of Guangdong held that from the chat logs on WeChat, the work of Wu Xiaobin was temporary, and both parties did not intend to establish a long-term and reliable labour relationship.

In the Civil Decision of Second Instance of the Case of Labour Dispute between Xiao Jiguang and Wuhan Guoxing Industrial Co., Ltd. (2020 E 01 CF 102), the Intermediate People's Court of Wuhan listed the following factors to identify the establishment of a labour relationship: (1) whether labour is provided independently or collaboratively; (2) whether instruments of labour and production materials are provided by an employing unit; (3) whether the work is continuous; and (4) whether the work is part of routine business.

2.3.1.4 The Payment of Remuneration

In the Civil Decision of Second Instance of the Case of Labour Contract between Tang Weiguo and Beijing Tongcheng Bing Technology Co., Ltd. (2020 Hu 02 CF 5544), the Second Intermediate People's Court of Shanghai held that the base pay was not agreed upon, the remuneration was paid for every single delivery instead of on a regular basis and that there was no labour relationship between the two parties. In the Civil Order of Retrial Reviewing and Hearing Supervision of the Case of Labour Contract between Liu Qinghong and Shenzhen Jiaajia Mother & Baby Technology Co., Ltd. (2019 Yue CA 10897), the Higher People's Court of Guangdong held that Liu Qinghong was paid by her clients instead of Shenzhen Jiajia Mother & Baby Technology Co., Ltd. and there was no labour relationship between the two parties.

2.3.2 Labour Relationships in the Context of the Gig Economy

2.3.2.1 The Prevailing Online Platform Work

The world is moving into a digitalised economy, and online platforms play a crucial role, impacting the economic process in various ways. Of course, they have an impact on the provision of labour. In particular, online platforms can play a role in the organisation of work in the production process, for instance, by constituting the method of dividing tasks on a project between a team of workers within a company or by matching a demand for a (digital or manual) work project with a worker who is willing to perform it, as well as in the (orgnisation of the) delivery/provision/sale of a good or service, for instance, by allowing consumers to book and pay a car driver via a smartphone application. This has given rise to what is widely referred to as "online platform work", which refers to all labour provided through, on or mediated by online platforms, and features a wide array of working arrangements/relationships, such as (versions of) casual work, dependent self-employment, informal work, piecework, home work and crowdwork, in a wide range of sectors. The actual work provided can be digital or manual, in-house or outsourced, high-skilled or low-skilled, on-site or off-site, large- or small- scale, permanent or temporary, all depending on the specific situation.

2.3.2.2 The Latest Court Opinion on Online Platform Workers in the UK

Different attitudes toward gig economy employment status show complexity. On 19 February 2021, the UK Supreme Court gave the Judgment of Uber BV and others (Appellants) v Aslam and others (Respondents). New ways of working organised through digital platforms pose pressing questions about the employment status of the people who do the work involved. The central question on this appeal is whether an employment tribunal was entitled to find that drivers whose work is arranged through Uber's smartphone application ("the Uber app") work for Uber under workers' contracts and so qualify for the national minimum wage, paid annual leave and other workers' rights; or whether, as Uber contends, the drivers do not have these rights because they work for themselves as independent contractors, performing services under contracts made with passengers through Uber as their booking agent.

The first appellant, Uber BV, is a Dutch company which owns the rights in the Uber app. The second appellant, Uber London Ltd ("Uber London"), is a UK subsidiary of Uber BV which, since May 2012, has been licensed to operate private hire vehicles in London. The third appellant, Uber Britannia Ltd, is another UK subsidiary of Uber BV which holds licences to operate such vehicles outside London. The claimants, and respondents to this appeal, are individuals who work or used to work as private hire vehicle drivers, performing driving services booked through the Uber app. Following a preliminary hearing, the Employment Tribunal found that the Respondents were "workers" and that they were "working" whenever they (a) had the Appellants' app switched on; (b) were within the territory in which they were authorised to work; and (c) were able and willing to accept assignments. These findings were upheld by the Employment Appeal Tribunal and the Court of Appeal. The Appellants then appealed to the Supreme Court.

The Supreme Court unanimously dismissed the appeal, with Lord Leggatt giving the main judgment. The Court held that the transportation service performed by drivers and offered to passengers through the Uber app is very tightly defined and controlled by Uber. Drivers are in a position of subordination and dependency in relation to Uber such that they have little or no ability to improve their economic position through professional or entrepreneurial skill. In practice the only way in which they can increase their earnings is by working longer hours while constantly meeting Uber's measures of performance. The Supreme Court considered that comparisons made by Uber with digital platforms which act as booking agents for hotels and other accommodation and with minicab drivers did not advance its case. The drivers were rightly found to be "workers".[2]

2.3.2.3 Problems with Online Platform Workers in China and Countermeasures

According to the 48th China Statistical Report on Internet Development, released by the China Internet Network Information Center on 27 August 2021, as of June 2021, China had 1.011 biliion netizens, the Internet Penetration had reached 71.6%, the number of mobile Internet users in China had reached 1.007 billion, and the proportion of China's netizens accessing the Internet via their mobile phones had amounted to 99.6%. As of June 2021, the number of apps monitored in China's domestic market was 3.02 million, and the number of daily tools, e-commerce and consumer service apps reached 465,000, 295,000 and 2710,000, respectively, and ranked second, third and fourth on the scale of mobile apps. The per capita weekly online duration of China's Internet users was 26.9 h. Up to June 2021, the user size of online meal ordering was 469 million or accounted for 46.4% of China's total netizen population.[3]

Traditional labour-related laws are also facing new challenges from the rapid development of the digitalised economy in China. Recent hotnews drew public attention to online platform workers. On 29 December 2020, a woman labourer aged 23 working on Pinduoduo Inc. was reported to have suffered sudden death on her way back home from work. On 11 January 2021, a delivery man was reported to try to burn himself to ask for delivery fees. At present, most courts tend to apply the Notice of Establishment of Labour Relationships to disputes concerning online platform work.

Contradicting Decisions on Establishment of Labour Relationships

Even if the Notice of Establishment of Labour Relations is repeatedly invoked in identifying the establishment of labour relationships, the courts are always making contradictory decisions.

---

[2] SUPREME COURT. (2019). *Uber BV and others (Appellants) v Aslam and others (Respondents)*. Retrieved 15 March 2021, from https://www.supremecourt.uk/cases/docs/uksc-2019-0029-judgment.pdf.

[3] CNNIC. (2021). *The 48th China Statistical Report on Internet Development*. Retrieved 28 August, 2021, from https://www.cnnic.com.cn/IDR/ReportDownloads/.

On 14 July 2015, Tang Ruiting was employed by Beijing Yisheng Health Technology Co., Ltd. and worked as a health care professional and was sent to work in Shenzhen. In December 2015, Tang Ruiting returned to Beijing, and no base pay was provided. Tang Ruiting provided services via the "Yisheng Massage" platform and obtained the commission from every order. There was no requirement of daily attendance. In the Civil Decision of First Instance of the Case of Labour Dispute between Tang Ruiting and Beijing Yisheng Health Technology Co., Ltd. (2019 Jing 0101 CF 12884), the People's Court of the Dongcheng District of Beijing held that there was no establishment of a labour relationship on grounds of flexible employment, nonfixed wages, and no work attendance management.

However, in the Civil Decision of Second Instance of the Case of Labour Dispute between Tang and Beijing Yisheng Health Technology Co., Ltd. (2020 Jing 02 CF 8125), the Second People's Court of Beijing held that there was a labour relationship if a labourer who provided services or labour via an online platform controlled by the platform operator in terms of work rules, working hours, work process, work supervision, remuneration, non-compete, or work appearance.

On 23 April 2014, Ge Peisheng, in the name of "Yufeng Company", signed the Fengniao Distribution and Delivery Agency Cooperation Agreement with Shanghai Rajax Information Technology Co., Ltd. The Distribution and Delivery Rules, the attachment to the Agreement, stipulated that "the Distributor shall purchase Fengniao Supplies (including a hamlet, working clothes, waist bag, and food box) and wearing pants and slippers is not allowed when providing services." On 15 December 2017, Zhou Guangli worked as a delivery boy, a member of Fengniao Team Platform, which was operated by Shanghai Rajax Information Technology Co., Ltd. Zhou Guangli provided the delivery services according to the messages from the Fengniao Team Platform. According to the registration information of Shanghai Rajax Information Technology Co., Ltd., Zhou Guangli was a member of Yufeng Company. In the Civil Decision of First Instance of the Case of Labour Contract between Zhou Guangli and Shanghai Rajax Information Technology Co., Ltd. (2017 Hu 0107 CF 27564), the People's Court of Putuo District in Shanghai held that there was a labour relationship between the two parties on the grounds (1) that there were the intentions of the two parties to establish the labour relationship, (2) that Zhou Guangli was subordinated to Shanghai Rajax Information Technology Co., Ltd. and (3) the work results of Zhou Guangli belonged to Shanghai Rajax Information Technology Co., Ltd.

However, in the Civil Decision of Second Instance of the Case of Labour Contract between Zhou Guangli and Shanghai Rajax Information Technology Co., Ltd. (2019 Hu 02 CF 3226), the Second Intermediate People's Court of Shanghai reversed the Civil Decision of First Instance of the Case of Labour Contract between Zhou Guangli and Shanghai Rajax Information Technology Co., Ltd. (2017 Hu 0107 CF 27564), ruled that there was no labour relationship between the two parties and further commented that the establishment of a labour relationship could not be generalised, the relationship between a platform company and a labourer was still subject to the test of subordination, and in deciding the nature of the relationship in the platform economy the following factors should be taken into account: whether the labourer was free to decide the work contents and working hours; whether the remuneration was comparatively stable; and whether the operation was at the labourer's own risks.

Countermeasures

It is right that the establishment of a labour relationship cannot be generalised. It is generally accepted that there is no labour relationship between network anchors or camgirls and live-streaming platforms, which is reflected in the Civil Decision of Second Instance of the Case of Labour Dispute between Li Linxia and Chongqing Man Ka Culture Communication Co., Ltd. (2019 Yu 01 CF 1910) made by the First Intermediate People's Court of Chongqing, released by the Gazette of the Supreme People's Court of the PRC of 2020 (Volume 10).

Problems with online platform work should be analyzed on a case-by-case basis. If an online platform only serves as an intermediary agency, there is no room for establishment of a labour relationship. If an online platform exercises the management power on a labourer, and in essence the labourer is subordinated to the online platform, there is a labour relationship.

To address the problems with online platform work, some guidance documents were released. On 18 July 2018, the Higher People's Court of Guangdong Province and the Labour Dispute Arbitration Commission of Guangdong Province jointly released Several Opinions concerning the Linkage between Labour Dispute Arbitration and Litigation, which provides that in principle the nature of the relationship between an online platform operator and a labourer shall be determined as stipulated; there is no establishment of a labour relationship where the system of sharing of risks and profits is in place by outsourcing contracts, operation contracts or investment contracts.

On 3 July 2017, Jiangsu Province Labour and Personnel Dispute Arbitration Commission released the Minutes on Jiangsu Province Workshop of Difficult Issues concerning Labour and Personnel Disputes, which provides that in confirming the labour relationship involving a platform enterprise the labour arbitration commissions shall strike a balance between the protection of the labourers' interests and the increase of flexibility of the labour market and separate a labour relationship from a civil relationship for provision of services in light of the operating mode of the platform, the occupation status, the degree of the management of the platform, the distribution mode of the wages and remuneration, and the allocation of the operating risks; in the case of an online platform as an intermediary, which only releases service information in exchange for management fees or information fees, there is no labour relationship; in the case of outsourcing contracts or entrustment contracts between a labourer and an online platform enterprise, generally there is no labour relationship, and it can be rebuttable if the relationship meets the conditions specified in the Notice of Establishment of Labour Relationships.

On 10 June 2019, the Higher People's Court of Shandong Province and Shandong Province Human Resources and Social Security Department jointly released the Meeting Minutes of Several Issues of Hearing the Case of Labour and Personnel Disputes, which provides that where a labourer (often as a delivery boy, a market sales promoter, or a water delivery man) uses his own tools to work for an enterprise via have similar interests to an entrustment contract, there is no labour relationship and the nature of the relationship shall be determined as stipulated by both parties, unless the labourer produces contrary evidence.

On 21 January 2020, Tianjin Market Supervision and Administration Commission released the Guidelines of Internet Management and Service for the Gig Workers on Sharing Economy Platform, which provides that the gig workers have the following characteristics: (1) Self-employed. Gig workers are not economically or organisationally subordinated to the sharing economy platform operator or service agency, and they can be free to decide and manage working hours, places of work, and workload. (2) Nonfixed Incomes. There is no base pay, and the incomes are not fixed. The profits and losses are at the gig workers' risk. (3) Operating costs. The gig workers use their own tools and production materials. (4) No labour relationship. There is no labour relationship in any form between the gig workers and the sharing economy platform operator or service agency. (5) Random transactions. The gig workers take the assignments at random. and (6) Via the online platform. The service demands and the service resources are integrated via the online platform. It is anticipated that the courts in Tianjin tend to decide the establishment of a labour relationship with reference to the abovementioned characteristics of the gig workers.

It is noteworthy that on 16 July 2021, the Guiding Opinions on Protection of Rights of Workers in New Form of Employment were issued jointly by the Ministry of Human Resources and Social Security, the National Development and Reform Commission, the Ministry of Transport, the Ministry of Emergency Management, the State Administration for Market Regulation, the National Healthcare Security Administration, the Supreme People's Court and All-China Federation of Trade Unions. The Guiding Opinions provide that (1) an enterprise is required to sign a labour contract where the conditions for establishment of a labour relationship are met; (2) an enterprise is expected to sign a written agreement to set forth the rights and obligations of the enterprise and its worker where despite that the enterprise exercises the labour management power, the conditions for establishment of a labour relationship are not fully met; and (3) civil law applies where an individual uses the platform to carry out his business or is self-employed.

2.3.3 Labour Relationships Between Top Managers and Employing Units

In accordance with Article 216 of the Company Law of 2018, top managers mean a manager, a vice manager, a person in charge of corporate finance, the board secretary of a listed company and other persons stipulated by the articles of association. There is nothing in law to prevent a senior executive or a shareholder from being a labourer. In case that a senior executive is removed from office in accordance with the procedure in the Company Law of 2018, the question arises whether the labour relationship between the senior executive and the employing unit is terminated.

In July 1991, Wang Zhuo was employed by Shanghai Jahwa United Co., Ltd. as the branding manager of the market department. In April 1997, Wang Zhuo resigned to study in the USA. On 1 January 2004, Wang Zhuo established the labour relationship again with Shanghai Jahwa United Co., Ltd. Wang Zhuo was appointed as the vice general manager on 21 January 2004, and then as the general manager on 18 December 2012. On 19 November 2013, Wang Zhuo and Shanghai Jahwa United Co., Ltd. signed an open-ended labour contract. On 12 May 2014, the meeting of directors passed a resolution to remove Wang Zhuo from the general manager. On 13 May 2014, Shanghai Jahwa United Co., Ltd. delivered a written notice to cancel the labour contract with Wang Zhuo.

In the Civil Decision of Second Instance of the Case of Labour Contract between Shanghai Jahwa United Co., Ltd and Wang Zhuo (2015 Hu SIC CTD CF 747), the Second Intermediate People's Court of Shanghai reversed the decision of first instance and held that (1) the system of professional managers that was independent from the labour relationship was not in place in China and the senior executives were subject to the labour laws and regulations and (2) the removal of Wang Zhuo from the general manager amounted to the modification of the position listed in the labour contract and did not necessarily lead to the termination of the labour contract with Wang Zhuo.

However, some courts in Beijing told a different story. On 1 December 2008, Luo Yafei established the labour relationship with Beijing Sunplusapp Technology Co., Ltd. In the labour contract, his position of the general manager was stipulated, and he was responsible for the board of directors, which had the power to remove him from the position. Luo Yafei was also one of the shareholders and a member of the board of directors of Beijing Sunplusapp Technology Co., Ltd. On 10 March 2018, in the meeting of the board of directors, Luo Yafei resigned from the position of the general manager on grounds of ill health. In the Civil Decision of First Instance of the Case of Labour Dispute between Luo Yafei and Beijing Sunplusapp Technology Co., Ltd. (2019 Jing CF 27900), the People's Court of Haidian District of Beijing held that his resignation as the general manager was in accordance with the procedure of the Company Law of 2018, and his resignation under the Company Law was different from the revocation of the labour contract. In the Civil Decision of Second Instance of the Case of Labour Dispute between Luo Yafei and Beijing Sunplusapp Technology Co., Ltd. (2019 Jing 01 CF 11111), the First Intermediate People's Court of Beijing held that (1) his resignation under the Company Law was different from the revocation of the labour contract; (2) the performance of the job duty was directly relevant to the labour relationship; and (3) before or after his resignation, Luo Yafei and Beijing Sunplusapp Technology Co., Ltd. did not agree to modify the labour contract or establish a fresh labour contract; and (4) that Beijing Sunplusapp Technology Co., Ltd. accepted his resignation suggested that the labour contract was revoked. The Higher People's Court of Beijing upheld the First Intermediate People's Court of Beijing ruling that the resignation from office amounted to the revocation of a labour contract in the Civil Order of the Case of Labour Dispute between Luo Yafei and Beijing Sunplusapp Technology Co., Ltd. (2020 Jing CA 2797).

The Supreme People's Court of the PRC held the same view as the Higher People's Court of Beijing in the Civil Decision of Retrial of the Case of Labour Dispute between Sun Qixiang and Jilin Midas Light Alloy Co., Ltd. (2020 SC CA 50). Sun Qixiang worked as the CFO of Jilin Midas Light Aluminum Co., Ltd. from March 2001 to June 2013 and as the vice manager from July 2013 to July 2017. From March 2011 to July 2017, he was sent to Luoyang Midas Aluminum Co., Ltd. to double as the general manager. On 20 July 2017, he was transferred by Midas Holdings Limited, the shareholder of Jilin Midas Light Alloy Co., Ltd., to Jilin Midas Light Alloy Co., Ltd. to work as the Chairman of the Board and the legal representative. On 7 February 2018, Sun Qixiang was removed by Midas Holdings Limited from the Chairman of the Board of Jilin Midas Light Alloy Co., Ltd. and from then on Jilin Midas Light Alloy Co., Ltd. has not paid him any wages or took out social insurance. The court of first instance held the same view as the Second Intermediate People's Court of Shanghai in the Civil Decision of Second Instance of the Case of Labour Contract between Shanghai Jahwa United Co., Ltd and Wang Zhuo (2015 Hu SIC CTD CF 747) and held that the removal from the Chairman of the Board was to modify the position specified in the labour contract but did not necessarily amount to the revocation of the labour contract.

However, in the Civil Decision of Second Instance of the Case of Labour Dispute between Jilin Midas Light Alloy Co., Ltd. and Sun Qixiang (2019 Ji CF 19), the Higher People's Court of Jilin held that (1) there were no intentions between Jilin Midas Light Alloy Co., Ltd. and Sun Qixiang to establish the labour relationship; (2) Sun Qixiang was appointed and removed by Midas Holdings Limited, and he was not recruited by Jilin Midas Light Alloy Co., Ltd.; and (3) there was the entrustment relationship between Midas Holdings Limited, the shareholder of Jilin Midas Light Alloy Co., Ltd. and Sun Qixiang.

In the Civil Decision of Retrial of the Case of Labour Dispute between Sun Qixiang and Jilin Midas Light Alloy Co., Ltd. (2020 SC CA 50), the Supreme People's Court of the PRC held that there was a de facto labour relationship between Sun Qixiang and Jilin Midas Light Alloy Co., Ltd. on the grounds that (1) there was an entrustment contract between Sun Qixiang and Jilin Midas Light Alloy Co., Ltd. In the sense of the Company Law of 2018; (2) the entrustment relationship did not exclude the existence of the labour relationship provided that the requirements of the Notice of Establishment of Labour Relationships were met; (3) despite that there was no written labour contract, in addition to the Chairman of the Board, Sun Qixiang worked as the legal representative of Jilin Midas Light Alloy Co., Ltd., was responsible for corporate financing and financial management and was subject to the rules of Jilin Midas Light Alloy Co. and got paid by Jilin Midas Light Alloy Co. With regard to the status quo of the de facto labour relationship, the Supreme People's Court of the PRC further held that the removal of Sun Qixiang from the general manager by Midas Holdings Limited led to the revocation of the de facto labour relationship on the grounds that the basis for the de facto labour relationship did not exist.

Reference

ILO. (2006). *Employment Relationship Recommendation, 2006 (No. 198)*. Retrieved 12 March, 2021, from https://ilo.org/dyn/normlex/en/f?p=NORMLEXPUB:12100:0::NO::P12100_INSTRUMENT_ID:312535.

Chapter 3
Labour Contracts

A labour contract is an agreement that establishes the labour relationship between a labourer and an employing unit and defines the rights and obligations of respective parties, which serves as the prima facie evidence that there exists the labour relationship and the basis on which a court judge makes a decision. The terms and conditions will be discussed. Quite unlike in a civil contract, the doctrine of restitution cannot come into play where a labour contract is held to be invalid. The amount of remuneration shall be determined mutatis mutandis with reference to that for the labourer holding the same or similar posts in the employing unit. In practice, many disputes often arise from the revocation and termination of a labour contract, and practical issues will be discussed.

3.1 Overview of Labour Contracts

3.1.1 Concept and Nature of a Labour Contract

3.1.1.1 Concept

A labour contract is an agreement that establishes the labour relationship between a labourer and an employing unit and defines the rights and obligations of respective parties. A labour contract is different from a civil contract in that the former is mainly subject to labour law, while the latter is governed by civil law. The labour contract system is the basic form of employment, and thus, a labour contract plays a fundamental role in labour laws and regulations.

Y. Wang, *Chinese Labour Law*, Understanding China,
https://doi.org/10.1007/978-981-16-8101-1_3

3.1.1.2 Nature

When the labour contract system was introduced to China, most had mixed feelings about labour contacts. The Third Plenary Session of the CPC 12th Central Committee, held in 1984, adopted the Decision on Restructuring the Economic System, which provided that while the wage system of enterprises, state organs and public institutions was reformed, the reform of the labour system should be accelerated. At that time, some argued that the labour contract system would change the role of the people as the masters of the country, which seems very absurd today.[1]

In essence, a labour contract is used as a tool of management that sets forth the rights and obligations and allocates the risks between both parties to a labour contract under labour law. The issue is to what degree the Civil Code applies to a labour contract. Specifically, a labour contract is subject to labour law and civil law. The courts have to resort to civil law to determine "fraud", "duress", "liability for breach of contract", "personal information" and "adjusting the stipulated damages".

3.1.2 History of the Labour Contract System in China

3.1.2.1 From the Foundation of the PRC to 1980

On 26 November 1949, the Interim Measures of Handling the Relations between Labourers and Private Business Proprietors were promulgated by the All-China Federation of Trade Unions, which provided that private business proprietors and their employed workers, clerks, apprentices, and odd-job men might sign labour contracts. On 15 May 1951, the Interim Regulations of Recruitment of Workers in Every Region were released by the Ministry of Labour, which provided that employing units and employees shall sign labour contracts to set forth wages, working hours, a probation period and resettlement allowances. At that time, labour contracts were used to stabilise labour relationships and carry out production plans. During the decade of the Cultural Revolution (1966–1976), the labour contract system was sharply criticised. On 30 November 1971, the Notice of Reforming Temporary Workers and Shift Workers was released by the State Council, by which most temporary workers and contract workers were converted into fixed workers and the labour contract system was abolished.

3.1.2.2 In the 1980s

Since 1980, the contract labour system has revived itself in some regions. On 22 February 1983, the Ministry of Labour and Personnel issued the Notice of Actively Implementing the Labour Contract System, which provided that the fundamental

[1] Gong (1986).

aims of implementing the labour contract system were to break the "*iron rice bowls*" and "*big rice pots*" and mobilise the masses to emancipate the productive forces, and that the labour contract system applied to all the units owned by the whole people and the units owned by the collectives. On 12 July 1986, the State Council issued the Notice of Implementing the Labour Contract System by State-operated Enterprises, which provided that state-operated enterprises utilised labour contracts to recruit long-term workers according to the planned quotas of state wages.

3.1.2.3 In the 1990 and Afterwards

Since 1990, the labour contract system has spread across China. After the Labour Law of 2018 was enacted, 80% of the labourers in enterprises were required to sign labour contracts. The full-scale labour contract system helped to abolish the fixed worker system gradually. The Labour Contract Law of 2012 was enacted on 29 June 2007 and was revised on 28 December 2012, which offered legal protection and support to the contract system.

3.1.3 Legal Framework of Labour Contracts

3.1.3.1 The Labour Law of 2018

The Labour Law of 2018 is the basic law for employment in China. Chapter 3 of the Labour Law of 2018 provides, among other things, the definition of a labour contract, invalidity, the forms and contents of a labour contract, the revocation of a labour contract, the revocation with a notice, the redundancies, and the revocation of a labour contract on the part of labourers.

3.1.3.2 The Labour Contract Law of 2012

The Labour Contract Law of 2012 is the Magna Carta of labour contracts. It was promulgated by the Standing Committee of the 10th National People's Congress on 29 June 2007 and was revised on 28 December 2012. The Labour Contract Law of 2012 covers all the aspects of labour contracts, which includes General Provisions (Chap. 1), Conclusion of Labour Contracts (Chap. 2), Performance and Modification of Labour Contracts (Chap. 3), Revocation and Termination of Labour Contracts (Chap. 4), Special Provisions (Chap. 5), Supervision and Inspection (Chap. 6), Legal Liabilities (Chap. 7) and Supplementary Provisions (Chap. 8).

3.1.3.3 The Regulations on the Implementation of the Labour Contract Law

To put the Labour Contract Law of 2012 into practice, the Regulations on the Implementation of the Labour Contract Law were promulgated by the State Council on 18 September 2008, which further clarified the issues related to the Labour Contract Law of 2012, such as the capacity of the subsidiary of an employing unit as a party to a labour contract, the conclusion of an open-ended labour contract, the compositions of training expenses, and the termination of a labour contract for completing an assignment.

3.1.3.4 Judicial Interpretations, Opinions or Meeting Minutes of People's Courts

Judicial Interpretations (No. 1) by the Supreme People's Court of Issues Concerning the Application of Law in Hearing the Cases of Labour Disputes entered into force as of 1 January 2021, which consolidated and replaced the four judicial interpretations released by the Supreme People's Court on hearing the case of labour disputes. Judicial interpretations (No. 1) clarify the consequences of invalid labour contracts (Article 41), oral modification of labour contracts (Article 43), revocation of labour contracts under pressure (Article 45), cumulation of working years (Article 46), notification of the trade union in the case of revocation (Article 47) and annulment of illegal revocation or dismissal (Article 53).

Some Higher People's Courts at the provincial level or Intermediate People's Courts at the municipal level, sometimes together with Labour Arbitration Commissions, released the opinions or meeting minutes related to hearing the case of labour disputes, which often involved some thorny issues related to labour contracts.

On 24 April 2017, the Higher People's Court of Beijing and Beijing Labour and Personnel Dispute Arbitration Commission jointly released the Replies to Issues of Application of Law in Hearing the Cases of Labour Disputes, which clarify the specific performance of labour contracts (Article 8), the circumstances where employing units are not in a position to continue performing labour contracts (Article 9), revocation of labour contracts under Item 1 of Article 39 of the Labour Contract Law of 2012 (Article 11), and interpretation of Item 3 of Article 40 of the Labour Contract Law of 2012 (Article 12).

On 10 June 2019, the Higher People's Court of Shandong Province and Shandong Province Human Resources and Social Security Department jointly released the Meeting Minutes of Several Issues of Hearing the Case of Labour and Personnel Disputes, which also provide for the circumstances where employing units are not in a position to continue performing labour contracts (Article 12) and the means of service of Notice of Termination (Article 22). The First Civil Division of the Higher People's Court of Zhejiang and Zhengjiang Labour Dispute Arbitration Commission have jointly released the Replies to Several Issues of Hearing the Cases of Labour Dispute (No. 1–5).

On 9 May 2020, the Higher People's Court of Jiangxi Province and Jiangxi Province Human Resources and Social Security Department jointly released the Replies to Several Issues of Hearing the Case of Labour Disputes, which address the problems with the conclusion and performance of labour contracts (section 2) and the revocation and termination of labour contracts (section 4). Some Higher People's Courts in Shanghai, Guangdong and Fujian also released similar guides or replies. It should be noted that the abovementioned replies or minutes only apply to relevant regions.

3.1.3.5 The Letter in Reply to the Issues Related to Conclusion of Electronic Labour Contracts

On 4 March 2020, the General Office of the Ministry of Human Resources and Social Security gave the Letter in Reply to the Issues related to Conclusion of Electronic Labour Contracts, which provides that an employing unit and a labourer may conclude a written labour contract in an electronic form, and the electronic labour contracts shall include the data message and reliable electronic signatures provided by the Electronic Signature Law, and the employing unit shall make sure that the production, transmitting and storage of electronic contracts shall comply with the provisions of the Electronic Signature Law.

3.1.3.6 Regulations of the Labour Contract Law at Local Levels

Nearly every province of China formulated its own regulations of the Labour Contract Law of 2012 according to its realities. Although most of the provisions of such regulations are identical to those of the Labour Contract Law of 2012, some regulations at local levels have their own highlights. The Regulations of Labour Contracts of Shandong Province were first promulgated on 28 October 2001 and revised on 1 October 2013, which provide that, among other things, employing units shall maintain the confidentiality of labourers' personal information and that a labour contract that is again signed with the same labourer within the interval of three months from termination of the former labour contract shall be deemed to have been signed consecutively twice. The Labour Contract Law of 2012 does not clarify the wording of "consecutively". The Regulations of Labour Contracts of Jiangsu Province were revised on 15 January 2013, which allowed a labour dispatch unit and a labourer to sign an open-ended labour contract by mutual consent.

3.1.4 *Types of Labour Contracts*

3.1.4.1 Fixed-Term Contracts, Open-Ended Contracts and Contracts for Completing a Specific Assignment

Under the Labour Contract Law of 2012, labour contracts can be classified into fixed-term contracts, open-ended contracts and contracts for completing a specific assignment.[2] A fixed-term labour contract is one the ending dates of which is agreed upon between an employing unit and a labourer.[3] An employing unit and a labourer may conclude a fixed-term labour contract upon reaching consensus through consultation. An open-ended labour contract is one where an employing unit and a labourer have agreed not to stipulate a definite ending date. An employing unit and a labourer may conclude an open-ended labour contract upon reaching consensus through consultation. If a labourer proposes or agrees to renew the labour contract or to conclude a labour contract in any of the following circumstances, an open-ended labour contract shall be concluded unless the labourer requests the conclusion of a fixed-term labour contract: (a) The labourer has been working for the employing unit for a consecutive period of 10 or more years; (b) The labourer has been working for the employing unit for a consecutive period of 10 or more years but less than 10 years away from the statutory retirement age when the employing unit introduces the labour contract system or when the state-owned enterprise has to conclude a new labour contract with him or her as a result of restructuring; or (c) The labourer intends to renew the labour contract after he has consecutively concluded a fixed-term labour contract with the employing unit twice and he has not been found in any of the specified circumstances in Article 39 or Subparagraph (1) or (2) in Article 40 of this Law after he has consecutively concluded a fixed-term labour contract.[4] If an employing unit fails to conclude a written labour contract with a labourer within one year as of the date when it employs him, it shall be deemed to have concluded an open-ended labour contract with the latter. A labour contract that expires upon completion of a given job is one in which an employing unit and a labourer have agreed that the period for completion of the given assignment is the term of the contract. An employing unit and a labourer may, upon reaching consensus through consultation, conclude a labour contract that expires upon completion of a given assignment.[5]

3.1.4.2 General Labour Contracts and Labour Contracts for Labour Dispatch

General labour contracts are the agreements between employing units and labourers, which are used for direct employment. Labour contracts for labour dispatch are the

[2] The Labour Contract Law of 2012, Article 12.

[3] The Labour Contract Law of 2012, Article 13.

[4] The Labour Contract Law of 2012, Article 14.

[5] The Labour Contract Law of 2012, Article 15.

agreements between labour dispatch units and dispatched labourers, where labour dispatch units fulfil the obligations of employing units under the Labour Contract Law of 2012. Because labour dispatch involves three parties, labour contracts for labour dipatch are more complicated than general labour contracts. Labour contracts for labour dispatch shall not be in the form of contracts for completing a specific assignment.[6] Whether the provisions of open-ended labour contracts in the Labour Contract Law of 2012 apply to labour contracts for labour dispatch remains in dispute.

3.1.4.3 Full-Time Labour Contracts and Part-Time Labour Contracts

Part-time employment is a form of employment under which remuneration is chiefly calculated by the hour and the labourers generally work for not more than 4 h per day on average and not more than an aggregate of 24 h per week for the same employing unit.[7] The two parties to part-time employment may conclude an oral agreement, which is quite distinct from full-time employment.[8] A labourer in part-time employment may conclude a labour contract with one or more employing units; however, the labour contract concluded later may not prejudice the performance of the one concluded earlier. The provisions of a probation period do not apply to part-time labour contracts.[9] Either party to part-time labour contracts may terminate the contracts without the liability of paying economic compensation.[10] In contrast, full-time labour contracts shall be in writing, and there are strict provisions related to the termination of labour contracts.

3.1.4.4 Written Labour Contracts and Oral Labour Contracts

Written labour contracts are necessary for full-time employment, without which an employing unit may bear the related liabilities. If the requisite terms provided for by the Labour Contract Law of 2012 are not clearly stated in the text of a labour contract provided by an employing unit or an employing unit fails to deliver a copy of the labour contract to its labourer, the administrative department of labour shall order it to rectify. If harm is done to the labourer, the employing unit shall be liable for compensation. If an employing unit fails to conclude a written labour contract with a labourer for more than a month but less than a year from the date it starts employing him, it shall pay the labourer two times his salary for each month. If an employing unit fails to conclude an open-ended labour contract with a labourer in violation of the provisions of the Labour Contract Law of 2012, it shall pay the

[6] The Labour Contract Law of 2012, Article 58.

[7] The Labour Contract Law of 2012, Article 68.

[8] The Labour Contract Law of 2012, Article 69.

[9] The Labour Contract Law of 2012, Article 70.

[10] The Labour Contract Law of 2012, Article 71.

labourer two times his salary for each month, starting from the date on which an open-ended labour contract should be concluded.[11]

It should be noted that written labour contracts may be in an electronic form. A document can be deemed to be a written labour contract provided that it contains the elements of a written labour contract and sets out the rights and obligations of both parties. In TPS v Shan Jingjing, released by the Gazette of the Supreme People's Court of the PRC of 2013 (Volume 12), the Approval Form of Recruitment of Labourers was deemed to be a written contract.

3.1.4.5 Individual Labour Contracts and Collective Labour Contracts

An individual labour contract is the agreement between an individual labourer and an employing unit, which sets forth, among other things, the contract period, work contents and a place of work, working hours and rest and holidays, labour remuneration, social insurance, labour protection, labour conditions, and occupational disease prevention. Usually, the stipulations of confidentiality, supplementary insurance and benefits and noncompeting are included in an individual labour contract. A collective labour contract is the agreement between labourers or the trade union, if applicable, and an employing unit, which sets forth labour remuneration, working hours, rest and holidays, labour security and health, and insurance and benefits. The draft collective contract shall be adopted by the meeting of labourer representatives or all the labourers.[12] Where the standards of an individual labour contract are inferior to those of a collective labour contract, the latter shall prevail.[13]

3.2 Standard Form of Labour Contracts

On 25 November 2019, the Ministry of Labour Resources and Social Security released the standard form of labour contracts.[14] Next, its terms and conditions will be introduced, on which comments will be made.

3.2.1 The Basic Information of the Parties

The basic information of an employing unit (Party A) shall include its name, uniform social credit code, legal representative (person in charge) or authorised representative, place of incorporation, place of business, and telephone number. The basic

[11] The Labour Contract Law of 2012, Article 82.

[12] The Labour Contract Law of 2012, Article 51.

[13] The Labour Contract Law of 2012, Article 55.

[14] Standard Form of Labour Contract (2021).

information of a labourer (Party B shall include the number of identification cards (or other valid certificates and their numbers), the domicile, the habitual address (contact address) and the telephone number.

Comment:

Basic information of the parities is necessary for any contract to identify the parties. The basic information shall be complete, precise and true. In case of the termination of a labour contract, the notice shall be delivered to the party and the address. It's better to include the information of the emergency contact in the labour contract. It is advisable that email addresses or webchat accounts be included. The service of notices or summons in an electronic way was confirmed by the Supreme People's Court.

3.2.2 Applicable Laws and Basic Principles

This contract is made in accordance with the Labour Law, the Labour Contract Law and other related laws, regulations and policies. Party A and Party B follow the principles of legality, fairness, equity, voluntariness, consensus and the bona fide doctrine to conclude this contract.

Comment:

Any dispute arising out of the Contract shall be settled in accordance with appliable laws. The Labour Law of 2018 and the Labour Contract Law of 2012 are the basis of dispute settlement. Such laws will apply to matters that are not stipulated by the Contract. The following principles shall be followed. Legality is first and foremost. Particularly, in the case of a labour contract with a foreigner worker, the work permit shall be taken into consideration. The minimum age of a labourer shall be 16 years. A labour contract shall be made on the basis of fairness and equity. If the stipulated damages are extremely high, the labour contract will be unfair to a labourer, which the court will adjust on the basis of fairness and equity. What voluntariness and consensus require is that a labour contract shall be understood and interpreted in favor of a labourer. The bona fide doctrine can be used to fill in the gaps of a labour contract.

3.2.3 Period of Labour Contracts

Party A and Party B establish the labour relationship from employment, and both parties agree on the period of the labour contract as follows:

(a) Fixed term: from_____(date/month/year) to_____ (date/month/year). The probation period is from the employment date to _____(date/month/year).

(b) Open ended: from _____(date/month/year) to the date when the labour contract is revoked or terminated. The probation period is from the employment date to _____(date/month/year).
(c) Completing a specific assignment: from_____(date/month/year) to the date when the assignment is completed. Party A shall notify Party B of the completion of the task in writing.

Comment:

There is no requirement for the duration of a fixed-term labour contract. A proper period of the labour contract should be selected according to realities. If the period is too short, it is very likely that an employing unit is subject to the provision of an open-ended labour contract. If the period is too long, it is not flexible for the management of human resources. If the period of a labour contract is more than three months but less than one year, the probation period may not exceed one month; if the period is more than one year but less than three years, the probation period may not exceed two months; and if the period is fixed for three or more years or is open-ended, the probation period may not exceed six months. An employing unit and a labourer may agree upon only one probation period. No probation period may be stipulated in a labour contract that expires upon completion of a given job or in a labour contract for a period of less than three months. The probation period shall be included in terms of a labour contract.[15] It is a misconception that an open-ended contract is a permanent labour contract. In fact, a labourer under an open ended labour contract is still subject to all the obligations under the Labour Contract Law of 2012, and an employing unit may revoke and terminate an open ended labour contract in accordance with the Labour Contract Law of 2012. Whether the probation period can be extended remains in dispute.

3.2.4 Work Contents and Place of Work

The job position of Party B is__________, and the duty is _____________. Party B's place of work is________________.

Party B shall love his or her job, devote himself or herself to work, be honest and trustworthy. Party B shall maintain the confidentiality of Party A's trade secrets, comply with the labour rules made by Party A, perform his duties, and finish the work in time. Where Party B violates Party A's discipline, Party A may take disciplinary actions against Party B in accordance with the labour rules duly made by law.

Comments:

(1) Job position and duty should be specific to judge whether Party B is competent for the job. Otherwise, there will be some difficulty in dismissing Party B in accordance with Item 2 of Article 40 in the Labour Contract Law of 2012. It

[15] The Labour Contract Law of 2012, Article 19.

is suggested that the right to transfer a labourer from the position be included so that Party A has the initiative in human resource management.

(2) The place of work should not be too specific or too broad. For example, the wording of "the place of work is in Beijing" may not be accepted because "in Beijing" is too broad. However, it is accepted that *the place of work in Beijing and Party B knows about the operation model of Party A and the nature of the job position*. Even if both parties agree that Party A has the uniliteral right to change the place of work, such change will be subject to the test of reasonableness by courts.

(3) The rules of Party A play an important role in human resource management. However, the rules of Party A shall comply with the procedural and substantial requirements of the Labour Contract Law of 2012. In practice, they may be subject to the test of reasonableness by court.

3.2.5 Working Hours, Rest and Holidays

According to the characteristics of the job position of Party B, Party B shall be subject to a _____working hour system:

(a) Standard Working Hour System. The working hours per day shall not exceed 8 h, and the working hours per week shall not exceed 40 h.[16] Both parties may agree to extend the working hours as necessitated by its production or business operation after consultation, but the extended working hours per day shall generally not exceed one hour; if such extension is needed for special reasons, the extended hours shall not exceed three hours per day. However, the total extended hours in a month shall not exceed thirty-six hours.[17] Party A shall not compel Party B to work overtime.

(b) Comprehensive Working Hour System with a week/month/quarter/year as a computation cycle. The aggregated working hours within the computation cycle shall not exceed the statutory aggregated working hours. Party A shall take proper actions to protect Party B's right to rest and holidays.

(c) Irregular Working Hour System. Party A shall take proper actions to protect Party B's rights to rest and holidays.

Party A arranges for Party B to work overtime, and Party A shall arrange compensatory time off or pay overtime wages.

Party A may be entitled to statutory holidays, paid annual leave, marital leave, funeral leave, maternal leave, etc.

Comments:

(1) Under the standard working hour system, Party A shall ensure that Party B has a day off in a week. Such day may be at weekends or on any working

[16] The Labour Law of 2018, Article 36.

[17] The Labour Law of 2018, Article 41.

day. Party A shall apply for an administrative permit in accordance with the Approval Measures for the Enterprises concerning Irregular Working Hour System and Comprehensive Working Hour System before adopting comprehensive working hour system or irregular working hour system. Party A shall also comply with the Regulations of Labourers' Paid Annual Leave.

(2) The irregular working hour system is applicable to (i) senior management, outdoor staff, salesmen and operators on duty; (ii) long-distance transport workers, taxi drivers and stevedores in a railway station, port, or warehouse; or (iii) others in special work positions that may arrange their own work and rest schedules.[18]

(3) The comprehensive working hour system is a system that calculates working hours over a "comprehensive calculation period" (e.g., weekly, monthly, quarterly, or yearly); however, the average daily working hours and average weekly working time shall meet the requirements of the standard working hours system. The comprehensive working hour system is applicable to (i) transportation industries, railway systems, telecommunications, water transport enterprises, air transport industries, and fisheries and (ii) geologic and resource exploration, construction, salt production, sugar production and tourism.[19]

(4) Under any of the following circumstances, Party A shall, according to the following standards, pay Party B remuneration that are higher than those for normal working hours: (i) to pay no less than 150% of the normal wages if an extension of working hours is arranged; (ii) to pay no less than 200% of the normal wages if work is arranged on off days and no make-up off days can be arranged; or (iii) to pay no less than 300% of the normal wages if work is arranged on statutory holidays.

3.2.6 Labour Remuneration

Party A shall pay Party B the wages in cash by the______day of every month as follows:

(a) Monthly wages______yuan.

(b) Piece wages. The piece rate is_____. Party A shall decide the reasonable quotas to ensure that Party B is reasonably paid if Party B provides normal labour.

(c) Combination of basic wages and performance wages: Party B's basic wages are_____yuan, and the performance wages are_________________.

(d) Other ways stipulated by both parties________________________.

Party B's wages in the probation period are___________________.

[18] The Approval Measures for the Enterprises concerning Irregular Working Hour System and Comprehensive Working Hour System, Article 4.

[19] The Approval Measures for the Enterprises concerning Irregular Working Hour System and Comprehensive Working Hour System, Article 5.

Party A shall reasonably adjust Party B's wages and benefits. Party A shall withhold and deduct the personal income tax payable by Party B from Party B's wages.

Comments:

(1) Party A shall pay the wages in accordance with the Interim Regulations of Wage Payment released by the Ministry of Labour on 6 December 1994 and the regulations of wage payment in every province. Liaoning Province released its wage payment regulations on 2 September 2006. Guangdong Province released its wage payment regulations on 19 January 2005 and revised them on 29 September 2016. The wages to be paid to Party B shall not be embezzled nor the payment thereof delayed for no reason. Party A shall pay wages Party B for their statutory holidays, marriage or funeral leave or periods when Party B participates in social activities in accordance with the law.
(2) If Party A owes Party B back pay, Party B may revoke the labour contract and claim economic compensation.
(3) It is suggested that both parties agree on the standard to calculate the overtime wages, even though such stipulated standard is deemed to be invalid in some provinces.
(4) The following items shall be deducted from Party B's wages: (a) personal income tax payable by Party B; (b) the expenses of social insurance and housing funds payable by Party B; (c) the alimonies decided by the court; (d) the damages to Party A where Party B does harm to Party A; or (e) other statutory items or stipulated items, provided the remaining after such deductions shall not be below the minimum wage standard at the local.[20]

3.2.7 Social Insurance and Benefits

Both parties shall take out social insurance by law, and Party A shall go through procedures related to social insurance for Party B and fulfil obligations related to social insurance. Party A shall deduct the expenses of the social insurance payable by Party B from Party B's wages.

Party A shall comply with the state regulations of labourers' benefits. In the case of work-related injuries or occupational diseases, Party B shall be entitled to the benefits under state laws and regulations. In the case of nonwork-related injuries or nonoccupational diseases, Party B shall be entitled to the benefits under the state laws and regulations and the rules of Party A.

Comments:

(1) Taking out social insurance is a statutory obligation for Party A. Such obligations may not be evaded or transferred. Party A shall take out the social insurance for foreigner workers employed in China unless the bilateral protocols

[20] The Interim Regulations of Wage Payment, Article 15.

between China and another country concerning social security are applicable. At present, China has signed totalisation agreements with German, Korea, Denmark, Canada, Finland, Switzerland, Holland, Spain, Luxembourg, Japan and Serbia.[21]

(2) Without taking out work-related injury insurance, Party A will be solely responsible for work-related injury and compensate Party B for the benefits under work-related injury insurance.

(3) Commercial insurance cannot take the place of social insurance.

(4) Party A shall comply with the Regulations on Management of Housing Provident Fund. It should be noted that in some cities, the payment of housing provident funds is not compulsory.

3.2.8 Vocational Training and Labour Protection

Party A shall provide Party B with the vocational training necessary for the job position. Party B shall take the initiative to study and take part in the training orgaised by Party A to improve vocational skills.

Party A shall strictly implement the laws and regulations related to labour security and hygiene, comply with the laws and regulations related to the special protection of women labourers and young labourers, make and perfect the rules related to labour security and hygiene, provide Party B with labour security education and operating procedure training, offer Party B necessary labour protection equipment and supplies, improve labour conditions and reduce occupational hazards. Where Party B's job position is exposed to occupational diseases, Party A shall notify Party B of potential occupational diseases and their consequences that may arise out of the employment, take necessary and reasonable measures to prevent the occupational diseases, and make sure that Party B has physical checkups before taking the job position, on the job position and after leaving the job position.

Party A shall strictly comply with safety operating procedures, and Party B may refuse to carry out the instructions that are against such procedures.

Comments:

(1) Party A shall strictly comply with the Law of the PRC on Work Safety of 2014. The principal leading members of production and business units are charged with the following responsibilities for work safety in their own units: (a) setting up and improving the responsibility system for work safety in their own units; (b) making arrangements for formulating rules and operating regulations for work safety in their own units; (c) guaranteeing an effective input into work safety in their own units; (d) supervising over and inspecting work safety in their own units and, in a timely manner, eliminating hidden dangers threatening work safety; (e) making arrangements for the formulation and implementation

[21] Totalisation Agreements (2021).

of their own units' rescue plans in the event of accidents; and (f) submitting to higher authorities timely and truthful report on accidents due to lack of work safety.[22] Labourers shall have the right to criticise and inform their work units of the problems with work safety. They shall have the right to refuse to comply with directions that are contrary to rules and regulations or arbitrary orders for risky operations.[23]

(2) Party B sustaining work-related injuries due to lack of work safety may, in addition to enjoying the benefits from social insurance in accordance with law, have the right to demand compensation from the Party under relevant civil laws.[24]

(3) Where Party A fails to comply with the Law of the PRC on Work Safety of 2014, Party A shall bear administrative liabilities and criminal liabilities, if applicable.

(4) Party A shall strictly comply with the Law of the PRC on Prevention and Control of Occupational Diseases of 2018. The workplace, set up by the employing unit, where occupational disease hazards are produced shall, apart from fulfilling the conditions specified by laws and administrative regulations, meet the following requirements for occupational health: (a) the strength or concentration of the factors of occupational disease hazards shall meet the national norms for occupational health; (b) there are facilities commensurate with the prevention of occupational disease hazards; (c) the production processes are arranged rationally and in conformity with the principle of separation the harmful from nonharmful processes; (d) there are supporting health facilities such as locker rooms, bathrooms and a lounge for pregnant women workers; (e) the equipment, tools, apparatus and other facilities meet the requirements for protecting workers' physiological and psychological health; and (f) the workplace meets the other requirements specified by laws administrative regulations and the public health administration department under the State Council regarding the protection of worker's health.[25]

(5) In addition to enjoying the benefits from social insurance, occupational disease patients who, according to related civil laws, still have the right to compensation, shall have the right to make a claim against the employing unit.[26]

(6) Where Party A fails to comply with the Law of the PRC on Prevention and Control of Occupational Diseases of 2018, Party A shall bear the administrative liabilities. In the case of a major accident caused by occupational disease hazards or other serious consequences, if a crime is constituted, the persons directly in charge and the other persons directly responsible shall be investigated for criminal responsibility according to law.

---

[22] The Law of the PRC on Work Safety of 2014, Article 18.

[23] The Law of the PRC on Work Safety of 2014, Article 51.

[24] The Law of the PRC on Work Safety of 2014, Article 53.

[25] The Law of the PRC on Prevention and Control of Occupational Diseases of 2018, Article 15.

[26] The Law of the PRC on Prevention and Control of Occupational Diseases of 2018, Article 58.

3.2.9 *Modification, Revocation and Termination of Labour Contracts*

Party A and Party B shall modify the labour contract in writing by law. Party A and Party B shall revoke or terminate the labour contract in accordance with related laws and regulations. In case of the revocation of the labour contract by both parties, Party B shall coordinate with Party A to hand over the work. Economic compensation may be paid to Party B by Party A after handing over the work. When Party A revokes or terminates the labour contract, Party A shall provide Certificate of Revoking/Terminating Labour Contracts for Party B and go through the procedures of personnel document transfer and social insurance transfer within 15 days.

Comment:

The modification, revocation and termination of labour contracts often give rise to many labour disputes. The topic will be discussed in Sect. 3.4.

3.2.10 *Other Matters Stipulated by Both Parties*

Party A may sign a nondisclosure or noncompete agreement with Party B with regard to Party A's trade secrets and intellectual property rights where they are involved in the course of employment of Party B. Where the vocational training is at the expense of Party A, Party A and Party B may sign a written agreement for a service period.

Other matters both parties agree on include ____________.

Comments:

(1) Trade secrets are of incalculable value to the development of enterprises, which provide enterprises with advantages over competitors. Trade secrets are information that has either actual or potential independent economic value by virtue of not being generally known, have value to others who cannot legitimately obtain the information and are subject to reasonable efforts to maintain their secrecy. On 10 September 2020, the Supreme People's Court released the Judicial Regulations on Several Issues of Legal Application of Hearing the Cases of Infringement on Trade Secrets, which sets forth the definitions of technological information and operation information (Article 1), the circumstances that are deemed to be generally known to the public (Article 4), the reasonable efforts to maintain the secrecy (Article 6), the scope of labourers that are subject to the obligations of confidentiality (Article 11), and the defence of reverse engineering (Article 14). In addition, Party A shall comply with the Anti Unfair Competition Law revised on 23 April 2019. Party A and Party B may incorporate a nondisclosure clause into the Labour Contract or sign a separate contract to protect the trade secrets of Party A.

(2) A noncompete contract is an agreement where a labourer promises not to enter into competition of any kind with any other employing unit after the contract period is over. An employing unit shall pay compensation in exchange for the promise. The labourers who are subject to a noncompete contract may include senior managers, senior technicians and other labourers in whose employment the obligations of confidentiality are involved.

3.2.11 Settlement of Labour Disputes

In case of any dispute arising out of this Contract, both parties may consult with each other first or apply for mediation or arbitration. Either Party that is not satisfied with the arbitral award may lodge a lawsuit in a competent court.

Comments:

(1) Labour arbitration is compulsory, and it is a procedural prerequisite to labour dispute litigation.
(2) Any agreement that a labour dispute shall be settled in the place where an employing unit is located is invalid. In the Civil Order of the Dispute of Jurisdiction between Cao Wen and Beijing Haitian Zhiyuan Labour Service Co., Ltd. (2020 SC CJ 28), the Supreme People's Court held that the legal relationship underlying the labour dispute was personal, and the stipulated jurisdiction of court was not applicable to the labour dispute.

3.2.12 Miscellaneous Matters

Party B's telephone number and contact address stated in this Contract shall be for the use of any notice and service. Party B shall notify Party A immediately of any change in the number and address.

Party A and Party B understand and acknowledge that they have read this Contract and understood their respective rights and obligations. Any matters not stipulated in this Contract shall be decided in accordance with the related laws, regulations and policies.

Each Party holds one copy of this Contract, and this Contract enters into force upon the signatures (seal) by both parties, and both parties shall strictly perform this Contract.

Party A (seal): ____________ Party B (signature): ____________.

Legal/Authorised Representative:

DD/MM/YY DD/MM/YY

Comments:

(1) It is suggested that the consequence of Party B's failure to notify A of such change be included in the Contract. It's better to make it clear that if Party B fails to notify Party A of the changed personal information, the delivery of any notice or legal documents by Party A to such address shall be deemed that the delivery is actually made.
(2) Party B shall sign the name in person before Party A so that the forged signature is avoided. Once the signature is forged, it can be inferred that there is no written labour contract between Party A and Party B, and Party A may bear the related liabilities, such as payment of double wages.

Attachment 1

Renewal of Labour Contract

Party A and Party B agree to renew this Contract as follows:

Article 1 Party A and Party B determine the Contract period in the ______form:

1. Fixed term: From DD/MM/YY to DD/MM/YY

2. Open ended: From DD/MM/YY to the date of the due revocation or termination of this Contract

Article 2 Both parties agree on the following matters:

1.

2.

3.

Article 3 With regard to other matters, both parties shall continue to perform this Contract dated DD/MM/YY.

Party A(seal):__________ Party B(signature):____________

Legal/Authorised Representative:

DD/MM/YY DD/MM/YY

Comments:

(1) Both parties shall renew the Contract in writing.
(2) Consensus of both parties is necessary for renewing the Contract.
(3) Renewing the Contract amounts the signing of the Contract on a consecutive basis, which may make Party B invoke the provision of an open-ended labour contract.

Attachment 2

Modification of Labour Contract

Article 1 On DD/MM/YY, Party A and Party B agree to modify this Contract as follows:

1.

2.

3.

Article 2 With regard to other matters, both parties shall continue to perform this Contract dated DD/MM/YY.

Party A(seal): ___________ Party B(signature): _____________

Legal/Authorised Representative:

DD/MM/YY DD/MM/YY

Comments:

(1) Consensus of both parties is necessary for modifying the Contract.
(2) Party A's unilateral right to modify the Contract may be subject to the test of reasonableness by courts.

3.3 Invalidity and Modification of Labour Contracts

3.3.1 Invalidity of Labour Contracts

3.3.1.1 Causes for Invalidity of Labour Contracts

Article 26 of the Labour Contract Law of 2012 provides that a labour contract shall be wholly or partially invalid under one of the following circumstances: (a) the labour contract is concluded or modified against a party's true intention by means of deception or coercion, or when the party is in precarious situations; (b) the employing unit disclaims its statutory responsibility or denies the labourer's rights; or (c) the labour contract is at variance with the mandatory provisions of laws or administrative regulations. If a dispute arises over the whole invalidity or partial invalidity of a labour contract, the matter shall be determined by a labour dispute arbitration institution or a people's court.

In the case of deception or coercion, a labour contract is invalid, while a civil contract is voidable in accordance with Article 148 and Article 150 of the Civil Code. Coerce is rare today. A labour contract is often held to be invalid on the grounds that a labourer provides a fake academic credential while applying for a position. In the Civil Decision of Second Instance of the Case of Labour Dispute between Shenzhen Road Innovation Technology Co., Ltd. and Li Weilan (2019 Yue03 CF 20539), the Intermediate People's Court of Shenzhen held that Shenzhen Road

Innovation Technology Co., Ltd. was entitled to revoke the labour contract because Li Weilan provided the fake academic credential when Li joined the company.

Under the Labour Contract Law of 2012, an employing unit has to fulfil some statutory obligations, such as taking out social insurance. Exclusion of such compulsory obligations is deemed to be invalid. In the Civil Decision of Second Instance of the Case of Labour Dispute between Sumitomo Electric Software (Dalian) Co., Ltd. and Hou Zhidong (2016 Liao 02 CF 2097), the Intermediate People's Court of Dalian held that Article 11 of the Overseas Dispatch Contract was invalid, which stipulated that Hou Zhidong shall refund the portion of the payment of social insurance and housing provident fund payable by Sumitomo Electric Software (Dalian) Co., Ltd. in case that he resigned during the dispatching period.

Any clause in a labour contract that goes against the compulsory provisions of laws or administrative regulations is invalid. For example, Article 25 of the Labour Contract Law of 2012 is compulsory, which provides that with the exception of the circumstances specified in Articles 22 (service period) and 23 (nondisclosure and noncompete) of the Labour Contract Law of 2012, an employing unit shall not enter into an agreement with a labourer on payment of stipulated damages by the labourer. In the Civil Decision of Second Instance of the Case of Labour Dispute between Beijing Uppoint Hengxin Consulting Co., Ltd. and Liang Yi (2014 CF 4000), the First Intermediate People's Court of Beijing held that Article 28 of the labour contract in dispute stipulated that where Party B resigned without permission, Party A could withhold the basis wage of one month as the stipulated damages, which went against the compulsory provision of the Labour Contract Law of 2012 and was invalid.

3.3.1.2 Effects of Invalid Labour Contracts

If part of a labour contract is invalid, which does not affect the validity of the rest of the contract, the rest shall remain valid. The doctrine of restitution cannot come into play where a labour contract is held to invalid. The labourer is still entitled to the remuneration if he has fulfiled the obligations under the labour contract. The amount of remuneration shall be determined mutatis mutandis with reference to that for the labourer holding the same or similar posts in the employing unit.

In the Civil Decision of Second Instance of the Case of Labour Contract between Ding Ding and CCPI (2019 Jing 03 CF 3356), Ding Ding confirmed that he practiced law on 26 April 2007 and worked as a full-time lawyer in Beijing Zhongwen Law Firm in January 2011. Ding Ding was employed as a senior lawyer in the investment center by CCPI on 1 July 2013 and signed a labour contract for the period from 1 July 2013 to 30 June 2019. On 30 December 2016, the CCPI delivered him a notice of termination of the labour contract on the grounds that (a) Ding Ding was absent from work for no good reason; (b) he kept the labour relationship with other units; and (c) he violated the financial rules of CCPI. On 12 January 2017, he applied to the Beijing Chaoyang Labour Arbitration Commission for arbitration, and the Commission held that the labour relationship between Ding Ding and CCPI shall be restituted. However, Beijing Chaoyang District People's Court held that (a) Article

10 of the Law of Lawyers was compulsory and the employment of Ding Ding by CCPI violated the compulsory provision, so the labour contract between Ding Ding and CCPI was invalid and (b) the invalidity of the labour contract did not prejudice Ding Ding's right to the remuneration, which was determined with reference to the remuneration of a labourer holding the same or similar position and the Third Intermediated People's Court of Beijing upheld the decision of first instance.

3.3.2 *Modification of Labour Contracts*

3.3.2.1 Modification of Labour Contracts by Agreement

An employing unit and its labourers may modify the labour contracts in writing through consensus in terms of work content, place of work, working hours, labour remuneration, etc. In accordance with Article 25 of the Labour Contract Law of 2012, modification of labour contracts entails consensus by both parties and the written form. The modification of labour contracts is often connected with the revocation of labour contracts. A labourer is entitled to refuse to perform an illegally modified labour contract. If an employing unit revokes the labour contract with a labourer on the grounds that the labourer refuses to perform the illegal modification, the employing unit shall bear the liability of illegal revocation of the labour contract in accordance with Article 48 of the Labour Contract of 2012.

In the Civil Decision of Second Instance of the Case of Labour Dispute between Jiaduobao (China) Drink Co., Ltd. and Xie Jianmin (2020 Jing 02 CF 6272), Xie Jianmin worked in Jiaduobao from 17 June 2010 and signed the labour contract for the period from 17 June 2010 to 16 June 2014, which stipulated that her job position was the business representative and that the working places were Beijing, Tianjin, Hebei, Shandong, Shanxi, Inner Mongolia, Shanxi, Qinghai, Xinjiang, Gansu, Heilongjiang, Jilin, Liaoning and Ningxia. On 17 June 2014, Jiaduobao and Xie Jianmin signed the labour contract for the period from 17 June 2014 to 16 June 2020, which stipulated that her job position was the senior business representative, and the working place was China. On 26 July 2019, Jiaduobao notified Xie Jianmin that she was transferred from the Shunyi District to the Chaoyang District in Beijing. However, Jiaduobao failed to compensate her for the inconvenience to her life and work arising from such transfer. On 30 July 2019, Xie Jianmin refused the transfer. On 9 October 2019, Xie Jianmin refused the transfer again and replied that the transfer was not justified. On 20 October 2019, Xie Jianmin replied that she was pregnant, and the transfer would bring inconveniences to her. The Second Intermediate People's Court of Beijing held that (a) a place of work mattered to a labourer, but Jiaduobao did not consult with Xie Jianmin before making the decision; (b) Jiaduobao did not reasonably compensate Xie Jianmin for the inconvenience caused by such transfer; and (c) Jiaduobao did not actively consult with Xie Jianmin even though it knew of her pregnancy and it was not proper for Jiaduobao to revoke the labour contract with Xie Jianmin. What is more important is that the stipulated unilateral right to modify the labour contract will be subject to the test of reasonableness by court. Therefore, Article 21 (unilateral right to modify the labour contract) of the labour contract was negated in this case. Finally, Jiaduobao paid Xie Jianmin the economic compensation incurred by the illegal revocation of the labour contract.

3.3.2.2 Statutory Modification of Labour Contracts by an Employing Unit

As an exception to Article 25 of the Labour Contract Law of 2012, statutory modification of labour contracts by an employing unit occurs in case of any of the following occurrences: (a) a labourer who contracted a disease or sustained a nonwork-related injury cannot do the stipulated work after the statutory medical treatment period expires; (b) a labourer is not competent for the stipulated work; and (c) a labourer's health is harmed by work-related factors, which is found in occupational health examinations for the purposes of the Law of the PRC on Prevention and Control of Occupational Diseases of 2018. To maintain the balance between the management rights of an employing unit and the legal rights of a labourer, the statutory modification of labour contracts is subject to the test of reasonableness by courts.

In the Civil Order of Second Instance of the Case of Labour Contract Dispute between Halla Visteon Climate Control (Dalian) Co., Ltd. and Wang Yan (2020 Liao 02 CF 318), the Intermediate People's Court of Dalian repealed the decision of first instance and remanded the dispute for retrial on the grounds that the court of first instance did not determine whether the wages of Wang Yan, the appellee, decreased sharply after the job transfer or whether the job transfer was insulting or punitive.

3.4 Revocation and Termination of Labour Contracts

3.4.1 Revocation and Termination

Often revocation is often confused with termination. According to Black's Law Dictionary, revocation means withdrawal of an offer by the offeror, while termination means the act of ending something, such as termination of conditional contract (the act of putting an end to all unperformed portions of a conditional contract) or termination of employment (the complete severance of an employer-employee relationship).[27] However, in accordance with Articles 26 and 27 of the Opinions of Several Issues of Implementing the Labour Law, the revocation of a labour means either party or both parties end the labour relationships in advance due to a certain reason after the labour contract is concluded before it is performed completely, while an invalid labour contract is the contract that does not meet the statutory conditions and has

[27] Garner (2014).

no binding forces as expected, and whether a labour contract is invalid shall be determined by a competent People's Court or a competent labour dispute arbitration commission. The effect of revocation is generally the same as that of termination. In Chinese labour law, revocation and termination are different in their respective grounds and procedures. However, from the perspective of the effect, revocation may be a special type of termination, both of which imply that all the rights and obligations under a labour contract come to an end.

It should be noted that before the Civil Code was enacted, there were revocation of contracts and termination of contracts in the Contract Law, but termination of contracts was deleted by the Civil Code.

3.4.2 Revocation of Labour Contracts

3.4.2.1 Revocation of Labour Contracts by Agreement

An employing unit and its labourer may revoke the labour contract by agreement. Sometimes, revocation of a labour contract may be confused with unilateral revocation of a labour contract. In accordance with Article 471 of the Civil Code, the parties may conclude a contract by making an offer and acceptance or other means. Therefore, revocation of labour contracts by agreement generally entails an offer and an acceptance. Identifying who makes an offer to revoke labour contact is very important. If an employing unit offers to revoke a labour contract, the unit will bear the liability in accordance with Item 2 of Article 46 of the Labour Law of 2018. In contrast, if a labourer offers to revoke a labour contract and Article 46 of the Labour Contract Law of 2012 does not apply, his employing unit will not bear any liabilities.

The reasoning behind it is that generally a job hopper who proposes to revoke the labour contract will not be faced with unemployment or has been well prepared for unemployment, and it is not fair for an employing unit to pay economic compensation in this case. In the Civil Decision of Second Instance of the Case of Labour Dispute between Wuhan Telecommunication Devices Co., Ltd. and Yang Jialong (2020 E01 CF 4316), on 1 April 2012 Yang Jialong and Wuhan Telecommunication Devices Co., Ltd. (WTD) signed the labour contract, the period of which was from 1 April 2012 to 31 March 2015, and renewed the labour contract in the form of Labour-Contract-Renewal Intention Feedback Table, where both parties agreed to the period of the labour contract was from 1 April 2015 to 31 March 2018. On 13 May 2019, Yang Jialong submitted to WTD an online application for resignation, ticked "others" and remarked "revocation by agreement". The Intermediate People's Court of Wuhan held that Article 37 of the Labour Contract Law of 2012 did not entail consultation with an employing unit, and WTD's argument that Yang Jialong offered to resign was rejected.

3.4.2.2 Revocation of Labour Contracts by an Employing Unit

Article 39 of the Labour Contract Law of 2012 provides that an employing unit may revoke the labour contract where a labourer:

(1) **Is found not to meet the requirements of recruitment in the probation period**

In accordance with the Several Opinions of Implementing the Labour Law released by the former Ministry of Labour, the probation period means the period of less than 6 months that an employing unit and a labourer agree on with a view to mutual understanding and two-way selection. In a broad sense, the requirements of recruitment refer to all the requirements of admission to an employing unit, which include the objective requirements (age, gender, degree of education, etc.) and the subjective requirements (teamwork spirit, loyalty, etc.). In a narrow sense, the requirements of recruitment refer to objective requirements, which mainly include the basic information of a labourer, such as the degree of education and working experience. Whether performance appraisals may be included in the requirements of recruitment remains in dispute.

(2) **Seriously violates the rules of the employing unit**

The rules of the employing unit shall meet the procedural and substantive requirements under the Labour Contract Law of 2012. To maintain the balance between the management rights and the labourers' rights, the rules of the employing unit are subject to legality and reasonableness tests. It is common that many employing units are not aware of such requirements. "seriously" shows the extent to which the rules are violated. "seriously" has different meanings in different scenarios and should be judged on a case-by-case basis.

(3) **Caused major losses to an employing unit due to serious dereliction of duty or engagement in malpractices for personal gain**

Similarly, major losses shall be determined on a case-by-case basis. In practice, the type of employing units and their rules are factors to be taken into account. Serious dereliction of duty is identified with reference to the job description. An employing unit has to produce sufficient evidence in terms of the alleged fact, the major loss, and the causal relationship. In the Civil Decision of Second Instance of the Case of Labour Dispute between Newlong Packaging Machinery (Beijing) Co., Ltd. and Li Jinsheng (2020 Jing 02 CF 7052), Li Jinsheng signed an open-ended contract with Newlong Packaging Machinery (Beijing) Co., Ltd. (Newlong), and worked as a factory manager; in the course of the employment, Li Jinsheng had Liu Wenqin, wife of Li Jinsheng, and Li Chunguang, son of Li Jinsheng, established and operated Beijing Dingge Technology Co., Ltd., from which Newlong made purchases at higher prices, Newlong produced as evidence the purchase orders, the invoices, the photos of warehouse inventories and the auditor's report to prove that Li Jinsheng caused major loss to Newlong, but the Second Intermediate People's Court of Beijing held that Newlong failed to prove the causative relationship between the alleged mismanagement and the major loss.

(4) **Concurrently establishes a labour relationship with another employing unit, which seriously affects the accomplishment of the task of the original employing unit, or refuses to rectify it after the original employing unit brings the matter to his attention**

Double labour relationships are not prohibited by law, which is generally accepted in legal practice. In the Civil Order of Retrial Review and Supervision Inspection of the Case of Labour Dispute between Presence Energy Technology (Beijing) Co., Ltd. and Jie Zhihua (2019 Jing CA 4954), the Higher People's Court of Beijing held that double labour relationships are not prohibited by law, and thus Presence Energy Technology (Beijing) Co., Ltd. could not deny the labour relationship with Jie Zhihua on the grounds that Jie Zhihua and another company had the labour relationship.

(5) **Invalidates the labour contract as a result of the circumstance specified in Subparagraph 1 of Paragraph 1 of Article 26 of the Labour Contract Law of 2012**

Where a labour contract is concluded or modified against a party's true intention by means of deception or coercion or when the party is in precarious situations, the labour contract is held to be invalid ab initio. Theoretically, the parties cannot revoke an invalid contract. This provision may be treated as a special provision in Chinese labour law. As explained earlier, it often invalidates the labour contract that a job hunter provides forged personal information. Whether the meanings of deception or coercion in labour law are the same as those in civil law should be reconsidered. This question will be addressed later.

or

(6) **Is investigated for criminal liability in accordance with law**

Paragraph 4 of Article 25 of the Several Opinions of Implementing the Labour Law released by the former Ministry of Labour, "being investigated for criminal liability" means that a labourer is (a) exempted from prosecution by a competent people's procuratorate; (b) imposed a criminal penalty on by court; (c) exempted from a criminal penalty by court in accordance with Article 37 of the Criminal Law of 2017;or (d) sentenced to a penal servitude or subject to a suspended prison sentence of less than three years.

3.4.2.3 Revocation of Labour Contracts with a 30-Day Notice

Article 40 of the Labour Law of 2018 provides that an employing unit may revoke the labour contract if it notifies in writing the labourer of its intention 30 days in advance, or after paying him or her an extra one-month wage in case of one of the following circumstances: (a) the labourer is unable to take up his original work or any other work arranged by the employing unit on the expiry of the specified period of medical treatment for illness or for a nonwork-related injury; (b) the labourer is incompetent for the post and remains incompetent after receiving a training or being transferred to another post; or (c) the objective conditions taken as the basis for conclusion of the contract have greatly changed, so that the original labour contract cannot be performed and, despite the consultation between the employing unit and the labourer, no agreement is reached on modification of the labour contract. In this case, it is not the labourer's fault that leads to the revocation of the labour contract.

It should be noted that in accordance with Article 35 of the Opinions of Several Issues of Implementing the Labour Law released by the Ministry of Labour on 4 August 1995, the Labour Appraisal Commission shall make the appraisal of labour capacity with reference to the appraisal standards for a labourer sustaining work-related injuries and occupational diseases before an employing unit revokes a labour contract on grounds of Item 2 of Article 40 of the Labour Contract Law of 2012. In accordance with Article 27 of the Explanations of Several Provisions of the Labour Law released by the Ministry of Labour on 5 September 1994, which was annulled on 1 January 2001, "incompetent for the post" means a labourer cannot complete the assignment stipulated in the labour contract as required or the workload of the same type of job or a labourer holding the same post, and the objective conditions mean act of God, or other circumstances that make the whole or partial provisions of a labour contract unenforceable, such as reallocation, M&A, and the transfer of the enterprise assets.

3.4.2.4 Redundancies

Article 41 of the Labour Contract Law of 2012 provides that, if an employing unit needs to reduce the workforce by more than 20 persons, or by less than 20 persons, which, however, accounts for more than 10% of the total number of the enterprise's labourers, it may do so after it explains the situation to the trade union or all of its labourers 30 days in advance, solicits opinions from among them and submit its plan for reducing the workforce to the administrative department of labour in any of the following circumstances: (a) it is to undergo reorganisation pursuant to the provisions of the Law on Enterprise Bankruptcy; (b) it is in dire straits in production and management; (c) it changes its line of production, introduces a major technological updating or adjusts its business method, and, after modification of the labour contracts, still needs to reduce its workforce; or (d) the objective economic conditions taken as the basis for conclusion of the labour cannot be performed. When reducing the workforce, the employing unit shall continue to employ the following persons by giving priority to them: (a) persons who have concluded fixed-term labour contracts for a relatively long term with the employing unit; (b) persons who have concluded open-ended labour contracts with the employing unit; and (c) persons whose family members are jobless or persons who have dependents. If an employing unit that has reduced its workforce reemploys labourers within six months, it shall give notification to the laid off persons and, under equal conditions, recruit them before others.

In practice, there are some disputes over the procedure of redundancies and the selection of redundant labourers. In the Civil Decision of Second Instance of the Case of Labour Dispute between Beijing Huidao Zhiyuan Technology Co., Ltd. and Chai Li (2020 Jing 03 CF 8023), the Third Intermediate People's Court held that it was groundless that Beijing Huidao Zhiyuan Technology Co., Ltd. argued that it had revoked the labour contract with Chai Li on grounds of redundancy specified in Article 41 of the Labour Contract Law of 2012, but it failed to submit the plan of reducing the workforce to the labour administrative department.

3.4.2.5 Exceptions to Articles 40–41 of the Labour Contract Law of 2012

Article 42 of the Labour Contract Law of 2012 provides exceptions where Articles 40–41 do not come into play. The employing unit may not revoke the labour contract concluded with the labourer, who is under one of the following circumstances: (a) Being engaged in operations exposed to occupational disease hazards, the labourer is not given predeparture occupational health examinations, or being suspected of an occupational disease, is in the process of being diagnosed or is under medical observation; (b) Having contracted an occupational disease or being injured at work, the labourer is confirmed to have totally or partially lost the ability to work; (c) The labourer is in the prescribed period of medical treatment for illness, or for injury incurred when not at work, and; (d) The labourer is during the pregnant, puerperal or breast-feeding stage; (e) The labourer has been working for the employing unit continuously for 15 years in full and is less than 5 years away from the statutory retirement age; or (f) The labourer is in any other circumstances as provided for laws or regulations.

It should be noted that Article 39 of the Labour Contract Law of 2012 prevails over Article 42 of the Labour Contract Law of 2012. In the Civil Decision of Second Instance of the Case of Labour Dispute between Wang Xinli and Jier Machine-tool Group Co., Ltd., etc. (2018 Lu 01 CF 4113), the Intermediate People's Court of Jinan held that even if it was true that Wang Xinli had not been given predeparture occupational health examinations before the revocation, it was not illegal that Jier Machine-tool Group Co., Ltd. revoked the labour contract in accordance with Article 39 of the Contract Labour Law. In the Civil Decision of Second Instance of the Case of Labour Dispute between Beijing Longxi Body-building Club Co., Ltd. and Li Li (2020 Jing 02 CF 1983), the Second Intermediate People's Court of Beijing held that Li Li, who was pregnant, failed to go through the procedure of asking for maternal leave and broke the rules of Beijing Longxi Body-building Club Co., Ltd. and it was not illegal that the labour contract was revoked in accordance with Article 39.

3.4.3 Revocation of Labour Contracts by a Labourer

3.4.3.1 Voluntary Resignation with a Notice

A labourer may give a 30-day notice in writing to an employing unit to revoke the labour contract, while a labourer in the probation period may revoke the labour contract by giving a 3-day written notice. It is generally accepted that such a notice is an obligation for the labouer who intends to resign. Failure to give such notice may impose the liability of compensation on the labourer in case the employing unit sustains losses due to immediate resignation. In addition, mutual consultation is not necessary for voluntary resignation, which, in nature, is a unilateral right of a labourer, and the view was held by the Intermediate People's Court of Wuhan in In the Civil Decision of Second Instance of the Case of Labour Dispute between Wuhan Telecommunication Devices Co., Ltd. and Yang Jialong (2020 E01CF 4316).

3.4.3.2 Immediate Revocation of Labour Contracts by a Labourer

Article 38 of the Labour Contract Law of 2012 provides that a labourer may have the labour contract revoked if the employing unit is found in any of the following circumstances: (a) failing to provide occupational protection or working conditions as agreed upon in the labour contract; (b) failing to pay labour remuneration on time and in full; (c) failing to pay the social insurance premiums for the labourer in accordance with law; (d) having rules that are at variance with laws or regulations, thereby impairing the labourer's rights and interests; (e) invalidating the labour contract as a result of one of the circumstances specified in Paragraph 1 of Article 26 of the Labour Contract Law of 2012; or (f) other circumstances in which a labourer may have the labour contract revoked as provided for by laws or administrative regulations. If an employing unit forces a person to work by means of violence, intimidation or illegal restriction of personal freedom, or if it gives instructions in violation of rules and regulations or gives peremptory orders to the labourer to perform hazardous operations, which endangers his or her personal safety, the latter may revoke the labour contract forthwith without notifying the employing unit of the intended revocation in advance.

3.4.4 Termination of Labour Contracts

The termination of labour contracts is prescribed in Article 44 of the Labour Contract Law of 2012. A labour contract shall be terminated under one of the following circumstances: (a) the period of the contract expires; (b) the labourer begins to enjoy the benefits of the basic old-age insurance pension in accordance with law; (c) the labourer dies, or is declared dead or missing by the people's court; (d) the employing unit is declared bankrupt in accordance with law; (e) the business licence of the employing unit is revoked, the employing unit is ordered to close down or to dissolve, or it decides to dissolve on an earlier date; or (f) any other circumstances provided for by laws and administrative regulations. The grounds of termination of labour contracts are added by the Implementation Regulations of the Labour Contract Law, which include that (a) the labourer reaches the age of retirement and (b) the job is completed in case of the labour contract that expires upon completion of a given job.

In practice, there may be contradictions between the entitlement to the benefits of the basic old-age insurance pension and the age of retirement. The nature of the legal relationship between an employing unit and a person who reaches the age of retirement but does not enjoy the benefits of the basic old-age insurance pension is controversial. Few courts hold that the legal relationship in issue is a labour contract instead of a contract for services. The Higher People's Court of Jiangxi Province held that in the Administrative Order of Retrial Review and Hearing Supervision of the Case of Labour and Social Security Administration between Jiangxi Huachunse Textile Technology Development Co., Ltd. and Hu Bin (2019 Gan AA589).

In contrast, most courts hold the view that the contract with a retired person was a contract for services. In the Civil Order of the Appeal for Labour Dispute between Zhao Changcui and Yangzhou Machinery Co., Ltd. (2018 Su CA 5600), the Higher People's Court of Jiangsu Province held that (a) in accordance of Article 21 of the Implementation Regulations of the Labour Contract Law, which provides that a labour contract is terminated where a labourer reaches the age of retirement, the labour contract between Zhao Changcui and Yangzhou Machinery Co., Ltd. was terminated of itself, and (b) the contract between Yangzhou Machinery Co., Ltd. and Zhao Changcui after her retirement was a special contract labour, which Yangzhou Machinery Co., Ltd. might revoke the contract without paying any economic compensation. In contrast, in the Civil Order of Retrial Review and Hearing Supervision of the Case of Labour Dispute between Liu Suna and Weihai Sanchang Foods Co., Ltd. (2020 Lu CA 4513), the Higher People's Court of Shandong Province held that (a) on 6 May 2013, Liu Suna reached the age of retirement, so the labour contract between Liu Suna and Weihai Sanchang Foods Co., Ltd. was terminated of itself; and (b) the contract after Liu Suna retired was a contract for services, which was subject to civil law. Some courts in Guangdong, Beijing, Zhejiang, Anhui, Fujian and Liaoning hold the same view as the courts in Shangdong Province. For example, the Intermediate People's Court of Guangzhou was of the same view in the Civil Decision of Second Instance of the Case of Labour Dispute between Liang Wanxia and Guangzhou Huantong Industry Co., Ltd. (2020 Yue 01 CF 11092).

3.4.5 *Obligations with Regard to Revocation and Termination of Labour Contracts*

3.4.5.1 Payment of Economic Compensation

In accordance with Article 46 of the Labour Contract Law of 2012, an employing unit shall pay economic compensation to a labourer in case of one of the following circumstances: (a) the labourer revokes the labour contract pursuant to the provisions in Article 38 of the Labour Contract Law of 2012; (b) the employing unit offers to revoke the labour contract pursuant to the provisions in Article 36 of the Labour Contract Law of 2012 and the parties reach an agreement thereon through consultation; (c) the employing unit revokes the labour contract pursuant to the provisions in Article 40 of the Labour Contract Law of 2012; (d) the employing unit revokes the labour contract pursuant to the provisions in the first paragraph of Article 41 of the Labour Contract Law of 2012; (e) the fixed-term labour contract is terminated pursuant to the provisions in Subparagraph (1) of Article 44 of the Labour Contract Law of 2012, except that the labourer does not agree to renew the contract even though the employing unit maintains the same conditions as, or offers better conditions than, the ones stipulated in the previous contract; (f) the labour contract is terminated pursuant to the provisions of Subparagraph (4) or (5) of Article 44 of the Labour Contract Law of 2012; or (g) under any other circumstances provided for by laws or administrative regulations.

Economic compensation shall be paid on the basis of the number of years a person works in an employing unit, the rate being one month's salary for the work of one full year. If he has worked for six months or more but less than one year, the time shall be calculated as one year; and if he has worked for less than six months, he shall be paid half of his monthly salary as economic compensation. If the monthly salary of a worker is three times the average monthly salary of the labourers of the region for the previous year, which is published by the people's government of the municipality directly under the Central Government or by that of the city divided into districts where the employing unit is located, the rate for his economic compensation payable shall be three times the average monthly salary of the labourers, and the number of years involved shall not exceed 12 years. The monthly salary means the average of a given labourer's monthly salary for the 12 months prior to the revocation or termination of the labour contract.

3.4.5.2 Post-contractual Obligations

In accordance with Article 50 of the Contract Labour Law of 2012, an employing unit shall issue a certificate of revocation or termination of the labour contract at the time of its revocation or termination and shall, within 15 days, go with the formalities for the transfer of the labourer's personal file and social insurance account. If an employing unit fails to fulfil the obligations, an affected labourer may lodge a lawsuit against the employing unit to have it performed such obligations and/or make a claim for compensation.

In the Civil Decision of Second Instance of the Case of Labour Dispute between Dashang Co., Ltd. and Fu Xiaowei (2020 Liao 02 CF 2473), Fu Xiaowei resigned from Dashang Co., Ltd. in January 2014, and Dashang Co., Ltd. kept Fu Xiaowei's personal file. On 28 June 2017, Fu Xiaowei reached the age of retirement, but Dashang Co., Ltd. did not go through the retirement procedure for him. The Intermediate People's Court of Dalian held that (a) Dashang Co., Ltd. handed over the personal file to Dalian Longxin Human Resources Service Center in charge of management of personal files; and (b) Dashang Co., Ltd. compensated Fu Xiaowei for the loss of his retirement benefit.

If violation of Article 50 of the Labour Contract Law of 2012 adversely affects the reemployment of a labourer, the affected labourer may lodge a lawsuit against his employing unit for the loss incurred by the unsuccessful reemployment. In the Civil Decision of Second Instance of the Case of Economic Compensation Dispute between Cai Yulong and Nanjing Jinzhongjian Curtain Wall Decoration Co., Ltd. (2016 Su 01 CF 652), which was released by the Gazette of the Supreme People's Court of the PRC of 2013 (Volume 12), the Intermediate People's Court of Nanjing held that if an employing unit fails to handle the procedures of personal files, social insurance and professional certificates so as that a labourer concerned cannot provide related certificates for a new employing unit or handle the procedures of reemployment, the new employing unit underestimates the labourer in terms of his working attitude and work ability and refused to employ him, the employing unit shall pay compensation for the unsuccessful reemployment.

The loss incurred to the affected labourer can be determined on the basis of the level of wages of the affected labourer in the former employing unit. In the Civil Decision of Second Instance of the Case of Labour Dispute between Dalian Machinery & Electronics Co., Ltd. and Jiang Yongbo (2020 Liao 02 CF 6247), the Intermediate People's Court of Dalian held that it was proper for the loss to be determined on the basis of the wages of Jiang Yongbo in Dalian Daxiang Machinery & Electronics Co., Ltd. Sometimes, some courts, at their discretion, decided on the loss to the affected labourer, which was reflected in the Civil Order by the Higher People's Court of Shandong of Retrial Review and Hearing Supervision of the Case of Labour Dispute between Doosan Infracore China Co., Ltd. (DICC) and Liu Fang (2020 Lu CA 2541).

3.4.5.3 Payment of Damages and Specific Performance

In accordance with Article 48 of the Labour Contract Law of 2012, if an employing unit revokes or terminates a labour contract in violation of the provisions of the Labour Contract Law of 2012 and the labourer involved demands continued performance of the labour contract, the employing unit shall continue performing the same. If the labourer does not demand so or if it becomes impossible for continued performance of the labour contract, the employing unit shall pay damages equivalent to double economic compensation pursuant to the provisions in Article 87 of the Labour Contract Law of 2012.

In the Civil Decision of Second Instance of the Case of Labour Dispute between Beijing Terminus Technology Group Co., Ltd. and Yang Fenglan (2020 Jing 02 CF 4601), the Second Intermediate People's Court of Beijing held that (a) Beijing Terminus Technology Group Co., Ltd. illegally revoked the labour contract with Yang Fenglan; and (b) Beijing Terminus Technology Group Co., Ltd. shall continue to perform the labour contract on the grounds that (i) the claim that the labour contract should be performed pursuant to Article 48 should be upheld; (ii) the fact that a new labourer filled Yang's post could not exempt Beijing Terminus Technology Group Co., Ltd. from continuing to perform the labour contract; and (iii) mutual trust between both parties remained in place.

3.5 Practical Issues Related to Labour Contracts

3.5.1 Conclusion of Labour Contracts

3.5.1.1 Understanding of Written Labour Contracts

In accordance with Article 10 of the Labour Contract Law of 2012, concluding a labour contract is a statutory obligation of an employing unit. In accordance with Article 82 of the Labour Contract Law of 2012, where an employing unit fails to conclude a written labour contract with a labourer for more than a month but less than a year from the date of employment, it shall pay the labourer double wages for each month. However, both the Labour Law of 2018 and the Labour Contract Law of 2012 are silent on what constitutes a written labour contract. There is no doubt that the legal document named Labour Contract is a written labour contract. What if a document containing the basic terms and conditions provided by Article 17 of the Labour Contract Law of 2012?

In TPS v Shan Jingjing, released by the Gazette of the Supreme People's Court of the PRC of 2013 (Volume 12), the Second Intermediate People's Court of Beijing held that the Approval Form of Recruitment of Labourers was deemed to be a written contract on grounds of (a) Aticle 82 of the Labour Contract Law of 2012 was designed to solve the problems that the percentage of the labour contracts signed by employing units was too low and that no legal consequences were prescribed for Article 16 of the Labour Law. The additional "wage" was not what a labourer earned in consideration of his labour but a kind of penalty imposed on the employing unit that failed to sign a written labour contract. The double wages aimed to increase the percentage of the signed labour contracts and clearly set out the rights and obligations by way of a labour contract. (b) The Approval Form of Recruitment of Labourers signed by the legal representative of TPS had functions similar to a labour contract in that in the Approval Form of Recruitment of Labourers, the working department, the place of work, the employment period, the probation period, the wages and the Approval Form were listed. The Approval Form contained the necessary elements of a labour contract, which not only evidenced the existence of a labour relationship but also set out the rights and obligations of both parties. Some courts held that the Approval Form of Recruitment of Labourers was not valid unless signed by a labourer; see the Civil Decision of Second Instance of the Case of Labour Dispute between Guangzhou Senteng Printing Co., Ltd. and Li Fukui (2019 Yue 01CF 2740).

The view that other written documents evidencing a labour relationship are deemed to be a labour contract and that the penalty of double wages is not applicable has been crystallised by some guiding documents, such as the Replies to Several Difficult Issues of Hearing the Case of Labour Disputes released by the Higher People's Court of Sichuan Province on 15 January 2016. Article 20 of the Replies to Several Difficult Issues of Hearing the Case of Labour Dispute released by the Higher People's Court of Sichuan Province provides written documents such as Registration Form for Job Applicants, Notice of Employment, Registration Form for Labourers that contains the employment period, labour remuneration, etc. and has been performed are considered to be labour contracts signed by both parties, and an employing unit is not subject to the penalty of double wages.

A labour contract in an electronic form is a written labour contract for the purpose of Article 10 of the Labour Contract Law of 2012. The Letter in Reply to the Issues related to Conclusion of Electronic Labour Contracts provides that an employing unit and a labourer may agree on concluding a written labour contract in an electronic form. However, a written labour contract that is sent to a labourer's email box is not deemed to be an electronic labour contract. In the Civil Decision of Second Instance of the Case of Labour Dispute between Beijing Dongfangfengruan Enterprise Management Consulting Co., Ltd. and Li Junqiang (2016 Jing 01 CF 5144), the First Intermediate People Court of Beijing held that both parties did not sign the labour contract or affix the seal, and they did not sign a letter of confirmation that the labour contract was concluded; thus, the argument of Beijing Dongfangfengruan Enterprise Management Consulting Co., Ltd. that an electronic labour contract was signed was rejected.

What if the labour contract is sent to a labourer by WeChat, a popular instant messenger in China? In the Civil Decision of Second Instance of the Case of Labour Dispute between Donghong Wuwei Space (Beijing) Decoration and Design Co. Ltd. and Zhao Zhiyuan (2020 Jing 03 CF 7483), Donghong Wuwei, the appellant, argued that the labour contract was concluded by WeChat because the appellant sent the labour contract to the appellee (Zhao Zhiyuan) by WeChat twice and asked for the confirmation by the appellee, and the appellee typed "Ok", inserted the name, address and contact information in the labour contract and sent it to the appellant by WeChat. The court of first instance, Beijing Miyun District People's Court held that the labour contract was not signed by both parties and the argument of the appellant was rejected; and the Third Intermediate People's Court of Beijing further held that (a) an employment and a labourer could conclude a written labour contract in an electronic form by consensus; (b) an electronic labour contract shall include the data message and reliable electronic signatures provided by the Electronic Signature Law, and the employing unit shall ensure that the production, transmission and storage of electronic contracts shall comply with the provisions of the Electronic Signature Law; (c) the historical records of chatting did not suggest that both parties agreed on the contents of the labour contract; and (d) there were no signatures or seals on the labour contract, which violated Article 16 of the Labour Contract Law of 2012 and Article 13 of the Electronic Signatures. Article 13 of the Electronic Signatures provides that an electronic signature is considered to be reliable if (i) the signature creation data are, within the context in which they used, linked to the signatory and to no other person; (ii) the signature creation data were, at the time of signing, under the control of the signatory and of no other person; (iii) any alteration to the electronic signature, made after the time of signing, is detectable; and (iv) any alteration made to the information to which the electronic signature relates after the time of signing is detectable.

3.5.1.2 Differential Application of Article 82 of the Labour Contract Law of 2012

Recently, it has become controversial that Article 82 of the Labour Contract Law of 2012 applies to all labourers equally. From the perspective of the wording of Article 82, it seems that there are no limits to labourers. However, some senior managers, such as those in charge of labour contract management, intentionally do not sign the labour contracts with themselves. In this case, it will be not fair for an employing unit to pay double wages under Article 82 of the Labour Contract Law of 2012. In the Civil Case of First Instance of the Case of Labour Dispute between Liu Danping and Nanjing Renchuang Materials Co., Ltd. (2015 Jiang Ning CF 4477), which was released by the Gazette of the Supreme People's Court of the PRC of 2018 (Volume 7), Nanjing Jiangning District People's Court held that (a) the defendant, Nanjing Renchuang Materials Co., Ltd. indeed did not sign the written labour contract with the claimant, Liu Danping and (b) however, the person in charge of human resources was responsible for labour contract management; the claimant was the head of the human resources department, and handling the matters related to labour contracts on behalf of the defendant fell into her scope of work; (c) the claimant should have known the provisions related to concluding written labour contracts and the legal consequences of not concluding labour contracts; (d) the claimant was obliged to request the defendant to conclude the labour contract with herself; (e) the claimant failed to evidence that she made such a request; and (f) the claim for double wages was rejected.

For the differential application of Article 82 of the Labour Contract Law of 2012, some courts and labour arbitration commissions jointly released the guiding documents. Article 5 of the Replies of the Higher People's Court of Shanghai to Several Issues of Labour, which were released in 2010, provides that where some managers, head of a human resources department and other persons in charge of human resources in enterprises concealed the written labour contracts so as that the employing unit cannot provide them and the managers or like make a claim for double wages, Article 82 of the Labour Contract Law of 2012 is not applicable provided that other evidence shows that the written contracts were concluded.

Article 6 of the Guiding Opinions (II) of Hearing Labour and Personnel Disputes, which were released by the Higher People's Court of Jiangsu on 8 November 2011, provides that although an employing unit does not sign the labour contract with a labourer, the claim that top management made for double wages on grounds of failure to sign the labour contract shall be rejected provided that the employing unit can present the letter of appointment to show that there exist rights and obligations and they have been performed.

Article 1 of the Replies by the First Civil Division of the Higher People's Court of Zhejiang to Serveral Difficult Issues of Hearing Labour Disputes, which were released in December 2012, provides that (a) signing labour contracts is the statutory obligation of an employing unit, but the claim that a labourer makes for double wages may be rejected provided that failure to signing the labour contract was not attributable to the employing unit; (b) it is not attributable to the employing unit in case of any of the following circumstances: (i) it has sufficient evidence to show that the labourer refused to sign the labourer contract or the labourer took advantage of the position in charge of human resources not to sign the labour contract; (ii) for other reasons the employing unit cannot sign the labaour contract with the labourer sustaining work-related injuries who is in the suspension-of-work-with-pay period, the woman labourer who is on maternity leave, or the labourer who is on sick leave.

Article 31 of the Meeting Minutes (II) of Several Issues of Application of Law concerning Labour Disputes, released by the Higher People's Court of Beijing and Beijing Labour Dispute Arbitration on 5 January 2015, provides that (a) where the legal representative makes a claim for double wages incurred by failure to signing a labour contract, generally a competent court may not uphold such claim; (b) where the top management of an employing units make a claim for double wages incurred by failure to signing a labour contract, a competent court may uphold such claim, unless the employing unit can prove that their scope of work covers the signing of labour contracts; if they further prove that they offered to request the employing unit to sign the labour contract but were refused, a competent court may uphold such claim; (c) where the head of the human resources department or the person who is mainly responsible for the human resources makes a claim for double wages incurred by failure to signing a labour contract and the employing unit can prove that their scope of work covers the signing of labour contracts, generally a competent court may not uphold such claim; the head of the human resources department or the person who is mainly responsible for the human resources prove that he offered to request the employing unit to sign the labour contract but were refused, a competent court may uphold such claim.

Similarly, Article 82 of the Replies to Several Difficult Issues of Hearing the Case of Labour Disputes, which were released by the Higher People's Court of Sichuan Province on 15 January 2016, provides the same except for the provision of the legal representative. The Intermediate People's Court of Xiaman and Xiamen Labour Artbiration Commission jointly released similar provisions on 31 December 2017.

In practice, top management is identified in accordance with Article 216 of the Company Law of 2018, under which top management means a manager, a vice manager, a person in charge of corporate finance, the board secretary of a listed company and other persons stipulated by the articles of association.

3.5.2 Terms and Conditions of Labour Contracts

3.5.2.1 Relationships Between Wages, Remuneration and Benefits

What the relationships between wages, remuneration and benefits are truly hard to answer. The main reason is that all the laws and regulations related to labour and employment in China are silent on them. Courts and labour arbitration commissions often take different views toward them. Therefore, it is urgent to clarify what they are.

Wages

In accordance with Article 1 of Protection of Wages Convention, 1949 (No. 95), the term "wages" means remuneration or earning, however designated or calculated, capable of being expressed in terms of money and fixed by mutual agreement or by national laws or regulations, which are payable in virtue of a written or unwritten contract of employment by an employer to an employed person for work done or to be done or for services rendered or to be rendered; wages payable in money shall be paid only in legal tender.[28] However, wages were not defined in the Labour Law of 2018. For the purposes of the Interim Regulations on Payment of Wages released by the Ministry of Labour on 6 December 1994, the term "wages" means the remuneration which is payable by an employing unit to labourers in various forms in accordance with a labour contract; wages payable in money shall be paid only in legal tender, and payment in the form of vouchers or coupons, or in kind, shall be prohibited. In accordance with the Opinions of Serval Issues of Implementing the Labour Law released by the Ministry of Labour Law on 4 August 1995, for the purposes of the Labour Law of 2018, the term "wages" means the remuneration which is payable in money by an employing unit directly to a labourer by national laws or regulations or by a labour contract, and which generally includes time wages, piece wages, bonus, allowances, subsidiaries, overtime pay, and wages paid under special circumstances. Wages are the main part of the incomes of a labourer. The following incomes of a labourer are not considered to be wages: (a) the benefits paid by an employing unit to a labourer, such as funeral pensions and subsistence allowances; (b) the expenses for labour protection, such as working clothes and antidote; and (c) other remuneration and incomes not listed in the total sum of wages.

[28] Protection of Wages Convention, 1949 (No. 95) (2021).

Remuneration

Remuneration is broader than wages. In the Interpretations of Several Issues of Application of Law concerning Hearing the Criminal Cases of Refusal to Payment of Remuneration released by the Supreme People's Court on 14 January 2013, the remuneration referred to in Article 267 of the Criminal Law means that what is payable to a labourer under the Labour Law of 2018 and the Labour Contract Law of 2012, including wages, bonus, allowances, subsidiaries, overtime pay, and wages paid under special circumstances.

Benefits

The term "benefits" is vogue. Most believe that benefits are less related to the quality and quantity of the labour offered by a labourer, and an employing unit may decide on them by itself. Benefits are not part of remuneration or wages. Benefits are different from remuneration in that (1) the former may be paid in money, in kind or by means of service while the latter shall be paid in money and (2) the former is subject to the general time limit of one year, while the latter the special time limit of one year.

Taking the wages for annual leave as an example, most courts, such as in Zhejiang, Jilin, Beijing, Jiangsu, Shanghai, Anhui, Guangzhou, and Dalian, take such wages as benefits, but few courts hold the opposite view. In the Civil Order of Second Instance of the Case of Benefits between Zhongshan Domestic Appliances Co., Ltd., Zhongshan Qianye Plastic Co., Ltd. and Chen Genjiao (2019 Yue 20 CF 5337), the Intermediate People's Court of Zhongshan held that the wages for the annual leave due were remuneration and were not subject to the general time limit of one year.

3.5.2.2 The Effect of Waiver of Paid Annual Leave

In accordance with the Regulations of Labourers' Paid Annual Leave, released by the State Council on 14 December 2007, a labourer who has worked for over one year in a consecutive way is entitled to paid annual leave in which the wages remain unchanged. It can be seen that paid annual leave is a right of a labourer. From the perspective of civil law, the subject of civil law may waive a right unless there is deception, duress or undue influence.

The waiver of paid annual leave often raises a storm of controversy. In the Civil Decision of Second Instance of the Case of Labour Dispute between Zeng Meng and Huawei Technologies Co., Ltd. (2019 Yue 03 CF 5236), Zeng Meng, the appellant, produced the Agreement of Strivers as evidence, which read as follows: *I, Zeng Meng, undertake to Huawei Investment Holding Co., Ltd. or its affiliated companies (hereinafter referred to be the Companies) that I fully and deeply understand that the industry of the Companies is full of risks and uncertainty, the competitions are fierce and ruthless, and thus following the old routine only gives rise to basic remuneration; no striving, no development, and in order to share the benefits arising out of the long-term development of the Companies, I volunteer to strive for them and waive my own partial benefits and I also understand that I will not merely a labourer if I share the benefits from the Companies. I undertake to volunteer to be a striver and waive the paid annual leave and the wages for the annual leave due and in the course of the employment I promise not to apply to take the paid annual leave and the wages for the annual leave due. Even if I resign from the Companies, I may not request the Companies to pay me the wages for the paid annual leave due.* Shenzhen Longgang Labour and Personnel Arbitration Commission rejected his claim for the wages for the paid annual leave due. The People's Court of Long Gang District again rejected his claim on the grounds that he volunteered to waive his paid annual leave and the wages for the paid annual leave due. Again, in the Civil Decision of Second Instance of the Case of Labour Dispute between Zeng Meng and Huawei Technologies Co., Ltd. (2019 Yue CF 5236), the Intermediate People's Court of Shenzhen upheld the decision of the first instance made by the People's Court of Long Gang District on the grounds that Zeng Meng failed to produce no evidence showing that there existed deception or duress when he signed the Agreement of Strivers. Finally, Zeng Meng applied to the Higher People's Court of Guangdong for a retrial. In the Civil Order of the Retrial of the Case of Labour Dispute between Zeng Meng and Huawei Technologies Co., Ltd. (2020 Yue CA 2577), the Higher People's Court of Guangdong held that with regard to the wages for the paid annual leave due, Zeng Meng undertook "to volunteer to waive the paid annual leave during the employment in the Companies in the Agreement of Strivers", and there was no evidence showing that he signed the Agreement under the influence of deception or duress or that the Companies took advantage of his precarious position and accordingly rejected his application for the retrial.

Apparently, what matters in this case is whether the provisions in civil law with regard to deception and duress can be directly applied in the field of the Labour Contract Law of 2012. However, the underlying problem is with which party the onus of proof is and how to identify the existence of deception and duress. Article 26 of the Labour Contract Law of 2012 provides that a labour contract shall be invalid where it is signed by means of deception and duress or one party takes advantage of the other party's precarious position. In my opinion, a labourer is affiliated with an employing unit, and as a matter of fact, it is more likely that a labourer is in a weaker position. In a labour relationship, obeying a man who pays is easy to understand. When an offer is presented by an employing unit, a labourer is faced with a take-it-or-leave-it option. Take it, and a labourer will waive his rights. Leave it, and he or she will be dismissed. The only freedom of a labourer before a strong employing unit is to obey. There is little room for the doctrine of free will in the field of labour law. Therefore, it is appropriate that an employing unit produce evidence to show that the agreement or contract was not made by means of deception, duress or undue influence. Alternatively, it should be made clear that some rights in the Labour Contract Law of 2012 cannot be waived in any case.

3.5.2.3 Irregular Working Hour System

Generally, the irregular working hour system is not invalid unless approved in advance, even if both parties agree on it. However, the courts in Beijing and Jiangsu hold that the irregular working hour system can directly apply to senior managers even if it is not approved in advance. Paragraph 2 of Article 16 of the Measures for Enterprises in Beijing to Implement Comprehensive Working Hour System and Irregular Working Hour System provides that without being approved, the irregular working hour system may apply to top management in enterprises. Similarly, Article 8 of the Guiding Opinions (II) of Hearing Labour and Personnel Disputes, which were released by the Higher People's Court of Jiangsu on 8 November 2011, provides that with regard to the dispute over overtime wages between a senior manager and an employing unit, it may be deemed that the irregular working hour system, even if not approved in advance, is applicable to the senior manager provided that (1)in nature it is suitable to his work and position or (2)that it is obviously not reasonable to calculate the overtime wages on the basis of the standard working hour system, or (3) that his working hours cannot be calculated on the basis of the standard working hour system.

However, despite the above provisions, it is still necessary for an employing unit to produce evidence showing the nature of a labourer's position. In the Civil Decision of Retrial of the Case of Labour Dispute between Pan Xiaoqiong and Zhenjiang Hanxiang Real Estate Co., Ltd. (2017 Su CA 68), the Higher People's Court of Jiangsu held that although Pan Xiaoqiong worked as a financial manager, Zhenjiang Hanxiang Real Estate Co., Ltd. failed to produce evidence showing (1) that her position had the characteristics that necessitated an irregular working hour system or (2) that it was obviously not reasonable to calculate the overtime wages on the basis of the standard working hour system.

It is noteworthy that the special working hour systems may apply where an employing unit may, after mutual consultation with its labourers, notify them of the implementation of the special working hour systems and they undertake to comply with it, provided that it is not feasible for the standard working hour systems to apply to the production and operation of the unit and the unit falls into the scope of the special working hour systems in accordance with the Regulations on Optimizing the Business Environment released by Shenzhen Special Economic Zone on 29 October 2020. In other words, enterprises in Shenzhen can implement special working hour systems without being approved in advance.

Incidentally, the working hour system of 996 is illegal, which means that the total working hours per day is more than 10 h, which is from 9 a.m. to 9 p.m. and 6 working days in a week. The system is popular among Internet enterprises. On 17 January 2019, Hangzhou Youzan Technology Co., Ltd. declared that it implemented the working hour system of 996, which sparked off controversy. Another company terminated the labour contract with Mr. J on the grounds that he did not pass the appraisal in the probation period. However, it was reported that it was due to J's refusal to 996 that he was dismissed. The working hour system of 996 is illegal under the Labour Law of 2018 and the Labour Contract Law of 2012. There are three types of working hour systems under the Labour Law of 2018: standard working hour systems, irregular working hour systems and comprehensive working hour systems. 996 does not belong to any type of working hour systems.

3.5.3 Revocation and Termination of Labour Contracts

3.5.3.1 The Role of Trade Unions

In accordance with the Trade Union Law and the Regulations of the Work of Trade Unions of 2006, all labourers performing physical or mental work in enterprises, public institutions and government organs within the Chinese territory, regardless of their nationality, race, sex, occupation, religious beliefs or level of education, who earn their living primarily from wages have the rights to participate in and set up trade unions. If an employing unit revokes or terminates a labour contract in violation of related laws, regulations or contractual stipulations, the trade union shall give advice with regard to improper revocation or termination and request the employing unit to notify the trade union of the rectification, which the trade union may approve or disapprove of. However, Article 47 of Judicial Interpretations (No.1) by the Supreme People's Court of Issues Concerning the Application of Law in Hearing the Cases of Labour Disputes released on 29 December 2020 provides that if any employing unit which has set up the trade union revokes a labour contract in accordance with Articles 39 and 40 of the Labour Contract Law of 2012 without giving an advance notice to the trade union in accordance with Article 43 of the Labour Contract Law of 2012, and if a labourer makes a claim for the damages on grounds of illegal revocation, the competent court shall uphold such claim, except that the employing unit gave such notice before the lodging of the lawsuit by the labourer.

The reality is that many employing units fail to establish trade unions, as required by the Trade Union Law. What if an employing unit has not set up the trade union? Has Article 43 of the Labour Contact Law of 2012 been softened by Article 47 of Judicial Interpretations (No. 1) by the Supreme People's Court of Issues Concerning the Application of Law in Hearing the Cases of Labour Disputes?

The courts in Dalian, Jiangsu, Chongqing take a prudent attitude to the role of the trade union. In the Civil Decision of Second Instance of the Case of Labour Dispute between Nanjing Military Region Guesthouse and Yang Tao (2020 Su 01 CF 4859), the Intermediate People's Court of Nanjing held that (a) the Regulations of the Labour Contracts in Jiangsu were applicable to this case; (b) before the revocation, Nanjing Military Region Guesthouse failed to notify the trade union where it was located of the grounds of the revocation and (c) the revocation was illegal in accordance with Article 31 of the Regulations of the Labour Contracts in Jiangsu. In the Civil Decision of Second Instance of the Case between Jian Jingmei and Shanghai Yinuosheng Advertising Co., Ltd. (2019 Su 01 CC 7706), the Intermediate People's Court of Nanjing held that before the lodging of the lawsuit, Shanghai Yinuosheng Advertising

Co., Ltd. had notified the trade union of the grounds of the revocation, which made the claim of Jian Jingmei groundless.

In contrast, the courts in Shanghai, Fujian, Guangzhou, Tianjin, Beijing and Qingdao take a remarkably liberal attitude. The reason is that an employing unit is not obliged to set up the trade union in accordance with Articles 2 and 3 of the Trade Union Law. In the Civil Decision of Hearing Supervision of the Case of Labour Contract between Zhong Zhiping and ESBJERG Ship Technology Consulting (Shanghai) Co., Ltd. (2019 Hu CA 849), the Higher People's Court of Shanghai held that although an employing unit unilaterally revoking the labour contract shall notify the trade union of the grounds in accordance with Article 43 of the Labour Contract Law of 2012, the provision was applicable on the condition that the trade union had been set up by the employing unit, and in this case ESBJERG Ship Technology Consulting (Shanghai) Co., Ltd. had not set up the trade union, so the revocation was not illegal. The same view was held by the Third Intermediate People's Court of Tianjin in the Civil Decision of Second Instance of the Case of Labour Dispute between Zhang Zhiguo and Tianjin Zhongsheng Car Leasing Co., Ltd. (2019 Jin 03 CF 915), the Intermediate People's Court of Guangzhou in the Civil Decision of Second Instance of the Case of Labour Dispute between Liu Yanbei and Guangdong Longxin Labour Service Co., Ltd. (2018 Yue 01CF 17030), and the Second Intermediate People's Court of Beijing in the Civil Decision of Second Instance of the Case of Labour Dispute between Beijing Dangdang Information Technology Co., Ltd. and Gao (2019 Jing 02 CF11084).

It should be noted that the Measures of Trade Unions on Labour Law Supervision were released by the All-China Federation of Trade Unions on 31 March 2021, which provided that trade unions at the grassroots or labourer representative meeting shall establish the Labour Law Supervision Commission or the Supervision Team. This implies that where there is no trade union in an employing unit, its labourer representative meeting shall the Labour Law Supervision Commission or the Supervision Team. Furthermore, at the provincial level, the Regulations of Shandong Trade Unions on Labour Law Supervision, released on 29 July 2021, provide that where an employing unit fails to establish a trade union, the trade union at the higher level may appoint a labourer of the employing unit as the supervisor of labour law, who is responsible for supervising labour law enforcement in his employing unit. To put it differently, the defence that there is no trade union in an employing unit, and it is not obliged to notify the trade union of the termination of a labour contract will no longer hold water.

3.5.3.2 Specific Performance of Labour Contracts

According to Black's Law Dictionary, specific performance is an equitable remedy that lies within the court's discretion to award whenever the common-law remedy is insufficient, either because damages would be inadequate or because the damages could not possibly be established.[29] Similar provisions are also seen in Chinese law. In accordance with Article 48 of the Labour Contract Law of 2012, in case of illegal revocation or termination by an employing unit, the labour contract shall continue to be performed unless it is impossible to be performed or the affected labourer does not request the employing unit to perform it.

However, both the Labour Contract Law of 2012 and the Implementation Regulations of the Labour Contract Law are silent on what constitutes the impossibility of continuing performance of the labour contract. Article 9 of the Replies to Issues of Application of Law in Hearing the Cases of Labour Disputes, which were released by the Higher People's Court of Beijing and Beijing Labour and Personnel Dispute Arbitration Commission on 24 April 2017, provides that a labour contract cannot be performed in case of any of the following circumstances: (a) an employing unit is declared bankrupt by law, a competent authority cancels its business licence, or orders it to be closed, or an employing unit decides to dissolve itself in advance; (b) the labourer reaches the statutory age of retirement during the course of the labour arbitration or the lawsuit; (c) the labour contract terminates upon the expiry during the course of the labour arbitration or the lawsuit unless Article 14 of the Labour Contract Law of 2012 applies; (d) as for the operation, the original position (like the general manager and the financial chief officer) that has been occupied is not replaceable and unique, and the employing unit and the labourer cannot agree on a new position; (e) the labourer is reemployed by another employing unit; (f) during the course of the labour arbitration or the lawsuit, the labourer refuses to continue to work as requested by the employing unit; or (g) other circumstances where it is obviously inappropriate for the employing unit to perform the labour contract. With regard to the impossibility of performance, the Higher People's Court of Shandong and the Higher People's Court of Jiangxi followed the example of the Higher People's Court of Beijing.

In the Civil Decision of Second Instance of the Case of Labour Dispute between Beijing Dangdang Information Technology Co., Ltd. and Gao (2019 Jing 02 CF11084), Beijing Dangdang Information Technology Co., Ltd. (the appellant) appealed that even if the revocation of the labour contract with Gao (the appellee) was illegal, the specific performance was impossible on the grounds that (a) the position of the appellee was the product director and she was the sole person in charge of the product department of the appellant, but her position had been occupied by another labourer; (b) the appellee developed transsexualism and other coworkers could not work together with her, but the Second Intermediate People's Court of Beijing rejected the arguments of the appellant on the grounds that (a) the appellee stated that she would take the position of UED or other position and the appellant said it would consider the appellee's request; and (b) with regard to the discomfort or embarrassment to other coworkers, the gender of the appellee had been changed from male to female by the Public Security Bureau in accordance with the Reply to Several Issues of Gender Change in Household Registration for Citizens Undergoing Transexual Operations and the appellee had the right to go to the women's toilet and other

[29] Garner (2014).

coworkers were expected to be tolerant toward her. It is a landmark case where the judge tried to solve the tricky problem with the employment of a person who underwent a transsexual operation. Transgender is a sensitive topic among the Chinese people. The judge took public policy into consideration in making the decision. The judge did not think that transgender did harm others, the country or society and further believed that we were expected to show respect for the personality, dignity, and legitimate rights of transgender and that the rights to employment should also be respected and protected.

Some courts think that mutual trust is the key basis of labour contracts. In the Civil Decision of Second Instance of the Case of Labour Contract between Lear (China) Investment Co., Ltd. and Shen Zhipeng (2020 Hu 02 CF3772), the Second Intermediate People's Court of Shanghai held that given that Lear (China) Investment Co., Ltd. and Shen Zhipeng were involved in six pending cases, the labour contract could not be performed due to a lack of mutual trust. Likewise, the Higher People's Court of Shanghai held that given that China Construction First Group Corporation Limited (Southwest Branch) had the position of Chen Wei filled by another person and insisted that it did not agree to restore the labour relationship with Chen Wei, lack of mutual trust made it impossible for the labour contract to be performed in the Civil Order of Hearing Supervision of the Case of Labour Contract between Chen Wei and China Construction First Group Corporation Limited (Southwest Branch) (2020 Hu CA 602).

References

Garner, B. A. (2014). Revocation. In *Black's Law Dictionary* (10th ed., p. 1515). Thomson Reuters.

Gong, J. (1986). On the nature of labour contracts and the legal status of parties. *China Labour Science, 6,* p. 8–9 [in Chinese].

ILO. (1949). *Protection of Wages Convention, 1949 (No. 95).* Retrieved 1 May, 2021, from https://www.ilo.org/dyn/normlex/en/f?p=NORMLEXPUB:12100:0::NO::P12100_ILO_CODE:C095.

MOHRSS. (2020). *Standard Form of Labour Contract.* Retrieved 5 January, 2021, from http://www.mohrss.gov.cn/xxgk2020/fdzdgknr/ldgx_4234/ldyg/202106/t20210602_415702.html.

MOHRSS. (2020). *Totalisation Agreements.* Retrieved 25 September, 2021, from http://www.mohrss.gov.cn/SYrlzyhshbzb/zhuanti/waiguorencanbao/sbsbhmxd/.

Chapter 4
Labour Dispatch

Dispatch labour is an atypical employment relationship that involves three parties: a labour dispatch unit, a dispatched labourer and a labour-user unit. Accordingly, it tends to give rise to complicated legal issues. Labour dispatch applies only to temporary, auxiliary and substitute vacancies. The relationship between the labour dispatch unit and the dispatched labourer is subject to labour law, while the relationship between the labour dispatch unit and the labour-user unit is subject to civil law.

4.1 Overview of Labour Dispatch

4.1.1 Labour Dispatch and Multiparty Employment Arrangement

From the global perspective, a multiparty employment arrangement seems more common. A multiparty employment relationship is a contractual arrangement involving multiple parties: a worker, an economic unit for which the work is performed and a third party. This means a type of contract where workers are not directly employed by the company to which they provide their services. Such relationships are variously referred to as triangular relationships, temporary agency work, outsourced employment and labour subcontracting. Labour dispatch is one type of multiparty employment relationship. Labour dispatch was recognised by ILO in Private Employment Agencies Convention, 1997 (No. 181), Subparagraph (b) of Paragraph 1 of Article 1 of which provides that services consisting of employing workers with a view to making them available to a third party, who may be a natural or legal person (referred to below as a "user enterprise") which assigns their tasks

Y. Wang, *Chinese Labour Law*, Understanding China,
https://doi.org/10.1007/978-981-16-8101-1_4

and supervises the execution of these tasks.[1] In China, there is no single statutory definition of labour dispatch. It is generally accepted that the term "labour dispatch" refers to the practice of hiring labourers through an employment service agency as opposed to direct employment.

4.1.2 *Development of Labour Dispatch in China*

4.1.2.1 The Late 1970s to Mid-1980s

On 30 October 1980, the Interim Regulations on Administration of Resident Representative Offices of Foreign Enterprises were released by the State Council, which provided that the employment of the resident offices shall be entrusted to the local foreign affair service unit or other units designated by the Chinese Government. Therefore, foreign affair services companies, often referred to labour dispatch companies, were established to provide services to resident representative offices of foreign enterprises in Beijing, Shanghai and other coastal cities. The Shanghai Foreign Agency Service Department (FASD) was set up in August 1975, and then Beijing Foreign Enterprise Service Group CO., Ltd. (FESCO) was set up in 1979.

4.1.2.2 The 1990s to the Beginning of the 2000s

To solve the problems with the reemployment of laid-off workers of state-owned enterprises and the surplus of rural labour forces, labour dispatch companies and labour service companies were established. Some state-owned enterprises established their own labour dispatch companies to provide services for laid-off workers. In 1999, Beijing Labour and Social Security Bereau released the Interim Measures for Administration of Beijing Labour Dispatch Organisations, which encouraged enterprises that had many laid-off workers to establish labour dispatch companies to promote the reemployment of their laid-off workers. In 2002, the CPC Central Committee and the State Council released the Notice of Further Strengthening the Reemployment of Laid-off Workers, which encouraged the laid-off workers to be reemployed in the form of part-time, temporary and flexible employment and encouraged labour dispatch companies and employment bases to provide services for the laid-off workers.

4.1.2.3 The Middle of the 2000s to the Present

Labour dispatch is developing in full scale. The number of labour dispatch companies is on the increase. An increasing number of sectors are using labour dispatch services.

---

[1] Private Employment Agencies Convention (2021).

Even the clerks of the courts are dispatched from the labour dispatch companies. Some laws and regulations related to labour dispatch were enacted.

4.1.3 Types of Labour Dispatch

4.1.3.1 Regular Labour Dispatch and Registered Labour Dispatch

Regular labour dispatch is the one by which dispatched labourers keep a stablised labour relationship with the labour dispatch unit, and the relationship will not be affected by the dismissal of the labourers by labour-user enterprises, while in registered labour dispatch, the dispatched labourers are temporarily employed by the labour dispatch unit only during the period when they are dispatched. Obviously, regular dispatch helps to promote the stabilisation of a labour relationship. In China, regular labour dispatch is prescribed by the Labour Contract Law of 2012.

4.1.3.2 Original Labour Dispatch and Reassigned Labour Dispatch

Original labaour dispatch means that the labour dispatch unit dispatches the labourers to the labour-user unit. Reassigned labour dispatch means that the labour-user unit reassigns the labourers to another unit. Reassigned labour dispatch gives rise to intricate relationships among the labour dispatch unit, the dispatched labourers, the employing unit and the labour-user unit, which tend to damage the interests of the dispatched labourers. Reassigned labour dispatch is not allowed in China.[2]

4.1.3.3 Labour Dispatch Toward Domestic Units and Labour Dispatch Toward Resident Foreign Agencies

Dispatched labourers can be dispatched to domestic labour-user units or to resident foreign agencies. Resident foreign agencies include resident offices of foreign enterprises, foreign governments, foreign news agencies, and UN agencies in China. In accordance with Regulations concerning Foreign Journalists and Permanent Offices of Foreign News Agencies and Provisional Measures for Administration of the Registration of Employees of Foreign Enterprise Representative Offices Stationed in Beijing, resident foreign agencies have no right to employ labourers in China.

[2] The Labour Contract Law of 2012, Paragraph 2 of Article 62.

4.1.4 *Characteristics of Labour Dispatch*

4.1.4.1 An Atypical Form of Employment

Typical employment means that there exists a labour relationship between a labourer and an employing unit, and they directly conclude a labour contract by which the labourer is directly employed by the employing unit and works under the direction of the employing unit and the labourer is well protected by labour laws and regulations. With regard to labour dispatch, the labourer and the labour-user unit do not conclude a labour contract, and the labourer is employed not by the labour-user unit but by the labour dispatch unit.

4.1.4.2 Involvement of Tripartite Relationships

Labour dispatch involves three parties: the labour dispatch unit, the dispatched labourer, and the labour-user unit. There exists a labour contract between the labour dispatch unit and the dispatched labourer and a dispatching service contract between the labour dispatch unit and the labour-user unit. The labour dispatch unit pays the wages to the dispatched labourer and takes out the social insurance contributions for the labourer. The labour-user unit pays the wages and the expenses of social insurance to the labour dispatch unit in accordance with the related law and the dispatching service contract.

4.1.4.3 Giving Rise to Complicated Legal Issues

Given that labour dispatch involves three parties, it tends to give rise to complicated legal issues, such as work-related injury insurance, the termination of the dispatching service contract and the labour contract, the relationship between the dispatching service contact and the labour contract, the joint and several liabilities and equal pay for equal work.

4.2 Legal Framework of Labour Dispatch in China

4.2.1 *The Labour Contract Law of 2012*

Labour dispatch is provided by Chap. 5 (special provisions) of the Labour Contract Law of 2012. Article 57 sets out the following requirements for establishing a labour dispatch unit: (a) its registered capital shall be not less than RMB 2,000,000 yuan; (b) it has a fixed business office and facilities suitable for its business; (c) it has the management system of labour dispatch required by the related laws and regulations;

(d) it meets other conditions prescribed by the related laws and regulations; and (e) it shall apply for and obtain an administrative permit in accordance with the relevant regulations from a local labour administrative department; if approved, it shall apply for business registration subject to related laws and regulations; if not, no company or individual is allowed to provide labour dispatch service. Article 58 sets out the rights and obligations of the labour dispatch unit, the labour-user unit and the dispatched labourer, which provides that the labour dispatch unit is the employing unit that discharges the obligations of an employing unit to its labourers. The labour contracts between a labour dispatch unit and the labourers shall be a fixed term contract with a term of no less than two years. The labour dispatch unit shall pay labour remuneration on a monthly basis. In cases where there is no job available for the labourers to be placed, the labour dispatch unit shall pay the labourers the minimum wage on a monthly basis. Article 59 sets out the terms and conditions of the labour dispatch contract. Article 60 sets out the obligations of the labour-user unit, which includes compliance with national work standards, provision of related work conditions and labour security, notifying the labourers of the work requirements and labour remuneration, payment of overtime wages, performance bonuses and benefits, provision of necessary labour training, and implementation of a regular wage adjustment in case of continuous placement of the labourers. Article 63 provides that the dispatched labourers are entitled to equal pay for equal work with the labourers directly employed by the labour-user unit. Article 65 provides that the dispatched labourers may terminate the labour contract with the labour dispatch unit in accordance with Articles 36 and 38. If a dispatched labourer is in any of the circumstances specified in Article 39 and Subparagraphs (1) or (2) of Article 40, the labour-user unit may send him back to the labour dispatch unit, which may revoke the labour contract with him or her in accordance with the relevant provisions. Article 66 provides that labourers are dispatched generally for temporary, auxiliary or substitute jobs.

Furthermore, the Regulation on the Implementation of the Labour Contract Law provides that any labour-user unit may not establish a labour dispatch unit to dispatch labourers to itself or its subsidiaries.

4.2.2 The Interim Provisions on Labour Dispatch

To clarify some issues related to labour dispatch, the Ministry of Human Resources and Social Security of the PRC released the Interim Provisions on Labour Dispatch on 24 January 2014, which entered into force as of 1 March 2014. In accordance with the Interim Provisions on Labour Dispatch, labour dispatch is only applicable to the following three types of vacancies: (a) a temporary position with a duration of no more than six months; (b) an auxiliary position that provides auxiliary services to the main or core business of the labour-user unit; or (c) a substitute position that can be performed by a dispatched labourer in place of a permanent labourer during the period when such labourer is away from work for study, vacation or other reasons.

The labour-user unit shall strictly control the number of dispatched employees to 10% of its total staff. In case of a work-related injury, the labour dispatch unit shall apply for identification of the work-related injury, and the labour-user unit shall assist in the investigation and verification of the work-related injury. Furthermore, the labour dispatch unit and the labour-user unit may agree on the compensation with regard to the work-related injury.

4.2.3 The Measures of Implementation of Administrative Permits for Labour Dispatch

On 20 June 2013, the Ministry of Human Resources and Social Security of the PRC released the Measures of Implementation of Administrative Permits for Labour Dispatch, which sets out the provisions of receipt and acceptance of the application for administrative permits for labour dispatch, examination and approval, and the related supervision and inspection.

4.2.4 Bylaws at Local Levels

The Notice of Further Regulating the Administration of the Employment of Dispatched Labourers, released by the Human Resources and Social Security Department of Jiangsu Province on 7 May 2019, provides that a labour-user unit violating the laws and regulations related to labour dispatch shall take the liabilities of an employing unit in accordance with the related provisions in the Labour Contract Law of 2012.

The Meeting Minutes of Several Issues of Law Application of Labour Dispatch released by Shanghai City Human Resources and Social Security Bureau and the Higher People's Court of Shanghai released on 31 December 2014 clarified the following issues concerning labour dispatch: (a) the provisions of being temporary, auxiliary and substitute are administrative, and violation of such provisions cannot invalidate the labour dispatch contract and the labour contract; and (b) the differences between labour dispatch and labour outsourcing.

On 18 July 2018, the Higher People's Court of Guangdong Province and the Labour Dispute Arbitration Commission of Guangdong Province jointly released Several Opinions concerning the Linkage between Labour Dispute Arbitration and Litigation, which provides that an open-ended labour contract is applicable to labour dispatch if Paragraph 2 or Paragraph 3 of Article 14 of the Labour Contract Law of 2012 is met and that violation of the application scope of labour dispatch and the percentage of dispatched labourers cannot invalidate labour dispatch contracts. Labour dispatch contracts shall be invalid if a labour dispatch unit does not gain the administrative permit for labour dispatch and the labour dispatch unit and the labour-user unit bear the joint and several liabilities to the affected labourers.

On 28 October 2020, the Human Resources and Social Security Department of Guangdong Province released the Guiding Opinions of further Regulating Labour Dispatch, which clarify the differences between labour dispatch and human resource outsourcing.

On 25 June 2018, Qingdao Human Resources and Social Bureau released the Measures of Labour Dispatch Administration, which includes the definition of labour dispatch, labour dispatch in disguise of labour outsourcing, a labour contract and social insurance, and the circumstances where a labour-user unit bears the liabilities of an employing unit.

The abovementioned legal documents further give rise to different understandings of labour dispatch. The Notice of Further Regulating the Administration of Domestic Labour Dispatch released by the General Office of Dalian City People's Government on 4 July 2007 provides that the labour relationship shall exist between a labour-user unit and dispatched labourers where the labour-user unit receives the dispatched labourers who do not sign labour contracts with a labour dispatch unit or where the labour-user unit does not sign a labour dispatch contract with the labour dispatch unit.

4.3 Terms and Conditions of Labour Dispatch Contracts

As noted earlier, labour dispatch involves three parties and two contracts. A labour dispatch unit and a labour-user unit shall sign a labour dispatch contract to set out their respective rights, obligations and liabilities. In nature, the labour dispatch contract is governed by the Civil Code. The labour dispatch contract often includes the following terms and conditions.

4.3.1 Parties to the Labour Dispatch Contract

The Labour Dispatch Registry Number is strongly recommended to be included. The fact that a labour dispatch unit without a valid labour dispatch registry will invalidate the labour dispatch in some areas will give rise to the liabilities of an employing unit.

4.3.2 The Number of Dispatched Labourers, Vacancies and Period

At the request of Party B (the labour-user unit), Party A (the labour dispatch unit) dispatches_____ [insert the number] labourers to Party B, and the dispatched labourers' vacancies shall be temporary, auxiliary, and substitute. The vacancies shall meet the requirements of the Interim Provisions on Labour Dispatch.

4.3.3 Settlement and Payment of Related Expenses

Both parties may agree on the settlement and payment of related expenses. It is recommended that such expenses be paid by Party B. Equal pay for equal work shall be included. Party B shall apply the same distribution of remuneration to the dispatched labourers. With regard to social insurance, Party B shall pay Party A the expenses for social insurance by the month, including endowment, medical treatment, work-related injuries, unemployment and maternity. Party B shall pay Party A the service expenses.

4.3.4 Labour Security and Hygiene, Occupational Diseases Prevention and Benefits

Party B shall ensure that it complies with the national standards related to employment and provides related labour conditions, labour protection and occupational disease prevention. Both parties shall be responsible for training and educating the dispatched labourers in terms of occupational skills, safety production and labour discipline. Party B shall be responsible for the life and health of the labourers. The dispatched labourers may complain of the violation of the related laws and regulations. In case of work-related injuries, Party B shall give a written notice to Party A, and Party A shall apply for the identification of work-related injuries and the appraisal of work capacity in accordance with related laws and regulations. The benefits during the medical treatment period shall be borne by Party B. Party B shall ensure that the dispatched labourers are entitled to statutory rest and holidays and paid annual leave. In the case of overtime work, the consent of dispatched labourers should be gained in advance. In the case of the special working hour system, Party B shall apply to the competent human resources and social security bureau for administrative approval.

4.3.5 Rights and Obligations of Party A

Party A may be well informed of the use of the dispatched labourers by Party B. Party A shall assist Party B in managing the dispatched labourers and cooperate with Party B to ensure that the dispatched labourers comply with the related laws and regulations and the rules of Party B. Party A shall maintain a valid labour dispatch certificate. Party A shall conclude labour contracts with the dispatched labourers and provide valid evidence for Party B within 30 days after the dispatched labourers work for Party B. Party A shall pay wages to the dispatched labourers by month and may not withhold or deduct wages for no good reason. The wages shall not be lower than the local minimum wage standard. Party A shall take out social insurance for the sake of dispatched labourers and be responsible for violating the laws and regulations related to social insurance.

4.3.6 Rights and Obligations of Party B

Party B may formulate, revise or decide on the rules concerning labour remuneration, working hours, rest and holidays, labour safety and hygiene, insurance and benefits, vocational training, labour discipline and other important matters and rules directly affecting the labourers of Party A, provided that such matters and rules meet the procedural and substantial requirements of the related laws and regulations. Party B may make an enquiry about the payment of wages and social insurance of the dispatched labourers. Party B shall not redispatch the dispatch labourers to other labour-user units. Party B shall pay Party A the wages, the expenses of social insurance, and the service fees in a timely and full manner. Party B shall perform the following contractual obligations: (a) implementing the national labour standards and providing the related labour conditions and labour protection; (b) informing the dispatched labourers of the work requirements and the labour remuneration; (c) paying overtime wages, performance bonuses, and benefits related to the job positions; (d) providing the training necessary for performing the duties of the dispatched labourers; (e) implementing the wage adjustment in case of continuous employment of the dispatched labourers; and (f) performing the duties prescribed by the related laws and regulations.

4.3.7 Modification, Revocation and Termination of Labour Dispatch Contracts

Both parties shall comply with the terms and conditions of the labour dispatch contract. One party shall not modify or revoke the contract without consent from the other party. If the contract cannot be performed due to any change of laws and regulations or force majeure, the affected party shall inform the other party in time, and both parties may modify and revoke the contract. Party B may send back the dispatched labourers in case of any of the following events: (a) Article 39 and Items 1 and 2 of Article 40 of the Labour Contract Law of 2012 are applicable to the dispatched labourers; (b) Item 3 of Article 40 and Article 41 of the Labour Contract Law of 2012 are applicable to Party B; (c) Party B is declared bankruptcy, Party B's business licence is revoked, or Party B is closed; (d) the dispatched labour contract expires; or (e) other stipulations.

4.4 Practical Issues Related to Labour Dispatch

4.4.1 The Implication of the Administrative Permit for Labour Dispatch on Labour Dispatch

Article 6 of the Measures of Implementation of Administrative Permits for Labour Dispatch provides that any enterprise engaging in labour dispatch shall apply to the local competent human resources and social security organ for an administrative permit and without it, no enterprise or individual shall not engage in labour dispatch. The administrative permit for labour dispatch shall not be obliterated, sold, rented or illegally transferred. The validity period of the administrative permit is three years. Article 31 provides that where any unit or individual violates the Labour Contract Law of 2012 and without authorisation engages in labour dispatch, the human resources and social security organ shall order the unit or the individual to stop the illegal act, confiscate the illegal earnings, if any, and impose a fine of not less than one time but not more than five times the earnings.

There are some controversies regarding the nature of the administrative permit. Some argue that the administrative permit is only to facilitate the administration of labour dispatch. Some courts in Shanghai, Hunan, Jilin and Henan hold this view. In the Civil Order of Retrial Review and Hearing Inspection of the Case of Confirming Labour Relation between Qian Hongtao and China Unicom Fan County Branch (2018 Yu CA 8742), the Higher People's Court of Henan Province held that Article 92 of the Labour Contract Law of 2012 was an administrative provision, and the violation of Article 92 would not invalidate the labour dispatch contract. The Higher People's Court of Hunan Province held the same view in the Civil Decision of the Retrial of Labour Dispute between Xiao Qinghong and China Unicom Changsha Branch (2018 Xiang CR 299). The view was also held by the Higher People's Court of Jinlin Province in the Civil Order of Retrial Review of Labour Dispute between Gao Hongchao and PICC Nongan Branch and Jilin Haichuang HR Service Co., Ltd., and Jilin Rainbow Talent Development and Consulting Service Co., Ltd. (2018 Ji CA 1453).

However, others argue that the administrative permit is statutory and compulsory, and the labour dispatch without the valid administrative permit shall be deemed the de facto labour contract. The Notice of Several Issues of Regulating Labour Dispatch, released by the Human Resources and Social Security Department of Shandong Province on 1 March 2015, provides that labour dispatch without an administrative permit imposes the liabilities of an employing unit under the Labour Contract Law of 2012 on a labour-user unit. The same provision is included in the Measures of Labour Dispatch Administration released by Qingdao Human Resources and Social Bureau on 25 June 2018, the Opinions of Handling the Issues of the Linkage of Arbitration and Hearing of Labour Disputes released by the Intermediate People's Court of Yantai and the Human Resources and Social Security Bureau of Yantai on 21 June 2019 and Several Opinions concerning the Linkage between Labour Dispute Arbitration and Litigation released by the Higher People's Court of Guangdong Province and the Labour Dispute Arbitration Commission of Guangdong Province on 18 July 2018.

4.4.2 Violating the Requirements of Being Temporary, Auxiliary and Substitute

According to the Interim Provisions on Labour Dispatch, labour dispatch is only applicable to temporary, auxiliary or substitute vacancies. The courts in China have not reached an agreement on whether such requirements are compulsory or not.

The courts in Shanghai, Yantai Fujian and Guangdong do not think that the violation of Article 3 of the Interim Provisions on Labour Dispatch invalidates the labour dispatch or gives rise to the de facto labour relationship between the dispatched labourers and the labour-user unit. The Meeting Minutes of Several Issues of Law Application of Labour Dispatch released by Shanghai City Human Resources and Social Security Bureau and the Higher People's Court of Shanghai released on 31 December 2014 clarified that the provisions of being temporary, auxiliary and substitute are administrative, and violation of such provisions cannot invalidate the labour dispatch contract and the labour contract. A similar provision is included in Several Opinions concerning the Linkage between Labour Dispute Arbitration and Litigation released by the Higher People's Court of Guangdong Province and the Labour Dispute Arbitration Commission of Guangdong Province and the Opinions of Handling the Issues of the Linkage of Arbitration and Hearing of Labour Disputes released by the Intermediate People's Court of Yantai and the Human Resources and Social Security Bureau of Yantai. In the Civil Decision of Second Instance of the Case of Labour Dispute between Zhang Zhujun and Shanghai Xuhui Human Resources Co. Ltd. (2019 Hu CF 14746), the First Intermediate People's Court of Shanghai held that Article 66 of the Labour Contract Law of 2012 was an administrative provision and the fact that Article 66 was violated did not invalidate the labour contract between Zhang Zhujun and Xuhui Human Resources Co. Ltd. The Higher People's Court of Fujian Province held the same view in the Civil Order of Retrial Review and Hearing Supervision of the Labour Dispute between Yan Zhengyin and Putian City Public Transportation Group Co., Ltd. (2017 Min CA 2763).

In contrast, some courts take the opposite view, especially in Chongqing, Liaoning Province, Xinjiang and Shantou. This view is reflected in the Regulations on Protecting the Rights and Interests of Employees in Chongqing, the Regulations on Protecting the Rights and Interests of Employees in Liaoning Province, the Regulations on Protecting the Rights and Interests of Employees in Xinjiang, and the Regulations on Protecting the Rights and Interests of Employees in Shantou.

It should be reconsidered where the dividing line between an administrative provision and a statutory provision is. From the perspective of civil law, it should be deemed to be statutory where a provision is (a) related to financial security, market order, national macroeconomic policies and other public order and good customs; (b) related to banned transactions such as drugs, guns and human organs; or (c) related to franchising law in accordance with the Meeting Minutes of National Courts Trials of Civil and Commercial Case released on 8 November 2019. However, whether the criteria mentioned in the Meeting Minutes of National Courts Trials of Civil and Commercial Case are applicable to labour law should be reconsidered. Labour dispatch would be doomed to be a castle in air if the provisions of an administrative permit for labour dispatch and the requirements of being temporary, auxiliary and substitute were deemed to be administrative.

4.4.3 Joint and Several Liability

The joint and several liabilities under labour dispatch underwent changes in the Labour Contract Law of 2012. Article 92 of the Labour Contract Law of 2008 provided that where a labour-dispatching unit violates the provisions of this Law, the administrative department of labour and other competent departments concerned shall order it to rectify; if the circumstances are serious, a fine shall be imposed on it, with not less than 1,000 yuan but not more than 5,000 yuan for each person, and its business licence shall be revoked by the administrative department for industry and commerce; if damage is caused to the dispatched labourers, the labour dispatch unit and the labour-user unit shall bear joint and several liability for compensation. However, Article 92 of the Labour Contract Law of 2012 provides where damage is caused to the labourers dispatched by the labour-user unit, the labour dispatch unit and the labour-user unit shall bear the joint and several liabilities for compensation. The joint and several liability under the Labour Contract Law of 2008 was two-way, while the joint and several liability under the Labour Contract Law of 2012 was one-way. Under the Labour Contract Law of 2012, the labour-user unit will not bear the joint and several liability if the damage to the dispatch labourers is caused by the labour dispatch unit. It can be seen that the liability of the labour-user unit has been mitigated under the Labour Contract Law of 2012.

However, at the provincial level, some higher courts released detailed rules concerning the joint and several liabilities. On 14 April 2014, the Replies to Several Issues of Hearing the Cases of Labour Dispute (No. 2) were released by the First Civil Division of the Higher People's Court of Zhejiang and Zhengjiang Labour Dispute

Arbitration Commission, which provide that the labour-user unit will not bear the joint and several liability if the damage to the dispatch labourers is caused by the labour dispatch unit, provided that there is intention or gross fault on the part of the labour-user unit. The same provision is included in the Minutes of Several Issues on Labour and Personnel Labour Dispute Case Hearing by Shandong Province Higher People's Court and Human Resources and Social Security Department of Shandong Province.

In practice, some courts still have different understandings of the circumstances where the labour-user unit takes the joint and several liabilities. In the Civil Order of Retrial Review and Hearing Supervision of the Case of Labour Dispute between Qingdao Beer (Weifang) Co., Ltd., and Geng Qiulan (2018 Lu CA 3895), the Higher People's Court of Shandong Province held that Qingdao Beer (Weifang) Co., Ltd. shall take the joint and several liability with Weifang Kunhong Labour Service Co., Ltd. (a labour dispatch unit) because Weifang Kunhong Labour Service Co., Ltd. failed to sign a labour contract with Geng Qiulan, and Qingdao Beer (Weifang) Co., Ltd. and Weifang Kunhong Labour Service Co., Ltd. shall pay Geng Qiulan double wages. Other courts think that contributary negligence shall be taken into account in deciding whether a labour-user unit takes the liability arising from the damage caused by a labour dispatch unit. In the Civil Order of Retrial Review and Hearing Supervision of the Case of Labour Dispatch Contract between APAC and Guangzhou Limide Enterprise Management and Consultation Co. Ltd. (2019 Yue CA 1789), the Higher People's Court of Guangdong Province held that although the labour dispatch contract between APAC and Limide did not stipulate which party shall bear the expenses for housing funds, such expenses were a part of employment costs and it was fair that APAC shall bear 70% of the liability and Limide shall bear 30% of the liability. Similarly, the Intermediate People's Court of Wuhan held that Wuhan Dexingtianxia HR Development Co. Ltd. employed Guan Chuanzhi and was obliged to take out the social insurance for the sake of its labourer and that it was groundless for Dexingtianxia to argue that Wuhan PepsiCo., Ltd. shall bear the whole liability on the grounds that Wuhan PepsiCo Co., Ltd. did not pay Dexingtianxia the wages and the expenses of social insurance in the Civil Decision of Second Instance of the Case of Recovery Right between Wuhan Dexingtianxia HR Development Co., Ltd. and Wuhan PepsiCo., Ltd. (2020 E01CF 1972).

4.4.4 Tort Liabilities Under Labour Dispatch

Article 1191 of the Civil Code provides that where an employee causes damage to another person in connection with the performance of his work, his employer shall assume tort liability. The employer may, after assuming tort liability, claim indemnification against the employee who acts intentionally or with gross negligence. During the period of labour dispatch, a dispatched labourer causes damage to another person in connection with the performance of his work, and the labour-user unit shall assume tort liability. The labour dispatch unit that is at fault shall assume corresponding liability. However, under the Torts Liability Law of 2010, the labour dispatch unit who is at fault shall assume corresponding supplementary liability. It is fair that the liability of the labour dispatch unit is determined on the basis of its fault.

The liability of a labour dispatch unit entails "in connection with the performance his work" and "at fault". Committing crimes is not "in connection with the performance his work". In the Civil Decision of Second Instance of the Case of Tort Liability of Dispatch Labourers between Li Junguo, Xi'an Tangcheng Hospital and Xi'an Jinhui Security Service Co., Ltd. (2018 Shan 01CF 9909) on 5 December 2016 Tangcheng Hospital and Jinhui Security Service Co., Ltd. signed the Contract for Security Services. Guo Tong and Liu Fengnian were dispatched to Tangcheng Hospital by Jinhui Security Service Co., Ltd. On 20 January 2017, Li Junguo came to Tangcheng Hospital to claim his payment in arrears, and Guo Tong and Liu Fengnian were on their duties. Guo Tong and Liu Fengnian beat Li Junguo using spontoons. Finally, Guo Tong and Liu Fengnian were found guilty of willful and malicious injury, the Second Intermediate People's Court of Xi'an held that the crime of willful and malicious injury was far beyond the scope of performance of the duties and thus the argument that Jinhui Security Service Co., Ltd. should assume the supplementary liability was rejected.

It can be anticipated that under the Civil Code, "corresponding liability" will be proportional to the degree of the fault on the part of the labour dispatch unit. It should be noted that "another person" means a person outside a labour-user unit. If a dispatched labourer does damage to a person employed by a labour-user unit, the labour-user unit may not claim indemnification against the dispatched labourer. Similarly, if a dispatched labourer does damage to a labour-user unit, it remains in dispute whether the labour-user unit may claim the loss from the dispatched labourer. It is generally accepted that a user employing unit may not claim the loss from a dispatched labourer where there is no intention or gross negligence on the part of the dispatched labourer. In the Civil Order of Retrial Review and Hearing Supervision of the Case of the Right to Recovery between Liaoning Changyuan Traveling Bus Co., Ltd. and De Libin (2020 Liao CA 55), the Higher People's Court of Liaoning Province held that the Road Traffic Accident Identification did not show that there was intention or gross negligence on the part of De Libin while he was performing his duties, and thus Liaoning Changyuan Traveling Bus Co., Ltd. could not claim the loss from De Libin. In accordance with the Replies to Several Issues of Hearing the Cases of Labour Dispute (No. 5) released by the First Civil Division of the Higher People's Court of Zhejiang and Zhengjiang Labour Dispute Arbitration Commission on 21 June 2019, where a labourer (including a dispatched labourer) damages an employing unit (labour-user unit), such damage should be at the risk of the employing unit. A labourer shall compensate an employing unit if the damage is caused due to the intention or gross fault on the part of the labouer. The amount of the compensation shall be determined on the basis of the degree of the fault, the causative potency, the amount of the loss, the level of labour remuneration and the continuing performance of the contract.

4.4.5 Open-Ended Labour Contracts in Labour Dispatch

Article 14 of the Labour Contract Law of 2012 sets forth the conditions for an open-ended labour contract, including (1) the worker has been working for the employing unit for a consecutive period of 10 or more years; (2) the worker has been working for the employing unit for a consecutive period of 10 or more years but less than 10 years away from the statutory retirement age when the employing unit adopts the labour contract system or when the state-owned enterprise has to conclude a new labour contract with him as a result of restructuring; (3) the worker intends to renew the labour contract after he has consecutively concluded a fixed-term labour contract with the employing unit twice and he has not been found in any of the circumstances specified in Article 39 or Subparagraph (1) or (2) in Article 40 of this Law. On the other hand, Article 50 of the Labour Contract Law of 2012 provides that the labour-dispatching unit shall conclude with the workers to be dispatched a fixed-term labour contract for a period of not less than two years and shall pay labour remuneration on a monthly basis.

The relationship between Article 14 and Article 50 is confusing. Does Article 50 exclude the application of Article 14? It is not easy to say yes or no. If Article 51 is a special provision, Article 14 does not apply to labour dispatch according to the legal maxim "*lex specialis derogat legi generali*". However, the conclusion that labour dispatch is exempt from Article 14 cannot be justified. There is no wonder that there are different understandings of the relationship between Article 14 and Article 50.

Some courts in Guangdong, Inner Mongolia, Beijing and Shenyang favour the view that Article 14 is applicable to labour dispatch. On 18 July 2018, the Higher People's Court of Guangdong Province and the Labour Dispute Arbitration Commission of Guangdong Province jointly released Several Opinions concerning the Linkage between Labour Dispute Arbitration and Litigation, which provides that an open-ended labour contract is applicable to labour dispatch if Paragraph 2 or Paragraph 3 of Article 14 of the Labour Contract Law of 2012 is met. A similar provision is included in the Guiding Opinions of Hearing the Cases of Labour and Personnel Disputes released by the Higher People's Court of Inner Mongolia and Labour Dispute Arbitration Commission of Inner Mongolia on 2 December 2015.

The reasoning can be seen in the Civil Decision of Retrial of the Case of Labour Dispute between Liaoning Zhongtian Talents Service Co., Ltd. and Niu Chunyu (2020 Liao 01 CR 26), where the Intermediate People's Court of Shenyang held that Zhongtian shall sign an open-ended labour contract with Niu Chunyu on the grounds that (a) Article 58 of the Labour Contract Law of 2012 provides that a labour dispatch unit is the employing unit under the Labour Contract Law of 2012 and shall fulfil the obligations toward labourers. Accordingly, a labour dispatch unit shall fulfil all the obligations of an employing unit set forth by the Labour Contract Law of 2012. Where the requirements in Article 14 are met, a labour dispatch unit shall sign an open-ended labour contract; (b) as opposed to the general fixed-term labour contract, which has no limit on the length of the contract period, a fixed-term labour contract of not less than two years applies to labour dispatch in Article 58. The purport of

Article 58 is that a fixed-term labour contract of less than two years is not allowed in the case of labour dispatch, and Article 58 does not naturally exclude the application of Article 14. (c) The legislative purpose of Article 58 is to prevent the short period of the labour dispatch and stabilise the labour relationships. If Article 58 was deemed to be exceptional to Article 14, an increasing number of employing units would resort to labour dispatch to evade signing open-ended labour contracts. Thus, an increasing number of labourers would be dispatched labourers, which would amount to cutting the ground from under Article 14's feet. In the Civil Order of the Appeal Case of Labour Dispute between China Energy Engineering Group Beijing Electric Power Construction Co., Ltd. (CEEGBEPC) and Li Huinian(2016 Jing CA 1007), the Higher People's Court of Beijing held that Li Huinian and Beijing Jingzhiye Human Resources Service Co., Ltd. consecutively signed the fixed-term labour contracts twice, Li Huinian might request that Beijing Jingzhiye Human Resources Service Co., Ltd. sign an open-ended labour contract with him, and that the termination of the labour contract by Beijing Jingzhihui Human Resources Service Co., Ltd. without his consent amounted to deprivation of his option to signing an open-ended labour contract.

Other courts in Jiangsu, Zhejiang, Shanghai and Dalian believe that Article 14 is not applicable to labour dispatch. This view is reflected in the Guiding Opinions concerning Hearing the Cases of Labour Disputes, which were released by the Higher People's Court of Jiangsu Province and the Labour Dispute Arbitration Commission of Jiangsu Province on 14 December 2009 (but interestingly, Article 13 of the Regulations of Labour Contracts of Jiangsu Province allows a dispatch unit and a labourer to sign an open-ended labour contract by mutual consent), and the Replies to Several Issues of Hearing the Cases of Labour Dispute (No. 5), which were released by the First Civil Division of the Higher People's Court of Zhejiang and Zhengjiang Labour Dispute Arbitration Commission on 21 June 2019. In the Civil Order of Hearing Supervision of the Case of Labour Contract Dispute between Zhu Yonghua, Shanghai Fuchu Labour Management Co., Ltd. and Volkswagen Car Renting Co., Ltd. (2020 Hu CA 644), Zhu Yonghua appealed that he signed the labour contract with Shanghai Fuchu Labour Management Co., Ltd. twice and might sign an open-ended labour contract, the Higher People's Court of Shanghai rejected his appeal and upheld the decision of second instance made by the Second Intermediate People's Court of Shanghai.

4.4.6 Autonomy of Sending Back Dispatched Labourers

A labour-user unit may send back its dispatched labourers if the conditions of Article 65 of the Labour Contract Law of 2012 and Article 12 of the Interim Regulations of Labour Dispatch are satisfied. If a labour-user unit sends back its dispatched labourers in accordance with Article 65 of the Labour Contract Law of 2012, the labour dispatch unit may terminate the labour contract with the dispatched labourers sent back by the labour-user unit. If a labour-user unit sends back its dispatched labourers in accordance with Article 12 of the Interim Regulations of Labour Dispatch, the labour dispatch unit may terminate the labour contract with the dispatched labourers sent back by the labour-user unit, the labour dispatch unit may terminate the labour contract with the dispatched labourers sent back by the labour-user unit, provided that the dispatched labourers refuse to be redispatched on the conditions equal or superior to those stipulated in the labour contract. If a labour-user unit sends back its dispatched labourers in accordance with Article 12 of the Interim Regulations of Labour Dispatch, the labour dispatch unit may not terminate the labour contract with the dispatched labourers sent back by the labour-user unit, provided that the dispatched labourers refuse to be redispatched on the conditions inferior to those stipulated in the labour contract. The ways the dispatched labourers are sent back may affect the rights and interests of the dispatched labourers. The problem is that given that the nature of the labour dispatch contract is a contract under civil law and that one of the distinguishing features of civil law is respect for autonomy, can the parties to the labour dispatch contract freely stipulate the circumstances where the dispatched labourers are sent back?

The courts in Shanghai say "yes". The Meeting Minutes of Several Issues of Law Application of Labour Dispatch released by Shanghai City Human Resources and Social Security Bureau and the Higher People's Court of Shanghai on 31December 2014, provides that Article 12 of the Interim Regulations of Labour Dispatch are not exclusive and only used for reference, a dispatch unit may withdraw its dispatched labourers, three parties may agree on sending back the dispatched labourers and the dispatched labourers may be sent back (a) upon the expiry of the labour dispatch contract, (b) in case that the labour dispatch contract is revoked; or (c) in case that the labour-user unit fails to fulfil the primary obligations under the labour dispatch contract.

In contrast, the courts in Guangdong are of the opposite view that any stipulations of sending back dispatched labourers are invalid, which can be seen in the Opinions of Guangzhou City Labour Arbitration Commission and the Intermediate People's Court of Guangzhou City concerning Trial of Labour Disputes released in 2015.

4.4.7 Reverse Labour Dispatch

Strictly speaking, reverse labour dispatch is not a legal term. Reverse labour dispatch means that at the request of an employing unit, a labour dispatch unit dispatches the labourer who the employing unit refuses to sign a labour contract although the labour relationship between them has been in place. It often occurs where an employing unit recruits a labourer but does not intend to sign the labour contract with him or where an employing unit terminates the labour contract with a labourer but expects him to continue to work for it. Taking no account of the former labour relationship with the employing unit, reverse labour dispatch would be within the meaning of labour dispatch under the Labour Contract Law of 2012.

There is considerable uncertainty as to whether reverse labour dispatch is valid. The courts in Beijing tend to hold that reverse dispatch labour is legal, and Article 67 of the Labour Contract Law of 2012 is in the nature of administrative provisions. In the Civil Order of Appeal and Application of the Case of Labour Dispute between Zhong Xiang, China Education Television and Beijing Guoshi Human Resources Management Co., Ltd. (2016 Jing CA 1443), the court of first instance and the court of second instance held that the labour contract between Zhong Yang and Beijing Guoshi Human Resources Management Co., Ltd. was valid on the grounds that Article 67 of the Labour Contract Law of 2012 was not mandatory but administrative, and the Higher People's Court of Beijing further held that even if reverse labour dispatch existed between Beijing Guoshi Human Resources Management Co., Ltd. and China Education Television after 1 January 2008, it did not necessarily invalidate the labour contract between Beijing Guoshi Human Resources Management Co., Ltd. and Zhong Yang and the argument put forward by Zhong Yang that the labour relationship between China Education Television and him was unfounded. In contrast, the courts in Shandong tend to be silent on whether reverse labour dispatch is valid and identify which party should take responsibility, and in the Civil Order Retrial of the Case of Labour Dispute between Liu Jiandong and China Construction Bank Zhaozhuang Branch (2020 Lu CR 3557), The Higher People's Court of Shandong Province held that it was legal for China Construction Bank Zhaozhuang Branch to terminate the labour contract with Liu Jiandong, who received the economic compensation provided by the Labour Contract Law of 2012. The handling of reverse labour dispatch in Shandong agreed with the provisions of the Opinions by the Higher People's Court of Shandong Province on Several Issues of Hearing Labour Disputes, which were released 26 November 2009. The courts in Shanghai followed the footsteps of the courts in Beijing in the Civil Decision of Second Instance of the Case of Labour Dispute between Zhao Xiaoqing, JUKI (Shanghai) Industrial Co., Ltd. and Shanghai Jiayang Labour Service Co., Ltd. (Hu 02 CF 137).

In accordance with the Guidance of the Higher People's Court of Jiangsu Province to Hearing the Cases of Labour Dispute released on 17 May 2010, the reverse labour dipatch was valid where an employing unit legally terminated or revoked the labour contract with a labourer and paid the economic compensation and reemployed him in temporary, auxiliary or substitute job positions through the labour dispatch, and it was invalid where an employing unit legally terminated or revoked the labour contract with a labourer and paid the economic compensation but reemployed him not in temporary, auxiliary or substitute job positions through the labour dispatch or where an employing unit illegally terminated or revoked the labour contract with a labourer and reemployed him through the labour dispatch. In the Civil Order of Appeal and Application of the Case of Labour Dispute between Cai Qinqin and Nantong Yaohan Commerce and Trade Co., Ltd. (2020 Su CA 7408), the Higher People's Court of Jiangsu Province held that the argument put forward by Cai Qinqin that the reverse labour dispatch was not legal was rejected.

Reference

ILO. (1997). *Private Employment Agencies Convention, 1997 (No. 181)*. Retrieved 15 May, 2021, from https://www.ilo.org/dyn/normlex/en/f?p=NORMLEXPUB:12100:0::NO::P12100_INSTRUMENT_ID:312326.

Chapter 5
Outsourcing

Outsourcing is the delegation of noncore operations or jobs from internal production to an external entity. Human resource outsourcing and manufacturing outsourcing are common forms of outsourcing. Labour dispatch in disguise of human resources outsourcing is not allowed, which will give rise to legal liabilities under labour law. Most of the courts tend to judge the nature of outsourcing from the perspectives of the exercise of management power, the payment of service fees, and the party paying such fees.

5.1 Overview of Outsourcing

5.1.1 Concept and Types of Outsourcing

Even if it is hardly a new or radical business practice, there is no concept of outsourcing within the context of Chinese labour law. Outsourcing can be defined as the delegation of noncore operations or functions from one entity to another for cost-cutting purposes. In terms of the delegated content, outsourcing may be grouped into human resource outsourcing and manufacturing outsourcing.

5.1.2 Advantages and Disadvantages of Outsourcing

5.1.2.1 Advantages

Improving Core Competencies

Core competencies are the capabilities and resources that an enterprise has access to, which are vital for its growth and survival in the market-oriented economy. An

Y. Wang, *Chinese Labour Law*, Understanding China,
https://doi.org/10.1007/978-981-16-8101-1_5

enterprise has to exploit its core competencies to succeed against competition. It is common that an enterprise cannot specialise in every field. If an enterprise allocates its limited resources to the field that it does not specialise in, its core competencies will be lowered.

Cutting Costs

The aim of an enterprise is to bring the best and most profits or advantages for the lowest possible costs. Specialisation can cut costs. Integrating all parts of production in a sole enterprise is not necessary or practical. For example, a motor manufacturing enterprise cannot manufacture all parts of a motor, and it may delegate the testing services to an external service provider or contractor. If it intends to test the motors on its own, it has to invest a lot to establish a motor testing lab and employ and manage its own professional employees.

Reducing Labour Disputes

Outsourcing is a firewall to isolate an enterprise from potential labour disputes. Without outsourcing, an enterprise has to recruit, employ and manage the labourers necessary for its operations. More labourers mean more labour disputes. In the case of outsourcing, some functions or noncore business will be delegated to an independent contractor, who will recruit, employ and manage the labourers in its name to finish the tasks. Usually, an enterprise will not be involved in the labour disputes between the independent contractor and its labourers. In this sense, outsourcing is a risk management tool.

5.1.2.2 Disadvantages

Discouraging Innovation

Innovation ability is an essential prerequisite for efficient management and sustainable growth. If too many tasks are outsourced by an enterprise to an independent contractor, it will lack the initiative to innovate management strategies. A growing dependence on outsourcing will decrease the profitability of an enterprise.

Potential Risks

Because labour laws and regulations are silent on outsourcing, there is no clear-cut dividing line between outsourcing and labour dispatch. The labour dispatch in disguise of outsourcing will give rise to legal liabilities under the Labour Contract Law of 2012.

5.1.3 *Specifications for Human Resources Outsourcing Service*

On 28 February 2017, Specifications for Human Resources Outsourcing Service were released by General Administration of Quality Supervision, Inspection and Quarantine of the People's Republic of China and the Standardisation Administration, and the Specifications are for reference only.

The specifications lay down the basic requirements for human resource outsourcing services. The human resources outsourcing agencies are expected to comply with the following requirements: (1) the agencies should gain business licences stating human resources outsourcing service and permit for human resources outsourcing, (2) the agencies should have their own offices and furniture, and (3) the agencies should have workers who are familiar with the basic knowledge of human resources outsourcing and process.

In accordance with Specifications for Human Resources Outsourcing Services, human resources outsourcing services mean human resources management, development, manning, and other related services. The contents of human resource outsourcing include without limitation management function outsourcing, human resources consulting outsourcing, human resource risks controlling service outsourcing and other types of outsourcing. In practice, there are more types, such as wages and remuneration outsourcing, wages and remuneration management outsourcing, benefits outsourcing, social insurance outsourcing, social insurance withholding, and personal income tax withholding. However, in accordance with Article 30 of the Interim Regulations on Human Resources Market released by the State Council on 29 October 2018, human resources service organisations providing human resources outsourcing services may not change the labour relationship between an employing unit and an individual labourer and may not, in collusion with an employing unit, infringe on the legitimate interests of an individual labourer.

5.1.4 *Process of Outsourcing*

5.1.4.1 Demand Analysis

Conducting a demand analysis helps an organisation better understand current and future workforce requirements. The analysis often involves the type of industry, the size of the organisation, the organisation chart, the necessity of establishing an in-house human resources department, the workload, the number of staff, etc.

5.1.4.2 Feasibility Study

Doing a feasibility study in terms of law and economy is a requisite for outsourcing. Laws and regulations related to human resource outsourcing must be well and fully understood. In China, there are few laws and regulations related to human resources in place. Therefore, positions in court decisions are particularly important to guide human resource outsourcing. Cost-benefits analysis is an important tool for human resource outsourcing decisions.

5.1.4.3 Analysis of Service Providers

The market of outsourcing service providers must be under scrutiny. Reputation and credit records are significant factors for the selection of service providers.

5.1.4.4 Procurement of Outsourcing Service

The process of procurement shall comply with the procurement laws and regulations, if applicable, and the related rules in enterprises. In the case of state-owned enterprises, the Law of the PRC on Tenders and Bids will apply. Generally, the Law of the PRC against Unfair Competition applies, particularly the provisions of bribery and corruption. Undertaking of No-bribery and No-corruption and Nondisclosure Agreement shall be signed.

5.1.4.5 Execution of Service Contract

A contract for outsourcing services shall be duly drafted and signed. Given that there are few laws and regulations related to outsourcing, the terms of contractual rights, obligations and liabilities shall be included, which are significant. The contract for outsourcing services is an important tool for risk allocation.

5.1.4.6 Appraisal of Service Performance

The service provider's performance should be appraised on a regular basis. In case of any deviation from the contract, both parties should consult with each other and try to find a correction measure. In the case of fundamental breach, the contracts may be terminated without prejudice to the remedies under law.

5.2 Manufacturing Outsourcing

As noted earlier, outsourcing is normally treated as involving contracting out of a business function or process performed in house to an external service provider. Some auxiliary functions or processes are split up and outsourced to an external provider, while the core business remains in house. The outsourced functions and processes often add less value to core business activities. Manufacturing outsourcing, a type of outsourcing, not only means that products are purchased from outside but also allocates risks and responsibilities to an external service provider.

5.2.1 The Nature of Manufacturing Outsourcing

Some argue that manufacturing outsourcing is in the nature of a work contract, which is prescribed by the Civil Code, while others argue that it is in the nature of a service contract, which the Civil Code is silent on. A work contract is a contract under which a contractor, in accordance with the requirements of a client, completes work and delivers the work product to the client who pays remuneration in return. Contracted work includes processing, manufacturing on order, repair, reproduction, testing, inspection, etc.[1] In contrast, the meaning of a service contract is a little vague. A service contract has to be performed with reference to the provisions of a contract similar to a service contract, and there is room for the application of the doctrine of autonomy in a service contract. In practice, manufacturing outsourcing may involve a work contract and a leasing contract, particularly where an external contractor does not own the premises or manufacturing facilities necessary for performing the work contract.

5.2.2 Key Terms of Manufacturing Outsourcing Contracts

At present, there are no standards for manufacturing outsourcing at the national level. In commercial practice, the following terms are popular.

5.2.2.1 Subject Matter of Manufacturing Outsourcing Contracts

The subject matter of manufacturing outsourcing contracts is a work result, which shall be clearly defined from the perspectives of quantity, quality, specifications and delivery.

[1] The Civil Code, Article 770.

5.2.2.2 Labourer Management

The contractor has an independent right to use labourers. The contractor may set out the rules with regard to wages and remuneration, working hours, rest and holidays, labour security and hygiene, social insurance and benefits, labour training, labour discipline and quota management.

5.2.2.3 On-Site Management

The contract-awarding party does not intervene in the management of the contractor but may retain the right to supervise quality control and work security. Regardless, the contractor shall directly exercise the management power. It is better to appoint a person responsible for on-site management.

5.2.2.4 Equipment and Premises Management

The contractor may use its own equipment and premises to carry out manufacturing outsourcing. Alternatively, the contractor can lease the equipment and premises from the contract-awarding party or a third party. The contractor is often responsible for the management, maintenance and inspection of equipment. The contractor and the contract-awarding party may agree on the sharing of the related expenses.

5.2.2.5 Materials Management

The contractor is responsible for receiving, delivering, storing and making an inventory of the materials.

5.2.2.6 Processing Management

The contractor is responsible for processing control and keeping records of processing. The contractor at its own discretion decides on the work schedules and the number of labourers. The contractor shall ensure that the production, storage and transportation meet the relevant requirements.

5.2.2.7 Quality Management

The contractor shall ensure that the work result meets the quality standards and constantly improve the quality.

5.2.2.8 Settlement of Service Expenses

Service expenses may be settled on the basis of the workload or the work result. The service expenses shall not be settled per capita. The contract-awarding party cannot pay service expenses in the form of wages and social insurance.

5.2.3 Problems with Manufacturing Outsourcing

Some enterprises try to evade the restrictive provisions related to labour dispatch and resort to manufacturing outsourcing. However, they still retain the direct management power of the labourers, which amounts to the loan of labourers from other enterprises or labour dispatch. Retaining direct management powers will always expose enterprises to joint and several liabilities or de factor labour relationships with labourers. Such enterprises tend to pay service expenses in the form of wages per capita, which enables the courts to deny the existence of manufacturing outsourcing and brings more disputes and liabilities. These problems will be addressed in Sects. 5.3.2 and 5.3.3. It should be noted that if the whole business is contracted out, the contractor always pays the contracting fees to the contract-awarding party, which is totally different from manufacturing outsourcing.

5.3 Practical Issues Related to Outsourcing

5.3.1 Doubtful Legitimacy of Human Resources Outsourcing

There is no doubt that human resource outsourcing is legitimate provided that it complies with Specifications for Human Resources Outsourcing Services and the Interim Regulations on Human Resources Market released by the State Council on 29 October 2018. However, in practice, there are newly emerging types of human resources outsourcing services, such as social insurance payment agency services. It is in disguise of human resources outsourcing. As noted earlier, payment of social insurance is a primary and statutory obligation of employing units. The obligation may not be derogated, excluded or transferred. An outsourcing service company often uses its account to take out social insurance for the labourers employed by other companies. From a legal perspective, there must be labour contracts between the outsourcing service company and the labourers. However, the truth is that the labourers are employed by other companies instead of the outsourcing service company. It is very likely that the outsourcing service company and the real employing units are in collusion with each other to evade the obligation of payment of social insurance. In the Civil Decision of Second Instance of the Case of Entrusting Contract between Qingdao Huizhong Taihe Enterprise Management Co., Ltd., and

Li Xianhong (2019, Lu 02 CF 1944), the Intermediate People's Court of Qingdao held that in accordance with Article 10 of the Social Insurance Law, payment of social insurance was a statutory obligation of an employing unit and the employing unit shall in its own name pay the social insurance on the basis of the real labour relationship with the labourers.

The payment of social insurance by means of forged labour contracts may expose outsourcing service companies to liabilities under the Labour law of 2018 and the Criminal law, at least in Qingdao, Wuhan, Beijing and Guangdong Provinces. The room for payment of social insurance by means of forged labourer contracts is being narrowed in the context of the Notice of Serval Issues concerning Participation in Social insurance by Labour Dispatch Enterprises and Human Resources Enterprises released by the Beijing City Human Resources and Social Security Bureau on 30 June 2020.

5.3.1.1 Liabilities Under the Labour Law of 2018

In accordance with Article 12 of the Opinions of Guangzhou City Labour Arbitration Commission and the Intermediate People's Court of Guangzhou City concerning Trial of Labour Disputes released in 2015, where an employing unit signs a labour contract with a labourer and establishes the labour relationship, is it legitimate for the employing unit to entrust another unit to pay the social insurance for the sake of its labourer? Is the employing unit obliged to pay economic compensation in case the labourer terminates the labour contract with his employing unit on the grounds that the employing unit does not pay social insurance? Answer: It is illegitimate in that the employing unit violates Articles 4 and 10 of the Social Insurance Law, and the employing unit shall pay economic compensation. In accordance with the Regulations of Supervision of Social insurance Fund of Guangdong Province, no unit or individual may cheat social security organs out of the eligibility of payment of social insurance by means of forged labour contracts or supporting documents, or such a unit or individual may be fined.

In the Civil Decision of Second Instance of the Case of Labour Dispute between Qiao Wei and Wuhan Guodan Pharmaceuticals Co., Ltd. (2018 E 01 CF 3245), Qiao Wei worked at Wuhan Guodan Pharmaceuticals Co., Ltd. and the labour contract period was from 1 September 2014 to 31 December 2018. Qiao Wei sustained a work-related injury on 25 December 2015. Wuhan Guodan Pharmaceuticals Co., Ltd. sent a notice of termination stating that the labour contract was terminated on 1 April 2016 on the grounds that Qiao Wei was not capable of performing her duty; Wuhan Guodan Pharmaceuticals Co., Ltd. entrusted Beijing Youbang Tongkang Pharmaceuticals Technology Development Co., Ltd. to pay social insurance for the sake of employees working in Beijing for the period of September 2014 to January 2016. However, the social security organ in Beijing refused to pay to Qiao Wei the benefits of the work-related injury insurance, the Intermediate People's Court of Wuhan held that in accordance with Articles 27 and 28 of Social Insurance Law, an employing unit shall, within thirty days from the date of establishment of the entity, proceed with the business licence, registration certificate or entity seal to the local social insurance agency to apply for social insurance registration. The social insurance agency shall complete the check and review process and issue social insurance registration certificate to the employing unit within fifteen days from receipt of the application, and an employing unit shall, within thirty days, proceed to the social insurance agency to apply for social insurance registrations on behalf of the employees. For those whose social insurance registrations are not processed, the assessed scale of social insurance contributions shall be set by the social insurance agency, and it was the employing unit that paid the social insurance for the sake of labourers, that it was illegal that the employing units entrusted other units to pay the social insurance and that payment of the social insurance in the name of a third party (Beijing Youbang Tongkang Pharmaceuticals Technology Development Co., Ltd.) was not in the nature of agency under civil law and that Wuhan Guodan Pharmaceuticals Co., Ltd. remained responsible for paying Qiao Wei the benefits of work-related injury insurance.

5.3.1.2 Liabilities Under the Criminal Law

Illegal payment of social insurance may be treated as a criminal offence. In accordance with the Interpretation of the NPC standing committee of Article 266 of the Criminal Law, swindling the endowment, medical work-related injury, unemployment, maternity and other social insurance funds or other social security benefits falls within the meaning of the criminal offence of swindling public or private property prescribed by Article 266 of the Criminal Law.

In the Criminal Decision of First Instance of Fraud Crime of Zhang Hong and Guan Yusong (2018 Ji 0102 CF 275), in March 2015, Guan Yusong and Sun Lili, the legal representative of Changchun Fenghuo Human Resources Service Co., Ltd., were aware that Zhang Hong lost her job and they forged the labour contract between Zhang Hong and Changchun Fenghuo Human Resources Service Co., Ltd. and Zhang Hong gained the maternity allowance of 2400 yuan by cheating, the court held that Zhang Hong and Guan Yusong were guilty of a fraud crime and was sentenced to one-year probation under suspended sentence of one-year imprisonment and was fined 2000 yuan, respectively.

The same view was held by the Intermediate People's Court of Jilin City in the Criminal Decision of Second Instance of Fraud Crime of Cao Hongmei (2016 Ji 02 CF 72). Similarly, in the Criminal Decision of First Instance of Fraud Crime of Feng (2014 Zhu Xiang CF 2422), the People's Court of Xiangzhou District Zhuhai City held that Feng forged the labour relationship with a barber shop, which paid the social insurance for the sake of Feng and that Feng was guilty of fraud crime and was sentenced to two-year probation under suspended sentence of one-year imprisonment and was fined 15,000 yuan.

5.3.2 Labour Dispatch in Disguise of Human Resources Outsourcing

In practice, human resources outsourcing and manufacturing outsourcing are often mixed up. Even some courts don't distinguish between the two terms. In accordance with the Regulations of Labour Contracts of Jiangsu Province, if the labourers of an outsourcing service provider work on the premises of a client unit, comply with the arrangement of the client unit and provide labour force using the equipment and devices of the client unit, such outsourcing service shall be treated as labour dispatch. Apparently, the premises, compliance with instructions, and ownership of production tools are taken into consideration when identifying the nature of human resource outsourcing.

In Guandong Province, the factors affecting the nature of human resource outsourcing are different. In accordance with the Guidance Opinions of further Regulating the Administration of Labour Dispatch released by Guangdong Human Resources and Social Security Department on 28 October 2020, the labour dispatch in disguise of human resources outsourcing exists if (a) the contract-awarding party manages the job contents, the workload and other aspects related to work; (b) the contract-awarding party manages the work hours, rest and holidays, overtime work, daily assessment and discipline related to the labourers of the human resources outsourcing provider; (c) the labourers have to comply with the discipline rules made by the contract-awarding party.

In contrast, the courts in Shanghai take a liberal attitude toward the power of management in distinguishing human resources outsourcing from the labour dispatch. In accordance with the Meeting Minutes of Several Issues of Law Application of Labour Dispatch released by Shanghai City Human Resources and Social Security Bureau and the Higher People's Court of Shanghai on 31 December 2014, the application of the rules of enterprises and the exercise of power of management shall be taken into consideration in differentiating human resources outsourcing from labour dispatch. Where the contract-awarding party partly exercises the power of management to meet the requirements of fire prevention, safety production, product and service quality and the order of workplaces, the labour dispute settlement organs should be prudent in judging whether the labour relationship is changed or not, and in other words, in case of human resources outsourcing, both parties may reasonably set a limit on the exercise of the power of management.

5.3.3 The Court Opinions in Related Decisions

Most courts tend to judge the nature of human resource outsourcing from the perspectives of the exercise of management power, the payment of service fees, and the party paying such fees. However, a few courts analyse the ownership of the premises and the production tools in deciding the nature of human resource outsourcing.

5.3.3.1 Dalian UENO Colour Printing Package Co., Ltd. v Yin Shuliang, Etc.

Yin Shuliang (defendant, appellee) knew of the recruitment information of Dalian UENO Colour Printing Package Co., Ltd. (claimant, appellant) through WeChat Moments and worked as a printing worker as of 20 September 2016. On 26 August 2016, the claimant and Dalian Blue Collar's Home Human Resources Service Co., Ltd. (a third party, appellee) signed a contract for enterprise services for a one-year period, which stipulated that the claimant entrusted the third party to render manufacturing outsourcing services, including HR management, inspection, operation, manual handling, packing, assembling and the assignments instructed by the claimant, and the claimant paid the third party the service fees by the month, and the services fees were composed of the wages and the expenses for social insurance. On 9 January 2017, the defendant made an arbitration application to the Dalian Free Trade Labour Arbitration Commission to confirm the existence of the labour relationship between the claimant and the defendant from 20 September 2016 to 6 February 2017. The Commission gave the arbitral award confirming the existence of the labour relationship. The third party was not legible for a labour dispatch service provider. In the Civil Decision of First Instance of the Case of Labour Dispute among Dalian UENO Colour Printing Package Co., Ltd. Yin Shuliang and Dalian Blue Collar's Home Human Resources Service Co., Ltd. (2018 Liao 0219 CF 236), the People's Court of Economic & Technological Development Zone held that in essence the contract for enterprise services was a contract for labour dispatch (instead of human resources outsourcing) on the grounds that (a) the claimant paid the third party the fees of labour management on the basis of the monthly wage instead of the assignment and the work schedule, and the means of payment was in the nature of the payment of service fees of labour dispatch; (b) the defendant was directly commanded, supervised or managed not by the third party but by the claimant, the defendant worked in working hours as the claimant required, and the claimant checked on defendant's work attendance record and decided on the defendant's wages; and (c) the third party was entrusted to pay the wages to the defendant on the behalf of the claimant. In other words, the third party did not directly manage the defendant, and the payment of the service fees was made per capita instead of on the basis of the assignment or the workload, which implied that the contract for enterprise services was a labour outsourcing contract rather than a labour dispatch contract. Furthermore, the third party was not legible for providing labour dispatch services, the contract for enterprise services was not protected by law, and there existed a de facto labour relationship between the claimant and the defendant. In the Civil Decision of Second Instance of the Case of Labour Dispute among Dalian UENO Colour Printing Package Co., Ltd., Yin Shuliang and Dalian Blue Collar's Home Human Resources Service Co., Ltd. (2018 Liao 02 CF 6858), the Intermediate People's Court of Dalian held that it was groundless that the appellant argued that there existed the labour relationship between Yin Shuliang and Dalian Blue Collar's Home Human Resources Service Co., Ltd.

5.3.3.2 Weng Liansheng v Shanghai Shenxin Human Resources Outsourcing Service Co., Ltd., Moet Hennessy Diageo (China) Company Limited (MHDC)

On 27 June 2005, Weng Liansheng and MHDC signed a labour contract for the period from 1 July 2005 to 30 June 2007 and signed several fixed-term labour contracts, and on 1 July 2013, they signed an open-ended labour contract. In June 2014, Weng Liansheng and Shanghai Shenxin Human Resources Outsourcing Service Co., Ltd. signed an open-ended labour contract, which stipulated that (a) whereas Weng Liansheng understood and acknowledged that (i) Shanghai Shenxin Human Resources Outsourcing Service Co. appointed Weng Liansheng and Weng Liansheng agreed to provide related services on the basis of the service contract between Shanghai Shenxin Human Resources Outsourcing Service Co. Ltd. and MHDC (the client), (ii) Shanghai Shenxin Human Resources Outsourcing Service Co. Ltd. was the sole employer of Weng Liansheng and that Weng Liansheng provided services for the client on behalf of his employer did not mean that there existed any labour relationship with the client; (b) Weng Liansheng's job title was a driver; (c) Weng Liansheng was subject to the nonregular working hours system; and (d) his basic monthly wage was 6646 yuan and his monthly subsidy was 1000 yuan; (e) his overtime work should be approved by Shanghai Shenxin Human Resources Outsourcing Service Co. Ltd. Weng Liansheng was notified that the contract was in the nature of service outsourcing, that Weng Liansheng shall comply with the rules made by the client and that the client might advise that Shanghai Shenxin Human Resources Outsourcing Service Co. Ltd. take disciplinary action against Weng Liansheng where he violated the rules of the client. On 1 June 2014, Weng Liansheng, Shanghai Shenxin Human Resources Outsourcing Service Co. Ltd. and MHDC signed a tripartite agreement, where they confirmed that Weng Liansheng and Shanghai Shenxin Human Resources Outsourcing Service Co. Ltd. signed an open-ended labour contract and that in addition to the rules of Shanghai Shenxin Human Resources Outsourcing Service Co. Ltd., Weng Liansheng shall comply with the rules of MHDC.

The court of first instance held that (a) labour outsourcing, also called assignment outsourcing or service outsourcing, was a management mode by which an enterprise integrated outside professional resources with a view to reducing costs and improving efficiency. In case of labour outsourcing, a labour-utilising unit often contracted its partial business or assignment out to a service provider, and the service provider, at its sole discretion, arranged for its labourer to do the related business or assignment as the labour-utilising unit instructed; (b) there was an entrusted service contract between the labour-utilising unit and the service provider, which was responsible for managing the labourers, and the service provider paid the labourers the wages; (c) it was groundless that Weng Liansheng argued that the contract with Shanghai Shenxin Human Resources Outsourcing Service Co. Ltd. was in the nature of labour dispatch; and (d) it was on the basis of the labour outsourcing relationship that Weng Liansheng complied with the rules of MHDC, and the fact that Weng Liansheng complied with the rules of MHDC could not navigate the formation of the labour outsourcing relationship. In the Civil Decision of Second Instance of the Case of Labour Dispute among Weng Liansheng, Shanghai Shenxin Human Resources Outsourcing Service Co., Ltd. and Moet Hennessy Diageo (China) Company Limited (MHDC) (2017 Hu 02 CF 794), the Intermediate People's Court of Shanaghai held the same view on the grounds that Weng Liansheng, the appellant, failed to produce the evidence supporting that there existed the labour dispatch relationship.

5.3.3.3 Panasonic Appliances Air-Conditioning and Refrigeration (Dalian) Co., Ltd. (PAPARDL) v Zhao Naishuang

Zhao Naishuang (claimant, appellee) and Dalian Guoji Enterprise Service Co., Ltd. (Guoji) (defendant, appellant) signed a labour contract on 1 November 2015, and the contract period was from 1 November 2015 to 31 December 2017. Guoji arranged for the claimant to work as a security guard at Panasonic Appliances Air-Conditioning and Refrigeration (Dalian) Co., Ltd. (PAPARDL). Neither Guoji nor PAPARDL took out the social insurance for the claimant. In 2016, the two defendants signed a contract for security services, whose period was from 1 January 2016 to 31 December 2016. The contract for security services was as follows: (a) Guoji provided the services under the guidance of PAPARDL; (b) Guoji dispatched 19 security guards to PAPARDL; and (c) the monthly expenses for security services were 2800 yuan per capita, which did not include wages, insurance, living allowance, training expenses, etc.; (d) PAPARDL might examine the work of the security guards and ensure that the security guards were entitled to a reasonable rest and holidays; and (e) the security guards shall strictly comply with the related rules of PAPARDL and might give advice with regard to potential risks and hidden danger.

The court of first instance held that the real bone of contention was whether the relationships among the claimant, Guoji and PAPARDL were labour dispatch or labour outsourcing. The labour dispatch was a tripartite mode by which a labour dispatch unit signed a dispatch agreement with a labour-user unit and dispatched its labourer to temporary, auxiliary and replaceable job positions in the labour-user unit. The dispatch unit received the expenses of dispatching services from the labour-user unit and paid wages to its labourers. Labour outsourcing was the mode in which the contract-awarding unit contracted its partial business or auxiliary work to the outside professional organisation, and the professional organisation by itself completed the business or work required by the labour-user unit. The two modes were different in that who had the power of management, whether the subject matter of the contract was labourers or work results and whether the payment was made per capita or on the basis of the workload. To be specific, in case of labour dispatch, the labourers were directly managed by the labour-user unit and provided labour force in the working hours and the form as required by the labour-user unit, while in case of labour outsourcing, the labourers were managed not just by the labour-user unit, and the professional organisation arranged the working hours and the working manners; in case of labour dispatch, what the labour-user unit bought was the labour force of the labourers and the subject matter was a human, while in case of labour outsourcing, what the labour-user unit bought was the work results, and the subject matter was a thing; in case of labour dispatch, the payment was made per capita, while in case of labour outsourcing, the payment was made according to the workload regardless of the wages and the social insurance.

Furthermore, the court of first instance held that the claimant was managed and supervised by PAPARDL, and the claimant had to comply with the rules of PAPARDL. The expenses of the security services included wages, social insurance, living allowances, training expenses and uniform expenses. Such expenses were not settled on the basis of the workload, and the court came to the conclusion that the contract was in the nature of labour dispatch in disguise of labour outsourcing. The Intermediate People's Court of Dalian held that it was groundless that PAPARDL argued that Guoji was not qualified for labour dispatch and that the labour dispatch relationship was invalidated and that providing labour dispatch services without authorisation should be subject to administrative punishment did not negate the existence of the labour dispatch relationship. The Higher People's Court of Liaoning Province held the same view in the Civil Order of the Retrial Review and Hearing Supervision of the Case of the Labour Contract between Panasonic Appliances Air-Conditioning and Refrigeration (Dalian) Co., Ltd. (PAPARDL) and Zhao Naishuang (2019 Liao CA 562).

Chapter 6
Employment of Foreigner Workers in China

The employment of foreigner workers is subject to strict regulation. A work permit is necessary for the employment of foreigner workers. Unlawful employment of foreigner workers gives rise to strict administrative liabilities, and foreigner workers in unlawful employment cannot be protected by labour law. Eligible foreign workers may be subject to labour law and civil law, and they are entitled to social insurance benefits.

6.1 Regulatory Framework of Employment of Foreigner Workers

With the growing pace of economic globalisation, migrant workers are more than ever before. Migrant workers contribute to the economies of their host countries, and the remittances they send home help to boost the economies of their countries of origin. However, migrant workers often benefit from inadequate social protection and are vulnerable to exploitation and human trafficking. Foreigners have been coming to China not just for travel but also for business and investment or cultural exchange. After joining the World Trade Organisation, China opened up fully to the world. Rapid growth has also been evident among foreigner workers, with the number rising almost six-fold between 2001 and 2018. China's determination to be a good host to expatriates was formalised in 2016 when the country became a member of the International Organisation for Migration, a related organisation of the UN. China has played an active role in the global governance of migration within the UN framework. Further reforms to the country's domestic immigration governance structure took effect in 2018 when the National Immigration Administration officially opened, strengthening the management of immigration and foreshadowing a concerted effort to attract global talent of all types to China.

Y. Wang, *Chinese Labour Law*, Understanding China,
https://doi.org/10.1007/978-981-16-8101-1_6

6.1.1 UN Provisions of the Migrant Workers

The International Convention on the Protection of the Rights of All Migrant Workers and Members of Their Families, adopted by General Assembly resolution 45/158 of 18 December 1990, is an important and comprehensive convention concerning the rights of migrant workers. For the purposes of the Convention, the term "migrant worker" refers to a person who is to be engaged, is engaged or has been engaged in a remunerated activity in a state in which he is not a national. Article 7 of the Convention provides that States Parties undertake, in accordance with the international instruments concerning human rights, to respect and to ensure to all migrant workers and members of their families within their territory or subject to their jurisdiction the rights provided for in the present Convention without distinction of any kind such as to sex, race, colour, language, religion or conviction, political or other opinion, national, ethnic or social origin, nationality, age, economic position, property, marital status, birth or other status. Therefore, all migrant workers shall be treated equal. For employment, Article 25 of the Convention provides that (1) migrant workers shall enjoy treatment not less favourable than that which applies to nationals of the State of employment in respect of remuneration and: (a) Other conditions of work, that is to say, overtime, hours of work, weekly rest, holidays with pay, safety, health, termination of the employment relationship and any other conditions of work which, according to national law and practice, are covered by these terms; (b) Other terms of employment, that is to say, minimum age of employment, restriction on work and any other matters which, according to national law and practice, are considered a term of employment. and (2) it shall not be lawful to derogate in private contracts of employment from the principle of equality of treatment referred to in paragraph 1 of the present article. As for freedom of association, Article 26 of the Convention provides that (1) States Parties recognise the right of migrant workers and members of their families: (a) To take part in meetings and activities of trade unions and of any other associations established in accordance with law, with a view to protecting their economic, social, cultural and other interests, subject only to the rules of the organisation concerned; (b) To join freely any trade union and any such association as aforesaid, subject only to the rules of the organisation concerned; (c) To seek the aid and assistance of any trade union and of any such association as aforesaid. For social security, Article 27 of the Convention provides that migrant workers and members of their families shall enjoy in the State of employment the same treatment granted to nationals in so far as they fulfil the requirements provided for by the applicable legislation of that State and the applicable bilateral and multilateral treaties. The competent authorities of the State of origin and the State of employment can at any time establish the necessary arrangements to determine the modalities of application of this norm.[1]

---

[1] International Convention on the Protection of the Rights of All Migrant Workers and Members of Their Families (2021).

6.1.2 Relevant ILO Instruments

6.1.2.1 Migration for Employment Convention (Revised), 1949 (No. 97)

For the purpose of this Convention, the term migrant for employment means a person who migrates from one country to another with a view to being employed otherwise than on his own account and includes any person regularly admitted as a migrant for employment. As for equal treatment in terms of substantial and procedural rights, Article 6 of Migration for Employment Convention (Revised), 1949 (No. 97) provides that Each Member for which this Convention is in force undertakes to apply, without discrimination in respect of nationality, race, religion or sex, to immigrants lawfully within its territory, treatment no less favourable than that which it applies to its own nationals in respect of the following matters: (a) in so far as such matters are regulated by law or regulations, or are subject to the control of administrative authorities—(i) remuneration, including family allowances where these form part of remuneration, hours of work, overtime arrangements, holidays with pay, restrictions on home work, minimum age for employment, apprenticeship and training, women's work and the work of young persons; (ii) membership of trade unions and enjoyment of the benefits of collective bargaining; (iii) accommodation; (b) social security (that is to say, legal provision in respect of employment injury, maternity, sickness, invalidity, old age, death, unemployment and family responsibilities, and any other contingency which, according to national laws or regulations, is covered by a social security scheme), subject to the following limitations: (i) there may be appropriate arrangements for the maintenance of acquired rights and rights in course of acquisition; (ii) national laws or regulations of immigration countries may prescribe special arrangements concerning benefits or portions of benefits which are payable wholly out of public funds, and concerning allowances paid to persons who do not fulfil the contribution conditions prescribed for the award of a normal pension; (c) employment taxes, dues or contributions payable in respect of the person employed; and (d) legal proceedings relating to the matters referred to in this Convention.[2]

6.1.2.2 Migrant Workers (Supplementary Provisions) Convention, 1975 (No. 143)

For illegal employment, Article 6 of Migrant Workers (Supplementary Provisions) Convention, 1975 (No. 143) provides that Provision shall be made under national laws or regulations for the effective detection of the illegal employment of migrant workers and for the definition and the application of administrative, civil and penal sanctions, which include imprisonment in their range, in respect of the illegal employment of migrant workers, in respect of the organisation of movements of migrants for employment defined as involving the abuses referred to in Article 2 of this Convention, and in respect of knowing assistance to such movements, whether for profit

[2] Migration for Employment Convention (Revised), 1949 (No. 97) (2021).

or otherwise. As for the remedy, Paragraph 2 of Article 9 provides that in case of dispute about the rights referred to in the preceding paragraph, the worker shall have the possibility of presenting his case to a competent body, either himself or through a representative.[3]

6.1.2.3 Equality of Treatment (Accident Compensation) Convention, 1925 (No. 19)

Article 1 of the Equality of Treatment (Accident Compensation) Convention, 1925 (No. 19) provides that each member of the International Labour Organisation which ratifies this Convention undertakes to grant to the nationals of any other Member which shall have ratified the Convention, who suffer personal injury due to industrial accidents happening in its territory, or to their dependants, the same treatment in respect of workmen's compensation as it grants to its own nationals.[4]

6.1.3 Regulation of Employment of Foreigner Workers in China

With regard to migrant workers, only the Equality of Treatment (Accident Compensation) Convention, 1925 (No. 19), and the Discrimination (Employment and Occupation) Convention, 1958 (No. 111), have been ratified by China. In spite of this, China has attached great importance to the protection of foreigner workers. As China builds an internationally competitive talent-based immigration system, foreigners are being encouraged to actively take part in its sustainable development. A clear process and legal protection that are part of a favorable environment are key to attracting and retaining them.

6.1.3.1 Administration of Exit and Entry of Foreigners

The provisions of administration of exit and entry of Foreigners in China are set forth in the Exit and Entry Administration Law and Regulations of the People's Republic of China on Administration of the Entry and Exit of Foreigners. In accordance with Articles 15 and 16 of the Exit and Entry Administration Law, foreigner workers shall apply to the visa-issuing authorities stationed abroad for ordinary visas before entering China. Article 21 of the Exit and Entry Administration Law sets forth the exceptions to issuing visas to foreigner workers if they (a) were deported or repatriated upon decision, and the No-Entry-into-China Period has not expired; (b)

---

[3] Migrant Workers (Supplementary Provisions) Convention, 1975 (No. 143) (2021).

[4] Equality of Treatment (Accident Compensation) Convention, 1925 (No. 19) (2021).

are suffering from serious mental disorders, infectious tuberculosis or other infectious diseases that may severely jeopardise public health; (c) may endanger China's national security or interests, disrupt social and public order, or engage in other illegal or criminal activities; (d) resort to fraudulent acts in visa application or cannot guarantee expected expenditures during their stay in China; (e) fail to submit relevant information required by the visa-issuing authorities; or (f) other circumstances in which visa authorities consider a visa should not be issued.[5] The validity period of a foreigner's work-type residence permit shall be 90 days at the minimum and five years at the maximum. Foreigner workers shall obtain work permits and work-type residence permits, and foreigner workers who fail to obtain such permits shall not be employed in China in accordance with Article 41 of the Exit and Entry Administration Law. In accordance with Regulations of the People's Republic of China on Administration of the Entry and Exit of Foreigners, employing units who employ foreigner workers shall report to the exit and entry administration authority of the public security organ if they resign or change employment location, or if they violate the provisions of administration of exit and entry. Employing units that unlawfully employ foreigner workers shall bear the related expenses for repatriation.

6.1.3.2 Rules for the Administration of Employment of Foreigners in China, 2017

In accordance with Rules for the Administration of Employment of Foreigners in China, 2017, "employment of foreigners in China" means acts of foreigners without permanent residence status to engage in remunerative work within Chinese territory in accordance with its laws. Employing units intending to employ foreigner workers shall apply for work permits and obtain "the PRC Employment Licence for Foreigners". Employing units and foreigner workers should conclude labour contracts, the term of which shall not exceed five years. The wage paid to foreign workers by employing units shall not be lower than the minimum wage in the locality. The working hours, rest and vacation, work safety and hygiene as well as the social security of foreigner workers in China shall follow the relevant provisions. Should labour disputes arise between employing units and foreigner workers, they should be handled in accordance with the Labour Law of 2018 and the Regulations of the People's Republic of China on Settlement of Labour Disputes in Enterprises.

6.2 Procedures for Employment of Foreigner Workers

As explained in Sect. 6.1, a work permit and a residence permit are requisites for the employment of foreigner workers in China. In this section, procedures of such permits will be introduced.

[5] Commission for Legislative Affairs of the NPC Standing Committee (2012).

6.2.1 *Work Permits*

6.2.1.1 Requirements for an Employing Unit

Any employing unit intending to employ foreigner workers shall be established by the Company Law and/or the Foreign Investment Law and has no historical records of violation of law or refusal to execute court decisions. The job title for foreigner workers shall be in need, and there are no proper candidates for it at home. The job title should be subject to relevant regulations, such as the Jiangsu Province Job Titles Management Catalogue for Employment of Foreigner Workers. The employing unit shall pay foreigner workers wages that exceed the local minimum wage standard. The employing unit shall comply with the relevant regulations of approval, if necessary.

6.2.1.2 Requirements for an Applicant

Any foreigner seeking employment in China shall meet the following requirements: (a) 18 years of age or older and in good health; (b) with professional skills and job experience required for the work of intended employment; (c) with no criminal record; (d) a clearly defined employing unit; and (e) with a valid passport or other international travel documents in lieu of the passport.

6.2.1.3 Necessary Documents and Approval

The employing unit shall register an account on the relevant official websites, such as http://www.safea.gov.cn, and submit Information Registry Form, Legal Certificate of Incorporation, Identification Certification of Person in Charge and Approval, if applicable. To apply for the Notification Letter of Foreigner's Work Permit in the People's Republic of China, the employing unit shall submit a Visa (Z or R) or a valid Residence Permit, Labour Contract, and Certification of Physical Examination. To apply for renewal of a work permit, the employing unit shall before 30 days submit Application Form for Extension of Work Permits, Labour Contract or Certificate of Job Title, Visa or valid Residence Permit, and Work Permit. In case of a change in job titles (for example, from professional job to administrative job) in the same employing unit, the application for Change and supporting documents shall be submitted. A work permit shall be cancelled if (a) it expires; (b) it is revoked or annulled; (c) the holder deceases or loses capacity for civil conduct; or (d) the labour contract is terminated. Within 10 working days, the employing unit shall submit an Application Form for Cancellation of Work Permits, Certificate of Termination of Labour Contract and other supporting documents. If a work permit is lost or damaged, the holder may submit the Application Form for Replacement of Work Permits and the statement. The application for a work permit may be rejected if the application materials are not incomplete, are falsified or do not meet the relevant requirements.

6.2.2 *Residence Permits*

In accordance with the Exit and Entry Administration Law and Regulations of the People's Republic of China on Administration of the Entry and Exit of Foreigners, a work-type residence permit is necessary for employment of foreigner workers. Foreigner workers shall submit a valid passport or other valid travelling documents, application form, certificate of physical examination which shows the applicant is free of mental disorders, contagious pulmonary tuberculosis or other contagious diseases that may endanger public health. The applicant who holds a Z-type visa shall provide a work permit issued by the local human resources and social security bureau and the certificate issued by the employing unit. In case of renewal or replacement of residence permits, the applicant shall provide relevant supporting documents or personal information.

6.2.3 *Liabilities of Unlawful Employment*

6.2.3.1 Definition of Unlawful Employment

Unlawful employment is defined in Article 43 of the Exit and Entry Administration Law, which provides that (a) work in China without obtaining work permits or work-type residence permits in accordance with relevant regulations; (b) work in China beyond the scope prescribed in the work permits; or (c) foreign students work in violation of the regulations on the administration of foreign students working to support their study in China and work beyond the prescribed scope of jobs or prescribed time limit. Under the Identification of Behaviors Violating the Exit and Entry Administration Law, which was enacted by the General Office of the Ministry of Public Security in 2017, any of the following circumstances shall be identified as unlawful employment: (a) the fact that foreigners work in China does not the requirements of work permits and residence permits; (b) foreigners work in the scope designated in work permits; or (c) foreigners work in other employing units not designated in work permits.

However, the meanings of "employment" are not clear. To solve this problem, the Administrative Office of the Ministry of Labour issued the Notice of Implementation of Rules for the Administration of Employment of Foreigners in China in 1996, which provides that any foreigner worker in China shall be deemed to be employed provided that he concludes a labour contract with an employing unit in China, no matter how long he works and that any foreigner worker in China shall be deemed to be employed if he concludes a labour contract with an employing unit abroad and works for more than three months. The Notice of further Strengthening the Administration of Employment of Foreigners in Guangdong Province was released by Guangdong Province Human Resources and Social Bureau Department and Guangdong Province Public Security Department in 2010. Under the Notice, unlawful employment means: (a) Without obtaining work and residence permits, foreigners without obtaining are employed by any state organ, enterprise, public institution, social orgaise or individual; (2) without obtaining work and residence permits, foreigners go in for profitable activities; (3) a foreigner's employer and occupation are not the ones stated in work permits; or (4) a foreigner falsifies, alters, transfers, or purchases a work permit and a residence permit.

It is generally accepted that whether remuneration is paid or not does not affect the identification of unlawful employment, which was affirmed in the Administrative Decision of Second Instance of the Case of Administrative Penalty Order between Shanghai Xiaomei Health Technology Co., Ltd., and Shanghai City Public Security Bureau Putuo Branch and Shanghai City Public Security Bureau (2019 Hu AF 361). In this case, the Third Intermediate People's Court of Shanaghai held that the fact that Xiaomei Company provided the expenses of board and lodging, and the expenses of flight rather because of the services offered by the foreigners showed that there existed the de facto employment of foreigners and rejected the argument of Xiaomei Company that temporary or one-off service was not in the nature of unlawful employment.

Dispatch services can be identified as employment. In the Administrative Decision of Second Instance of the Case between Tianhe Auto Technology (Shanaghai) Co., Ltd. and Shanghai City Public Security Bureau Baoshan Branch (2015 Hu 2nd Intermediate AF 628), the Second Intermediate People's Court of Shanghai held that unlawful employment of 6 Indian workers was true on the grounds that (a) 6 Indian workers concluded labour contracts with HOK Information Consultation Company, and were paid by HOK Information Consultation Company, which handled the procedures of Work Permits for them; (b) the labour contracts kept silent on the job contents of them and they went to the appellant, Tianhe Auto Technology (Shanghai) Co., Ltd. directly; (c) the appellant arranged the job contents for them and appraised their performance and there existed de facto labour contracts between them and the appellant; (d) the appellant failed to produce any supportive evidence that there existed an outsourcing relationship with HOK; and (e) the argument that the appellant was not aware that they were employed by HOK and did not check their work permits did not hold water in that it was against Several Opinions concerning Implementation of Rules for the Administration of Employment of Foreigners in China, released by Shanghai City Labour Bureau in 1998. Article 2 of Several Opinions concerning Implementation of Rules for the Administration of Employment of Foreigners in China provides that employment of foreigner workers in Shanghai is subject to work permits and foreigner workers who receive wages from overseas and work for at least three months in Shanghai shall obtain work permits.

6.2.3.2 Liabilities of Unlawful Employment

Foreigners who work without the Employment Permit or employing units that hire foreigners without the Employment Licence shall be handled by the public security organs in accordance with Article 44 of the Rules Governing the Implementation of the Law of the People's Republic of China on the Entry and Exit of Aliens. For Foreigners who refuse to have their Employment Permit inspected by the labour administrative authorities, change their employing units and professions at will or extend their term of employment without permission, the labour administrative authorities shall withdraw their employment permits and recommend that their residence status be canceled by the public security organs. In the case of deportation, the costs and expenses shall be borne by the foreigners or their employing units. For foreigners and employing units who forge, alter, falsely use, transfer, buy and sell the Employment Permit and the Employment Licence, the labour administrative authorities shall take over the Employment Permit and the Employment Licence in question, confiscate the illegal proceeds and impose a fine between ten thousand and one hundred thousand RMB yuan. In serious cases that constitute a crime, their criminal responsibility of the perpetrators shall be looked into by the judicial authorities.

In accordance with the Discretion Standards for Disciplining Who Violates the Exit and Entry Administration Law, released by the Administrative Office of the Ministry of Public Security in 2017, in case of unlawful employment, a fine of 5000 yuan to 10,000 yuan is imposed where foreigner workers are employed for less than 30 days; a fine of 10,000 yuan to 20,000 yuan is imposed where foreigner workers are employed for 30 days to 90 days; a detain of 5 days to 10 days and a fine of 5,000 yuan to 10,000 yuan are imposed where (a) foreigner workers are employed for 90 days to one year; or (b) the earning arising out of unlawful employment is 30,000 yuan to 50,000 yuan. A detain of 10 days to 15 days and a fine of 10,000 yuan to 20,000 yuan are imposed where (a) foreigner workers are employed for more than one year; (b) the earning arising out of unlawful employment is more than 50,000 yuan; (c) the same unlawful act is repeated within one year after such act was disciplined.

6.3 Practical Issues Related to Employment of Foreigners

6.3.1 Influence of Work Permits on Labour Contracts

6.3.1.1 The Nature of Work Permits

There is a dispute concerning the nature of work permits. Some argue that work permits are for registry of employment because there is no definition of a labourer in the Labour Contract Law of 2012, and there are no restrictions of labourers in terms of nationality and race. Furthermore, Rules for the Administration of Employment of Foreigners in China, 2017 are in the nature of ministerial rules, by which administrative permits shall not be granted in accordance with the Administrative Permit Law. Others argue that work permits are characteristic of administrative permits because Rules for the Administration of Employment of Foreigners in China, 2017 provide that in case of employment of foreigner workers, employing units shall apply for work permits and work permits are requisite for the capacity of foreigner worker as labourers in the Labour Law of 2018.

The latter argument is prevailing in practice. The reasons are as follows. First, in accordance with the Decision of Establishment of Permits on Items that must be subject to Administrative Approval, work permits are the items subject to approval, and in accordance with paragraph 2 of Article 14 of the Administrative Permit Law, the State Council may establish administrative permits in the form of decisions. Second, it is not practical for foreigner workers to have freedom of employment in China. It is true that the EU enacted Directive 2014/54/EU OF THE EUROPEAN PARLIAMENT AND OF THE COUNCIL of 16 April 2014 on measures facilitating the exercise of rights conferred on workers in the context of freedom of movement for workers. However, the freedom of employment for foreigner workers is relevant to the development of politics, law, economy and culture. It is a general rule that reasonable restrictions are imposed on the employment of foreigners.

6.3.1.2 The Legal Relationship with Foreigner Workers in Breach of the Requirements of Work Permits

The importance of work permits cannot be overemphasised. Obtaining no work permits, delay in renewal of work permits, failure to renew or change work permits are in breach of the requirements of work permits. In practice, the legal relationships with foreigner workers in breach of the requirements of work permits are treated differently.

Some argue that the legal relationship is a contract for services, under which employing units are obliged to pay the stipulated wages and foreigner workers are not entitled to economic compensation and other rights under the Labour Law of 2018 and the Labour Contract Law of 2012. Early in 2002, the First Civil Division of the Higher People's Court of Shanghai released the Reply to Several Issues concerning Trial of the Case of Labour Disputes, which made it clear that the dispute concerning foreigners holding no work permit may be directly accepted as ordinary civil case by the competent People's court provided that such dispute meets the conditions of case acceptance set forth by the Civil Procedure Law. In the Civil Order of the Trial Supervision of the Case of the Contract for Services between Shanghai Jiangtai International Logistics Co., Ltd. and Kim Yeo Su Yun (2018 Hu CA 2755), the Higher People's Court of Shanghai held that the contract between Kim Yeo Su Yun holding no work permit and Shanghai Jiangtai International Logistics Co., Ltd. was a contract for services and was regulated by the Contract Law. In the Civil Decision of Second Instance of the Case of the Contract for Serives between Misawa Eiji and Hubei Juntengfa Automatic Welding Equipment Co., Ltd. (2016 E CF 1614), the Higher People's Court of Hubei Province held that the contract with Misawa Eiji holding no work permit was the contract for services and the stipulations of termination of the contract were much looser than the relevant provisions under the Labour Contract Law of 2012.

Other argue that it is an invalid labour contract. In this case, some courts hold that employing units are obliged to pay the stipulated wages and foreigner workers are not entitled to economic compensation, which is supported by Article 18 of Guiding Opinions released by Guangdong Province Higher People's Court and Guangdong Province Labour Dispute Arbitration Commission concerning Several Issues of Implementation of the Labour Dispute Mediation and Arbitration Law and the Labour Contract Law of 2012, while other courts hold that whether foreigner workers are entitled to economic compensation or not depends on who is responsible for the invalidity of labour contracts. If employing units fail to apply for work permits, foreigner workers are entitled to economic compensation. If foreigner workers do not provide support or assistance in applying for work permits, employing units may terminate labour contracts, but foreigner workers are entitled to economic compensation. In the Retrial of the Labour Dispute between Michael Deng and Zhongshan Shenbao Electronical Devices Manufacturing Co., Ltd. (2008 Yue HCTSCT 63), the Higher People's Court of Guangdong Province held that the contract with Michael Deng holding no work permit was an invalid labour contract, and it was due to Deng's fault that made the contract invalid and Deng was not entitled to economic compensation.

I am of the opinion that the legal relationship with foreigner workers holding no work permits and employing units is an invalid labour contract on the grounds that (a) since labour contracts between illegible employing units and eligible labourers are invalid, it's logical that labour contracts between illegible labourers and legible employing units are invalid. Article 29 of Judicial Interpretations (No. 1) by the Supreme People's Court of Issues Concerning the Application of Law in Hearing the Cases of Labour Disputes released on 29 December 2020 provides that the employing unit or its investor shall be a party to the lawsuit where there is any dispute between a labourer and an employing unit that does not hold a Business Licence, or whose Business Licence is revoked or that go on operating after expiry of Business Licence; (b) a foreigner worker holding no work permit complies with the discipline and rules of his employing unit and his employing unit treats him to be a labourer as if he was Chinese in terms of wage payment, working hours, rest and holidays and occupational health and safety; (c) a contract for services is not the only conclusion that may be drawn from Article 33 of Judicial Interpretations (No. 1) by the Supreme People's Court of Issues Concerning the Application of Law in Hearing the Cases of Labour Disputes released on 29 December 2020, which provides that where a foreigner or a stateless person holding no work permit concludes a labour contract with an employing unit in China, the People's Court shall reject the request that a party concerned intends to confirm the existence of a labour relationship. The existence of an invalid labour contract is also a logical conclusion. (d) Article 18 of the Labour Law of 2018 provides that a labour contract is invalid where it is against the provisions of laws and regulations. It is apparent that the fact that a foreigner worker has not obtained a work permit is against the relevant laws and regulations; or (e) the dispute arising out of such contracts with foreigner workers holding no work permits does not fall into the scope of Article 2 of Article 29 of Judicial Interpretations (No. 1) by the Supreme People's Court of Issues Concerning the Application of Law in Hearing the Cases of Labour Disputes released on 29 December 2020, which provides for the disputes not arising out of a labour relationship.

6.3.2 *Work Permits as Prima Facie Evidence of Labour Contracts*

As explained earlier, work permits are necessary for valid labour contracts. However, work permits do not necessarily show that labour contracts exist, particularly when a foreigner worker is dispatched by an overseas company. Work permits are used only as prima facie evidence of labour contracts. Opposite evidence, if any, may negate the existence of a labour contract. This is because of the various meanings of the employment of foreigner workers.

In the Guidance to Elements of Trial of Labour Disputes released by the Higher People's Court of Shanghai in 2013, a labour relationship does not exist in case of any of the following events: (a) a foreigner is dispatched by an overseas legal person to a Chinese enterprise; (b) a foreigner is a chief representative or representative of resident offices in China of foreign enterprises; or (c) a foreigner comes to China for investment but does not directly participate in the management of his enterprise.

In the Civil Order of the Case of Trial Supervision of the Labour Dispute between Changshu Yoneyama Chemical Co., Ltd. and Akitomo (2014 Su TSCA 009), Japan Yoneyama Chemical Co., Ltd. signed a contract labour with Akitomo, paid him wages and took out social insurance in Japan. Therefore, the Higher People's Court of Jiangsu Province held that if a foreigner worker was recruited and then dispatched by a parent company overseas to its affiliated company in China, a work permit and a labour contract that was signed to go through the procedures of the work permit did not necessarily show a labour relationship between the foreigner worker and the affiliated company.

Similarly, in the Civil Order of Retrial of the Case of Remuneration Recovery between Jiang and SS company (2011 Su TSCA 525), SS company in China was wholly invested by S company in the US., Jiang signed the employment contract with SS company and was appointed as the deputy director of SS company, Jiang was paid by S company, and therefore, the Higher People's Court of Jiangsu Province held that there existed no labour relationship between Jiang and SS company for the purposes of the Labour Contract Law of 2012.

6.3.3 *Liabilities of Contracts for Services and of Invalid Labour Contracts*

Whether the contracts with foreigner workers holding no work permits are contracts for services or invalid labour contracts, foreigner workers may be entitled to the stipulated wages. It seems that there is no point discussing the nature of the contracts with foreigner workers holding no work permits. In fact, the nature of such contracts may affect the legal remedy to which foreigner workers resort. On the one hand, a labour arbitration commission often rejects the dispute arising out of a civil contract, and on the other hand, foreigner workers holding no work permits are not entitled to economic compensation under civil law. Particularly, in addition to the stipulated remuneration, economic compensation is added in case of invalid labour contracts in accordance with Article 41 of Judicial Interpretations (No. 1) by the Supreme People's Court of Issues Concerning the Application of Law in Hearing the Cases of Labour Disputes released on 29 December 2020, which is more favorable to foreigner workers than Article 28 of the Labour Contract Law of 2012. Under these circumstances, the identification of the nature of the contracts with foreigner workers holding no work permits does make much difference.

6.3.4 *Application of the Labour Contract Law of 2012 on Eligible Foreigner Workers*

6.3.4.1 Stipulated Damages

Under the Labour Contract Law of 2012, stipulated damages borne by a labourer are prohibited except for the following cases: (a) a labourer breaches the stipulation of the period of service and (b) a labourer breaches a noncompeting agreement. However, some courts are supportive of the view that stipulated damages are allowed in labour contracts with foreigner workers. In the Civil Decision of Second Instance of the Case of the Labour Contract between Shanghai Minhang District Morgen Henry Kindergarten and Amanda Marie Redden (2020 Hu01CF 2047), the First Intermediate People's Court of Shanghai held that in accordance with Articles 22 and 23 of Rules for the Administration of Employment of Foreigners in China,2017, the working hours, rest and vacation, work safety and hygiene as well as the social security of the foreign employees in China shall follow the relevant provisions of the state, and other rights and obligations shall be determined and performed on the basis of the stipulation or the separate agreement and that both parties thereto may agree on the stipulated damages in their labour contract, and the decision of first instance was revoked that Shanghai Minhang District People's Court held that the stipulated damages was invalid.

6.3.4.2 The Age of Retirement

In accordance with Article 21 of the Regulations of Implementation of the Labour Contract Law, a labour contract terminates where a labourer reaches the statutory age of retirement. Whether a foreign worker is subject to this provision is in dispute. In Beijing, a foreigner worker shall be aged 18–60 in accordance with the Notice of Further Strengthening the Employment of Foreigners in Beijing in 2014, while a foreigner worker who is employed in Shanghai shall meet the following requirement that, generally, the male shall be aged 18–60, and the female shall be aged 18–55, which is provided in the Notice of Implementation of Rules for the Administration of Employment of Foreigners in China released by Shanghai City Labour Bureau.

In the Civil Order of Retrial Inspection and Supervision of the Labour Dispute between Beijing SYNERGY Vacuum Glass Technology Co., Ltd. and Tang Jianzheng (2018 Jing CR 311), the Higher People's Court of Beijing held that the argument that there existed a labour relationship was groundless given that Tang had reached the statutory age of retirement. In the Civil Decision of Second Instance of the Case of the Labour Contract between Hu Lianping and ICON Clinical Research (Beijing) Co., Ltd. (2018 Jing 01 CF 6371), the First Intermediate People's Court of Beijing held that in accordance with Article 21 of Regulations of Implementation of the Labour Contract Law, a labour contract terminated where a labourer reached the statutory age of retirement, and in this case, Hu Lianping reached the statutory age of 60 years on 16 April 2018 and the argument of ICON Clinical Research (Beijing) Co., Ltd. that the labour contract with Hu Lianping terminated on 16 April 2018 was tenable, and Hu Lianping's argument that the statutory age of retirement was 65 years in Canada and that the labour contract terminated upon the age of 65 years did not hold water. The view was once again held by the First Intermediate People's Court of Beijing in the Civil Decision of Second Instance of the Case of the Contract for Services between Beijing Manet International Business Club Management Co., Ltd. and John E. Deal (2015 FICF 4402). The Third Intermediate People's Court of Beijing held the same view in the Civil Decision of Second Instance of the Case of the Labour Dispute between He Chufei and Mondelēz China (2017 Jing 03 CF 11619).

In contrast, in the Civil Decision of Second Instance of the Case of the Labour Contract between IMR (Shanghai) Machinery Co., Ltd. and Malek M (2013 Hu SICTCF 527), the Second Intermediate People's Court of Shanghai held that Malek M had reached the statutory age of retirement before he and IMR (Shanghai) Machinery Co., Ltd. signed a labour contract, the valid period of which was from 1 May 2011 to 30 April 2013 and that the rule that a labour contract terminates where a labourer reaches the statutory age of retirement did not apply in this case. Additionally, in the Civil Decision of First Instance of the Case of the Labour Contract between Wang and Saint-Gobain (China) Investment Co., Ltd. (2010 Huang CF 3498), the People's Court of Huangpu District, Shanghai held that the wording of "generally" in the Notice of Implementation of Rules for the Administration of Employment of Foreigners in China released by Shanghai City Labour Bureau did not prohibit foreigner workers above 60 years from being employed in Shanghai, and the Second

People's Court of Shanghai held the same view in the appeal by Saint-Gobain (China) Investment Co., Ltd.

The courts in Zhuhai and Guangzhou in Guangdong Provinces follow the example of the courts in Beijing, which can be seen in the Civil Decision of First Instance of the Case of Contract for Services between Huang Jingxian and Zhuhai City Precise Plastic Co., Ltd. (2018 Yue 0491 CF 810), the Civil Decision of First Instance of the Case of the Labour Dispute between Wu Liwei and Guangzhou City Huamei English Experimental School (2017 Yue 0106 CF1517).

6.3.4.3 The Causes of Termination of Labour Contracts

The causes of termination of the labour contract under Chap. 4 of the Labour Contract Law of 2012 are statutory and shall not be derogated or expanded by agreement. Whether Chap. 4 of the Labour Contract Law of 2012 applies to labour contracts with eligible foreigner workers remains in dispute.

Most courts in China say "yes". In the Civil Decision of Retrial of the Case of the Labour Dispute between Corbett Daimon John and Guangzhou City Chateau Star River Hotle Co., Ltd. (2018 Yue CR 267), Corbett Daimon John was employed by Guangzhou City Chateau Star River Hotle Co., Ltd. on 4 October 2012 and signed a labour contract for one year, and then the contract was renewed to 4 October 2016. On 22 March 2016, Guangzhou City Chateau Star River Hotle Co., Ltd. delivered a notice of termination to Corbett Daimon John, who was notified that the labour contract would be terminated on 1 April 2016. The fact that the labour contract was illegally terminated by Guangzhou City Chateau Star River Hotle Co., Ltd. was affirmed by the labour arbitration commission and the court of first instance. The Intermediate People's Court of Guangzhou held that the labour contract was terminated by agreement. Guangzhou City Chateau Star River Hotle Co., Ltd. argued that in the labour contract dated 5 October 2013, both parties stipulated that either party to the labour contract might terminate the contract unilaterally, provided that a one-month written notice of termination was delivered or the wages of one month was paid in lieu of such notice, and such was the intention of both parties and not prohibited by law. With regard to the application of law, the Higher People's Court of Guangdong Province held that the contract labour between Corbett Daimon John and Guangzhou City Chateau Star River Hotle Co., Ltd. was subject to the Labour Law of 2018 and the Labour Contract Law of 2012 and although Article 23 of Rules for the Administration of Employment of Foreigners in China provides that the working hours, rest and vacation, work safety and hygiene as well as the social security of the foreign employees in China shall follow the relevant provisions of the state, termination and relevant compensation were not mentioned, which did not imply that Article 23 of Rules for the Administration of Employment of Foreigners excluded the application of the Labour Law of 2018 and the Labour Contract Law of 2012 in case of termination of labour contracts with Foreigner workers and finally, the argument of Guangzhou City Chateau Star River Hotel Co., Ltd. was rejected.

The courts in Shanghai adopt a liberal attitude toward the autonomy of both parties to the labour contract of foreigner workers. On 31 January 2001, Shanghai City Labour and Social Security Bureau released the Rules for Administration of Employment of Labourers Residing Abroad in Shanghai, which provide that an employing unit and its labourer residing abroad may conclude a labour contract in terms of period, job title, remuneration, insurance, working hours, conditions of and liabilities of termination of a labour contract. The Reply of the Higher People's Court of Shanghai to Serval Issues concerning Trial of the Case of Labour Disputes (Shanghai Higher Court First Civil Division 2006 No. 17) provides that (a) the organ of labour dispute settlement may uphold the request where any party concerned requests that the provisions of minimum wages, working hours, rest and holiday, labour safety and health and social insurance in Rules for the Administration of Employment of Foreigners in China should apply; or (b) other rights and obligations not mentioned in (a) shall be determined and performed on the basis of the stipulations of the written labour contract or the separate agreement or what is actually performed. Again, the same view was affirmed by the Guidance to Elements of Trial of Labour Disputes released by the Higher People's Court of Shanghai in 2013.

6.3.4.4 Languages of Labour Contracts with Foreigner Workers

Interestingly, in the Civil Decision of Second Instance of the Case of the Labour Contract between Shanghai Minhang District Morgen Henry Kindergarten and Amanda Marie Redden (2020 Hu01CF 2047), there was an English labour contract and a Chinese labour contract, and there was no agreement that which language prevailed in case of any discrepancies. The First Intermediate People's Court of Shanghai held that the Chinese contract prevailed in accordance with Regulations of Labour Contracts of Shanghai. In accordance with the Reply of the General Office of the Ministry of Labour to the Issues related to Implementation of Rules of Labour Management in Foreign-invested Enterprises released in 1995, the labour contract between a foreign-invested enterprise and a labourer shall be in Chinese. Additionally, it can be in English, provided that the English contract shall be consistent with the Chinese contract. Otherwise, the Chinese contract will prevail. In the Civil Decision of Second Instance of the Case of the Labour Dispute between AJMERSINGHKAIRON and Oerlikon (China) Technology Co., Ltd. (2018 Su 05 CF 5317), the Intermediate People's Court of Suzhou City held that both parties signed two contracts in Chinese and in English and they were partly different, stipulated damages was set forth in the English contract, which the Chinese contract was silent on, and further that the Chinese contract was used by Oerlikon (China) Technology Co., Ltd. for going through the procedure of work permits and shall be the basis of dispute settlement.

It is worth noting that the rule that the Chinese contract prevails only applies to the labour contract with foreigner workers. More generally, with regard to the interpretation of a contract, Paragraph 1 of Article 466 of the Civil Code provides that where a contract is made in two or more languages which are agreed to be equally authentic, the words and sentences used in each text shall be presumed to have the same meaning; where the words and sentences used in each text are inconsistent, interpretation thereof shall be made in accordance with the related clauses, nature, and purpose of the contract, and the principle of good faith, and the like. It is suggested that for contracts other than labour contracts with foreigner workers, a clause of choice of languages should be inserted; otherwise, Article 466 of the Civil Code will apply, which may give rise to uncertainty.

6.3.4.5 Paid Annual Leave

In accordance with the Regulation of Paid Annual Leave for Employees, employees who have worked continuously for one year or more are entitled to paid annual leave. The days of annual leave may be taken by an employee shall be determined on the basis of the accumulative working time, which shall cover the working time in the same or different employers and the hours treated as working time by law, administrative regulation or provisions of the State Council. For a foreigner worker, the question may arise whether the working time when he worked for an overseas employing unit should be included for the purposes of the basis of paid annual leave. In the Civil Decision of Second Instance of the Case of Labour Dispute between Sasaki Gakuto and the Liquidating Group of Beijing Kyori International Trade Co., Ltd. (2018 Jing 03 CF 5060), the Third Intermediate People's Court of Beijing held that the work permit was issued on 15 November 2013 and from then Sasaki Gakuto was an eligible labourer under the Chinese law and rejected Sasaki Gakuto's argument that his working experiences abroad shall be included for the basis of the computation of paid annual leave.

6.3.5 Social Security for Foreigner Workers

6.3.5.1 The Interim Measures for Social Insurance System Coverage of Foreigners Working Within the Territory of China

With a view to securing the legitimate rights and interests of foreigners working within the territory of China to social insurance participation and benefits in accordance with the law, as well as strengthening social insurance administration, the Interim Measures for Social Insurance System Coverage of Foreigners Working within the Territory of China were enacted by the Ministry of Human Resources and Social Security on 6 September 2011 and took effect on 15 October 2011. Foreigners employed in the territory of China means non-Chinese labourers holding Work Permits for Foreigners, Foreign Experts Certificate, Resident Foreign Correspondents Certificate, Residence Permit or Permanent Residence Permit for Foreigners. Foreigners employed in China shall participate in basic endowment insurance, basic medical insurance, work-related injury insurance, unemployment insurance and maternity insurance unless the bilateral protocols between China and their native countries concerning social security are applicable. Foreigners dispatched by an overseas employing unit are also covered by social insurance. Foreigners covered in the social insurance system shall be entitled to social insurance benefits in accordance with the law once the qualifying conditions are met. For a foreigner who leaves China before reaching the statutory pension age, the social insurance individual account shall be retained and shall be renewed on a cumulative basis when the person in question returns to work in China. Alternatively, upon written application for closing the social insurance account from the person in question, the proceeds in the individual account can be paid lump-sum to the said person. If a dispute occurs over social insurance between a foreigner legally covered in the social insurance system and his employer or host service entity, the person in question may apply for mediation, arbitration, or file a lawsuit in accordance with the law. A foreigner whose social insurance rights and interests are infringed upon by his employer or host service entity may demand redress from an administrative agency of social insurance or the agency responsible for the collection of social insurance contributions in accordance with the law. Furthermore, at the local level, Beijing, Shanghai, Guangzhou and Suzhou released detailed implementation measures.

6.3.5.2 Social Insurance in the Case of Unlawful Employment of Foreigner Workers

It is a statutory obligation for an employing unit to pay social insurance for foreigner workers holding work permits. However, whether unlawful employment affects social insurance remains unclear. In the Administrative Decision of Second Instance of the Case of Revoking Administrative Order between Shenyang Tongsen Education and Training School, Shengyang City Human Resources and Social Security Bureau and David John Harrison (2018 Liao 01 AF 1819), David worked in Shenyang Tongsen Education and Training School from March 2015 to November 2016 but signed the labour contract with Beijing Haidian District Paitesen Education and Training School, and the contract period was from 1 March 2015 to 29 February 2016. David signed the labour contract with Beijing Chaoyang District Paitesen Education and Training School, and the contract period was from 1 March 2016 to 28 January 2017. Shenyang Tongsen Education and Training School paid David wages and withheld the personal income tax but refused to take out social insurance for David. Dai Xu was the legal representative of Shenyang Tongsen Education and Training School, Beijing Haidian District Paitesen Education and Training School, and Beijing Chaoyang District Paitesen Education and Training School, but the offices of the latter two schools in Beijing were unknown, and the Intermediate People's Court of Shenyang held that (a) Shenyang Tongsen Education and Training School was a de facto employer of David; (b) having known that David signed the labour contracts with Beijing Haidian District Paitesen Education and Training School, and Beijing Chaoyang District Paitesen Education and Training

School and that his work permit was obtained in Beijing, Shenyang Tongsen Education and Training School arranged for David to work in Shenyang but refused to pay the social insurance for David, which was apparently against law and infringed on David's legitimate rights.

Before the Regulations for Administration of Employment of Residents from Taiwan, Hong Kong and Macao in the Mainland was revoked on 28 July 2018, work permits were necessary for residents from Taiwan, Hong Kong and Macao to work in the Mainland.[6] In the Administrative Decision of Second Instance of the Case of Labour and Social Security Administration between Zeng Yuzhe and Jiangmen City Xinhui District Human Resources and Social Security Bureau (2019 Yue AF 479), the Higher People's Court of Guangdong Province held that Zeng Yuzhe, as a resident from Chinese Taiwan, did not obtain the relevant work permit, so the contract between Zeng Yuzhe and Jiangmen Dingfeng Company was not a labour contract for the purposes of the Labour Law of 2018. We can infer from the decision that in the case of unlawful employment of foreigner workers without work permits, employing units are not obliged to pay social insurance for foreigner workers.

References

Commission for Legislative Affairs of the NPC Standing Committee. (2012). *Interpretations of and practical guides to exit and entry administration law of the People's Republic of China*. Beijing: China Democracy and Legal Press [in Chinese].

ILO. (1925). *Equality of Treatment (Accident Compensation) Convention, 1925 (No. 19). (2021)*. Retrieved 1 July, 2021, from https://www.ilo.org/dyn/normlex/en/f?p=NORMLEXPUB:12100:0::NO:12100:P12100_INSTRUMENT_ID:312164:NO.

OHCHR. (1990). *International Convention on the Protection of the Rights of All Migrant Workers and Members of Their Families*. Retrieved 1 July, 2021, from https://www.ohchr.org/EN/ProfessionalInterest/Pages/CMW.aspx.

ILO. (1975). *Migrant Workers (Supplementary Provisions) Convention, 1975 (No. 143)*. Retrieved 1 July, 2021, from https://www.ilo.org/dyn/normlex/en/f?p=NORMLEXPUB:12100:0::NO::P12100_ILO_CODE:C14.

ILO. (1949). *Migration for Employment Convention (Revised), 1949 (No. 97)*. Retrieved 1 July, 2021, from https://www.ilo.org/dyn/normlex/en/f?p=NORMLEXPUB:12100:0::NO::P12100_INSTRUMENT_ID:312242.

The First Tribunal of the Supreme People's Court. (2014). *Understanding and application of the interpretations (No. 4) by the supreme people's court of issues concerning the application of law in hearing the cases of labour disputes*. Beijing: People's Court Press [in Chinese].

[6] The First Tribunal of the Supreme People's Court (2014).

Chapter 7
Employment of Seafarers

Seafarers play an important role in international trade and maritime transportation. The occupational security of seafarers is of the utmost importance and includes insurance, workplace security, paid annual leave and repatriation. The Maritime Labour Convention, 2006, known as the "seafarers' bills of rights", provides seafarers with extensive protection. China revised the Regulations of Seafarers of the PRC several times to align with the Maritime Labour Convention, 2006. It is unique that several types of seafarers' claims are subject to maritime liens. The model format for seafarer employment agreements released by the International Labour Organisation and the standard contracts released by the China Maritime Arbitration Commission (CMAC) are introduced. Common practical issues related to the employment of seafarers are also discussed.

7.1 Overview of Employment of Seafarers

7.1.1 Current Situations of Chinese Seafarers

In accordance with the Chinese Seafarers Development Report for 2020, which was released by the Press Office of the Ministry of Transport of the PRC in June 2021, there were 1,716,866 registered seafarers in China by the end of 2020, among which 808,183 were for seagoing vessels (including active seafarers of 377,016) and 908,683 were for inland vessels, and in 2020, the number of seafarers dispatched aboard foreign-owned ships was 122,304. In 2020, the number of overseas seafarers dispatching service agencies was 250. The flag states included Hong Kong SAR,

Y. Wang, *Chinese Labour Law*, Understanding China,
https://doi.org/10.1007/978-981-16-8101-1_7

the Republic of Panama, Singapore, Libya, the Republic of the Marshall Islands, the Commonwealth of the Bahamas and other countries and regions.[1]

7.1.2 *Concept of Seafarers*

In accordance with the Maritime Code of the PRC, the term "crew" means the entire complement of the ship, including the master[2]; the master, deck officers, chief engineer, engineers, electrical engineer and radio operator must be in possession of appropriate certificates of competency,[3] and Chinese "crew" engaged in international voyages must possess Seaman's Book and other relevant certificates issued by the harbour superintendency authorities of the People's Republic of China.[4] For the purposes of the Regulations of Seafarers of the PRC of 2020, seafarers mean those who gain the certificates of competency, including the master, senior officers and officers.[5] Seafarers who apply for the certificates of competency shall meet the following conditions: (a) those reach the age of 18 and those are less than 60 years in case of first application; (b) those meet the requirements of the health for the positions; and (c) those undergo the basic security trainings.[6]

7.1.3 *Occupational Security of Seafarers*

7.1.3.1 Insurances

Employing units and seafarers shall take out social insurance by law, including work-related injury insurance, medical insurance, endowment insurance, unemployment insurance and other social insurance, and pay the contributions of social insurance in time and in full. Employing units shall take out special life insurance and health insurance and take protection measures for seafarers who work aboard vessels that are bound for or through war zones or epidemic zones or that carry toxic and hazardous cargo.[7]

---

[1] The State Council. (2020). *The Chinese Seafarers Development Report for 2020.* Retrieved 1 August, 2021, from http://www.gov.cn/xinwen/2021-06/25/5620861/files/a1c49282205f4e18a6b5026bd8813abc.pdf.

[2] the Maritime Code, Article 31.

[3] the Maritime Code, Article 32.

[4] the Maritime Code, Article 33.

[5] the Regulations of Seafarers of the PRC of 2020, Article 4.

[6] the Regulations of Seafarers of the PRC of 2020, Article 5.

[7] the Regulations of Seafarers of the PRC of 2020, Article 21.

7.1.3.2 Workplace Security

The places of living and work shall meet the requirements specified in the living environment, operation security and protection of vessel survey regulations. Employing units shall provide necessary living, protection and medical supplies, maintain the files of seafarers' health, conduct regular physical examinations and prevent occupational diseases.[8]

7.1.3.3 Paid Annual Leave

Unlike the labourers on the land, seafarers servicing on ships are entitled to take the annual leave of not less than 5 days for the employment of 2 months in addition to the statutory holidays. The level of pay for annual leave shall not be lower than the average wages during the period of employment aboard.[9]

7.1.3.4 Repatriation of Seafarers

Seafarers serving on ships may have a right to be repatriated in the following circumstances: (a) if the labour contract expires or is revoked by law; (b) when the seafarers are no longer able to carry out their duties on ships; (c) in the event of shipwreck; (d) if the ships are bound for a war zone or an epidemic zone to which the seafarer does not consent to go; or (e) in the event of the shipowner not being able to continue to fulfil their legal or contractual obligations as an employer of the seafarers because of insolvency, sale of ship, change of ship's registration or any other similar reason.[10] Seafarers have a right to choose from among the following destinations the place to which they to be repatriated: (a) the place at which the seafarer agreed at the time of engagement or the place at which the seafarer went abroad the ship; (b) the seafarer's residence, the place of the household registration or the country of ship registration; or(c)such other place as was mutually agreed on by the seafarer and the employing unit or the shipowner.[11] The expenses of a repatriation shall be borne by the shipowner, which was reflected in the Civil Decision of Second Instance of the Case of Contract for Services between Shanghai Yizhou Channel Engineering Co., Ltd. and Lin (2016 Hu CF 56), which was made by the Higher People's Court of Shanghai.

---

[8] the Regulations of Seafarers of the PRC of 2020, Article 22.

[9] the Regulations of Seafarers of the PRC of 2020, Article 26.

[10] Lujun (2017).

[11] the Regulations of Seafarers of the PRC of 2020, Article 27.

7.1.4 Administration System of Employment of Seafarers

7.1.4.1 Administration of Seafarers

The Ministry of Transport of the PRC is in charge of the administration of seafarers in China, and the Maritime Safety Administration of the PRC and the local maritime safety administrations of the PRC are responsible for carrying out the work-related to seafarers, including the training, examination and certification for the competency of seafarers, pilots and magnetic compass adjustors.

7.1.4.2 Employment of Seafarers on Ships Flying a Chinese Flag

The employment of seafarers on ships flying a Chinese flag is subject to the Labour Law of 2018, the Labour Contract Law of 2012 and the Interim Regulations of Labour Dispatch. In the case of typical employment, an employing unit (often a shipowner) signs a labour contract with a labourer (a seafarer). Sometimes, a shipowner signs a contract for services with a free seafarer (a self-employed seafarer) through an intermediatory, and the labour contract for services is often held to be the labour contract. In the case of atypical employment (labour dispatch), a seafarer dispatching agency signs a labour contract with a dispatched seafarer; a seafarer dispatching agency signs a dispatch contract with a shipowner; and the relationship between a dispatched seafarer and a shipowner is the de facto labour relationship. Articles 3 and 4 of the Interim Regulations of Labour Dispatch are not applicable where an employing unit employs dispatched ocean-going seafarers.[12]

7.1.4.3 Employment of Seafarers on Ships Flying a Foreign Flag

The employment of seafarers on ships flying a foreign flag is subject to the Regulations of the PRC on the Administration of Seafarers Employed Abroad of 2019. Whoever dispatches seafarers overseas is responsible for the seafarers employed abroad. In accordance with Article 23 of the Regulations of the PRC on the Administration of Seafarers Employed Abroad of 2019, an international seafarer manning agency shall ensure that the dispatched seafarer employed abroad signs a labour contract with one of the following units: (a) the manning agency itself; (b) an overseas shipowner; or (c) a shipping company or other related companies in China. Where the dispatched seafarer employed abroad signs a labour contract with an overseas shipowner, the international seafarer manning agency shall be responsible for reviewing the labour contract. In practice, it is common that an international seafarer manning agency chooses to sign a labour contract with its dispatched seafarer employed abroad. In other words, the dispatched seafarer is the self-owned seafarer of the international seafarer manning agency. Sometimes, a self-employed seafarer,

---

[12] the Interim Regulations of Labour Dispatch, Article 25.

referred to as a free seafarer, signs a labour contract with a foreign shipowner through an international seafarer manning agency, which acts as an intermediary. It is noteworthy that international seafarer manning services are not subject to the Interim Regulations of Labour Dispatch. Accordingly, the rights and obligations related to international seafarer management cannot be identified in accordance with the Interim Regulations of Labour Dispatch.

7.2 The LIO and the Maritime Labour Convention, 2006

7.2.1 The LIO

The ILO stands for the International Labour Organisation. The ILO was formed in 1919 after the end of World War I as part of the peace settlement under the Treaty of Versailles. It was formed to set labour standards, develop policies and devise programmes promoting decent work for all women and men. The unique tripartite structure of the ILO gives an equal voice to workers, employers and governments to ensure that the views of the social partners are closely reflected in labour standards and in shaping policies and programmes. The main aims of the ILO are to promote rights at work, encourage decent employment opportunities, enhance social protection and strengthen dialogue on work-related issues.

7.2.2 Structures and Contents of the Maritime Labour Convention, 2006

Widely known as the "seafarers' bill of rights," the Maritime Labour Convention, 2006 was adopted by governments, employers and worker representatives at a special ILO International Labour Conference in February 2006 to provide international standards for the world's first genuinely global industry. China ratified the Maritime Labour Convention, 2006, which entered into force for the Chinese mainland on 12 November 2016. On 6 August 2018, the Ambassador of the People's Republic of China deposited with the International Labour Office (ILO) the declaration of application of the Maritime Labour Convention, 2006, as amended (MLC, 2006) to the Hong Kong Special Administrative Region of the People's Republic of China (Hong Kong SAR). The Maritime Labour Convention, 2006, became applicable to Hong Kong SAR on 20 December 2018.

7.2.2.1 Structures

The Maritime Labour Convention, 2006 comprises three different but related parts: the Articles, the Regulations and the Code. The Articles include the preamble, general obligations (Article I), definitions and scope of application (Article II), fundamental rights and principles (Article III), seafarers' employment and social rights (Article IV), implementation and enforcement responsibilities (Article V), regulations and Parts A and B of the Code (Article VI), consultation with shipowners' and seafarers' organisations (Article VII), entry into force (Article VIII), denunciation (Article IX), effect of entry into force (Article X), depositary functions (Article XI and Article XII), special tripartite committee (Article XIII), amendment of this convention (Article XIV), amendments to the Code (Article XV), authoritative languages (Article XVI). The Articles and Regulations set out the core rights and principles and the basic obligations of members ratifying the Convention. The Code contains the details for the implementation of the Regulations. It comprises Part A (mandatory Standards) and Part B (nonmandatory Guidelines). The Regulations and the Code are organised into general areas under five titles: Title 1: Minimum requirements for seafarers to work on a ship; Title 2: Conditions of employment; Title 3: Accommodation, recreational facilities, food and catering; Title 4: Health protection, medical care, welfare and social security protection and Title 5: Compliance and enforcement.

7.2.2.2 Contents

The Maritime Labour Convention, 2006 sets out in one place seafarers' rights to decent conditions of work on almost every aspect of their working and living conditions including among others, minimum age, training and qualifications, recruitment and placement, employment agreements, hours of work or rest, payment of wages, paid annual leave, repatriation at the end of contract, onboard medical care, the use of licensed private recruitment and placement services, accommodation, food and catering, health and safety protection and accident prevention and seafarers' complaint handling, which is a single, coherent instrument embodying as far as possible all up-to-date standards of existing international maritime labour Conventions and Recommendations, as well as the fundamental principles to be found in other international labour Conventions, such as the Forced Labour Convention, 1930 (No. 29), and the Right to Organise and Collective Bargaining Convention, 1949 (No. 98). It was designed to be applicable globally, easy to understand, readily updatable and uniformly enforced and will become the "fourth pillar" of the international regulatory regime for quality shipping, complementing the key Conventions of the International Maritime Organisation (IMO) dealing with safety and security of ships and protection of the marine environment.[13]

[13] Yuzhuo (2015).

7.2.3 Amendments to the Maritime Labour Convention, 2006

The 2014 amendments to the Maritime Labour Convention, 2006, which were brought about to better address the specific problems faced in cases of abandonment of seafarers and to better address the problems faced by seafarers and their families and to elabourate on the requirement in the MLC, 2006, were approved by the 103rd session of the International Labour Conference at its One in Geneva on 11 June 2014. These Amendments relate to the Standard A2.5 Repatriation (abandonment of seafarers) and Standard A4.2 Shipowners Liability (claims for compensation in the case of a seafarer's death or long-term disability due to occupational injury or illness). The implementation date for these amendments was 18 January 2017.

The 2016 amendments to the Maritime Labour Convention, 2006 relate to the MLC Guideline B4.3.1 concerning provisions on occupational accidents, injuries and diseases, and add the text "Account should also be taken of the latest version of the Guidance on eliminating shipboard harassment and bullying jointly published by the International Chamber of Shipping and the International Transport Workers' Federation", and the Maritime Labour Convention Guideline B4.3.1 is amended such that implications for health and safety will also include harassment and bullying.

The 2018 amendments to the Maritime Labour Convention, 2006, entered into force on 26 December 2020. The amendment to Standard A2.1 requires a Seafarer's Employment Agreement (SEA) to remain in effect while a seafarer is held captive on or off the ship due to piracy or armed robbery, regardless of whether the date fixed for its expiry has passed or any notice to terminate it has been issued. The amendment to Standard A2.2 requires that wages and other entitlements, under the SEA and any Collective Bargaining Agreement (CBA), including allotments, shall continue to be paid during the entire period of captivity until the seafarer is released and repatriated in accordance with MLC 2006 requirements or dies in captivity. The date of any death in captivity will be determined in accordance with national laws and recommendations.

7.2.4 Implementation of the Maritime Labour Convention, 2006

China revised the Regulations of Seafarers of the PRC several times to align with the Maritime Labour Convention, 2006. In practice, the Maritime Labour Convention, 2006, may not be directly applicable in court in China. Paragraph 1 of Article V of the Martime Labour Convention, 2006 provides that each member shall implement and enforce laws or regulations or other measures that it has adopted to fulfil its commitments under this Convention with respect to ships and seafarers under its jurisdiction. In the Civil Decision of the Case of At-sea Personal Injury Compensation between Guangzhou BFL Shipping Co., Ltd., PICC Guangdong Branch, Liang

Jintang and Zhang Minhai (2018 Yue CF 593), the Higher People's Court of Guangdong held that(a) China has enacted the Labour Law, the Labour Contract Law, the Social insurance Law and the Regulations of Seafarers of the PRC and other laws and regulations, and the Supreme People's Court has released the Interpretations of Several Issues of Application of Law of Hearing Personal Injury Compensation, which have laid the legal ground to enforce the Martime Labour Convention, 2006.

7.3 The Regulations on Several Issues of Hearing the Cases of Seafarers-Related Disputes

The Supreme People's Court of the PRC released the Regulations on Several Issues of Hearing the Cases of Seafarers-related Disputes on 27 September 2020, which entered into force as of 29 September 2020, which address the issues related to the division of jurisdictions between maritime courts and labour arbitration commissions, forum shopping, the differences between labour contracts, contracts for services, labour dispatch contracts, brokerage contracts and entrustment contracts, the liability of work-related injury insurances, the linkage between labour arbitration commissions and maritime courts in case of ship arrest, the claims subject to maritime liens, overtime pay, the defence against personal injuries and the application of law in case of foreign-related contracts.

7.3.1 Jurisdiction of Maritime Courts

Under the Regulations on Several Issues of Hearing the Cases of Seafarers-related Disputes, a maritime court has the exclusive jurisdiction over the labour disputes related to seafarers' embarking, working on a ship and disembarking and repatriation. Other labour disputes between a seafarer and a shipowner shall be handled in accordance with the Labour Dispute Mediation and Arbitration Law.

In the Civil Order of First Instance of the Case of Labour Contract between Dong Lijian and COSCO Shipping Seafarer Management Co., Ltd. (Dalian Branch) (2019 Liao 72CF57-1), Dong Lijian made claims for the refunding of personal income tax upon the wages and the contribution of social insurance, year-end bonus and the economic compensation, and Dalian Maritime Court held that the complaint was rejected on the grounds that the claims were irreverent to the payment of remuneration arising out of seafarers' embarking, working on a ship, disembarking and repatriation and compensation for personal injury and death and they did not fall into the scope of the case acceptance by maritime courts in accordance with Article 24 of the Rules of the Supreme People's Court of the Scope of the Case Acceptance by Maritime Courts.

However, in the Civil Order of Second Instance of the Case of Labour Dispute between Wang Mingxia and COSCO Shipping Seafarer Management Co., Ltd. (2020 Liao CF 921), the Higher People's Court of Liaoning held that for the convenience of the affected labourer, Dalian Maritime Court shall accept the case related to the contribution of social insurance, year-end bonus, and refunding of personal income tax on her wages and such case was not subject to the preconditional labour arbitration. The above orders were made before the Regulations on Several Issues of Hearing the Cases of Seafarers-related Disputes. From my point of view, the dispute between a seafarer and a shipowner often involves wages, social insurance and double wages, economic compensation and overtime pay and can be directly handled by maritime courts, which can reduce the time cost.

7.3.2 Entrustment Contracts and Brokerage Contracts

Article 3 provides that if a seafarer service agency only goes through the related procedures on behalf of seafarers or only provides employment information for seafarers, which are not deemed to be the labour dispatch, the contract between the agency and a concerned seafarer is a brokerage contract or entrustment contract. Under the Labour Contract Law of 2012, a labour dispatch unit and a dispatched labourer shall conclude a labour contract. Sometimes, a service agency only provides the information related to employment of seafarers or handles the procedures of employment, especially when they are free seafarers and, in this case, there are no labour contracts between the agency and the seafarers and the disputes between them are subject to civil law. In the Civil Decision of Second Instance of the Case of the Labour Contract between Wang Houyin and Beijing Xinyusheng Ship Management Co., Ltd. (2017 Jin CF 60), the Higher People's Court held that (a) Beijing Xinyusheng Ship Management Co., Ltd. was an agency providing the services related to crew manning for sea-going vessels and the services of seafarer management on behalf of the employer of seafarers and it was not the employer of seafarers; and (b) the argument was groundless that there was a labour relationship between Wang Houyin and Beijing Xinyusheng Ship Management Co., Ltd.

7.3.3 Claims Subject to Maritime Liens

Article 8 provides that maritime court shall uphold the seafarer's claim that the following wages and remuneration are subject to maritime liens: (a) remuneration or base pay during the normal working hours; (b) overtime pay and rest day pay and statutory holiday pay; (c) the bonus, allowances and subsidiaries during the employment on ships, and the wages under the special circumstances and (d) the fruits arising out of the above unpaid items and further provides that the economic compensation, economic damages and double wages and the fruits arising out of them are not subject to maritime liens. In the Civil Decision of the Case of Seafarer Contract for Service between Zheng Kanlong and Zhanjiang Donghao Port Service Co., Ltd. (2018 Yue CC 1647), the Higher People's Court of Guangdong held that the double wages and economic compensation were punitive, and they were not the wages and remuneration in consideration of services on ships and it was groundless for Zheng Kanlong to argue that the double wages and economic compensation were subject to the maritime liens.

7.3.4 *Application of Law*

Article 17 provides that where the labour contract between a seafarer and a shipowner involves foreign factors, the applicable law shall be determined in accordance with Article 43 of the Law of the PRC on Application of Law for Foreign-related Civil Relations. Where both parties fail to choose the applicable law with regard to the contract for services between a seafarer and a shipowner, the law of the dispatching place, the shipowner's principal place of business, and the flag state shall be applied. In the case of a brokerage contract or entrustment contract between a seafarer and a service agency or between a service agency and a shipowner and if both parties fail to choose the applicable law, the doctrine of the most significant relationship shall be followed in determining the applicable law. In the Civil Decision of First Instance of the Case of Seafarer Contract for Services between Kurylov Oleksandr, Aronia Maritime S.A. and Avlemonas Shipping Co., Ltd. (2018 Zhe 72 CF 515), the vessel of AVLEMON was owned by Avlemonas Shipping Co. and managed by Aronia Maritime S.A., and on 18 November 2015, the vessel was repaired by Pacific Ocean Engineering (Zhoushan) Co., Ltd. However, the expenses of repairs, agency and the wages and remuneration of the seafarers were unpaid. The vessel was arrested by her creditors. On 29 March 2017, Kurylov Oleksandr signed the contract of employment with Aronia Maritime S.A. Later, the seafarers were in poor condition due to a lack of water, power and food. Ningbo Maritime Court held that (a)the port of disembarkation was Zhoushan Port, Zhejiang and Article 43 of the Law of the PRC on Application of Law for Foreign-related Civil Relations shall apply to this case, so the law of the place where a labourer worked shall be the applicable law; (b) from the end of 2017, Kurylov Oleksandr had been living ashore, performing the duty of looking after the vessel; and (c) the place of work of Kurylov Oleksandr was in China, and thus Chinese law was applicable in this case.

7.4 Terms of Seafarer Labour Contracts

Seafarer labour contracts play a very important role in protecting the rights of seafarers. In practice, every employing unit may use its own labour contract. As far as foreign labour employing units in different jurisdictions are concerned, the labour contracts are diverse, which may involve private international law. Therefore, the model format for seafarer employment agreements released by the International Labour Organisation and the standard contracts released by the China Maritime Arbitration Commission (CMAC) are introduced.

7.4.1 Model Format for Seafarer Employment Agreement[14]

7.4.1.1 Basic Information of the Parties

This Agreement is between_______ (insert Seafarer's full name) _______ (insert date of birth) ____________ (insert place of birth-town and country) and__________ (insert Shipowner's name) ____________ (insert Shipowner's full address).

7.4.1.2 Place of Work

You will be employed on______________________________(insert name of vessel or state any vessel owned, managed or chartered by the shipowner).

7.4.1.3 Wages and Means of Payment of Wages

Your wages will be_________________ (insert amount and currency) per week/month/year (delete as appropriate) or formula for determining wages.

Your wages will be payable by______________ (insert method of payment) at weekly/monthly (delete as appropriate) intervals on the___________ (insert number) day of each_________ week/month (delete as appropriate).

(Overtime hours, i.e., hours worked outside of normal working hours will be paid at a rate of____________ (insert overtime rate) (Delete this sentence if not applicable).

7.4.1.4 Paid Annual Leave

You are entitled to take_____________ (insert number) working days as paid leave in each year of employment.

If your employment commenced or terminated part way through the holiday year, your entitlement to paid annual leave will be assessed on a pro rata basis.

---

[14] ILO. (2006). *Model Format for Seafarer Employment Agreement*. Retrieved 1 July, 2021, from The International Labour Organisation. www.ilo.org/dyn/normlex/en/f?p=1000:53:0:::53:P53_FILE_ID:313082

Deductions from final salary due to you on termination of employment will be made in respect of any paid annal leave taken in excess of your entitlement.

There is no provision for the transfer of paid annual leave from one year to the next. All paid annual leave must be taken in the year in which it accrues. There is also no provision for payment to be made in lieu of untaken leave except where paid annual leave has accrued but has not been taken at the date of termination of employment.

7.4.1.5 Notice of Termination of Employment (Delete Whichever is not Applicable)

Definite Period Agreement

Your employment is for a period commencing on _____________ (insert date) and ending on _____________ (insert date) unless it is terminated for justified reasons in advance of this point or the ship is at sea at that point of time in which event it will continue until its arrival in port at which point it will terminate.

or

Indefinite Agreement

The length of notice that you are obliged to give to terminate your employment is (insert notice period which is to be not less than seven days).

The length of notice that you are entitled to receive from the shipowner to terminate your employment is _____________ (insert notice period which is to be not less than seven days).

or

Voyage Agreement

Your employment is for the length of the voyage of [ship] commencing on _____________ (insert date) from the port of_____________ (insert name of port) until _____________ (insert date) or the vessel' arrival in the port of_____________ (insert name of port) at which point it will terminate, unless it is terminated for justified reasons in advance of this point.

7.4.1.6 Health and Social Security Benefits

If you become sick or injured while on a voyage, you will be paid your normal basic wages until you have been repatriated in accordance with the repatriation provisions set out below. After you have been repatriated, you will be paid_____________percent (insert number) of your normal basic wages up to a maximum of _____________weeks. (insert number which shall be 16 or above) less the amount of any Statutory Sick Pay or Social security Sickness Benefit to which you may be entitled for ______________ (insert number) working days in total in any one sick pay year).

If you require medical care while you are on-board, this will be provided free of charge, including access to necessary medicines, medical equipment and facilities for diagnosis and treatment and medical information and expertise. Where practicable and appropriate, you will be given leave to visit a qualified medical doctor or dentists in ports of call for the purpose of obtaining treatment.

In the event of sickness or incapacity, you will be provided with medical care, including medical treatment and the supply of necessary medicines and therapeutic devices and board and lodging away from home until your recovery or until your sickness or incapacity has been declared of a permanent character, subject to a maximum period of______________weeks (insert number which shall be 16 or above). In addition, the shipowner will meet the cost of the return of your property left on board to you or your next of kin.

In the event of your death occurring on board or ashore during a voyage, the shipowner will meet the cost of burial expenses, cremation where appropriate or required by local legislation, and the return of your property left on board to your next of kin.

7.4.1.7 Repatriation

You will be entitled to repatriation, at the expense of the shipowner, if you are away from your country of residence when this agreement is terminated:

by the shipowner

☐ by you in the event of illness or injury or other medical condition requiring your repatriation, the event that the ship is proceeding to a Warlike Operations Area or the event of termination or interruption of employment in accordance with an industrial award or collective agreement.

☐ in circumstances where you are no longer able to carry out your duties under this agreement or cannot be expected to do so, e.g., shipwreck, the sale of your ship or a change in your ship's registration.

The entitlement to repatriation entails transport by ______________ (insert means of transport) to______________ (insert place name or country).:

Note: You may not be entitled to repatriation at the expense of the shipowner in circumstances where you have been dismissed on disciplinary grounds or have breached your obligations under this Agreement. In such circumstances, the shipowner will still be liable to repatriate you but is entitled to recover from any wages due to you the cost of doing so.

Maximum Duration of Service Periods after which You are Entitled to Repatriation

The maximum period of service following which you will be entitled to repatriation at no cost to you is _______________months (insert number of months –no more than 12 months).

7.4.1.8 Applicable Collective Bargaining Agreement(s) (Delete if not Applicable)

Your employment will also be subject to the Collective Bargaining Agreement(s) entered into on_______________ (insert date(s)) between the shipowner and _______________ (insert details of the other parties to the collective bargaining agreement(s) contains additional terms and conditions and forms part of this Seafarers' Employment Agreement, as attached.

7.4.1.9 Hours of Work

Your normal hours of work are from _______________ (insert time) to _______________ (insert time) from _______________ (insert day of week) to_______________ (insert day of week) inclusive.

Your hours of work will be arranged such as to ensure that you receive a minimum of 10 h available for rest in each 24-h period and a minimum of 77 h rest in each seven-day period. This minimum period of rest may not be reduced below 10 h except in an emergency.

You may be required, at the absolute discretion of the master, to work additional hours during an emergency affecting the safety of the ship, its passengers, crew or cargo or the marine environment or to give assistance to other ships or persons in peril. You may also be required to work additional hours for safety drills such as musters, firefighting and lifeboat drills. In such circumstances, you will be provided subsequently with (a) compensatory rest period(s).

7.4.1.10 Complaints and Disciplinary Procedures

(a) Complaints

If you have a complaint regarding your employment, you should follow the shipowner's complaints procedure, a copy of which will be provided to you when you join the vessel.

(b) Disciplinary Rules and Procedure

The disciplinary rules applicable to you are set out in the

☐ Merchant Shipping Law No. 106(I)/2000 on Criminal and Disciplinary Liability of Seafarers.

ADDITIONAL PROVISIONS INCLUDED BY SHIPOWNER.

____

7.4.1.11 Signatures and Signing Place

Signature of Seafarer

____

Signature of Shipowner or Shipowner's representative

______________ (State position held)

Place where this Agreement is entered into ______________

Date when this Agreement is entered into______________.

7.4.2 *Contracts in Case of Labour Dispatch Recommended by CMAC*

7.4.2.1 Seafarer Labour Contract[15]

Definitions

For the purposes of the Seafarer Labour Contract, an employing unit means the unit duly incorporated in the territory of China, which signs a labour contract with a seafarer. An employing unit may be a ship company, a ship management company, a seafarer service agency or other unit; a labour-user unit means the unit that uses the service of a seafarer. Seafarers means those who were registered and gained the Seafarer Service Certificates in accordance with the Regulations of Seafarers, including the Master, Senior Officers, and Officers.

Contract Period

Article 3 lists three types of contract periods, i.e., fixed-term contract, open-ended contract and contract for the completion of a specified task.

---

[15] CMAC. (2021). *Seafarer Labour Contract (Recommendation)*. Retrieved 2 July, 2021, from http://www.cmac.org.cn/uncategorized/598.html. Accessed 2 July 2021

Work Contents and Places of Work

Party B's place of work is the ship owned, controlled or managed by Party A in case of direct employment or by the labour-user unit (shipowner) in case of labour dispatch.

Working hours and Rest and Holidays

Article 6 lists two types of working hour systems, i.e., the comprehensive working hour system, and the standard working hour system. It should be noted that working hours should meet the requirements of related international conventions, such as the Maritime Labour Convention, 2006. Even if the standard working system is selected, Article 42 of the Labour Law may come into play. Article 7 stipulates that the period for the seafarer's consecutive working on ships shall not exceed 8 months and that the period may expire 2 months ahead or be delayed 2 months if crew replacement is not convenient for the port of call or the routine.

Wages

Different wages are paid for the period when a seafarer is not dispatched and the period when a seafarer is dispatched.

Insurances

In the case of labour dispatch, the dispatch unit shall ensure that the labour-user unit, by convention, takes out commercial insurance, such as personal injury and death insurance and medical insurance.

Training

Article 30 situates for the service period of at least 5 years, and a seafarer revoking the contract shall refund the training expenses to the employing unit.

Dispute Settlement

Article 42 stipulates that any dispute arising from the contract shall be referred to CMAC. It is noteworthy that Article 42 may be invalid, the reason for which is that the labour dispute between a seafarer and an employing unit shall be settled by court or labour arbitration commission.

7.4.3 *CMAC Seafarers' Employment Agreement*[16]

7.4.3.1 Trading Area

The ship Party B serves on board shall sail within the trading area of ________________. If the trading area is to be modified, consultation should be

[16] CMAC. (2021). *Seafarers' Employment Agreement*. Retrieved 2 July, 2021, from http://www.cmac.org.cn/uncategorized/608.html

made in advance with Party B and his recruitment and placement service. In the event it is necessary for the ship on board which Party B serves to be bound for a war zone or an affected area with serious life-threatening infectious diseases, Party A shall obtain the consent of Party B and may pay to him special allowances. If Party B refuses to go, Party A shall arrange repatriation for Party B and pay the cost of repatriation therefor. In the event the ship is trading to a pirate-infested area, Party A shall disclose such information in time and consult with Party B and shall take measures in pursuance of relevant legal provisions of states and international organisations.

7.4.3.2 Wages and Payments

Party A shall pay in time the wages and payments due to Party B at the agreed time in this Agreement. The wages and payments of Party B include basic wages and extra payments. The extra payments include overtime payments, paid annual leave (commencing from the date Party B left China), bonuses, allowances and other extra payments. The basic wages shall be paid monthly commencing from the day signing on the ship and terminating on the date returning to China, with the period of service less than a month to be paid on a pro rata basis. The overtime payment shall be not less than one and one-quarter times the basic wages per hour, payments shall be not less than 3 times the daily basic wages when Party B works on Chinese statutory holidays.

7.4.3.3 Working Hours and Overtime

The normal working hours of Party B shall not exceed 8 h per day, 44 h per week; the working hours over 44 h per week shall be overtime. The overtime per month shall not exceed 36 h. The overtime shall be deemed to be 1 h if less than 1 h, 1 and half hours if less than 90 min, and 2 h if less than 2 h, and so on. The work during an emergency that will, at the discretion of the Master, affect the safety of the ship, its passengers, crew or cargo, or the assistance rendered to other ships or persons in peril shall not be deemed to be overtime.

7.4.3.4 Hours of Rest

Party A Shall ensure that the maximum hours of work of Party B shall not exceed 14 h in any 24-h period or exceed 72 h in any seven-day period. Party A Shall ensure that minimum hours of rest shall not be less than 10 h in any 24-h period or less than 77 h in any seven-day period. Hours of rest may be divided into no more than 2 periods, one of which shall be at least 6 h in length, and the interval between 2 consecutive periods of rest shall not exceed 14 h.

7.4.3.5 Leave

The national statutory holidays of China are holidays for the general public, and Party A shall arrange leave for Party B. The statutory holidays include New Year's Day (1 January, one day off), the Spring Festival (Chinese lunar new year's eve, the first and second days of the lunar new year, 3 days off), the Labour Day (1 May, one day off), the National Day (1, 2, and 3 October, 3 days off), the Ching Ming Festival (one day off), the Dragon Boat Festival (one day off), and the Mid-Autumn Festival (one day off). Party B, apart from having the national statutory holidays, is also entitled to paid annual leave calculated on the basis of a minimum of 5 days per 2 months of employment.

7.4.3.6 Medical Care and Insurance

In case of injury or sickness of Party B during his employment, Party A shall be liable to bear all the costs, such as hospitalisation, treatment and accommodation and shall pay the basic wages. The treatment shall terminate when he has recovered, the injury or sickness has been declared of a permanent character, or the agreed period of treatment has expired. In case Party B intentionally conceals or fails to disclose his previous medical treatment, injury or disability as well as medical history before his employment, he shall not be entitled to the above rights.

During employment of Party B, including on the way joining the ship or repatriation from the ship, Party B is entitled to adequate compensation from Party A for his death or permanent disability arising from an accident.

Party A shall apply to prestigious P&I clubs or insurance companies to effect shipowners' liability insurance or to effect all personal accident (including sickness) insurance to cover the sickness, injury, disability or death of Party B and shall be responsible for the claims. Party A shall ensure that all the insurance compensation will be paid in total directly to, or via Party B's recruitment and placement service, forwarded to, Party B or his testamentary successor(s) or heir(s) at law.

7.4.3.7 Costs of Joining and Repatriation

Party A shall bear the costs of Party B commencing from leaving his domestic address to joining ship, including travelling expenses, accommodation and food expenses. The above costs shall be borne by Party B himself in case he abandons or misses the ship due to reasons on his own part.

7.4.3.8 Ship's Manning and Compliance with Regulations and Rules

Party A shall ensure that the ship is seaworthy (up to IMO and ILO convention standards) and manned with adequate and duly qualified seafarers to maintain safe operation and necessary watchkeeping of the ship. Under no circumstances shall the manning level be under the minimum safe manning standard set out by appropriate authorities in accordance with the provisions of relevant international conventions and national law and regulations. Party B shall abide by the instructions of the master or other superiors with honesty, good faith and due diligence and shall observe the following requirements: Properly perform his own duties required of his capacity; Do not keep any contraband knives, guns and ammunitions; Do not abuse drugs and alcohol or start up fights or quarrels; Observe the rules and regulations (including safety regulations) formulated by the employer for the normal navigation and mooring operation of the ship.

7.4.3.9 Party B's Claims for Compensation When Terminating This Agreement

For the unemployment of Party B due to termination of this Agreement resulting from the ship's loss or floundering, the indemnity by Party A against such unemployment will be limited to 2 months' basic wages in total. For the early termination of this Agreement, Party A shall, apart from the cost of repatriation payable to Party B, pay to Party B the compensation for his discharge, which is 2 months' basic wages when Party B's service on board is less than 6 months, or 1 month's basic wage when more than 6 months. If loss of, or damage to, Party B's personal effects occurs due to force majeure, an indemnity shall be paid by Party A, which will not exceed USD____________. (a) this Agreement must be terminated due to shipwreck. Party A shall also arrange for necessary medical examination for Party B, where appropriate; (b) this Agreement is terminated due to sale of the ship, her detention, or her being unable to continue her voyages, unless Party B is transferred to Party A's another ship to continue the execution of this Agreement with consent of Party B and his manning company that assigned him to Party A; (c) this Agreement is terminated due to unseaworthiness of the ship as declared so by her classification society, a port state or her flag state.

7.4.3.10 Settlement of Disputes

Any disputes arising from the performance of this Agreement shall, first of all, be settled through negotiation by Party A and Party B. The recruitment and placement service or the manning company of Party B and his next of kin are entitled to take part in the negotiation. If the negotiation fails, any dispute arising from or in connection with this Agreement shall be submitted to the China Maritime Arbitration Commission (Bei Jing/Shang Hai) for arbitration, which shall be conducted in accordance with the commission's arbitration rules in effect at the time of arbitration application. The arbitral award is final and binding upon both parties.

7.5 Practical Issues Related to Employment of Seafarers

7.5.1 The Protean Face of Employment of Seafarers in China

In accordance with the Provisions on Causes of Action for Civil Cases promulgated by the Supreme People's Court on 29 December 2020, there are three causes of action that may relate to seafarers: the dispute over contracts for services (No. 139), the dispute over labour contracts (No. 186) and the dispute over contracts for seafarers' services. In practice, the term "seafarer employment agreement/contract" is also used. The labour contracts, the contracts for seafarers' services and the seafarer employment contracts are intertwined together. Scholars of maritime law in China tend to think that the contracts for seafarers' services are contracts for services. Some maritime courts think that the contracts for seafarers' services are labour contracts. The Supreme People's Court thinks that the contracts for seafarers' services can be labour contracts or contracts for services. In the Speech by Judge Liu Guixiang, the Director of the Fourth Civil Division of the Supreme People's Court, on the National Maritime Trials Work Conference, Judge Liu pointed out that the differences between the labour contracts and the contracts for services were vogue in the early maritime legislation and sometimes they were interchangeable; the disputes of the labour contracts and the contracts for seafarers' services subject to the jurisdiction of maritime courts should be limited to those related to the employment of seafarers on ships.

The role of a service agency should be the first factor to be taken into account. If the service agency is an intermediary that only provides information related to the employment of seafarers, no matter what the contract between a shipowner and a seafarer is titled, it should be treated as a labour contract between them. In the Civil Decision of Second Instance of the Case of Contracts for Seafarers' services between Liu Wenlei, Searay Shipping Co., Ltd. and Shandong Tongda International Shipping Management Co., Ltd. and Qingdao Shipu Maritime Service Co., Ltd. (2020 Lu CF 452), the Higher People's Court of Shandong held that (1) the case was related to the dispute over the labour contract; (2) the labour relationship existed between Liu Wenlei and Searay Shipping Co., Ltd. and the contract set out the basic information of both parties, the post and duties, the wages and the contract period; (3) Shandong Tongda International Shipping Management Co., Ltd. acted as an intermediary; and (4) Qingdao Shipu Maritime Service Co., Ltd. was entrusted to pay wages on behalf of Shandong Tongda International Shipping Management Co., Ltd. It should be noted that the Interim Regulations of Labour Dispatch do not come into play where Chinese seafarers are dispatched to a ship flying a foreign flag.

In the case of labour dispatch, the seafarers are dispatched to the vessel flying the Chinese flag, and it was often thought that de facto labour relationships existed between the seafarers and the shipowner although there were no contracts between them. However, this view may not hold water because it contradicts the provisions of labour dispatch under the Labour Contract Law of 2012. In the Civil Decision of Second Instance of the Case of Liability for At-sea Personal Injury between Zhang

Wei, Liu Hongli, Meng Fanhua and (2020 Hu CF 40), the Higher People's Court of Shanghai held that (1) COSCO Shipping Seafarer Management Co., Ltd. Shanghai Branch was a labour dispatch unit; (2) COSCO Shipping Development Co., Ltd. and COSCO Shipping Seafarer Management Co., Ltd. signed a seafarer management service agreement on 1 January 2018, which stipulated that the latter provided crew manning services; (3) Liu signed a seafarer employment agreement with COSCO Shipping Development Co., Ltd. on 14 July 2018; (4) the seafarer employment agreement only was supplementary to the seafarer management service agreement; and (5) there was no separate employment relationship between Liu and COSCO Shipping Development Co., Ltd. Particularly in the case of work-related injuries, the dispatched seafarers might not make a claim for personal injury compensation against the shipowner in accordance with torts law, and the benefits from social insurance would be their last resort.

In the Civil Decision of Second Instance of the Case of Liability for At-sea Personal Injury between Zhang Wei, Liu Hongli, Meng Fanhua and (2020 Hu CF 40), the Higher People's Court of Shanghai rejected the claim against COSCO Shipping Development Co., Ltd. for the personal injury compensation. In contrast, a seafarer employed on a ship flying a foreign flag can claim personal injury compensation against the foreign shipowner under torts law, which was reflected in the Civil Decision of Second Instance of the Case of At-sea/waterway connected to the sea Personal Injury Compensation between Lao Xinlong, Qingdao Kunteng International Shipping Management Co., Ltd, Hong Kong Hehe International Shipping Co., Ltd. (2020 Lu CF1666) made by the Higher People's Court of Shandong.

7.5.2 Personal Insurance in the Contracts for Seafarers' Services

Where a seafarer provides services for an individual employer, the contract between them will be held to be a contract for services, which is common in the fishing industry. The individual employer often takes out personal accident insurance for the employed seafarer. In the case of personal injury or death, whether personal accident insurance can offset the compensation borne by the individual employer under torts law remains controversial.

In the Civil Decision of the Case of At-sea/waterway connected to the sea Personal Injury Compensation between Fan Huilan, Linyin and Han Guoliang (2019 Liao CF 569), Dalian Maritime Court held that (1) Han Guoliang took out the personal accident insurance for Lin Changbin, and the beneficiary should be the close relatives of Lin Changbin other than his employer, Han Guoliang; and (2) Han Guoliang could have be relieved or be exempted from his liability for compensation provided that there existed intention or gross negligence on the part of Lin Changbin.

In contrast, in the Civil Decision of Second Instance of the Case At-sea/waterway connected to the sea Personal Injury Compensation between Fan Huilan, Linyin and

Han Guoliang (2020 Liao CF 288), the Higher People's Court of Liaoning held that the benefits from the personal accident insurance should offset the compensation paid by Han Guoliang on the grounds that: (1) compensatory damages were awarded to a victim as compensation, indemnity or restitution for the harm sustained. An employer was encouraged to take out proper commercial insurance to reduce the risks related to employment; (2) the offset was justified in that it both protected the interests of the seafarer and achieved the aim of the insurance contract; (3) Paragraph 2 of Article 39 was designed to eliminate moral hazard, and the employer could indirectly benefit from the commercial insurance it took out for the seafarer; and (4) from the perspective of economy, to allow the employer to indirectly benefit from commercial insurance helped to fully compensate the seafarer, which would stabilise society and protect the interests of seafarers in the long run.

In the Civil Decision of Second Instance of the Case of Contracts for Seafarers' Services between Meng Xianwen, Zhang Yuai, Xiamen Xiangyu Shipping Co., Ltd., Xiamen Xinrongsheng Shipping Co., Ltd., and Tianjin Hengshengtai Logistics Co., Ltd. (2020 Min CF 862), the Higher People's Court of Fujian held that personal insurance in issue should be an additional benefit to the seafarer given by Xiamen Xinrongsheng Shipping Co., Ltd. The same view was held by the Higher People's Court of Guangdong in the Civil Decision of Second Instance of the case of Contract for Services between Shenzhen City Shuiwan Ocean Fishing Co., Ltd. and An Minzhong (2016 Yue CF 711), which was released by the Gazette of the Supreme People's Court of the PRC of 2017 (Volume 12).

Interestingly, in the disputes not involving seafarers, the majority of courts have agreed that commercial insurance, such as personal accident insurance and group life accident insurance, is an additional benefit to labourers and that employing units may not relieve or release itself from tort liability by offsetting insurance benefits against compensation. It is strongly recommended that employers liability insurance be taken out, which can actually relieve the liability of an employing unit.

7.5.3 Taking Out the Social Insurance of Seafarers

In the disputes not involving seafarers, it is generally accepted that an employing unit is obliged to take out social insurance for its labourers and that the obligation is compulsory. Wuhan Maritime Court and the Higher People's Court of Hubei held this view in the Civil Decision of Second Instance of the Case of Contracts for Seafarers' Services between NASCO and Wang Meijin, etc. (2016 E CF 36). Commonly, it is agreed by a shipowner and a seafarer that the wages and remuneration paid by the shipowner include the expenses for social insurance and that the seafarers take out social insurance by themselves. Such agreement is held to be valid by some courts. In the Civil Decision (2018 Min CF 1066), the Higher People's Court of Fujian held that it was not necessary that an employing unit took out the social insurance for its labourers where Article 60 of the Social Insurance Law applied. However, in this case, the appellants were not those (part-time labourers or labourers under the precarious employment) specified in Article 60 of the Social Insurance Law. In the Civil Decision of the Case of Contracts of Seafarers' Services between Wang Houyin and Beijing Xinyusheng Shipping Management Co., Ltd. (2017 Jin CF 60), the Higher People's Court of Tianjin held that with regard to the social insurance, it was agreed that Wang Houyin handled the procedure of the social insurance by himself and the expenses of the social insurance borne by the shipowner were paid along with the wages and that it was groundless for him to claim the expenses from Beijing Xinyusheng Shipping Management Co., Ltd.

References

Lujun, Z. (2017). *Ships and crew law*. Dalian: Dalian Maritime University Press [in Chinese].
Yuzhuo, S. (2015). *Maritime law monograph* (3rd ed.,). Beijing: China University of Political Science and Law Press [in Chinese].

Chapter 8
Work-Related Injury Insurance

Work-related injury insurance, the main part of social insurance, always gives rise to practical problems. Identifying work-related injuries is the first and most important thing, which is a tedious and sometimes lengthy process. The types of work-related injuries include statutory work-related injuries and presumed work-related injuries. The application of criteria for work-related injuries is complex. It is generally accepted that the three elements related to work, that is, working hours, a place of work and arising out of employment, are determinants for work-related injuries. In some special cases, a labour relationship is not a prerequisite to work-related injuries. Some practical issues are discussed.

8.1 Overview of Work-Related Injuries

In accordance with Social Security Programs Throughout the World, by the end of 2019, 183 countries and territories had maintained their own social security programmes. Work-related injury insurance plays an important role in social security programmes. In 1884, the Accident Insurance Law was enacted in Germany, which followed the principle of no fault. Since then, many countries have followed the German example. In 1951, labour insurance regulations of the PRC were enacted, which contained the provisions of work-related injury insurance. In 2003, work-related injury insurance regulations were enacted, which were revised in 2010. In 2004, Opinions on Several Issues concerning Implementation of Work-related Injury Insurance Regulations were released by the Ministry of Labour and Social Security. To implement the Work-related Injury Insurance Regulations of 2010, Opinions on Several Issues concerning Implementation of Work-related Injury Insurance Regulations were released by the Ministry of Human Resources and Social Security of the People's Republic of China in 2013. In 2016, Opinions on Several Issues concerning Implementation of Work-related Injury Insurance Regulations (No. 2) were released by the Ministry of Human Resources and Social Security

Y. Wang, *Chinese Labour Law*, Understanding China,
https://doi.org/10.1007/978-981-16-8101-1_8

of the People's Republic of China in 2016. To identify work-related injuries, Judicial Provisions of the Supreme People's Court on Several Issues concerning Hearing Administrative Cases of Work-related Injury Insurance were released in 2014.

8.1.1 Concept of Work-Related Injuries

In Workmen's Compensation (Agriculture) Convention, 1921 (No. 12), personal injury by accident arising out of or in the course of employment can be compensated.[1] In the Employment Injury Benefits Convention, 1964 (No. 121), a commuting accident that is considered to be an industrial accident and an occupational disease can be covered by employment injury schemes.[2] In accordance with the Work-related Injury Insurance Regulations of 2010, work-related injuries can be defined as personal injuries caused by accidents arising out of employment or occupational diseases. Occupational diseases are diseases contracted by the labourers of an enterprise, a public institution, an individual economic entity and other employing units as a result of exposure to dust, radioactive substances and other toxic or harmful factors in occupational activities in accordance with the Law of the People's Republic of China on the Prevention and Control of Occupational Diseases of 2018.

8.1.2 Nature of Work-Related Injury Insurance

Taking out work-related injury insurance is a statutory obligation for employing units. Any agreement intending to exclude the obligation or waiver of work-related injury insurance is invalid. This view can be seen in the Administrative Decision of Second Instance of the case of Identification of Work-related Injury between Beijing OTTEC Cleaning Service Co. Ltd. (Shanghai Branch) and Shanghai City Changning District Human Resources and Social Security Bureau (2019 Hu 03 AF 101), which was released by the Gazette of the Supreme People's Court of the PRC of 2020 (Volume 1).

Taking out commercial insurance does not exempt employing units from their liabilities under work-related injury insurance, which can be seen in the Civil Decision of Second Instance of the case of Contract for Services between Shenzhen City Shuiwan Ocean Fishing Co., Ltd. and An Minzhong (2016 Yue CF 711), which was released by the Gazette of the Supreme People's Court of the PRC of 2017 (Volume 12).

---

[1] ILO. (1921). *Workmen's Compensation (Agriculture) Convention, 1921 (No. 12)*. Retrieved 3 August, 2021, from https://ilo.org/dyn/normlex/en/f?p=NORMLEXPUB:12100:0::NO::P12100_INSTRUMLENT_ID:312157

[2] ILO. (1964). *Employment Injury Benefits Convention, 1964 (No. 121)*. Retrieved 3 August, 2021, from https://www.ilo.org/dyn/normlex/en/f?p=NORMLEXPUB:12100:0::NO::P12100_ILO_CODE:C121

Work-related injury insurance is based on the principle of no fault. Despite a fault in employment, a labourer is entitled to the benefits from work-related injury insurance, which can be seen in the case of Administrative Confirmation of the case of Identification of Work-related Injuries between Sun Lixing and Tianjin City Industries Park Labour Bureau, which was released by the Gazette of the Supreme People's Court of the PRC of 2006 (Volume 5).

8.1.3 Types of Work-Related Injuries

In accordance with the Work-related Injury Insurance Regulations of 2010, work-related injuries can be classified into statutory work-related injuries and presumed work-related injuries.

8.1.3.1 Statutory Work-Related Injuries

Article 14 of the Work-related Injury Insurance Regulations of 2010 provides that work-related injuries shall be identified in case that any of the following events occurs: (1) a labourer suffers from an injury arising out of employment at the place of work and during work hours; (2) a labourer suffers from an injury arising out of preparative work or the closing stage of work; (3) a labourer suffers from an unexpected injury arising out of violence in the course of the performance of duties at the place of work and during work hours; (4) a labourer develops occupational diseases; (5) a labourer sustains injuries arising out of the employment or his whereabouts is unknown due to an accident when he is out on duty; (6) a labourer sustains injuries arising out of a traffic accident related to urban rail transport, passenger ferries or trains, for which he does not take main responsibilities; or (7) other events prescribed by laws and administrative regulations where work-related injuries shall be identified.

8.1.3.2 Presumed Work-Related Injuries

Article 15 of the Work-related Injury Insurance Regulations of 2010 provides that any of the following events shall be presumed as a work-related injury: (1) a labourer dies of sudden illness during work hours and in the course of the performance of duties or dies within 48 h after rescue measures are ineffectual, (2) a labourer is injured in rescue and relief work and other activities for the sake of national interest and public interest, or (3) old injuries recrudesce after a labourer, who was injured as a result of war or duty when he served the army and gained a disabled solider certificate, is employed by an employing unit. In accordance with Opinions on Several Issues concerning Implementation of Work-related Injury Insurance Regulations, the period of 48 h commences from the time when the first diagnosis is made by medical institutions. This was affirmed by the Supreme Court of the People's Republic of

China in the Administrative Order of Retrial Inspection and Supervision of Case of Labour and Social Security Administration between Wei Shunjuan and Gansu Province Dingxi City Human Resources and Social Security Bureau (2017 SC AA 7363).

At the provincial level, the list of presumed work-related injuries is longer. In Guangdong Province Work-related Injury Insurance Regulations of 2019, acute poisoning induced by toxic and hazardous substances in working conditions or acute poisoning that occurs in the dining room on the premises is a presumed work-related injury, and an infectious disease is a presumed work-related injury if a labourer is sent on duty to an epidemic area declared by the government.

In Implementation Measures for Liaoning Province Work-related Injury Insurance of 2017, a labourer is injured in working hours at the place of work if he protects the interest of the employing unit in case of emergency and his injury is identified as a presumed work-related injury, even if his behavior is beyond his duty. Any personal injury or acute poisoning that occurs in working hours and is caused by insufficient safety facilities, bad working conditions and operating environment or blurring warning signs is a presumed work-related injury, regardless of whether he is on duty or not. It should be noted that the phrase "sending to a medical institution" is inserted as a restrictive condition of 48 h in Implementation Measures for Liaoning Province Work-related Injury Insurance of 2017. This means that for the purpose of presumed work-related injuries, the place where the affected labourer dies should be a medical institution.

In the Administrative Decision of Retrial of Case of Labour and Social Security Administration between Gao Yuanxiang and Shenyang Economic and Technological Development Zone (2020 Liao 01 AR 27), the court held that at 10 on 4 September 2018, Jin Xiangzhe felt bad in the course of employment and told the general manager that he would go back home to take medicine and fetch his Medical Insurance Card and go to hospital, and that after he went back home his condition became severe, his relatives called the emergency call and he died in despite of medical rescue and that his death did not fall into the scope of presumed work-related injuries.

8.1.4 Exceptions

Article 16 of the Work-related Injury Insurance Regulations of 2010 provides three exceptions to work-related injuries. Without prejudice to Article 15 and Article 16 of Work-related Injury Insurance Regulations of 2010, any of the following events shall not be identified as a statutory work-related injury or a presumed work-related injury: (1) intentional crime; (2) intoxication or drug abuse; or (3) self-mutilation or suicide.

Apparently, suicide is an exception to work-related injuries. Article 16 of the Work-related Injury Insurance Regulations of 2010 does not take into account the nature or cause of suicide. However, in practice, some courts may take a different view that the cause of suicide could play a role in identifying a work-related injury. In the

Administrative Decision of Second Instance of Sanming City Intimidate People's Court of Sanming City Human Resources and Social Security Bureau and Chen Xiaofang (2019 MIN 04 AF 13), the court held that Chen Junmian was injured by a student when he was on duty in Taixi Middle School, and as a result of posttraumatic stress disorder, he committed suicide, and the suicide under the influence of the injury identified as a work-related injury was different from suicide provided by Article 16 of the Work-related Injury Insurance Regulations of 2010, which is intentional and irrelevant to employment. Chen Junmian suffered from work-related injury, and then posttraumatic stress disorder developed and induced suicide. There is a causal link between Chen's injury and suicide. In the Administrative Decision of Second Instance of Sanming City Intimidate People's Court of Sanming City Human Resources and Social Security Bureau and Lei (2020 MIN 04 AF 46), the court took the same view that the fact that Wei Kexi committed suicide was a work-related injury because Sanming Human Resources and Social Security Bureau failed to produce sufficient evidence that Wei's suicide was irrelevant to employment. Therefore, we can conclude that if suicide is caused by employment or a previous work-related injury, it will be identified as a work-related injury. The conclusion is supported by the Supreme People's Court of the People's Republic of China. In the Administrative Order of Retrial Inspection and Supervision of Zhang Hongren and Gansu Province Jinchang City Human Resources and Social Security Bureau (2018 SC AA 332), Zhang Hongren appealed that he developed schizophrenia under the influence of severe working conditions and pollution and the Supreme Court held that with reference to Appraisal Standards of Disability Degrees caused by Workmen Work-related Injuries and Occupational Diseases (GB/T16180-2006), schizophrenia and bipolar disorder were endogenous and biological qualities were major determinants of these disease, and the appellant did not suffer from accidental injury or occupational disease. Therefore, schizophrenia was not directly caused by severe working conditions. Finally, Zhang's appeal for retrial was rejected.

8.2 Understanding and Application of Criteria of Work-Related Injuries

8.2.1 Three Elements Related to Work

It is generally accepted that the three elements related to work, that is, working hours, a place of work and arising out of employment, are determinants for work-related injuries. However, some think that each of the three elements plays a different role in identifying work-related injuries: arising out of employment is a sufficient element, while working hours and a place of work are subsidiary elements. Some think each of the three elements is necessary and plays the same role in identifying work-related injuries, while others think that each is sufficient for what constitutes work-related injuries. I am of the view that arising out of employment is a sufficient and core determinant for work-related injuries and working hours, and a place of work further demonstrates "arising out of employment". This view is supported by Article 36 of the Social Insurance Law of 2018, which provides that a labourer sustaining an injury by accident arising out of employment or contracting an occupational disease is entitled to the benefits from work-related injury insurance.

With it in mind, it can help to solve many problems with the identification of work-related injuries. Take sudden death at home as an example. Feng Fangdi was a mathematics teacher in Qiongshan middle school. After two classes in the late evening of 15 November 2011, Feng Fangdi went back home. At approximately 7 a.m. of the next day, Feng Fangdi was found dead, which was certified by Qiongshan People's Hospital. The Medical Certificate of Resident Death issued by Qiongshan People's Hospital stated that Feng Fangdi died of myocardial infarction at home on 16 November 2011. Qiongshan middle school applied the Haikou City Human Resources and Social Security Bureau for the identification of a work-related injury on 15 December 2011 on the grounds that as a result of fatigue for a long time, Feng Fangdi died of sudden myocardial infarction on the job during the working hours. The Haikou City Human Resources and Social Security Bureau refused to identify Feng's sudden death as a work-related injury on 23 May 2012. Yu Junjie, Feng's wife, was not satisfactory with the identification by the Haikou City Human Resources and Social Security Bureau and lodged an administrative suit against the Haikou City Human Resources and Social Security Bureau. The second intermediate People's Court of Haikou City ordered that the Haikou City Human Resources and Social Security Bureau identify the nature of Feng's sudden death again. On 17 January 2015, the Haikou City Human Resources and Social Security Bureau identified Feng's sudden death as a nonwork-related injury on the grounds that (a) at approximately 10 p.m. on 15 November 2011, Feng Fangdi, together with his daughter, went back home; (b) Feng lay on the bed when sudden myocardial infarction occurred.; (c) no teaching activities were arranged for the morning of 16 November 2011; (d) the school rules stipulated that no lesson or test was allowed at night; and (e) the school denied that a teacher was obliged to finish score testing papers that very day.

In the Administrative Order of Retrial Inspection and Supervision of the case of Labour and Social Security Administration between Haikou City Human Resources and Social Security Bureau of Hainan Province and Yu Junjie (2017 SC AA 6467), the Supreme Court held that it was generally accepted that "working hours and on the job" should be the working hours and the place of work designated by an employing unit and that the fact that a labourer worked at home for the sake of his employing unit should fall within the meanings of "working hours and on the job" on the grounds that (a)taking the teaching task home and finishing it in his private time was encouraging, which fulfiled the legislative objectives of the Work-related Injury Insurance Regulations of 2010; and (b) "on the job" of presumed work-related injuries was different from "a place of work" of statutory work-related injuries in that "on the job" meant "duty" rather than "place" and the meaning of "on the job" was broader. (see the case of Administrative Confirmation of Work-related Injuries between Wang Changwei and Jiangshu Province Xuyu County Labour and Social

Security Bureau, which was released by the Gazette of the Supreme People's Court of the PRC of 2011 (Volume 9)). "on the job" covers overtime work at home.

In other words, to solve the practical problems with the identification of work-related injuries, we are expected that in understanding the three elements related to work, the following principles should be followed: for the purpose of "arising out of employment", whether a labourer fulfils his duty, whether a labourer is designated to do a task, whether the behavior of a labourer is relevant to his duty, or whether a labourer behaves for the sake of his employing unit should be taken into consideration; for the purpose of working hours, whether the time is necessary for his duty should be taken into consideration; and for the purpose of a place of work, whether the area is a reasonably extended area for his duty should be taken into consideration.

8.2.2 Being Out on Duty

In accordance with Article 5 of Judicial Provisions of the Supreme People's Court on Several Issues concerning Hearing Administrative Cases of Work-related Injury Insurance, being out on duty means the period (a) when a labourer is dispatched to a place outside his place of work, or he goes to a place required by his work and carries out the activities related to his duty; (b) when a labourer is sent out to study or attend a meeting; or (c) when a labourer is out to carry out other activities required by his work. Where a labourer is out on duty and sustains an injury by accident arising out of an activity irrelevant to his work, the injury shall not be identified as work-related injury.

However, it should be noted that the party who intends to deny a work-related injury should bear the burden of proof that the injury was not caused by accidents arising out of employment. If the party fails to produce the proof, the court will render the injury a work-related injury. Mr. X was sent out by Tuanshan Middle School to undergo job-related training. Changsha Huihe Lujing Hotel was where Mr. X stayed and received the training. At 5 a.m. on 11 December 2018, Mr. X asked Wang Xionghui, head of the team for leave to go out for a breath of fresh air. In addition, Mr. X was found to fall dead on the ground. Shaoyang City Human Resources and Social Security Bureau insisted that Mr. X's death was not caused by accident arising out of employment or did not meet Item 5 of Article 14 of the Work-related Injury Insurance Regulations of 2010. In the Administrative Order of the Case of Retrial Inspection and Supervision between Shaoyang City Human Resources and Social Security Bureau and Li Menghua (2020 Xiang AA 412), the Higher People's Court of Hunan Province held that the public security bureau decided that Mr. X's death was not caused by a criminal offence and Mr. X did not commit suicide and further held that Shaoyang City Human Resources and Social Security Bureau failed to produce the proof that the death was not caused by accident arising out of employment and the application for a retrial was rejected.

8.2.3 *Participation in Activities Organised by an Employing Unit*

If a labourer is injured when he participates in the activities organised by his employing unit or is sent by his employing unit to participate in the activities organised by other employing units, the injury shall be identified as a work-related injury. It is generally accepted that such activities are related to work if his employing unit requires that labourers participate in them.

On 5 September 2006, Lang Yina executed the Labour Contract with Beijing Foreign Enterprises Services Company and was dispatched to BMW China. Beijing Foreign Enterprises Services Company took out social insurance for her. On 20 July 2007, BMW China arranged the labourers of the sales department to participate in the two-day teambuilding activities. The next morning, Lang Yina fell down from horseback during the course of equestrian training. She was diagnosed with a compression fracture. In the Administrative Decision of the case of Administrative Confirmation between Lang Yina and Beijing City Chaoyang District Labour and Social Employment Bureau (2008 Chao AC F131), which is No. 34 of Administrative Trial Guidance Case, the People's Court of Chaoyang District of Beijing held that in deciding whether the activities a labourer participates in are related to work, the forms, contents, objectives, nature and organiser of the activities shall be taken into consideration and that the equestrian trainings were part of the teambuilding activities of BMW China, and BMW China paid the expenses for the trainings and that the trainings were work-related.

However, if travelling activities are of the nature of benefits and are not imperative, an injury occurring in the course of travelling activities is not a work-related injury. Ke Jinglong worked at Sanhemingdi Company, and together with Mr. Zhang and Mr. Tan was honored with the title of 2016 Year Excellent Employees. Each of them was given a bonus of 3,000 yuan as travelling expenses and had the option of travelling. Ke Jinglong chose to travel in Vietnam. At 7:00 p.m. on 6 April 2018, Ke Jinglong went for a walk in the sands and drowned in the sea. On 9 April 2018, his body was found by the Vietnamese Police. Sanhemingdi Company applied the Panzhihua Human Resources and Social Security Bureau for the identification of work-related injuries. On 2 August 2018, the Panzhihua City Human Resources and Social Security Bureau gave a Decision of Non-Work-related Injuries. The court of first instance held that the company-sponsored activity, which was organised by Sanhemingdi Company, was different from the one that labourers themselves launched and the objectives of such activity were to encourage labourers, improve working performance and enhance the cohesive force among labourers and that in nature such activity was relevant to employment. In the second instance trial, the intermediate People's Court of Panzhihua City held that the period when Ke Jinglong traveled was not considered an absence from duty. Sanhemingdi Company provided financial support for travelling, and the travelling destination was a reasonable extension of his place of work and rejected the application for appeal by the Panzhihua Human Resources and Social Security Bureau and Sichuan Province Department of Human Resources and

Social Security. Interestingly, in the Administrative Decision of Retrial of the case of Labour and Social Security Administration between Sichuan Province Department of Human Resources and Social Security, Panzhihua City Human Resources and Social Security Bureau and Ke Xingmao and Sanhejingdi Company (2020 Chuan 04 AR 1), the Intermediate People's Court of Panzhihua City held that Ke's death was not of the nature of work-related injuries and that the travelling activity was a kind of paid annual leave, and Ke had the option of travelling.

8.2.4 Preparative Work and Concluding Work

Preparative work and concluding work are not defined by law. Article 5 of Employment Injury Benefits Convention, 1964 (No. 121) provides that each member should, under prescribed conditions, treat the following as industrial accidents: (a) accidents, regardless of their cause, sustained during working hours at or near the place of work or at any place where the worker would not have been except for his employment; (b) accidents sustained within reasonable periods before and after working hours in connection with transporting, cleaning, preparing, securing, conserving, storing and packing work tools or clothes; (c) accidents sustained while on the direct way between the place of work and–(i) the employee's principal or secondary residence; or (ii) the place where the employee usually takes his meals; or (iii) the place where he usually receives his remuneration.[3]

Roughly speaking, Item (b) of Article 5 of Employment Injury Benefits Convention, 1964 (No. 121) has the same meaning as "preparative work and concluding work" under Item 2 of Article 14 of the Work-related Injury Insurance Regulations of 2010. The scope of preparative work and concluding work varies from one industry to another. In the Administrative Decision of the case of Administrative Confirmation between Chen Shanju and Shanghai City Songjiang District Human Resources and Social Security, which was released by the Gazette of the Supreme People's Court of the PRC of 2013 (Volume 9), the first intermediate People's Court of Shanghai City held that "sustaining an injury by violence" meant the injury occurred when he was fulfiling his duty, that the injury caused by a personal vendetta was not of the nature of work-related injuries even if it occurred during the working hours and at the place of work, and further held that "preparative work and concluding work" meant the practice provided by law or the rules of an employing unit or other established practice. In this case, bathing was not necessary for employment, there were no such rules of the employing unit, and bathing was not concluding work.

[3] ILO. (1964). *Employment Injury Benefits Convention, 1964 (No. 121).* Retrieved 3 August, 2021, from https://www.ilo.org/dyn/normlex/en/f?p=NORMLEXPUB:12100:0::NO::P12100_ILO_CODE:C121

8.3 Work-Related Injury Insurance Benefits

8.3.1 Application for Identification of Work-Related Injuries

The identification of work-related injuries is in the nature of administrative confirmation, which is initiated by application. An employing unit shall make an application to the competent work-related insurance administrative authority for the identification of work-related injuries 30 days after an injury occurs or an occupational disease is diagnosed. If an employing unit fails to do this, the injured labourer, his close relatives or the trade union may make an application to the competent work-related insurance administrative authority for the identification of work-related injuries one year after an injury occurs or an occupational disease is diagnosed. The period of one year may commence from the day when the outcome of work-related injury appears. (see the case of Administrative Confirmation of the case of identification of Work-related Injuries between Yang Qingfeng and Jiangsu Province Wuxi City Human Resources and Social Security Bureau, which was released by the Gazette of the Supreme People's Court of the PRC of 2008 (Volume 1)). To make a valid application, the following documents shall be produced: (1) Application form for identification of work-related injuries stating the time and place of an injury, the cause of an injury, and his conditions; (2) documents supporting that there exists a labour relationship (including a de facto labour relationship) between the employing unit and the injured labourer; and (3) a medical certificate of diagnosis or a certificate of diagnosis of occupational diseases (or appraisal of occupational diseases). After receipt of the documents, the competent work-related insurance administrative authority may, at its discretion, investigate and verify the injuries by accident and give a letter of verification within 60 days. If the employing unit does not think that the injury is of the nature of work-related injuries, it shall bear the burden of proof. If the injured labourer or his close relative do not agree with the letter of verification, he could resort to administrative remedies.

8.3.2 Insurance Benefits

8.3.2.1 Medical Treatment

Treatment that is required to cure or relieve the effects of the injury is paid by work related insurance funds, provided that the expenses for medical treatment meet the standards listed by work related injury insurance diagnosis and medical item catalogues, work-related injury insurance drug catalogues and work related insurance hospitalisation services.

8.3.2.2 Food and Traffic Allowances

Food allowance for the period when a labourer who sustains a work-related injury is in hospital is paid by work-related insurance funds, provided that such an allowance is certified by a medical institution. Traffic allowances for medical treatment beyond the area where insurance is taken out are paid by work-related insurance funds.

8.3.2.3 Auxiliary Devices

Artificial limbs, orthotic devices, artificial eyes, false teeth, and wheelchairs that facilitate daily life or work are paid by work-related insurance funds, provided that these devices are confirmed by a labour capacity assessment committee.

8.3.2.4 Disability Benefits

A labourer who sustains a work-related injury is entitled to paid suspension from work for at most 12 months. If the injury is particularly severe, the paid suspension may be extended to 12 months. The wages during the suspension from work shall be paid by an employing unit. When the disability degree is assessed, paid suspension from work ceases, and an injured labourer is entitled to disability benefits and nursing expenses paid by work-related insurance funds.

Disability Degrees I–IV

A labourer whose injury is assessed between disability degree I and disability degree IV leaves his post but remains employed by his employing unit and is entitled to the following benefits:

(1) Lump-sum disability benefits of 27-month wages for disability degree I, 25-month wages for disability degree II, 23-month wages for disability degree III, and 21-month wages for disability degree IV, all of which are paid by work-related insurance funds.
(2) Monthly disability allowance of 90% of his wages for disability degree I, 85% of his wages for disability degree II, 80% of his wages for disability degree III, and 75% of his wages for disability degree IV, all of which are paid by work-related insurance funds.
(3) The disability allowance shall cease, and the labourer is entitled to basic endowment insurance benefits when he reaches the mandatory age for retirement and goes through retirement procedures.

Disability Degrees V and VI

A labourer whose injury is assessed between disability degree V and disability degree VI is entitled to the following benefits:

(1) Lump-sum disability benefits of 18-month wages for disability degree V and 16-month wages for disability degree VI, both of which are paid by work-related insurance funds.
(2) Monthly disability allowance of 90% of his wages for disability degree I, 85% of his wages for disability degree II, 80% of his wages for disability degree III, and 75% of his wages for disability degree IV, all of which are paid by work-related insurance funds.
(3) If he remains to be employed by his employing unit, the employing unit shall provide a job suitable for him. If such a job is not available, the employing unit shall pay a monthly disability allowance of 70% of his wages for disability degree V and 60% of his wages for disability degree VI. If he volunteers to terminate or cancel the labour relationship with his employing unit, he is entitled to a one-off medical treatment allowance paid by work-related insurance funds and a lump-sum employment allowance for the disabled paid by his employing unit, both of which are different in different provinces.

Disability Degrees VII and X

A labourer whose injury is assessed between disability degrees VII and X is entitled to the following benefits:

(1) Lump-sum disability benefits of 13-month wages for disability degree VII, 11-month wages for disability degree VIII, 9-month wages for disability degree IX, and 7-month wages for disability degree X, all of which are paid by work-related insurance funds.
(2) If he volunteers to terminate or cancel the labour relationship with his employing unit, he is entitled to lump-sum medical treatment allowance paid by work-related insurance funds and one-off employment allowance for the disabled paid by his employing unit, both of which are different in different provinces.

8.3.2.5 Death Benefits

If a labourer dies from a work-related injury, his close relatives may be entitled to (1) funeral allowance of 6-month average wages of labourers in the preceding year in the pooling area; (2) compensation payment to the surviving dependents and (3) death compensation of 20 times per capita disposable income of national urban and rural residents.

8.3.3 Termination of Insurance Benefits

Insurance benefits may be terminated in case of any of the following events: (1) a labourer sustaining a work-related injury fails to meet the conditions for insurance benefits; (2) a labour sustaining a work-related injury refuses to receive a labour capacity assessment or (3) a labour sustaining a work-related injury refuses to be treated.

8.4 Practical Issues with Work-Related Injury Insurance

According to Statistical Communiqué of 2020 Human Resources and Social Security Undertakings Development released by the Ministry of Human Resources and Social Security of the PRC on 26 July 2021, 267,630,000 labourers are covered by work-related insurance and 1,120,000 cases of identification of work-related injuries had been handled by the end of 2020.[4] According to the search results on the website of China Judgments Online, there were 30,999 cases concerning the identification of work-related injuries in 2019. In practice, there are a great number of disputes with regard to the identification of work-related injuries.

8.4.1 Labour Relationships and Work-Related Injuries

In accordance with Article 18 of the Work-related Injury Insurance Regulations of 2010, a labour relationship is a requisite for the identification of work-related injuries. However, Judicial Provisions of the Supreme People's Court on Several Issues concerning Hearing Administrative Cases of Work-related Injury Insurance further provides for the party who shall bear the liability of work-related injury insurance in some special circumstances where there exist concurrent labour relationships, a labour dispatch or illegal outsourcing. In the case of illegal outsourcing, a labour relationship is not a requisite for the identification of work-related injuries. We can conclude that a labour relationship is a requisite for the identification of work-related injuries except for special circumstances.

In the Administrative Decision for Retrial of the Case of Labour and Social Security Administration between Lin Jiquan and Chongqing Xingping Construction Labour Service Co., Ltd. (2018 SC AR 151), the Supreme Court held that the system of work-related injury insurance was established to ensure that labourers sustaining injuries by accident in the course of employment or contracting occupational diseases were entitled to medical treatment and economic compensation, that, generally, the labour relationship between an injured labourer and an employing unit shall be a requisite for the competent social insurance administrative authority to identify work-related injuries, expect as otherwise provided by law, regulations and judicial interpretations. Subparagraph 1 of Article 3 of Judicial Provisions of

[4] MOHRSS. (2020). *Statistical Communiqué of 2020 Human Resources and Social Security Undertakings Development*. Retrieved 31 August, 2021, from http://www.mohrss.gov.cn/SYrlzyhshbzb/zwgk/szrs/tjgb/202107/W020210728376021444478.pdf

the Supreme People's Court on Several Issues concerning Hearing Administrative Cases of Work-related Injury Insurance provides that if any unit which illegally outsources the assignments to a natural person or a unit which is not eligible for the purpose of employing unit under the Labour Contract Law of 2012, and a labourer who is recruited by the said person or unit sustains work-related injuries, the unit which illegally outsources the assignments shall bear the liability of work-related insurance.

This view was affirmed by the Administrative Decision of Second Instance of the Case of Labour and Social Security Administration between Tianjin Yuhao Construction Engineering Group Co., Ltd. and Tianjin City Human Resources and Social Security Bureau (2020 Jin 01 AF 172), where the First Intermediate People's Court of Tianjin rejected the argument of the appellant, Tianjin Yuhao Construction Engineering Group Co., Ltd. that a labour relationship was a requisite for the identification of work-related injuries in circumstances where the appellant illegally outsourced the assignments to Wang Fei, who recruited Xing Fengzhi, and Xing Fengzhi sustained a work-related injury.

8.4.2 Who is Covered by Work-Related Injury Insurance

Generally, a labour relationship is a requisite for the identification of work-related injuries. However, not all persons who work for enterprises are labourers for the purpose of the Labour Contract Law of 2012. It has been accepted that the persons who reach the age of retirement are interns or other persons who are under a contract for services and are not covered by work-related injury insurance.

In the Civil Decision of Second Instance of the Case of Life Right, Health Right and Body Right between Kong and Guangzhou Liuhua Hotel Group Co., Ltd. (2020 Yue 01 CF 8850), the Intermediate Court of Guangzhou City held that interns were not the labourers within the meaning of the Labour Law of 2018 and therefore Kong, being an intern, was not entitled to the insurance benefits under the Work-related Injury Insurance Regulations of 2010.

For the persons who reach the age of retirement, Paragraph 1 of Article 2 of Opinions on Several Issues concerning Implementation of Work-related Injury Insurance Regulations (No. 2) provides that where persons who reach or exceed the age of retirement but do not handle the retirement procedures or enjoy the benefits of basic endowment insurance sustain injuries by accident in the course of employment or contracts occupational diseases, the employing unit shall bear the liability of work-related injury insurance, which was affirmed by Jilin Higher People's Court in the Administrative Order of Retrial Inspection of the Case of Administrative Confirmation and Reconsideration between Jilin Hengchang Technology Co., Ltd. and Jilin Province Human Resources and Social Security Department (2018 Ji AA 141), where Xiao Xuejun finished retirement procedures in January 2012 and enjoyed the benefits of basic endowment insurance.

To protect the interests of the persons who reach the age of retirement and interns, practical measures are taken at provincial levels. Taking Jiangsu Province as an example, there are nearly 600,000 interns and 6 million persons exceeding the age of retirement who continue to be employed. On 14 December 2020, Jiangsu Province Measures for Persons Exceeding the Statutory Age of Retirement and Interns to Take out Work-related Injury Insurance were released, by which the persons under 65 years that handles the retirement procedures and interns of more than 16 years would be covered by Work-related Injury Insurance. Guangdong Province is expected to follow the footsteps of Jiangsu Province.

8.4.3 Concurrent Claims Under Work-Related Injury Insurance and Civil Tort Liability

Work-related injury insurance, an important part of the social security system, has a great influence on civil tort liability. Work-related injuries could give rise to claims under work-related injury insurance and civil torts law. However, different jurisdictions address the relationships of the claims between work-related injury insurance and civil torts law. An employee injured at work in the UK is able to claim not only no-fault social security benefit from the state under the industrial injuries compensation scheme but also damages from the employer if liability in tort can be established. The use of one system of compensation does not lead to exclusion from the other; there is no "employer privilege" preventing an employee claiming from both workers' compensation and tort. Intentional misconduct of the employer may give rise to added benefits under a state's workers' compensation statute or may expose the employer to a separate cause of action. In Massachusetts Section 28 of the compensation statute doubles all benefits where the injury was caused by the employer's "serious and willful misconduct". In Arkansas, for example, an employee may elect a tort remedy in such an instance. In Connecticut, an employee may be able to overcome an exclusivity defence if he can establish an intentional tort claim, Suarez v Dickmont, 242 Conn. 255 (1997). Each individual jurisdiction of the US will have its own body of law on this issue.

In China, the fact that a labourer sustaining a work-related injury is entitled to insurance benefits does not exclude his claim under civil torts law under circumstances where the work-related injury is caused by safety accidents, occupational diseases, traffic accidents or a third party. In accordance with Article 3 of Implementation Measures for Safety Production Liability Insurance of 2017, the economic compensation under the Measures shall not prejudice the right to the benefits under the work-related injury insurance. Article 58 of Law of the People's Republic of China on the Prevention and Control of Occupational Diseases of 2018 also provides that in addition to the benefits from the work-related injury insurance, a labourer contracting occupational diseases may make a claim for damages against his employing unit. Article 8 of Judicial Provisions of the Supreme People's Court on Several Issues concerning Hearing Administrative Cases of Work-related Injury Insurance further makes it clear that if a labourer is injured by a third party, he is entitled to both the benefits from work-related injury insurance and the claims against a third party.

The Civil Decision of Second Instance of the Case of the Labour Dispute between Fu Hengsheng, Zhang Zhenghua and Lianyungang Development Zone Huayuan Urban Gardening Engineering Co., Ltd. (2015 Lian CF 00159), which was released by the Gazette of the Supreme People's Court of the PRC of 2018 (Volume 3), affirmed that double compensation was allowed where a work-related injury was caused by a traffic accident. Unfortunately, the Civil Code of 2020 is silent on the relationship between claims under work-related injury insurance and civil torts. However, it can be expected that the principle of concurrent claims under work-related injury insurance and civil tort liability stated here will prevail in the future.

8.4.4 Right of Contribution Against a Third Party or an Employing Unit

In accordance with Provisional Measures for Advance Payment from Social Insurance Fund of 2018, if a labourer is injured by a third party (tortfeasor) and the work-related injury is identified but the tortfeasor refuses to pay the expenses for medical treatment of the work-related injury or the tortfeasor is not unknown, he or his close relative may make a written application to the competent social insurance authority for advance payment of the said expenses from work-related injury insurance fund. After a work-related injury is identified, a labourer or his close relative may make a written application to the competent social insurance authority for advance payment of the insurance benefits from work-related injury insurance funds if the business licence of the employing unit is cancelled or revoked, the employing unit refuses to pay relative expenses, or the execution of recovery for insurance benefits is suspended by court. The competent social insurance authority may have a right of contribution for the expenses for medical treatment of the work-related injury or the insurance benefits against a third party or employing unit, which was affirmed by the Civil Decision of Retrial of the case of Right to Contribution between Xiamen City Social Insurance Management Center and Xin Yong (2017 Min CR 269), where the Higher People's Court of Fujian Province held that Xin Yong shall refund the medical expenses in issue to the appellant, Xiamen City Social Insurance Management Center in accordance with Paragraph 1 of Article 11 of Provisional Measures for Advance Payment from Social Insurance Fund of 2018.

The problems with advance payment are that it takes a long time and that complicated procedures have to be gone through. Therefore, advance payment is called "the clause of Sleeping Beauty". In practice, a claimant may lodge an administrative suit against a competent social insurance authority for advance payment. In the Administrative Decision of Second Instance of the case of Nonfulfillment of Statutory Duties between Chongqing Shapingba District Social Bureau and Zhu Mingbi (2019 Yu

01 AF 324), the First Intermediate People's Court of Chongqing City held that the appellant shall prepay the insurance benefits to Zhu Mingbi since Zhu's application met the requirements of advance payment.

Chapter 9
Legal Liabilities

Legal liabilities under labour law vary and tend to overlap with those under civil law, administrative law and criminal law. The principles of the Civil Code should be limited in some circumstances. Tort liability and liability for breach of contract are common forms of civil liability. The Administrative Penalty Law sets out the types of administrative penalty, and the Labour Contract Law of 2012 and other administrative laws related to labour contracts also provide administrative liabilities. Common criminal offences in the course of employment are also introduced.

9.1 Civil Liabilities

9.1.1 Overlapping of the Labour Law and the Civil Code

Article 2 of the Civil Code provides that civil law regulates personal and proprietary relationships among the persons of civil law, namely, natural persons, legal persons, and unincorporated organisations that are equal in status. The term "status" means the legal status. "Equal in status" refers to being "equal in legal status in the abstract". Even if the doctrine of economic control is followed, a labourer in labour law remains a natural person in civil law who has personality rights and property rights. In this regard, a labourer is comparatively independent. In the context of labour law, the civil relationships between a labourer and an employing unit often have distinctive features, which may be neglected in legal practice. It is noteworthy that the provision of Book Three (Contracts) may be applied mutatis mutandis according to the nature of the agreements on establishing a marriage, adoption, guardianship or the like personal relationships,[1] while the Contract Law was not applied to such agreements

Y. Wang, *Chinese Labour Law*, Understanding China,
https://doi.org/10.1007/978-981-16-8101-1_9

before the Civil Code took effect. It can be inferred that the Labour Law and the Civil Code overlap to some extent.

In 2018, the dispute over equal employment rights and the dispute over liabilities for damages incurred by sexual harassment were recognised as causes of action. The dispute over equal employment rights, which is closely related to the Labour Law of 2018 and the Labour Contract Law of 2012, often occurs before the conclusion of a labour contract or during the performance of a labour contract. Sexual harassment at work is unwelcome conduct that involves sexual advances, requests for sexual favors, physical contract of a sexual nature or other verbal or physical of a sexual nature that creates an intimidating, hostile or offensive work environment.

9.1.2 Types of Civil Liabilities

The main types of civil labilities include: (a) cessation of the infringement; (b) removal of the nuisance; (c) elimination of the danger; (d) restitution; (e) restoration; (f) repair, redoing or replacement; (g) continuance of performance; (h) compensation for losses; (i) payment of liquidated damages; (j) elimination of adverse effects and rehabilitation of reputation; and (k) extension of apologies.[2] Where punitive damages are provided by law, such provisions shall be followed. The types of civil labilities provided in Article 179 may be applied separately or concurrently. The abovementioned forms can be applied where the property right, the contractual right or the personality right is infringed on. Intellectual property rights may be infringed on. In the case of disputes over intellectual property rights, related liabilities, which are subtly different from general tort liabilities, should be assumed. The issue related to the ownership of copyright in the course of employment was addressed by the Beijing Intellectual Property Court in the Civil Decision of Second Instance of the Case of Copyright Ownership and Infringement between Tianjin University Press Co., Ltd. and Feng Xian (2019 Jing 73 CF 639), where the ownership of the copyright was not stipulated in the labour contract.

9.1.3 Tort Liabilities and Practical Issues

9.1.3.1 Tort Liabilities

Book 7 of the Civil Code is about tort liabilities, which means a person's legal obligation to be liable for the legal consequences of infringing on others' property or personal rights. Its primary aims are to provide relief to injured parities for the harm caused by others, to impose liability on parties responsible for the harm and to deter

[1] The Civil Code, Paragraph 2 of Article 464.

[2] The Civil Code, Article 179.

others from committing unlawful acts. The doctrine of four elements of tort liability prevails in Chinese scholars and legal practice, although the Civil Code is silent on it. In establishing tort liability, the claimant should prove an unlawful act, damage, causation and subjective fault.

9.1.3.2 Practical Issues

Personality Right

In the course of recruitment, some employing units often impose some requirements of height, *hukou* (China's *hukou* system is a family registration programme that serves as a domestic passport, administrating population distribution and rural-to-urban migration) and other unreasonable items for the posts. Unreasonable requirements may be held to infringe on the equal employment rights provided by the Constitution, the Labour Law of 2018 and the Employment Promotion Law. In the Civil Decision of Second Instance of the Case of Equal Employment Right between Yan Jialin and Zhejiang XLD Resort Co., Ltd. (2020 Zhe CF 736), Zhejiang XLD Resort Co., Ltd. (the appellee) published the recruitment advertisement on the Zhaopin website in July 2019 and Yan Jialin (the appellant) submitted her resume online, which stated that her place of *hukou* was in Nanyang Henan province; the HR of the appellee thought the appellant was not fit for the post on the grounds that the appellant was a Henan person; and the Intermediate People's Court of Hangzhou held that (1) an employment cannot discriminate against people (applicants or employees) on grounds of sex, *hukou*, features and other inherent factors that were irrelevant to the work; (2) an employing unit may, at its discretion, choose its labourers on grounds of levels of education and working experience that were relevant to the work; (3) the appellee failed to reasonably explain the relationship between *hukou* and the post the appellant applied for; (4) the appellee infringed on the equal employment right and the dignity of the appellant by refusing to give the employment opportunity to the appellant; and (5) upheld the court of first instance ruling that the appellee compensated the appellant 10,000 yuan for the mental loss and made an apology to the appellant in the Legal Daily.

However, the test of reasonableness may be problematic. In the Civil Decision of First Instance of the Case of the General Right of Personality between Ning Jiaqi and Anxiang Rural Credit Cooperatives (2014 An CF 331), the height of not less than 157 cm was listed as one of the recruitment requirements, and Anxiang People's Court held that (1) Anxiang Rural Credit Cooperatives did not violate the statutory and prohibitive provisions related to employment by setting the requirement of height, (2) it might at its discretion choose the applicants according to the requirement of height, (3) it lacked the element of intention, which was fundamental to establish tort liabilities and (4) that the requirement of height set by Anxiang Rural Credit Cooperatives did not constitute employment discrimination. However, the court did not further explain why it was legitimate that Anxiang Rural Credit Cooperatives set the requirement of height. In fact, the improvement of staff quality could not justify the requirement of height, and Ning's height was not inherently relevant to the post she applied for.

In practice, it is rare that a labourer makes a successful claim against an employing unit on grounds of the right to privacy and reputation. In the Civil Decision of First Instance of the Case of Right to Privacy between Lu Songjie and Shanghai Found Automation Equipment Co., Ltd. (2018 Hu 0113 CF 19063), Shanghai Found Automation Equipment Co., Ltd. admitted that after revoking the labour contract with Lu Songjie and recovering the computer from him, it obtained the QQ chat history of Lu Songjie and Wu Hengling on the computer, the People's Court of Baoshan District, Shanghai held that (1) the QQ chat history was within the meaning of the privacy of correspondence between Long Songjie and Wu Hengling, and without authorisation, no one was allowed to check, capture, publicise, and disseminate it; (2) Shanghai Found Automation Equipment Co., Ltd. failed to prove that it gained his consent before obtaining it and further publicised it in the arbitration process; (3) Shanghai Found Automation Equipment Co., Ltd. infringed on the right to privacy of Lu Songjie; and (4) Shanghai Found Automation Equipment Co., Ltd. shall stop publicising the privacy of Lu Songjie and make a written apology to him.

As usual, the courts do not think the right to privacy is infringed on in the following circumstances: (1) making an announcement to revoke or terminate a labour contract in the newspaper (the Civil Decision of Second Instance of the Case of Right to Privacy between Gu Huairong and Hongze Fuda Textiles Co., Ltd. and Huai Daily (2019 Su 08 CC 3198), the People's Court of Huaian); (2) Verifying the illness of a labourer with his doctor (the Civil Decision of First Instance of the Case of Right to Privacy between Wang Xiaoguang and Nestle China (2015 Tian 3 CD 193), made by the People's Court of Tianqiao District, Jinan); (3) Publicizing the civil decision (the Civil Decision of First Instance of the Case of Right to Privacy between Li Xiaohong and Beijing Golden Dike Technology Co., Ltd. (2018 Jing 0108 CF 62250) made by the People's Court of Haidian District, Beijing); (4) Retrieving the historical employment information of a labourer contained in online civil decisions (the Civil Decision of First Instance of the Case of Privacy between Wang Yi and Tutorabc (Shanghai Branch) (2018 Hu 0109 CC 24914), made by the People's Court of Hongkou District, Shanghai); and (5) Using the GPS information for the purpose of employment (the Civil Decision of First Instance of the Case of Right to Privacy between Geng Zhicheng, Guangdong Chaoren Kitchen Appliances Co., Ltd. and China Telecom (Zhongshan Branch) (2017 Yue 2017 CC 5281), made by the First People's Court of Zhongshan, Guangdong).

It is noteworthy that an employing unit is entitled to the right to reputation in China. If a labourer defames his employing unit among the clients, the labourer is liable for his tortious act. In the Civil Decision of Second Instance of the Case of Right to Reputation between Sun Jianfeng and Shanghai Chiko Solar Technology Co., Ltd., Chiko failed to take out the social insurance on behalf of Sun Jianfeng, and he sent several emails to the clients of Chiko in which he referred Chiko to be *Laolai*, a defamatory word in Chinese (deadbeat in English). The Second Intermediate People's Court of Shanghai held that (1) Sun's act was beyond reasonable limits and he infringed on Chiko's right to reputation and (2) Sun was obliged to make an apology to Chico, restore its reputation and eliminate the adverse effects among the clients.

If a labourer protects his right not by resorting to labour arbitration or lawsuits but in an unlawful way, he may infringe on the right of reputation of the employing unit. In the Civil Decision of Second Instance of the Case of Right to Reputation between Fang Yan and Shanghai ShenSu Environmental Technology Group Co., Ltd. (2019 Hu 02 CF 11407), Fang Yan put up the big-character posters that read that "CONTRACTS FORGED" and "SHENSU BACK PAY", hung the placards by her neck which read that "DESPICABLE SHENSU"and "WARNING OF SHENSU BOSS, DEADBEAT", and publicised the photos of the posters and placards in Wechat Moments, and the Second Intermediate People's Court of Shanghai held that Fang's act was beyond reasonable limits.

However, the courts do not think the right to reputation is infringed on in the following circumstances: (1) Publicising the disciplinary result inside an employing unit (the Civil Order of First Instance of the Case of Right to Reputation between Wulei and Hangxiao Steel Structure Co., Ltd. (2020 Zhe 0109 CC 6734), made by the People's Court of Xiaoshan District, Hangzhou; the Civil Decision of Second Instance of the Case of Right to Reputation between Gao Linjing and Hangjin Technology Co., Ltd. (2020 Liao 14 CC 1253), made by the Intermediate People's Court of Huludao, Liaoning; and the Civil Order of Second Instance of the Case of Right to Reputation between Li Yiming and FESCO (2020 Jing 03 CC 6409), made by the Third Intermediate People's Court of Beijing); and (2) Internal management of a labourer (the Civil Order of Retrial Review and Hearing Supervision of the Case of Right to Reputation between Li Wenbin and Lianbao Investment Group Co., Ltd. (2019 Jing CA 5192), made by the Higher People's Court of Beijing).

Property Rights

Normally, only if intention or gross negligence exists on the part of a labourer can an employing unit make a claim for the loss against him, which was reflected in the Civil Decision of First Instance of the Case of Compensation for Damage to Property between Howag-Swisspur (Zhongshan) Ltd. and Li Qionghua (2017 Yue 2071 CF 21976) made by the First People's Court of Zhongshan, Guangdong. If the loss occurs when a labourer is fulfilling his duties, the dispute over the loss shall be referred to labour arbitration first, which was held by the Intermediate People's Court of Hangzhou, Zhejiang in the Civil Decision of Second Instance of the Case of Compensation for Damage to Property between Hangzhou Linkforever Brand Management Co., Ltd. and Liu Lina (2020 Zhe 01 CF 5033).

Likewise, the Higher People's Court of Beijing held the same view in the Civil Order of Retrial Review and Hearing Supervision of the Case of Compensation for Damage to Property between Shixi Holdings (Beijing) Co., Ltd. and Yang Xiaoying (2019 Jing CA 5596), in which the court rejected the lawsuit lodged by Shixi Holdings (Beijing) Co., Ltd. on the grounds that the dispute occurring when Yang Xiaoying was performing her duty was not a civil dispute but a labour dispute, and the dispute shall be referred to labour arbitration first. In establishing the liability for compensation for damage to property, the claimant shall prove(1) he has a legal ownership of the property in issue; (2) the tortfeasor did a unlawful act; (3) the unlawful act caused damage to the property; (4) there exists a causal relationship between the tortious act and the damage to the owner; and (5) the presence of fault on the part of the tortfeasor, which was reflected in the Civil Decision of Second Instance of the Case of Compensation for Damage to Property between Qingdao Audis Biotechnology Co., Ltd. and Li Yujun (2020 Lu 02 CF 3642).

In the Civil Decision of Second Instance of the Case of Compensation for Damage to Property between Sun Shijing, Shanghai Norden Digital Technology Co., Ltd. and Li Yiguang (2019 Hu 02 CF 11243), (1) Shanghai Norden Digital Technology Co., Ltd. (the appellee) was incorporated on 28 January 2016,developing online game software and online animation design; (2) Sun Shijing (the appellant) signed the labour contract with the appellee on 5 April 2016 and worked as the general manager assistant, Li Yiguang worked as the operation director assistant; (3) on 19 May 2017, the appellant send the email to the legal representative of the appellee to resign; (4) the appellant ordered Li Yiguang to format all the disks and delete all the data on the computer of the appellee; (5) At 21:24 on 19 May 2017, the appellee reported to the local police station that all the data on its computer were deleted by the appellant, and the Second Intermediate People's Court of Shanghai held that: (1) the appellant could exercise the management power over Li Yiguang and Li Yiguang deleted all the data as was ordered by the appellant, and Li Yiguang was thinking that he performed his duties by deleting the data and Li Yiguang assumed no liability for the loss of the appellee; and (2) the appellant shall compensate all the operating expenses of the appellee for the period from March 2016 to May 2017.

9.1.4 Liabilities for Breach of Contract and Practical Issues

9.1.4.1 Liabilities for Breach of Contract

Chapter 8 of Book 7 of the Civil Code focuses on liabilities for breach of contract. Breach of contract occurs when there is a failure to preform what is stipulated by all or part of the contract. Article 577 of the Civil Code provides that where a party fails to perform his contractual obligation or his performance does not conform to the agreement, he shall bear default liability such as continuing to perform his obligations, taking remedial measures, or compensating for losses. Generally, the principle of strict liability applies in determining the liability for breach of contracts. The party in breach shall continue to perform the contract, if possible, and/or compensate for the loss. The loss can be in the form of liquidated damages. Article 585 of the Civil Code provides that the parties may agree that, upon default by a party, a certain amount of liquidated damages shall be paid to the other party according to the circumstance of the breach, or the parties may agree on the method of calculating the compensation for losses arising from the breach; where the agreed liquidated damages are lower than the loss caused, the people's court or an arbitration institution may increase the amount upon request of a party; where the liquidated damages are excessively higher than the loss caused, the people's court or an arbitration institution may make appropriate reduction upon request of a party.

9.1.4.2 Practical Issues

Scope of Application of Liquated Damages

It seems that the scope of application of liquidated damages is limited to Article 22 and Article 90 of the Labour Contract Law of 2012. Article 22 of the Labour Contract Law of 2012 provides that if the labourer breaches the agreement on the term of service, he shall pay a penalty to the employing unit as agreed upon. The sum of the penalty may not exceed the training expenses paid by the employing unit. The penalty that the employing unit requires the labourer to pay may not exceed the portion of the training expenses allocable to the unperformed portion of the term of service. Article 90 of the Labour Contract Law of 2012 provides that where a labourer revokes the labour contract in violation of the provisions of this Law or breaches the confidentiality obligation or competition restriction stipulated in the labour contract, thus causing loss to the employing unit, he shall be liable for compensation.

However, some courts in Beijing think that liquidated damages may be applicable to other circumstances. Take the registration of *hukou* at Beijing for example. On 15 July 2015, Nutrichem Co., Ltd. (Party A) and Li Yaqian (Party B) signed the agreement as follows: (1) Party A agreed to handle the procedure of the registration of Party B's *hukou* at Beijing; (2) Party A agreed to bear the expenses for handling the procedure, including personnel agency expenses, consulting expenses, and *hukou* administration expenses; (3) Party B shall, on the basis of the bona fide doctrine, sign the labour contract with Party A and the service period was not less than 5 years; (4) Party B shall reimburse the aforesaid expenses to Party A where the labour contract was revoked by Party B; and (5) Party B shall compensate 150,000 yuan to Party A where the labour contract was revoked by Party B. In the Civil Decision of Second Instance of the Case of Labour Dispute between Nutrichem Co., Ltd. and Li Yaqian (2017 Jing 01CF 3780), the First Intermediate People's Court of Beijing held that (1) Nutrichem Co., Ltd. had fulfilled the contractual obligation in the agreement; (2) the nature of 150,000 yuan was not the liquidated damages but the compensation; and (3) Li Yaqian went against of the bona fide doctrine, revoked the labour contract, and shall be liable for the loss to Nutrichem Co., Ltd.

The reasoning behind the civil decision in favor of employing units is that (1) a labourer violates the bona fide doctrine under labour law (the Civil Order of Retrial Reviewing and Hearing Supervision of the Case of Labour Dispute between Tong Cunyu and China Securities Co., Ltd. (2020 Jing 0102 CA 38), and a similar view was also reflected in the Civil Decision of Second Instance of the Case of Labour Dispute between Beijing IQIYI Technology Co. Ltd. and Peng Bo (2021 Jing 01 CF 818) made by the First Intermediate People's Court of Beijing. (2) A labourer violates the bona fide doctrine under civil law (the Civil Decision of Second Instance of the

Case of Labour Contract between Landscape Architecture Corporation of China and Zhang Hui (2020 Jing 02 CF 6662); (3) the stipulated compensation for the loss to employing units is not liquidated damages (the Civil Decision of Second Instance of the Case of Labour Dispute between Nutrichem Co., Ltd. and Li Yaqian (2017 Jing 01CF 3780); and (4) the stipulated compensation for the loss to employing units is the *hukou* administration expenses (the Civil Decision of Second Instance of the Case of Labour Dispute between Pan Nian and China Aerospace Times Electronics Co., Ltd. (2018 Jing 01CF 4576).

In contrast, although agreement on the registration of *hukou* is also common in Shanghai, the courts often hold that such agreement is invalid. In the Civil Decision of First Instance of the Case of Labour Contract between Shanghai Yaspeed Information Technology Co., Ltd. and Xu Shanshan (2018 Hu 0112 CF 22681), the People's Court of Minhang District, Shanghai held that the agreement on the registration of *hukou* at Shanghai went against the prohibitive provision of the Labour Contract Law of 2012 and shall be *void ab initio.*

In my opinion, the agreement on the registration of *hukou* is tinged with the nature of a civil contract because the registration of *hukou* is not the statutory obligation under the Labour Law of 2018. The capacities of employing units and a labourer do not hinder them from signing a civil contract. In this case, Article 25 of the Labour Contract Law of 2012 does not come into play.

Restitution of Special Benefits

In addition to normal remuneration, an employing unit may offer special benefits, such as a car, a house and housing allowances to a labourer, especially when he is a high-end talent. If they agree on the service period and the labourer revokes the labour contract, the employing unit may refuse to continue to offer such benefits to the labourer and recover the offered benefits from the labourer pro rata. The view was crystallised in the Replies to Issues of Application of Law in Hearing the Cases of Labour Disputes released by the Higher People's Court of Beijing and Beijing Labour and Personnel Dispute Arbitration Commission on 24 April 2017 and the Opinions on Several Issues of Application of the Labour Contract Law released by the Higher People's Court of Shanghai on 3 March 2009.

Additionally, the view was reflected in the Civil Decision of Second Instance of the Case of Labour Contract between Zhong Xiongguang and ESSEMI (2018 Hu 02 CF 1671) made by the Second Intermediate People's Court of Shanghai. In my opinion, the labourers entitled to such benefits are not in a weaker position, and they can bargain on an equal footing with employing units. In this case, the principle of autonomy of will should be followed.

9.2 Administrative Liabilities

Administrative liability means a person's legal obligation to be liable for the legal consequences of violating administrative laws, also known as regulatory law, which is an arm of public law and is the body of law that regulates government decision making. The aims of the Labour law of 2018 are to protect the legitimate rights of labourers, regulate the relationships between employing units and labourers, establish and maintain the labour system meeting the requirements of the socialist market economy and advance economic development and social progress. In achieving those aims, administration law and administrative liability are indispensable. Administrative law plays a vital role in maintaining a harmonious labour relation, implementing labour policies and laws and protecting the legitimate rights of labourers. Generally, the elements of administrative liability include (1) the presence of unlawful acts in contravention of administrative law; (2) the existence of legal grounds; and (3) full capacity.

9.2.1 Types of Administrative Liabilities

9.2.1.1 The Administrative Penalty Law, 2021

The Administrative Penalty Law was officially promulgated by the Standing Committee of the NPC of China on 22 January 2021 and entered into force as of 15 July 2021. For the purpose of the Administrative Penal Law, the term "administrative penalty" means the administrative organs penalise a citizen, legal person or other orgaisations that break the administrative order by derogating rights and interests or imposing obligations. New types of administrative penalties were introduced, such as behavior penalties and qualification penalties. Article 9 of the Administrative Penalty Law provides that types of administrative penalty include disciplinary warning, announced criticism, fine, confiscation of illegal gains or confiscation of unlawful property or things of value, ordering for suspension of production or business, degrading qualifications, temporary suspension or rescission of permit or temporary suspension or rescission of licence, limiting the production and operation, ordering for closing, restricting the practice, administrative detention, and others as prescribed by laws and administrative rules and regulations.

9.2.1.2 The Regulations on Labour Security Supervision and Inspection

Labour security supervision and inspection means the administrative departments for labour security, according to law, supervises and inspects compliance with labour laws and regulations by employing units. In accordance with the Regulations on Labour Security Supervision and Inspection, administrative liability includes order for redressing, fine, written warning, and confiscation of illegal gains.

9.2.1.3 Administrative Provisions of the Labour Law and the Labour Contract Law

Most provisions in Chapter 12 of the Labour Law of 2018 are administrative liability. For example, Article 89 of the Labour Law provides that where the rules related to labour made by an employing unit go against the provisions of the laws and regulations, a competent labour administrative department will give a warning to the employing unit and order it to redress its unlawful act. For another example, Article 90 of the Labour Law of 2018 provides that where an employing unit extends the working hours against the provisions of the Labour Law, a competent labour administrative department will give a warning to the employing unit and order it to redress its unlawful act or may impose a fine on it. The Labour Law centers on the conclusion, performance, modification, revocation and termination of a labour contract, as well as the labour dispatch. Chapter 7 of the Labour Contract Law of 2012 addresses legal liability. For instance, Article 89 of the Labour Contract Law of 2012 provides that where an employing unit fails to deliver the written certificates of revocation or termination of the labour contract, a competent labour administrative department will order it to redress its unlawful act.

9.2.2 *Administrative Remedies*

9.2.2.1 Administrative Reconsideration

Citizens, legal persons or other organisations may apply to administrative organs for administrative reconsideration when they consider that certain specific administrative acts infringe upon their lawful rights or interests. Article of 6 the Admirative Reconsideration Law provides that citizens, legal persons and other organisations may apply for administrative reconsideration according to this Law, if they (1) refuse to accept decisions made by administrative organs to impose on them administrative penalties such as disciplinary warning, fine, confiscation of illegal gains, confiscation of unlawful property or things of value, order for suspension of production or business operation, temporary suspension or rescission of permit, temporary suspension or rescission of licence, and administrative detention; (2) refuse to accept decisions made by administrative organs to impose on them compulsory administrative measures including restriction of the freedom of person and sealing up, distraining or freezing of property; (3)refuse to accept decisions made by administrative organs concerning alteration, suspension or revocation of such documents as permits, licences and qualification certificates; (4) consider that administrative organs infringe upon their lawful decision-making power for operation; (5) consider that administrative organs fail to deal with, according to law, their applications for such documents as permits, licences and qualification certificates, or their applications for examination and approval and registration of affairs concerned, while the applications meet the requirements as prescribed by law; (6) apply to administrative organs requesting them to pay, according to law, pensions for the disabled or for the families of the deceased, social insurance money or the guaranteed minimum for living expenses, but the said organs fail to do so in accordance with law. In accordance with Article 9 of the Administrative Reconsideration Law, citizens, legal persons and other organisations that consider that certain specific administrative acts infringe upon their lawful rights or interests may apply for administrative reconsideration within 60 days from the date when they come to know such administrative acts, except where the time limit for application is more than 60 days as prescribed by law.

9.2.2.2 Administrative Litigation

Where a citizen, a legal person or any other organisation considers that his or its lawful rights and interests have been infringed upon by a specific administrative act of an administrative organ or its personnel, he or it has the right to bring a suit before court. Article 12 of the Admirative Procedure Law provides that citizens, legal persons and other organisations may apply for administrative reconsideration according to this Law if they (1) an administrative sanction, such as detention, fine, rescission of a licence or permit, order to suspend production or business or confiscation of property, which one refuses to accept; (2) a compulsory administrative measure, such as restricting freedom of the person or the sealing up, seizing or freezing of property, which one refuses to accept; (3) infringement upon one's managerial decision-making powers, which is considered to have been perpetrated by an administrative organ; (4) refusal by an administrative organ to issue a permit or licence, which one considers oneself legally qualified to apply for, or its failure to respond to the application; (5) refusal by an administrative organ to perform its statutory duty of protecting one's rights of the person and of property, as one has applied or its failure to respond to the application. (6) cases where an administrative organ is considered to have failed to issue a pension according to law; (7) cases where an administrative organ is considered to have illegally demanded the performance of duties; and (8) cases where an administrative organ is considered to have infringed upon other rights of the person and of property.

9.2.3 Practical Issues Related to Administrative Liability

9.2.3.1 Time Limit of Two Years

Article 20 of the Regulations on Labour Security Supervision and Inspection provides that a competent labour security department may not inspect the act in contravention of labour security laws, regulations or bylaws if it is not found by the competent labour security department, not reported or complained of within two years from the day it occurred. In the Administrative Order of Retrial Reviewing and Hearing Supervision of the Case of Labour and Social Security Administration between Mo Beining and Jiangmen Xinhui District Human Resources and Social Bureau (2019 Yue AA 796), the Higher People's Court of Guangdong held that (1) Mo Beining began to work on 26 September 1997 and resigned on 31 January 2009; (2)on 4 December 2017, Mo Beining reported to Jiangmen Xinhui District Human Resources and Social Bureau that his former employing unit failed to take out the social insurance for him and violated the labour security laws; and (3) it was proper that Jiangmen Xinhui District Human Resources and Social Bureau refused to accept his case.

In contrast, it is generally accepted that the audit of social insurance is not subject to the time limit of two years. In the Administrative Order of Retrial Reviewing and Hearing Supervision of the Case of Labour and Social Security Administration between STS Gems Ltd. and Guangzhou Fanyu District Social Insurance Fund Administration Office (2018 Yue AA 991), the Higher People's Court of Guangzhou held that the time limit for the audit of social insurance was not prescribed by the related laws and regulations, and Article 20 of the Regulations on Labour Security Supervision and Inspection was not applicable to it. Similarly, to demand payment of the Housing Provident Fund was not subject to the time limit of two years, which was reflected in the Administrative Decision of Second Instance of the Case of Other Administrative Disputes between Dongguan Qingxi Xingshi Curtain Plant, Dongguan Housing Provident Fund Management Center and Yang Xinfu (2020 Yue 19 AF 339) made by the Intermediate People's Court of Dongguan.

9.2.3.2 Common Defences

An employing unit may raise the following defences to the supervision and inspection of a competent labour security department: (1) the matter in issue is not the scope of case acceptance of labour security supervision and inspection. The Second Intermediate People's Court of Shanghai held that the restoration of a labour relationship did not fall into the scope of the case acceptance of labour security supervision and inspection in the Administrative Decision of Second Instance of the Case of Labour and Social Security between Li Jiawen and Shanghai Pudong New District Human Resources and Social Security Bureau (2020 Hu 02 AF 168). (2) Erroneous application of the laws.

In the Administrative Decision of Second Instance of the Case of Labour and Social Security Administration between Changsha Human Resources and Social Security Bureau and Changsha Juxing Lightweight Building Materials Co., Ltd. (2020 Xiang 01AF 149), (i) on 17 October 2018, Changsha Human Resources and Social Security Bureau delivering the Order for Rectification within the Specified Time Limit to Changsha Juxing Lightweight Building Materials Co., Ltd., ordered that it pay the contribution of the social insurance for Li Zhenghua, (ii) Changsha Juxing Lightweight Building Materials Co., Ltd. failed to do it within the time limit, (iii) on 15 January 2019, the Decision of Administrative Penalty was made and a fine of 15,000 yuan was imposed on Changsha Juxing Lightweight Building Materials

Co., Ltd. and the Intermediate People's Court of Changsha held that Changsha Human Resources and Social Security Bureau applied the law erroneously and the Decision of Administrative Penalty shall be revoked.

9.3 Criminal Liabilities

Companies may be hardest hit by criminal offences. According to the report released by the Anti-fraud Department of the Tencent Group on 2 February 2021, over 60 cases were found touching "the high-tension wire" of the Group, over 100 persons were fired, and over 40 labourers suspected of criminal offences were handed over to the competent public security bureau. Again, according to the report released by DiDi, an online car-hailing platform in China on 4 February 2021, 64 cases related to fraud and corruption were found in 2020, 70 labourers were fired and 11 persons were handed over to the competent public security bureau.

9.3.1 Elements of Criminal Liability

It is generally accepted among Chinese scholars that criminal liability requires four elements: (1) the subject matter, which means the social relationships protected by criminal law; (2) the guilty act or omission known as the "*actus reus*"; (3) the subject, which means a person (including a natural person or an entity) who has criminal capacity and is subject to criminal law; and (4) the prohibited state of mind or guilty mind (including intention or negligence) known as the "*mens rea*".

9.3.2 Labour-Related Criminal Offences in the Criminal Law

The doctrine of *nulla poena sine lege* is one of the cornerstones of the Criminal Law. Unlawful acts, no matter how severe they are, cannot be penalised unless prescribed by criminal law. Common labour-related criminal offences in the Criminal Law are as follows.

9.3.2.1 Forced Labour

Anyone who forces others to provide labour by violence, threat or restriction of personal freedom shall be sentenced to fixed-term imprisonment of not more than three years or criminal detention and be fined; or if the circumstances are serious, shall be sentenced to fixed-term imprisonment of not less than three years but not more than ten years and be fined. Where any entity commits the offence of forced labour, it shall be fined, and the directly liable person in charge and other directly liable persons shall be punished under the applicable paragraph.[3]

Forced labour is rarely seen. Deaf persons or mute persons are vulnerable to the offence of forced labour. In the Criminal Order of Second Instance of the Case of Forced Labour by Fan and Wang (2014 SI CF 138), the Second Intermediate People's Court of Tianjin confirmed that Fan and Wang, the accused, recruited nine deaf-and-mute persons and forced them to do heavy work by violence and threat and paid nothing to them and upheld the criminal decision of first instance ruling that the accused was sentenced to fixed term imprisonment of three years and was fined 10,000 yuan.

9.3.2.2 Refusal to Pay the Labour Remuneration

Anyone who evades paying the labour remuneration by transferring properties or escaping or has financial ability but refuses to pay the labour remuneration, still refuses to pay after the related governmental departments requires it be paid shall be sentenced to fixed-term imprisonment of not more than three years or criminal detention and/or be fined; or if the circumstances are serious, shall be not less than three years but not more than seven years and be fined. Where any entity commits the offence of refusal to pay the labour remuneration, it shall be fined and the directly liable person in charge and other directly liable persons shall be punished under the applicable paragraph. Where serious consequences are not caused, labour remuneration is paid before public prosecution is instituted, compensation is in place, and criminal punishment may be relieved or exempted.[4] In the Judicial Interpretations of Refusal to Pay the Labour Remuneration of 2013, the meaning of labour remuneration, the criteria for identifying "transferring properties" and "escaping" and other matters were clarified.

9.3.2.3 Commercial Bribery and Corruption

In accordance with Articles 163 and 164 of the Criminal Law, anyone who works in companies, enterprises or other entities takes advantage of his or her position to extract or illegally receives the properties from others and seeks benefits for others shall be sentenced to fixed term imprisonment of not more than three years or criminal detention and be fined, to fixed term imprisonment of not less than three years but not more than ten years and be fined, or fixed term imprisonment of not less than ten years or life imprisonment and be fined; anyone who provides properties or cashes for the employees of other companies or units in order to seek illegal benefits shall be sentenced to fixed term imprisonment of not less than three years or criminal

[3] The Criminal Law, Article 234.

[4] The Criminal Law, Article 276.

detention and be fined; or if the amount is enormous, shall be not less than three years but not more than ten years and be fined.

9.3.2.4 Criminal Offences Related to Property

Article 266 (Fraud), Article 271 (Embezzlement), Article 272 (Misappropriation of Corporate Fund) and Article 276 (Sabotaging Production and Business) are commonly criminal offences in the course of the corporate operation.

Anyone who deprives of public or private properties by fraud shall be sentenced to fixed term imprisonment of not more than three years, criminal detention or public surveillance and/to be fined; in case of the great amount or other serious circumstances, shall be not less than three years but not more than ten years and be fined; or in case of the extremely great amount or other extremely serious circumstances, shall be not less than ten years or life imprisonment, and be fined or his/her properties shall be confiscated. The offence of fraud is common in the field of social insurance.

Embezzlement occurs where employees working in companies, enterprises or other entities take advantage of their positions to embezzle the properties of their employers. Anyone who commits the offence of embezzlement shall be sentenced to fixed term imprisonment of not more than three years, not less than three years but not more than ten years, or not less than ten years or life imprisonment and/or be fined according to the degree of severity.

Misappropriation of Corporate Fund occurs where the employees working in companies, enterprises or other entities take advantage of their positions to misappropriate the corporate fund to personal use or lend it to others but fail to repay it in over three months, where the misappropriated fund is comparatively large and used for profit-making activities, or where the misappropriated fund is used for illegal activities. Anyone who commits the offence of misappropriation of corporate fund shall be sentenced to fixed term imprisonment of not more than three years or criminal detention, not less than three years but not more than seven years, or not less than seven years according to the degree of severity.

Sabotaging Production and Business occurs where anyone, with a view to venting his/her resentment, retaliating or for other private purposes, damages machines and equipment, injure or kill draught animals, or otherwise sabotages production and business, shall be sentenced to fixed term imprisonment of not more than three years, criminal detention, or public surveillance or shall be not less than three years but not more than seven years according to the degree of severity.

9.3.2.5 Trade Secret Infringement

The offence of trade secret infringement, also called misappropriation, is provided in Article 219 of the Criminal Law. Anyone shall be sentenced to fixed-term imprisonment of not more than three years and/or be fined; or if the circumstances are extremely serious, shall be not less than three years but not more than ten years and be fined in case of any of the following circumstance where he: (1)acquires a trade secret by theft, bribery, fraud, duress, electronic invasion or in other improper ways; (2) discloses, uses or allows other people to use the trade secret acquired in the aforesaid ways; and (3) discloses, uses or allows other people to use the trade secret he is in possession of in contravention of the obligation of confidentiality or the requirements of the trade secret owner. Anyone who steals, pries, buys, or illegally provides a trade secret for overseas agencies, organisations or persons shall be sentenced to fixed-term imprisonment of not more than five years and/or to be fined; if the circumstances are serious, shall be not less than five years and be fined.[5]

9.3.3 Practical Issues Related to Criminal Liabilities

9.3.3.1 Common Circumstances that Can Be Prosecuted as the Offence of Fraud

Perversion or concealment of truth can be in various forms. The offence of fraud may be established where (1) a labourer forges medical diagnosis documents to ask for sick leave. In the Criminal Decision of First Instance of the Case of Offence of Fraud (2018 Yue 5122 CF 40), You Ziang obtained a blank medical record from Shenzhen People's Hospital, forged the diagnosis results, asked for sick leave and finally defrauded his employer of sick pay, and the People's Court of Raoping, Guangdong held that You was convicted of the offence of fraud. (2) A labourer fabricates the labour relationship or a work-related injury to swindle the medical insurance benefits. In the Criminal Order of Second Instance of the Case of Offence of Fraud by Meng Hao and Shi Kaikai (2018 Min CF 169), the Higher People's Court of Fujian held that the accused forged the supporting evidence to swindle the medical insurance benefits and was convicted of offence of fraud. Likely, in the Criminal Order of Second Instance of the Case of Offence of Fraud by Ji Wenchao (2017 Hu 01 CF 2205), the accused professed that he was injured in the course of employment, but it was not true, the First Intermediate People's Court of Shanghai held that the accused was convicted of offence of fraud. The Measures of Investigation into Acts Infringing on the Social Insurance Fund, released by Guangdong Province Human Resources and Social Security Department and Guangdong Province Public Security Department on 26 November 2020, also provides that it is illegal to fabricate the labour relationship, work-related injuries and the evidence to swindle the social insurance benefits. Or (3) a labourer forges his or her signature on the labour contract or steals the labour contract to obtain double wages. It was reflected in the Criminal Decision of First Instance of the Case of Offence of Fraud (2017 Zhe 0304 CF 481) made by the People's Court of Ouhai District, Wenzhou and in the Criminal Order of Second Instance of the Case of Offence of Fraud (2014 Xi CSC 00078) made by the Intermediate People's Court of Wuxi, Jiangsu.

[5] The Criminal Law, Article 219.

9.3.3.2 The Effects of Labour Contract on Embezzlement and Misappropriation of Corporate Fund

The subject of the offence of embezzlement and the offence of misappropriation of corporate funds is a person who works in companies, enterprises or other entities. The subject of these offences is qualified if he performs some duties or holds a position in a company, enterprise or other entities, regardless of whether a labour contract was signed or renewed or not. The view can be found in Case No. 516 (The Offence of Embezzlement by Liu Hong) of Reference to Criminal Trial (Issue 65, 2008). The dispatched labourer can also be the subject of these offences. In the Criminal Order of Second Instance of the Case of the Offence of Embezzlement by Zhang Xing and Lin Fa (2019 Min 01 CF 984), Zhang Xing, the accused, was dispatched to Fuzhou Yili Electric Co., Ltd. as the project manager, took advantage of his duties to forge orders of purchase and sold the copper bars to make profits, and the Intermediate People's Court of Fuzhou upheld the criminal decision of first instance ruling that Zhang Xin was convicted of the offence of embezzlement.

Chapter 10
Labour Dispute Settlement

Labour disputes arise out of labour relationships and are the object of labour dispute settlement. In China, the forms of labour dispute settlement are consultation, mediation, labour arbitration and labour dispute litigation. The four forms are integrated, among which consultation and mediation are optional and labour arbitration is compulsory and is a procedural prerequisite to labour dispute litigation. The harmonious labour relationship depends on effective and efficient labour dispute settlement. Limitations in the Civil Code and the Labour Dispute Mediation and Arbitration Law are introduced. The practical issues are also discussed.

10.1 Labour Disputes

10.1.1 Concept and Characteristics of Labour Disputes

Labour disputes can be understood from two senses. In a broad sense, labour disputes are all disputes related to the field of labour law, including disputes of labour contracts, labour insurance and labour administration. In a narrow sense, labour disputes are all disputes arising out of a labour relationship. Labour disputes have the following characteristics: (1) Labour disputes are between employing units and labourers. Commonly, one labourer is employed by one employing unit. Regarding labour dispatch, which is a three-party employment model, a labour service provider and an employing unit will be a coparty (often as a codefendant). (2) For the purpose of labour dispute settlement, the scope of labour disputes is specific and limited. Labour disputes focus on the rights and obligations of labour contracts. (3) Some labour disputes are subject to the general time limit of one year in labour arbitration. The special time limit of one year applies to the disputes related to remuneration, which commences from the termination date of labour contracts. In this chapter, labour disputes in the latter sense will be addressed.

Y. Wang, *Chinese Labour Law*, Understanding China,
https://doi.org/10.1007/978-981-16-8101-1_10

10.1.2 Scope of Labour Dispute Settlement

In 2007, the Labour Dispute Mediation and Arbitration Law was enacted, which is a procedural law in nature. Article 2 of the Labour Dispute Mediation and Arbitration Law sets out the following scope of labour disputes.

Disputes Related to Confirming the Existence of a Labour Relationship

The existence of a labour relationship is a starting point for all legal issues in labour law. Without the existence of the labour relationship, there would be no room for the application of labour law. and the party, which is within the meaning of a labourer in labour law and offers services, would have to resort to the remedies in civil law. To protect the legitimate interests of labourers, disputes related to confirming the existence of the labour relationship are included in the scope of labour dispute settlement.

Disputes Related to Concluding, Executing, Modifying, Revoking and Terminating Labour Contracts

Labour contracts reflect the labour relationships and set out the rights and obligations of the parties to the labour relationship. Before the Labour Contract Law of 2012 was enacted, it was common that employing units did not conclude labour contracts with labourers, which was an obstacle to safeguarding the legitimate interests of labourers. To conclude a written labour contract is the legal obligation of employing units. Failure to do it will enable employing units to pay double monthly salary for the period from the second month to the twelfth month. Where no written contract is concluded after one year elapsed, it is deemed that employing units have entered into nonfixed-term contracts with labourers. In practice, there is doubt about the legitimacy of the execution, modification, revocation and termination of labour contracts, which often gives rise to many disputes.

Disputes Related to Expulsion, Dismissal of Labourers, Resignation from a Post or Quitting a Job

For the purpose of the Regulations of the PRC on Settlement of Labour Disputes in Enterprises, which were annulled in 2011, expulsion applies to labourers who are absent from work frequently for no good reason and in defiance of criticism and education remain absent from work for over 15 days continuously or for over 30 days cumulatively in one year. Dismissal means employing units terminate labour relationships with labourers in accordance with the conditions and procedure provided by law. Resignation from a post means labourers volunteer to resign from their posts but remain employed by their employing units. Quitting a job means labourers terminate the labour relationships with their employing units. The above four concepts are generally used in the context of corporate management. Roughly speaking, expulsion and dismissal have the same effect, which can be seen as termination of labour contracts by employing units and resignation from a post and quitting a job have the same effect, which can be seen as termination of labour contracts by labourers.

Disputes Related to Working Hours, Rest and Holidays, Social Insurance, Welfare, Training and Labour Protection

Three working hour systems are provided by law in China, that is, the standard working system, comprehensive working hour system and irregular working hour system, the latter two of which are subject to approval. Overtime pay and paid annual leave give rise to many disputes. Not all disputes related to social insurance fall within the scope of labour disputes. Labourers may claim the loss from employing units where employing units fail to take out social insurance for the benefit of labourers and cannot pay insurance contributions afterwards and labourers are not entitled to social insurance benefits in accordance to Article 1 of the Interpretations (No. 3) by the Supreme People's Court of Issues Concerning the Application of Law in Hearing the Cases of Labour Disputes, which were adopted by the Judicial Commission of the Supreme People's Court on 12 July 2010, was promulgated and came into effect on 14 September 2010. It should be noted that the claim on the social insurance contribution payment does not fall into the scope of labour disputes. Disputes related to the period of service and stipulated damages are common. Whether stipulated damages can be adjusted is controversial. Failure to provide sufficient labour protection always leads to occupational diseases and industrial injuries.

Disputes Related to Labour Remuneration, Medical Expenses for Industrial Injuries, Economic Compensation or Economic Damages and so on

To pay labour remuneration in full and on time is the primary obligation of employing units. How to pay wages can be found in Provisional Regulations on Wage Payment, which came into effect as of 1 January 1995. Economic compensation shall be paid to labourers where employing units revoke or terminate labour contracts. The termination of labour contracts by agreement entails economic compensation. Economic damages shall be paid to labourers where employing units revoke or terminate labour contracts against the law. In contrast, stipulated damages shall be paid to employing units where labourers breach the confidentiality agreement or noncompete agreement.

Other Disputes Provided by Laws or Regulations

It is a catch-all clause. As time goes on, more types of labour disputes may emerge. For example, disputes related to employment discrimination were rare in the past but are more common today. The clause makes it possible to include new types of labour disputes.

10.1.3 Trends in Labour Disputes

As the economy is developing fast, labour disputes show the following trends.

10.1.3.1 The Parties to Labour Disputes Are Diversified

Traditionally, the labourers involved in labour disputes were manual workers. With the marketing economy growing fast, new types of labourers are emerging, such as senior managers, new generations of migrant workers, college students and retirees. The cyber economy makes network platform operators, internet celebrities, and drivers cooperating with car-hailing platforms more likely to be involved in labour disputes.

10.1.3.2 Various Modes of Employment Give Rise to More Labour Disputes

Labour dispatch, outsourcing, shared employees and blended workforces make employment relationships more complicated. The existence of a labour relationship, the identification of employing units, the sharing of responsibility and the allocation of risks remain unsolved. In particular, labour dispatch involves three parties and two contracts, that is, labour contracts and labour service dispatch contracts. Outsourcing may be concurrently subject to civil law and labour law.

10.1.3.3 Claims of Labourers Are Multiple

Disputes involving a single claim are rare. The low cost of safeguarding labour rights urges labourers to solve all the problems in legal action. Multiple claims may include interest in back pay, apology, economic compensation, economic damages, specific performance of labour contracts and so on.

10.2 Consultation and Mediation

Consultation and mediation are provided by the Labour Dispute Mediation and Arbitration Law, which came into effect as of 1 May 2008. To make the provisions of consultation and mediation more practical, the Regulations on Enterprise Labour Dispute Consultation and Mediation were enacted by the Ministry of Human Resources and Social Security of the People's Republic of China on November 30, 2011. Consultation and mediation are optional.

10.2.1 Consultation

Consultation is the most efficient means of labour dispute settlement. In the case of a labour dispute, one party, an employing unit or labourer, may meet and consult with the other party to solve it. If necessary, the labourer may require the trade union to participate in the consultation or to provide possible help. The labourer may consult with the employing unit in person or a person, or an organisation may be delegated to consult with the employing unit. When one party expresses the willingness to consult, the other party is supposed to give a reply orally or in writing within five days. Failure to do it shows a reluctance to consult. After a successful consultation, a settlement agreement may be signed in writing. However, consultation depends on the voluntariness of the two parties to labour disputes. Even though the settlement agreement is signed, the agreement cannot be enforced by law. If one party fails to perform the settlement agreement within the stipulated period, the party may apply to a mediation organisation for mediation or to a labour and personnel dispute arbitration commission for arbitration. The settlement agreement can be used as evidence in the labour arbitration tribunal if the tribunal confirms that the process of the consultation and the contents of the settlement agreement are valid. In practice, employing units are always in a strong position and reluctant to give in to labourers. It should be noted that consultation is an optional mode of labour dispute settlement.

10.2.2 Mediation

Mediation means a third party mediates between labourers and employing units to reach an agreement on labour disputes. In terms of the nature of the party who presides over the mediation, mediation can be classified into civil mediation, administrative mediation, judicial mediation, and arbitration mediation. Here the civil mediation will be addressed.

10.2.2.1 Establishment of Enterprise Labour Dispute Mediation Commission

Civil mediation is presided over by civil organisations. In accordance with Article 10 of the Labour Dispute Mediation and Arbitration Law, such organisations include the Enterprise Labour Dispute Mediation Commission, Grassroots People's Mediation Organisations, and Mediation Organisations for Labour Disputes at the town or neighborhood level. In accordance with Article 13 and Article 14 of the Regulations on Enterprise Labour Dispute Consultation and Mediation, the mediation commission shall be established by medium and large enterprises. The mediation commission may be established by the branches of medium and large enterprises or small enterprises. The mediation commission consists of labourers' representatives and employing unit's representatives. The director of the mediation commission is a member of the trade union commission or a person who is recommended jointly by labourers and an employing unit.

10.2.2.2 Functions of Enterprise Mediation Commission

The Enterprise Mediation Commission has the following functions: (a) to publicise the laws, regulations and policies related to labour protection; (b) to preside over the mediation of labour disputes in the enterprise; (c) to supervise the execution of consultation and mediation agreements; (d) to recruit, dismiss and administrate conciliators; (e) to coordinate in executing labour contracts and collective contracts and solving the problems with the application of enterprises' rules and regulations; (f) to do research in important plans concerning the interests of labourers; and (g) to assist the enterprise in forming the labour dispute prevention and prewarning system.

10.2.2.3 Procedure for Enterprise Mediation Commission

In case of labour disputes, the party concerned may submit a written mediation application or orally apply to the enterprise mediation commission for mediation, and the mediation commission shall record the request of the party concerned. After receipt of the mediation application, the mediation commission shall confirm whether the labour dispute falls into the scope of the labour dispute settlement and whether both parties agree on mediation. If so, the mediation commission shall accept the labour dispute within 3 days. If not, the mediation commission shall send a written notice of refusal to the applicant. Alternatively, in the absence of such application, the mediation may volunteer to mediate between the two parties to labour disputes provided that they are willing. The mediation of the labour dispute shall be done within 15 days or the period otherwise agreed on. If the two parties reach an agreement, the mediation commission shall make a mediation agreement, and the two parties shall perform it after it is served on the two parties.

10.2.2.4 Binding Force of a Mediation Agreement

The binding force is limited even if the mediation agreement is signed. If one party fails to perform the mediation agreement within the stipulated period, the other party may apply for arbitration. To enhance the binding force of the mediation agreement, both parties may apply to the labour and personnel arbitration commission for review of the mediation agreement. The labour and personnel arbitration commission may issue the mediation paper after confirming that the mediation agreement is valid in terms of process and contents. For the mediation agreement with regard to remuneration, medical expenses of work-related injuries, economic compensation or economic damages, in case employing units fail to perform it, a labourer may apply to the People's Court for a payment warrant. The People's Court may enforce the payment warrant if an employing unit does not raise an objection or the People's Court rejects the objection raised by an employing unit.

10.2.3 *Practical Issues Related to Consultation and Mediation*

10.2.3.1 Lack of Confidence in Consultation and Mediation

Generally, labourers are in a weaker position. When labour disputes arise, both parties are dissatisfied with each other, and neither party is willing to comprise. In fact, there is little chance for two parities to reach a consultation agreement. For mediation, it appears that the enterprise mediation commission is impartial. The fact that the enterprise Mediation commission operates with the support of the enterprise makes labourers show less confidence in mediation.

To enhance the impartiality of mediation, it is suggested that lawyers be introduced into the enterprise mediation commission. The role of lawyers in mediation was confirmed in the Opinions on the Launching-Lawyer-Mediation Pilot Cities by the Supreme Court and the Ministry of Justice in 2017. Lawyers will be impartial in mediating labour disputes between the two parties. The mediation presided over by lawyers will be more convincing.

10.2.3.2 Weakening Authority of Consultation and Mediation

It is common that only after a tiring consultation or mediation can both parties reach an agreement. If the fate of the agreement is uncertain and cannot be enforced by law, consultation and mediation will be less attractive. Labourers would rather resort to the labour and personnel arbitration commission than waste time on consultation or mediation. In accordance with the Law of People's Mediation, juridical confirmation applies to the mediation agreement by the People's Mediation Commission. It is suggested that juridical confirmation extend to enterprise mediation agreements. When both parties may apply to the People's Court for juridical confirmation within 30 days after the mediation agreement came into effect. Once confirmed by the People's Court, it can be enforced if one party refuses to perform the agreement. Alternatively, the mediation agreement can be replaced by the mediation paper after it is reviewed by the labour and personnel arbitration commission.[1]

---

[1] The First Civil Tribunal of the People's Supreme Court (2021).

10.3 Labour Arbitration

10.3.1 Concept and Characteristics of Labour Arbitration

Labour arbitration refers to a mode of labour dispute settlement by which an impartial third party (a labour arbitration commission) arbitrates labour disputes between a labourer and an employing unit and renders an arbitral award.

Labour arbitration has the following characteristics: (1) Being speedy. In accordance with Article 45 of Rules on Labour and Personnel Case Handling, the arbitration of cases by an arbitration tribunal shall be completed 45 days after the arbitration commission accepts an arbitration application. In the case of a complicated case, the extension period shall not exceed 15 days. In contrast, the time limit for the ordinary procedure of the court trial of first instance is 6 months, which is lengthy. (2) Being compulsory. Unlike commercial arbitration, which is optional, labour arbitration is compulsory. The parties to labour disputes cannot detour it to lodge a lawsuit. The reason is that labour disputes are expected to solve in a mild way. (3) Being impartial. The arbitration commission consists of representatives from the local government, trade unions and enterprises. The composition guarantees the impartiality of labour arbitration. It should be noted that labour arbitration is different from commercial arbitration, which is regulated by the Arbitration Law revised in 2017. (4) Be heard in public. In accordance with Article 26 of the Labour Dispute Mediation and Arbitration Law, labour disputes shall be heard in public, with the exception of the cases otherwise agreed upon by the parties or the cases involving state secretes, trade secrets, or personal privacy. In contrast, commercial arbitration is characteristic of privacy and confidentiality and is very attractive to commercial entities.

10.3.2 Composition and Functions of Labour Dispute Arbitral Body

The labour dispute arbitral body is composed of an arbitration commission, offices, arbitration tribunals and arbitrators. An arbitration commission is in charge of labour dispute arbitration, whose functions include (1) recruiting, dismissing full-time or part-time arbitrators; (2) accepting the cases of labour disputes; (3) discussing important or hard cases; and (4) supervising the process of labour dispute arbitration. As mentioned above, the composition of an arbitration commission observes the tripartite principle, that is, the arbitration commission is composed of the labour administration agency on behalf of the local government, the trade union on behalf of labourers, and the economic administration department on behalf of employing units. Offices are responsible for the daily routines of the arbitration commission. On the whole, the functions of an arbitration commission are administrative. An arbitration tribunal is the basic form of handling the cases of labour disputes. Former judges, legal researchers or teachers, those working in the fields of law and human resources, or trade unions for at least five years, and lawyers practicing for over three years are qualified as arbitrators.

10.3.3 Procedure for Labour Arbitration

Application

The party concerned shall submit a written application, and the counterparts of the application correspond to the number of respondents. The written application is expected to include the personal information of the labourer, such as name, sex, age, occupation and address, and the information of the employing unit, claims and facts and grounds on which the claims are based, evidence and the name and address of the witness. If one party has difficulty with literacy, the arbitration commission may take notes of the particulars of the application.

Acceptance

The arbitration commission shall accept the application 5 days after receipt of it and give a written notice of acceptance to the applicant if it meets the requirements of case acceptance. If the arbitration commission deems that such application does not meet the requirements, it shall give a notice of refusal within 5 days after receipt of such application. Labour dispute cases are accepted if they meet all the following requirements: (1) the labour dispute in issue falls into the scope of labour disputes provided by Article 2 of Rules on Labour and Personnel Case Handling; (2) the claims and facts and grounds on which the caims are based are clear and definite; (3) the applicant has a stake in the labour dispute in issue, and the respondent is ascertainable; and (4) the labour dispute is under the jurisdiction of the labour arbitration commission.

Defence

The arbitration commission shall deliver the copy of the application to the respondent within 5 days after it accepts the application for labour disputes. The respondent shall submit a statement of defence to the arbitration commission within 10 days after receipt of the copy of the application. Failure to submit the statement of defence does not affect the procedure for labour arbitration. Within the defence period of 10 days, the respondent may file counterclaims. The counterclaims are handled according to the same procedure as the application.

Constitution of an Arbitral Tribunal and Notice of Case Hearing

The arbitral tribunal shall be constituted 5 days prior to the commencement of the hearing, and the written notice of the hearing date and place shall be served on both parties. With some justification, one party may apply to the arbitration commission for putting off the hearing date. In regard to this, the arbitration commission may at its own discretion make a decision.

Hearing

Both parties shall appear in arbitration on time. If either party, after receiving the written notice of case hearing, refuses to appear in arbitration for no good reason or withdraws from arbitration without permission, in case of an applicant, the case shall be deemed as being withdrawn; in case of a respondent, an arbitral award may be rendered against the respondent by default. Before the case hearing, the clerk shall handle some procedural matters. During the case hearing, the arbitrators listen to claims and defences, presides over the investigation, cross-examination of evidence, arguments, and, if possible, mediation.

Mediation

Mediation can take place after the submission of the application, before the commencement of the hearing or during the hearing. If an agreement is reached after the mediation, a mediation paper shall be prepared by the arbitration tribunal and shall take effect as of the date when it is signed and served on both parties.

Arbitral Award

Generally, the hearing of labour disputes by an arbitral tribunal shall be concluded in 45 days; in the event of hard cases, the time limit can be extended to 60 days. An arbitral award shall specify claims, facts in issue, reasons, results, remedies and dates. The arbitral award shall be signed by arbitrators. Dissenting arbitrators may not sign the award.

10.3.4 Practical Issues Related to Labour Arbitration

10.3.4.1 Scope of Labour Arbitration

The scope of labour arbitration seems to be clear and definite. However, there are some problems with it as new labour disputes emerge. For example, in the first case of employment discrimination on grounds of household register in China, Ms. Jiang Yaping, a graduate from the Law School of Anhui Normal University, wanted to accept an offer of telephonist from Nanjing City Human Resources and Social Security Bureau. She was refused because her household register was not in Nanjing. Nanjing City Human Resources and Social Security Bureau explained that the wage was too low and if she was not a native Nanjinger, too high living expenses would scare her away and further she could not understand the dialect in Nanjing, which was unacceptable to her. On 15 April 2013, she lodged a lawsuit against Nanjing City Human Resources and Social Security Bureau in Xuanwu District People's Court, but on 31 April 2013, the court held that the case was in the nature of a labour dispute and did not accept the lawsuit. On 23 July 2013, she applied to the Nanjing Labour Arbitration Commission for labour arbitration, but the Commission held that the case was not in the nature of a labour dispute, and she did not produce evidence of a labour relationship and refused her application. On 7 August 2013, she filed a lawsuit in Jianye District People's Court, and the court accepted her case. However, on 13 November 2013, the court rejected her lawsuit in that the defendant was not qualified. Then, she lodged the lawsuit against Nanjing Gulou Human and Resources Service Center in Gulou District People's Court, and the court refused the case in that the defendant was not interested in this case. She made an appeal to Nanjing Intermediate People's Court, and in accordance with the Order of (2014) Ning Civil Lawsuit Final No. 5, the court held that the refusal of the case by Gulou District People's Court was wrong. On 30 July 2014, the judge of Gulou District People's Court presided over the mediation, and 11,000 yuan was paid to Ms. Jiang.

In Provisions on Causes of Action for Civil Cases promulgated by the Supreme People's Court, Dispute of Equal Employment Right was added, which would open up the possibility of the lawsuit before court directly. However, it remains uncertain what kind of remedies are available to the party concerned if he was dismissed on grounds of employment discrimination. Some courts tend to hold that the party concerned could first apply for labour arbitration to claim economic damages and then make the lawsuit on the grounds that his personality was infringed on. See the Second Instance Civil Judgment for Equal Employment Right Dispute between Yang Zichen and Hangzhou Dimension Cultural and Creative Co. Ltd. (2020 Zhe 01 Civil Final No. 2725).

It should be noted that after the revocation of or the termination of a labour relationship, the disputes related to the refund of the deposit and the collateral and the disputes related to the transfer of personal records and social insurance also fall into the scope of labour arbitration.

10.3.4.2 Claims Subject to Time Limit

On the one hand, Paragraph 1 of Article 27 of the Labour Dispute Mediation and Arbitration Law provides that the time limit for the application for labour arbitration is one year, which commences from the date when the party concerned knows that or should have known that his rights were infringed on. On the other hand, Paragraph 4 of Article 27 of the Labour Dispute Mediation and Arbitration Law provides that the claim on unpaid remuneration for the duration of the labour relationship is not subject to the time limit in Paragraph 1 of Article 27, provided that, in case of the termination of labour relationship, the application shall be made within one year after the labour relationship is terminated. The former time limit is referred to as the general time limit for labour arbitration, and the latter is a special time limit.

In practice, what claims are subject to the special time limit is always controversial. For example, people take different views on whether the wages for annual leave due and not taken are subject to a special time limit. In accordance with Paragraph 2 of Article 5 in Regulations on Paid Annual Leave for Employees, where an entity fails to offer annual leave to a labourer, it is allowed to do as long as it gets the labourer's consent. For the annual leave due and not taken by the labourer, the entity shall pay the employee 300% of his daily wage for each day of the annual leave due and not taken. Some argue that the wages for the annual leave due and not taken are within the meaning of the wages in the Labour Law of 2018 and accordingly fall into the scope of remuneration, so such wages are subject to the special time limit. In accordance with Article 19 of Answers to Law Application of Labour Dispute Case Hearing issued by Beijing Higher People's Court in 2017, the time limit of the labourer's claim on unpaid wages (200%) for the annual leave due and not taken shall be subject to Paragraph 1 of Article 27 of the Labour Dispute Mediation and Arbitration Law. Likewise, the Liaoning Province Higher People's Court, Jilin Province Higher People's Court, Jiangsu Province Higher People's Court, Shanghai Higher People's Court, Zhejiang Province Higher People's Court, and Anhui Higher People's Court issued similar guidelines.

In contrast, others argue that the wages for the annual leave due and not taken are composed of two parts: one is normal wages, the other (200%) is punitive damages, and therefore, normal wages are subject to the special time limit, and 200% is subject to the general limit. Such an argument prevails in Yunnan Province and Inner Mongolia. According to Ministry of Human Resources and Social Security of the People's Republic of China's Rely to No. 3852 Proposal of the first Session of the 13th National People's Congress, the wages for the annual leave due and not taken fall into the scope of remuneration and are subject to the special time limit, which will protect the labourers' entitlement to paid annual leave. In the Civil Order of Retrial Review and Trial Supervision between COSCO Shipping Seafarer Management Co., Ltd., Dalian Branch and Dong Lijian Seafarer Labour Service Contract Dispute (2019) SPCA No. 6216, the Supreme People's Court of the People's Republic of China held that the wages for annual leave were within the meaning of the remuneration referred to in Paragraph 4 of Article 27 of the Labour Dispute Mediation and Arbitration Law, and Dong Lijian retired on 13 January 2018 and made an application for labour arbitration on 14 March 2018; therefore, the time limit did not elapse, and the argument that Dong Lijian's claim on the wages for annual leave before 2016 exceeded the general time limit could not hold water.

As a whole, the view that the wages for annual leave due and not taken are subject to the general time limit is popular among many provinces. However, such a view will encourage employing units to encroach on the entitlement to the paid annual leave and will pose a big obstacle to the protection of labourers' rights. The reasoning behind this view is that essentially paid annual leave is the vocation and falls into the scope of welfare, and therefore the wages for the annual leave due and not taken is the punitive damages instead of wages. The reasoning is wrong in that the wages for the annual leave due and not taken (200%) is the consideration for the annual leave due and not taken. In fact, the price of the labour provided during vacation is necessarily higher than that during normal working days, similar to fruits out of season definitely cost more than those in season. The wages for annual leave due and not taken (200%) are in the nature of much higher wages, not punitive damages. It is suggested that the wages for annual leave due and not taken be subject to a special time limit.

Similarly, double wages are also controversial. Some argue that double wages are subject to the general time limit, which prevails. Article 21 of the Minutes of Several

Issues on Labour and Personnel Labour Dispute Case Hearing by Shandong Province Higher People's Court and Human Resources and Social Security Department of Shandong Province provides that the double wages in Article 82 of Labour Contract Law is in the nature of punitive damages instead of remuneration. So double wages are subject to the general limit. The courts in Shanghai take the same view. Others argue that they are subject to the special time limit. which is reflected by Article 31 of the Minutes of Hubei Province Higher People's Court Civil Trial Forum.

10.3.4.3 Finality of Arbitral Awards

The finality of arbitral awards means that the arbitral tribunal's decision is final and binding, which is valuable to the parties in terms of time and cost because it minimises the risks of an appeal or challenge of arbitral awards before court. The courts in China manifest the highest respect for the decision of the parties to submit their disputes to arbitration and interfere as little as possible with the freedom of consenting parties to submit disputes to arbitration. Six standards for challenging arbitral awards are set forth in Article 18 of the Arbitration Law, five of which are about the procedure and evidence.

However, the strict finality abovementioned is not true of labour arbitral awards. In China, one-arbitration two-trials is the mechanism of labour dispute settlement; that is, a labour dispute goes through labour arbitration and a trial before the court of first instance and an appeal before the court of second instance. Labour arbitration is a procedural prerequisite for a labour lawsuit. Obviously, one-arbitration two-trials is not efficient. Therefore, the loose finality of labour arbitral awards was introduced in the Labour Dispute Mediation and Arbitration Law. In accordance with Article 47 of the Labour Dispute Mediation and Arbitration Law, the finality of labour arbitral awards applies to (1) claims on remuneration, expenses for medical injuries, economic compensation or damages, the amount of which is not higher than the amount 12 times the minimum wage at the local level and (2) disputes on working hours, rest and vacations, social insurance and so on. The arbitral awards related to the above items are final and binding, which take effect as of the date when they are rendered. However, Article 48 of the Labour Dispute Mediation and Arbitration Law provides that labourers may lodge lawsuits before court within 15 days after receipt of arbitral awards if they object to the arbitral awards specified by Article 47. Article 49 offers employing units the right to annul the arbitral awards on grounds of one of the following events: the mistake in the law application, without arbitral jurisdiction, violation of legal procedure, forged evidence, concealment of the evidence which are important enough to affect the imparity of the awards and arbitrators' bribe-taking.

How to identify and determine the finality of an arbitral award may be problematic. For the disputes specified by Article 48, the arbitral award states that "if you don't accept this Award, you may file a lawsuit before a competent court within 15 days after receipt of this Award." Does a court have power to review the finality of the arbitral award without regard to the statement in it? The answer may be no. With regard to the identification of the finality of an arbitral award, Article 2 of the Interpretations

(No. 4) by the Supreme People's Court of Issues Concerning the Application of Law in Hearing the Cases of Labour Disputes provides that the type of an arbitral award shall be subject to the statement of the finality/nonfinality in the award. Where there is no statement of finality or nonfinality in the award and an employing unit lodges a lawsuit before court, the court shall review the award and accept the lawsuit if it deems the award to be nonfinal or shall refuse the lawsuit and notify the employing unit that it may make an application to the intermediate court for annulling the award if it deems the award to be final. Therefore, the statement of finality/nonfinality is decisive to determine the type of arbitral award.

In the Civil Decision of Hangzhou Intermediate People's Court of the Case of Labour Dispute between Beierfenge Water Treatment Technology (Hangzhou) Co., Ltd. and Chen Feng, the applellant, Chen Feng, argued that the labour arbitral award (2013 No. 293) rendered by Hangzhou Binjiang Labour Dispute Arbitration Commission was related to economic damages and was final in accordance with Article 47 of the Labour Dispute Mediation and Arbitration Law and the court of first instance shall refuse the lawsuit lodged by the appellee, Beierfenge Water Treatment Technology (Hangzhou) Co., Ltd, and that the court of first instance should have reviewed the finality of the arbitral award despite the fact that the arbitral award stated that "if you don't accept this Award, you may file a lawsuit before a competent court within 15 days after receipt of this Award." The appellee argued that the arbitral award was not final in accordance with Paragraph 1 of Article 2 of the Interpretations (No. 4) by the Supreme People's Court of Issues Concerning the Application of Law in Hearing the Cases of Labour Disputes. The Court of Appeal was for the appellee's argument.

However, in the Civil Order (2019 Zhe 0110 First Civil No. 19616), Hangzhou Yuhang District People's Court ruled that the arbitral award rendered by Qingdao Labour Dispute Arbitration Commission shall be final on the grounds that Article 47 of the Labour Dispute Mediation and Arbitration Law applied to the claimed remuneration in spite of the fact that the arbitral award stated that "if either party does not accept the arbitral award, the party may file a lawsuit before a competent court within 15 days after receipt of this Award". Finally, Hangzhou Intermediate People's Court annulled the order and ruled that the arbitral award was final.

10.4 Labour Dispute Litigation

10.4.1 Concept of Labour Dispute Litigation and Causes of Civil Action

Litigation means the act of settling a dispute in a court of law. In this section, litigation related to labour disputes will be addressed. Litigation is the last resort to settle labour disputes. In accordance with Provisions on Causes of Action for Civil Cases promulgated by the Supreme People's Court, the causes of action for labour disputes include disputes related to the confirmation of labour relationships, collective contracts, labour dispatch contracts, part-time labour, claims on labour remuneration, economic compensation, noncompete restrictions, which are under the heading of labour contract disputes, disputes related to social insurance, disputes related to welfare and benefits, and disputes related to personnel affairs.

10.4.2 Scope of Labour Dispute Litigation

In accordance with Article 1 of Judicial Interpretations (No. 1) by the Supreme People's Court of Issues Concerning the Application of Law in Hearing the Cases of Labour Disputes, where a party concerned is dissatisfied with an arbitral award rendered by the labour dispute arbitration commission, the party may lodge a lawsuit before court of law provided that the arbitral award is about (1) the dispute between labourers and employing units during the performance of the labour contract, or (2) the dispute that arises after the labour relationship is formed in spite that there is no written labour contract between labourers and employing units, or (3) the dispute related to the claims on pensions, medical expenses, industrial injury insurance benefits and other social insurance premium. At the same time, exceptions are provided by Article 2 of Judicial Interpretations (No. 1) by the Supreme People's Court of Issues Concerning the Application of Law in Hearing the Cases of Labour Disputes. The court has no jurisdiction to hear the following disputes: (1) related to the payment of social insurance benefits; (2) related to the transfer of public houses; (3) related to the dissatisfaction with expert conclusion of gradation of disability caused by work-related injuries and occupational diseases; (4) with a household or personal employer and housekeeper; (5) related to the apprenticeship; and (6) between the rural contracting household and farming workers.

10.4.3 Procedure for Litigation

10.4.3.1 Procedure for Labour Dispute Litigation

With regard to the arbitral award specified by Article 47 of the Labour Dispute Mediation and Arbitration Law, a labourer who is dissatisfied may lodge a lawsuit before court within 15 days after receipt of the arbitral award. In addition, either party concerned may lodge a lawsuit before court within 15 days after receipt of the arbitral award that is not final.

In accordance with the Civil Procedure Law of the People's Republic of China, the procedure for labour dispute ligation is as follows.

Ordinary Procedure at First Instance

Lodging and Accepting a Lawsuit

A party concerned shall lodge a labour dispute lawsuit that meets all of the following requirements: the plaintiff is a natural or legal person or any other organisation with a direct interest in the case; the defendant is ascertainable; claims, facts and grounds are specific; the case is within the scope of labour disputes accepted by the People's Court and the court has jurisdiction over it. The plaintiff shall submit a written complaint stating the identification information of the plaintiff and the defendant, the claims, facts and grounds, the evidence and the names and domiciles of witnesses.

Prehearing Preparations

The court shall, within five days after docketing a case, serve a copy of the written complaint on the defendant, and the defendant shall submit a written statement of defence 15 days after receiving the complaint. The court shall, within five days after receipt of the written statement of defence, serve a copy of it on the plaintiff. The defendant's failure to submit a written statement of defence does not affect the hearing of the case by court.

Hearing

The court shall hear the case in public, except those related to any state secrets, personal privacy or as otherwise provided by law. The court investigation is conducted in the following order: the parties each present a statement, witnesses are notified of their rights and duties, witnesses testify, and the statements of absent witnesses are read; documentary evidence, physical evidence, audio-visual recordings and electronic data are adduced, expert opinions are read, transcripts of survey are read.

The court debate is conducted in the following order: the plaintiff and his representative present their case, the defendant and his representative present their arguments, a third party and his representative present their case or their arguments, and debate among the parties. At the end of the court debate, the plaintiff, defendant and third party make final statements. After the end of the court debate, a judgment shall be entered in accordance with law. Mediation is allowed before a judgment is entered.

Procedure for Appeal

If a party concerned is dissatisfied with a judgment or ruling by the court of first instance, the party may file an appeal before an appeal court, which is at the next high level. An appellant shall submit a written appeal, which includes the information of an appellant and an appellee, the claims in appeal and grounds for the appeal. An appellee shall, within 15 days after receipt of the copy of the written appeal, submit the written statements of defence. The appeal court shall review the facts and the application of law in relation to the claims in appeal. After hearing, the appeal court shall handle the appeal in accordance with the following circumstances: dismissing the appeal and sustaining the original judgment or ruling, reversing, revoking or modifying the original ruling, or issuing a ruling to revoke the original judgment and remand the case to the original trial court for retrial.

10.4.3.2 Procedure for Annulation of Final Labour Arbitral Awards

With regard to the arbitral award specified by Article 47 of the Labour Dispute Mediation and Arbitration Law, an employing unit may lodge a lawsuit to annul it before court within 30 days after receipt of the arbitral award on grounds of one of the following events: the mistake in the law application, without jurisdiction, the violation of legal procedure, forged evidence, the concealment of the evidence which are important enough to affect the imparity of the awards and arbitrators' bribe-taking.

The Civil Procedure Law keeps silent on the procedure for annulation of final labour arbitral awards. In accordance with Article 23 of Judicial Interpretations (No. 1) by the Supreme People's Court of Issues Concerning the Application of Law in Hearing, the Cases of Labour Disputes provides that where the employing unit makes an application to the intermediate court for annulling a final labour arbitral award, a collegial panel shall be formed to hear the case in public. The collegial panel may decide to try the case by record if no new facts, evidence or grounds are found after reviewing case files, making investigations and conducting enquiries. Of course, the intermediate court may mediate between two parties.

10.4.4 Practical Issues Related to Litigation

10.4.4.1 Understanding of Inseparability of Added Claims

In accordance with Article 14 of Judicial Interpretations (No. 1) by the Supreme People's Court of Issues Concerning the Application of Law in Hearing the Cases of Labour Disputes, where a party concerned adds claims after the people's court accepts a labour dispute case and the added claims are inseparable from the labour dispute in issue, the added claims shall be adjudicated together with the labour dispute in issue. Where the added claims arise from a separate labour dispute, the court shall notify that the party concerned shall make an application for labour arbitration first.

Obviously, the inseparability of added claims from the labour dispute in issue is a decisive factor in the consolidation of actions. However, it remains controversial what inseparability is. Theoretically, if the added claims and the claims in issue arise from the same fact, it can be said that the added claims are inseparable from the claims in issue. It is supported by the Opinions on Several Issues of Hearing Labour Dispute Cases by Fujian Province Higher People's Court in 2001. However, the understandings of the inseparability of added claims are different among the courts.

Most courts fail to state the reasons why they think the added claims are inseparable or separable from the claims in issue, which will make the inseparability of added claims more obscure and uncertain. In the Civil Decision of Second Instance of the Case of Labour Dispute between Teng Liheng v Dalian Tenglong Tengchuan Car Sales Service Co. Ltd. (2020 Liao 02 Civil Final No. 2950), the appellant claimed the economic compensation on grounds of the termination of the labour contract as well as the economic damages on grounds of the illegal termination of the labour contract, the court of first instance held that the economic damages were added and arose from the termination of the labour contract, and shall be adjudicated altogether, which was affirmed by Dalian Intermediate People's Court.

If the amount of the claim before the court of law is higher than that of the claims stated in the application for labour arbitration, the claim before the court of law is deemed inseparable from the claim in labour arbitration. In the Civil Decision of Second Instance of the Case of Labour Dispute between Guangzhou RISTON Cosmetic Manufacturing Co., Ltd. and Lin Wangting (2020 YUE 01 Civil Final 14862), which was made by Guangzhou Intermediate People's Court, Lin Wangting claimed the year-end bonus of 2124 yuan in labour arbitration, but claimed the year-end bonus of 12,124 yuan before the court of first instance, the court of first instance held that Guangzhou RISTON Cosmetic Manufacturing Co., Ltd. paid the year-end bonus of 12,214 yuan to Lin Wangting. Guangzhou RISTON Cosmetic Manufacturing Co., Ltd. lodged an appeal against Lin Wangting before Guangzhou Intermediate People's Court and argued that Lin's claim before the court of first instance exceeded his claim in labour arbitration and that the court of first instance had no jurisdiction over Lin's claim. Guangzhou Intermediate People's Court held that the increase in the year-end bonus did not impair the inseparability of the claim itself and rejected the appeal. The decision of the court of first instance was affirmed. The same view was taken by Shandong Higher People's Court in the Retrial of the Case of Labour Contract between Zhao Ruiqing and Hunan Tianyan Machinery Stocks Co. Ltd. (2020 LU Civil Retrial No. 340), where the addition of the balance of wages from December 2013 to May 2014, which was not stated in the application in labour arbitration, was inseparable.

Given that there may be different understandings of the inseparability of added claims among different courts, it is strongly suggested that all possible claims be made in labour arbitration.

10.4.4.2 Cohesive Mechanism Between Labour Arbitration and Labour Litigation

One-arbitration-two trials is the regime of labour dispute settlement in China. Almost all labour disputes shall go through labour arbitration first. In some sense, labour arbitration is under the review and supervision of labour litigation. In practice, the arbitration commissions and the courts have different understandings of the Labour Dispute Mediation and Arbitration Law, the Labour Law of 2018 and the Labour Contract Law of 2012 and the judicial interpretations issued by the Supreme People's Court, which is a big obstacle to a stable expectation of labour protection.

In 2017, the Ministry of Human Resources and Social Security of the People's Republic of China and the Supreme People's Court of the People's Republic of China jointly issued the Opinions on Enhancing the Construction of Cohesive Mechanism between Labour and Personnel Dispute Arbitration and Litigation, which laid down the following requirements: unification of the scope of arbitration and litigation and of standards for law application; regulation of cohesion of case acceptance, conservatory measures and enforcement between arbitration and litigation; establishment of joint conference, information sharing, guides to hard case handling, and joint training.

In this regard, a series of implementation opinions were issued by local Human Resources and Social Security Departments and Higher People's Courts in Beijing, Shandong, Liaoning, Jiangsu and other provinces. Particularly, on 24 April 2017, the Beijing Higher People's Court and Beijing Labour and Personnel Arbitration Commission jointly released Answers to the Law Application of Labour Dispute Case Hearing, which addressed many practical issues, such as the meaning and scope of fundamental changes in circumstances and double labour relationships. On 3 July 2017, the Minutes of Forum for Jiangsu Province Labour and Personnel Dispute Difficult Issues addressed the confirmation of labour relationships, the execution and termination of labour contracts and other issues.

To harmonise different opinions on the same issues between courts and labour arbitration commissions in different provinces, it is strongly advised that juridical interpretations and a series of guiding cases related to labour disputes be issued by the Supreme People's Court of the People's Republic of China, which will greatly advance the unification of the understanding and application of the labour law across China.

10.5 Limitation

Vigilantibus non dormientibus aequitas subvenit, which means equity aids the vigilant and not those who slumber on their rights and is a maxim in equity. There is no law of equity in China, but limitations play the same role. Unlike some countries that have separate limitation acts, there are provisions of limitation scattered in different laws in China.

10.5.1 General Provisions of Limitations of Actions in the Civil Code

Chapter 9 of the Civil Code is titled Limitations of Actions. Paragraph 1 of Article 188 of the Civil Code provides that the time limit for applying for the People's Court to protect civil rights is three years, unless otherwise provided by law. Furthermore, Article 198 of the Civil Code provides that where other laws provide for the time limit for arbitration, such provisions shall prevail and where there are no such provisions, the time limit for actions shall apply.

Under Chinese law, the time limits, commencement, suspension and interruption of causes are legally prescribed, any agreement to changes of which is invalid and any prior waiver of benefits from limitations of actions are prohibited. In accordance with Article 193 of the Civil Code, People's courts may not invoke the provisions of limitations of actions on their own initiative, so the lapse of time limits of actions doesn't mean that the claims are barred unless the defence of time limits are invoked. In fact, there are no provisions in regard to the limitation of arbitration except for Article 594 of the Civil Code, Article 82 of the Labour Law of 2018 and Article 27 of the Labour Dispute Mediation and Arbitration Law. Article 74 of the Arbitration Law has the same wording as Article 198 of the Civil Code and does not specify the time limits for arbitration. It can be concluded that in China, the provisions of limitation of actions generally apply to commercial arbitration, although actions and arbitration are two different things.

10.5.2 Limitations in Labour Arbitration

Following the doctrine of *lex specialis derogat legi generali*, Chapter 9 of the Civil Code does not apply to labour arbitration, which has special provisions.

10.5.2.1 Time Limit of 60 Days

Article 82 of the Labour Law of 1995 provided that one party who applied for arbitration shall submit a written application to a labour dispute arbitration commission within 60 days from the date when a labour dispute arose. In accordance with Article 85 of Opinions on Several Issues regarding Implementation of the Labour Law of the PRC in 1995, the date when a labour dispute arose refers to the date when the party concerned knew or should have known that his rights were infringed on. The short period and the commencement of the time limit of 60 days make it impractical for labourers in a weak position to resort to labour arbitration. Therefore, in 2006, the Interpretations (No. 2) by the Supreme People's Court of Issues Concerning the Application of Law in Hearing the Cases of Labour Disputes were passed, Article 1 of which provides that the date when a labour dispute arose referred to by Article 82 of the Labour Law of 2018 is determined as follows: (1) the date when a written notice was delivered where a dispute of wage payment arose during the period of the labour relationship and employing units can prove that the labourer was given a written notice that they refuse to pay the wages. Where employing units fails to prove that, the date when the labourer claims on his rights is the date when a labour dispute arose. (2) the date when the labourer claims on his rights is the date when a labour dispute arose, where the labour dispute is related to cancellation or termination of the labour relationship and employing units fail to prove the date when the labourer received the written notice of cancellation or termination of labour relation, and (3) the date when employing units promise to pay is the date when a labour dispute arose, where the labour dispute is related to the payment of wages, economic compensation and benefits after the revocation or termination of the labour relationship and a labourer can prove the date when employing units promise so is a specific date the revocation or termination of the labour relationship. The time limit of 60 days remains unchanged even if the Labour Law was revised in 2009 and 2018.

10.5.2.2 Time Limit of One Year

Article 27 of the Labour Dispute Mediation and Arbitration Law provides that the time limit of application for labour arbitration is one year and that the time limit commences on the date when the party concerned knew or should have known that his or her rights were infringed on. The time limit of one year is referred to as the general time limit. The time limit is interrupted where one party makes a claim, resorts to relevant authorities for remedies, or agrees to discharge the obligations. The time limit commences anew from the time of interruption. The time limit is suspended in cases where due to force majeure or other justified reasons, the party concerned is unable to apply for labour arbitration during the time limit specified in Paragraph 1 of Article 27. The time limit resumes on the day when the grounds for the suspension of the time limit is eliminated.

A labour dispute arising from remuneration in arrears during the period of a labour relationship is not subject to the general time limit, provided that an application for labour arbitration shall be made within one year after the labour relationship is terminated.

10.5.3 Practical Issues Related to Time Limit of Labour Dispute Arbitration

10.5.3.1 Choice of Time Limit

The time limit provided by the Labour Law of 2018 and the time limit provided by the Labour Dispute Mediation and Arbitration Law appear to contradict each other. In fact, the two time limits have different scopes of application. The Labour Dispute Mediation and Arbitration Law entered into effect as of 1 May 2008. With regard to the disputes that arose before 1 May 2008, the provisions related to the time limit of one year in the Labour Dispute Mediation and Arbitration Law are not retroactive and do not apply. In other words, the disputes that arose before 1 May 2008 were subject to the time limit of 60 days. In the Civil Decision of Second Instance of the Case of Labour Dispute between Wang Yonglei and Zhejiang Province Second Construction Group Co., Ltd. (2020 Zhe 02 Final 1663), the court held that the labour dispute in issue arose on 24 April 2003, when the Labour Dispute Mediation and Arbitration Law did not enter into effect, and that following the doctrine that *lex prospicit non respicit*, the time limit provided by the Labour Dispute Mediation and Arbitration Law does not apply.

10.5.3.2 Understanding of Relevant Authorities in Article 27

To interrupt the time limit, the requirements specified in Article 27 have to be met. The wording of relevant authorities is obscure. In practice, some labourers tend to resort to the local government or the public security bureau for remedies, which cannot interrupt the time limit. In the Civil Order of Retrial Examination and Trial Supervision of the Case of Labour Dispute between Ma Chuanmei and Shandong Rongbang Anticorrosion Engeering Co. Ltd. (2017 Lu CA 361), Higher People's Court of Shandong Province held that the fact that the party concerned lodged complaints to the local government, the committee of the Party, the procuratorate, the local Bureau for Petitions, law firms in the form of letters and visits does not interrupt the time limit in that such organisations are not in a position to handle labour disputes, and that labour dispute mediation commissions, labour dispute arbitration commissions, labour supervision departments, labour unions and people's courts are within the meaning of the relevant authorities in Article 27 of the Labour Dispute Mediation and Arbitration Law.

Reference

The First Civil Tribunal of the People's Supreme Court. (2021). *Understanding and Application of New Judicial Interpretations of the People's Supreme Court on Labour Disputes*. Beijing: People's Court Press [in Chinese].

Appendix

Guiding Cases[1]

(1) **Guiding Case No. 18**

Zhongxing Telecom Hangzhou Co., Ltd. v Wang Peng (the Case of Labour Contracts)

(Issued on 8 November 2013 as deliberated and adopted by the Judicial Committee of the Supreme People's Court).

Keywords: Civil, Labour Contracts, Unilateral Termination.

Gist of Decision: A labourer ranks as the last place of the performance assessment of the employing unit, which does not mean he is "incompetent", and he does not meet the prescribed condition of unilateral termination of labour contracts. The employing unit may not terminate the labour contract with him or her on grounds of the said ranking.

Relevant Legal Provisions:

Articles 39 and 40 of the Labour Contract Law of 2012.

Case Background:

In July 2005, Wang Peng, the defendant, was employed by Zhongxing Telecom Hangzhou Co., Ltd. (ZTC), the plaintiff. The labour contract stipulated that the defendant worked as a salesperson, and the basic monthly wage was 3000 Yuan. According to the Measures of Employee Performance Assessment, there were four

[1] With a view of treating like case alike, the Guiding Cases were released by the Supreme People's Court of the PRC. In accordance with Article 7 of the Regulations by the Supreme People's Court on Case Guiding Work, the courts at different levels shall refer to the Guiding Cases when hearing the similar cases. The Guiding Cases are translated by the author.

Y. Wang, *Chinese Labour Law*, Understanding China,
https://doi.org/10.1007/978-981-16-8101-1

grades: S, A, C1 and C2. Employees who ranked as Grade S accounted for 20%, employees who ranked as Grade A 70%, and employees who ranked as Grade C (C1 and C2) 10%. Employees who ranked as Grade C2 were considered incompetent. Wang Peng worked as a salesperson in the department of distribution. In January 2009, he was transferred to the East China District. In the second half of 2008, the first half of 2009 and the second half of 2010, Wang Peng ranked as Grade C2. ZTC treated him to be incompetent, and after the transfer to a new job, he was thought to be incompetent. Accordingly, ZTC paid him economic compensation and terminated the labour contract.

On 27 July 2011, Wang Peng made the application for labour arbitration, and the arbitral award was made that it was illegal for ZTC to terminate the labour contract. On 11 December 2011, ZTC lodged a lawsuit against Wang Peng.

Decision: The People's Court of Binjiang District, Hangzhou city, made a decision in favor of Wang Peng, where the court held that ZTC's termination of the labour contract was illegal.

Grounds of Decision: To protect the legal rights and interests of labourers and construct and develop harmonious and stable labour relationships, the conditions of employing the unit's unilateral termination of labour contracts were prescribed by the Labour Law and the Labour Contract Law. ZTC should take the burden of proof that Wang Peng was incompetent for his job and after the transfer he was still incompetent for a new job. According to the Measures of Employee Performance Assessment, the employees who ranked as Grade C (C1 and C2) accounted for 10%. However, C2 did not mean that Wang Peng was not competent for his job. There was no sufficient evidence that he was not competent for his job. In addition, the decision was made against ZTC.

(2) **Guiding Case No. 28**

Hu Kejin's Refusal to Pay Remuneration (Crime of Refusal to Pay Remuneration)

(Issued on 23 June 2014 as deliberated and adopted by the Judicial Committee of the Supreme People's Court).

Keywords: Criminal, Crime of Refusal to Pay Remuneration, Units or Individuals who are ineligible Employers.

Gist of Decision:

a. Any unit or individual who is not eligible for employment shall be convicted of the crime of refusal to pay remuneration if the said unit or individual employs labourers illegally, refuses to pay remuneration and again refuses to pay remuneration in spite of the governmental instruction.
b. The payment of remuneration by other units or individuals on behalf of the guilty unit or individual does not affect the criminal liability.

Relevant Legal Provisions:

Paragraph 1 of Article 276 of the Criminal Law.

Case Background:

In December 2010, Hu Kejin, the accused, employed many rural workers to construct landscape engineering and paid 510,000 yuan. After the completion of the construction, the accused defaulted on the wages of 120,000 yuan. On 9 June 2011, the accused was instructed by the Shuangliu Human Resources and Social Security Bureau to pay wages to rural workers. However, the accused booked a flight and fled. On 30 June 2011, the prime contractor paid wages of 120,000 yuan on behalf of the accused. On 12 July 2011, the accused was arrested in Zhejiang Province.

Decision: Hu Kejin was convicted of the crime of refusal to pay remuneration, was sentenced to one-year imprisonment and was fined 20,000 yuan.

Grounds of Decision: The accused was not eligible for an employer and had no construction qualification, which would not prevent him from taking the criminal liability.

(3) **Guiding Case No. 40**

Sun Lixing v Tianjin City Industries Park Labour Bureau (Administrative Confirmation of Identification of Work-related Injuries)

(Issued on 25 December 2014 as deliberated and adopted by the Judicial Committee of the Supreme People's Court).

Keywords: Administrative Confirmation of Work-related Injuries, Arising out of the Employment, Place of work, Work-related Negligence.

Gist of Decision:

a. Arising out of the employment prescribed in Paragraph 1 of Article 14 of the Work-related Injury Insurance Regulations of 2010 means that there exists a relationship between the injury and the work.
b. The place of work prescribed in Paragraph 1 of Article 14 of the Work-related Injury Insurance Regulations of 2010 means the place where a labourer works and includes, in the case of many places of work, the reasonable area where a labourer shuttles back and forth.
c. Negligence in the course of employment other than intentional crimes, intoxication or drug abuse, self-mutilation or suicide mentioned in Article 16 of the Work-related Injury Insurance Regulations of 2010 does not affect the identification of work-related injuries.

Relevant Legal Provisions:

Paragraph 1 of Article 14 and Article 16 of the Work-related Injury Insurance Regulations of 2010.

Case Background:

Sun Lixing, the plaintiff, argued that he fell down on the ground and was injured in the course of employment in the place of work and during working hours, and his injury fell into the scope of work-related injuries prescribed by the Work-related Injury Insurance Regulations of 2010. The decision made by the Tianjin City Industries Park Labour Bureau that his injury was not in the nature of work-related injuries was wrong, the decision was based on the wrong facts, and the Work-related Injury Insurance Regulations of 2010 were applied in an incorrect way.

Tianjin City Industries Park Labour Bureau, the defendant, responded that the plaintiff's injury did not arise out of employment but was incurred by his carelessness and that there was no obvious causal relationship between the injury and employment.

After the hearing, the court found that Sun Lixing was sent to Beijing Airport to pick up a client on 10 June 2003, and when the plaintiff step down from the door footsteps, he fell down and was injured. The Tianjin City Industries Park Labour Bureau made the administrative decision that his injury was not in the nature of work-related injuries.

Decision:

The First Intermediate People's Court of Tianjin made the decision that the administrative decision by Tianjin City Industries Park Labour Bureau shall be revoked and that Tianjin City Industries Park Labour Bureau shall remake an administrative decision within 60 days after the court decision's entry into force. The appeal to the Higher People's Court of Tianjin was rejected.

Grounds of Decision:

a. **Whether the place where Sun Lixing fell down was the place of work?**

In accordance with Paragraph 1 of Article 14 of the Work-related Injury Insurance Regulations of 2010, the injuries arising out of employment in the place of work and during working hours shall be identified as work-related injuries. The place of work in this Article means the place that is related to the duty of a labourer, and in the case of more than one place of work, the reasonable area where a labourer shuttles back and forth. In this case, the office on the 8th floor of the business building was his place of work, and the place where the car he would drive was parked was another place of work. The car was parked out of the door to the 1st floor of the business building. The steps between the 8th floor and the 1st floor were a reasonable area between two places of work and should be considered as his place of work. The conclusion that the place where Sun Lixing fell down and was injured was not his place of work went against the legislative purposes of the Work-related Injury Insurance Regulations of 2010.

b. **Whether Sun's injury arose out of the employment?**

Arising out of the employment prescribed in Paragraph 1 of Article 14 of the Work-related Injury Insurance Regulations of 2010 means there is a certain relationship between the injury and the employment. To pick up the client, Sun Lixing had to move out of the building center to the place where the car was parked. His movement was closely related to his employment and was not for his benefit. It was groundless that the Tianjin City Industries Park Labour Bureau defended that there was no direct causal relationship between his injury and his employment.

c. **Does Sun's negligence affect the identification of work-related injuries?**

There are three exceptions to work-related injuries, and according to Article 16 of the Work-related Injury Insurance Regulations of 2010, any of the following events shall not be identified as a statutory work-related injury or a presumed work-related injury: (1) intentional crime; (2) intoxication or drug abuse; or (3) self-mutilation or suicide. The negligence of a labourer is not among the three exceptions. The aims of work-related injury insurance are to diversify risks arising out of employment and provide labour security. It is against the basic principle of no-fault compensation to treat the labourer's carelessness as an exception to work-related injuries.

(4) **Guiding Case No. 69**

Wang Mingde v Leshan City Human Resources and Social Security Bureau (Identification of Work-related Injuries).

(Issued on 19 September 2016 as deliberated and adopted by the Judicial Committee of the Supreme People's Court).

Keywords: Administrative Litigation, Identification of Work-related Injuries, Procedural Administrative Act, Case Acceptance.

Gist of Decision:

The court shall accept the dispute over a procedural administrative act provided that the personal rights or property rights are, the affected party believes, damaged by the procedural act made by the administrative authority and are materially and physically influenced by the act and that the affected party cannot lodge litigation against the related substantive administrative act.

Relevant Legal Provisions :

Articles 12 and 13 of the Administrative Procedure Law.

Case Background:

Wang Mingde, the plaintiff, was son of Wang Leibing. His father, Wang Leibing, was employed by the Emeishan branch of Sicuan Jiabao Asset Management Group Co., Ltd. On 18 March 2013, Wang Leibing died in a traffic incident. The reason why the motorcycle he rode on fell down and rolled over could not be identified, so the traffic police of Emeishan issued the certificate of traffic incident, which stated that on 18 March 2013, Wang Leibing rode on his motorcycle and ran into the edge of the median strip and that the motorcycle rolled over and over on the median trip and Wang Leibing died in the accident.

On 10 April 2013, Emeishan branch, the third party, applied to Leshan City Human Resources and Social Security Bureau for administrative confirmation of work-related injuries and presented the certificate of traffic incident to it. On the same day, the defendant issued the notice of suspension to the plaintiff and the third party. On 24 June 2013, the plaintiff sent the application of resumption to the defendant, and the application was rejected. On 30 July, the plaintiff lodged litigation to revoke the notice of suspension made by the defendant.

Decision:

The court of first instance made the administrative decision in favor of the plaintiff and held that the notice of suspension made by the defendant was revoked. The defendant was not satisfactory with the administrative decision of first instance and appealed to the Intermediate People's Court of Leshan and then withdrew its appeal, and the administrative decision of first instance came into force.

Grounds of Decision:

a. **Whether the notice of suspension was actionable**

The court of first instance held: (1) that generally the notice of suspension made by the defendant was in the nature of a procedural administrative act in the course of administrative confirmation of work-related injuries; (2) that the notice of suspension was not actionable provided that the procedural administrative act was not final or did not substantively affect the rights and obligations of the party subject to administration; and (3) that the notice of suspension was actionable in this case where it was final and substantively affected the rights and obligation of the party subject to administration, who could not lodge a lawsuit against the related substantive administrative act.

In practice, the certificate of traffic incidents was not actionable, and the affected party, who was subject to administration, could not lodge an administrative lawsuit against the competent traffic police authority. It was legal for the competent traffic police authority to issue the certificate of traffic incidents provided that the cause of traffic incidents could not be identified. In this case, the certificate of traffic incidents was one of the conclusions defined in Paragraph 3 of Article 20 of the Work-related Injury Insurance Regulations of 2010.

b. **Whether the notice of suspension was revoked**

The court of first instance held: (1) that in accordance with Paragraph 3 of Article 20 of the Work-related Injury Insurance Regulations of 2010, the prescribed period was suspended where the conclusions made by judicial or administrative organs were necessary for the administrative confirmation of work-related injuries but such organs failed to make them; (2) that the third party had presented the certificate of traffic incidents, which was one of the conclusions prescribed by law, and it was not legal or groundless for the defendant to issue the notice of suspension; and (3) the notice of suspension should be revoked and the administrative confirmation should be resumed.

(5) Guiding Case No. 94

Chongqing Fuling Zhida Property Management Co., Ltd. v Chongqing Fuling Human Resources and Social Security Bureau (the Case of Administrative Confirmation of Social Security).

(Issued on 20 June 2018 as deliberated and adopted by the Judicial Committee of the Supreme People's Court).

Keywords: Administration, Administrative Confirmation, Presumed Work-related Injuries, Acting Bravely for a just Cause.

Gist of Decision:

An injury due to fighting against crimes shall be presumed to be a work-related injury, which falls into the scope of injuries caused by protection of public interests defined in Paragraph 2 of Article 15 of the Work-related Injury Insurance Regulations of 2010.

Relevant Legal Provisions:

Paragraph 2 of Article 15 of the Work-related Injury Insurance Regulations of 2010.

Case Background:

Luo Renjun was employed as a security guard by Chongqing Fuling Zhida Property Management Co., Ltd. (hereinafter referred to Fuling company). On 24 December 2011, Luo Renjun was working at the apartment complexes, where Fuling company provided services. At approximately 08:30, Luo Renjun heard loud shouts near the Hongfu Building. Luo Renjun blocked the robber's way and fought against him, finally fell down from the footsteps and was injured. On 12 June 2012, Luo Renjun made the application for Chongqing Fuling Human Resources and Social Security Bureau (hereinafter referred to Fuling bureau) for confirmation of work-related injuries and later presented the proof of Brave Act for a Just Cause to Fuling bureau. On 8 August 2012, the Administrative Decision of Work-related Injury Confirmation (2012 No. 676) was made, by which Luo's injury was identified as a statutory work-related injury. Fuling company was not stratified at the administrative decision and lodged an administrative lawsuit. In the course of the lawsuit, Fuling Bureau revoked the Administrative Decision of Work-related Injury Confirmation (2012 No. 676) and made the Administrative Decision of Work-related Injury Confirmation (2013 No. 524), by which Luo's injury was identified as the presumed work-related injury. Fuling was not satisfied at the Administrative Decision of Work-related Injury Confirmation (2013 No. 524) and applied to Chongqing Human Resources and Social Security Bureau for reconsideration. On 21 August 2013, the Administrative Decision of Work-related Injury Confirmation (2013 No. 524) was affirmed. Then, Fulin company thought that the Work-related Injury Insurance Regulations of 2010 were applied in a wrong way and lodged an administrative lawsuit against Fulin company.

Additionally, the court found that the competent authority of Fuling District issued the Notice of Praising Luo Renjun for Brave Acts.

Decision:

The People's Court of Fuling District made the administrative decision, holding that the claim was rejected that the Administrative Decision of Work-related Injury Confirmation (2013 No. 524) was revoked. Neither the Fuling company nor the Fuling bureau appealed to the court of second instance, and the administrative decision of first instance came into force.

Grounds of Decision:

The People's Court of Fuling District held: (1) that Fulin bureau, the defendant, had the administrative power to accept the application for confirmation of work-related injuries and confirm whether an injury was identified as work-related injuries or not; (2) that it was sufficient for Luo's injury to be identified as work-related injuries on grounds of the Notice of Praising Luo Renjun for Brave Acts. In accordance with Subparagraph 2, Paragraph 1 of Article 15 of the Work-related Injury Insurance Regulations of 2010, the injury incurred by protecting national or public interests shall be presumed work-related injuries. Fighting against crimes was also to protect public interests, which fulfilled the legislative purposes of the Work-related Injury Insurance Regulations of 2010.

Gazette Cases[2]

(1) **Dai Weijun v TG Changjiang Glass Co., Ltd. (the Case of Recovery of Labour Remuneration)**

(Gazette of the Supreme People's Court of the People's Republic of China, Issue 2, 2021).

Gist of Decision:

An employing unit may adjust positions and remuneration on the basis of rank and yank, which falls into the scope of autonomy in management, provided that the adjustment of positions and remuneration are based on the reasonable requirements of management and does not go against the laws and the rules and policies duly made by the employing unit.

(2) **Liang Haimei v Guangdong Huishijia Economic Development Co., Ltd. and Minghaoxuan Shark Fin Seafood Restaurant of Yuexiu District, Guangzhou (the Case of Personality Rights)**

(Gazette of the Supreme People's Court of the People's Republic of China, Issue 1, 2021).

[2] Gazette Cases are released on the gazettes of the Supreme People's Court of the PRC. The Gazette Cases are selected here to show how the courts understand and apply Chinese labour laws and regulations, despite that they may not be cited in court decisions. The Gazette Cases are translated by the author.

Gist of Decision:

Employment equity concerns labour rights and personality rights. Where the recruitment advertisement does not exclude women applicants and the job positions are not specially for men applicants, unreasonable differentiation, restriction and exclusion of women applicants on the basis of gender with no good reason constitutes gender discrimination in employment. The employment equity of labourers is infringed on.

(3) **Li Linxia v Chongqing Manka Cultural Communication Co., Ltd. (the Case of Labour Disputes)**

(Gazette of the Supreme People's Court of the People's Republic of China, Issue 10, 2020).

Gist of Decision:

A live streamer and her collaborator, a company, signed the exclusive collaboration agreement, by which the company packages her, she signs an account on the third party live video streaming flatform and they share the revenues from live streaming. There is no labour relationship between the live streamer and the company in that (1) the live streamer is not subject to the management of the company; (2) live streaming is not the main part of the company's business; and (3) the revenues gained by the live streamer are not the labour remuneration defined by labour law.

(4) **Wu Jiwei v Nanjing Bovon Power Tools Co., Ltd. (the Case of Labour Contracts)**

(Gazette of the Supreme People's Court of the People's Republic of China, Issue 9, 2020).

Gist of Decision:

Whether the change of the workplace and the prolonging of the commuting time as the result of relocation are the significant changes of the circumstances contemplated by the labour contracts depends on the distance of relocation, the convenience of commuting, the provision of commuting vehicles, the adjustment of working hours or the increase in traffic allowance. Relocation will not affect the performance of the labour contract, and labourers may not refuse to provide labour on grounds of relocation if reasonable actions have been taken to reduce the adverse effect on them.

(5) **Cai Yulong v Nanjing Jinzhongjian Curtain Wall Decoration Co., Ltd. (the Case of Labour Contracts)**

(Gazette of the Supreme People's Court of the People's Republic of China, Issue 4, 2020).

Gist of Decision:

If an employing unit fails to handle the procedures of personal files, social insurance and professional certificates so that a labourer concerned cannot provide related certificates for a new employing unit or handle the procedures of reemployment, the new employing unit underestimates the labourer in terms of his working attitude and work ability and refuses to employ him, and the employing unit shall pay compensation for the unsuccessful reemployment. The losses incurred to the affected labourer can be determined on the basis of the level of wages of the affected labourer in the former employing unit.

(6) **JSOGL v Zeng Guangfeng (the Case of Confirming Labour Relationships)**

(Gazette of the Supreme People's Court of the People's Republic of China, Issue 12, 2019).

Gist of Decision:

The labour relationships between a labourer and an employing unit exist if the requirements of labour relationships are met, that is, the labourer provides labour as required by the employing unit, the labourer is subject to the management of the employing unit and the labourer gains the remuneration in exchange for the labour. The other relationship between the labourer and another unit does not affect the labour relationships if the other contract with another unit is not performed and the income from the unit is not enough to sustain his or her living.

(7) **Liu Danping v Nanjing Renchuang Materials Co., Ltd. (the Case of Labour Dispute)**

(Gazette of the Supreme People's Court of the People's Republic of China, Issue 7, 2018).

Gist of Decision:

The person in charge of human resources was responsible for labour contract management and handled the matters related to labour contracts on behalf of the defendant. To conclude, a written labour contract fell into the scope of work. The claim for double wages was rejected where (1) the claimant should have known the provisions related to concluding written labour contracts and the legal consequences of not concluding labour contracts; (2) the claimant was obliged to request the defendant to conclude the labour contract with herself; and (3) the claimant failed to evidence that she made such a request.

(8) **Zhang Chuanjie v Shanghai Jinghao Labour Services Co., Ltd. (the Case of Labour contract)**

(Gazette of the Supreme People's Court of the People's Republic of China, Issue 5, 2017).

Gist of Decision:

The employing unit may not cancel or terminate the labour contract with the labourer unless he, whose employment was exposed to occupational diseases, failed to undergo a prior-resignation physical test. The termination agreement, even though made on the basis of consultation by the employing unit and the labourer, shall be invalidated.

(9) **Bao Liying v Shanghai Shenmei Food &Beverage Co., Ltd. (the Case of Labour Contract)**

(Gazette of the Supreme People's Court of the People's Republic of China, Issue 12, 2016).

Gist of Decision:

The working years shall be computed consecutively where the former employing unit was changed into a new unit but the place of work and the position of the labourer remain the same. To ascertain "not due to the labourer's own reason", the court shall examine what the cause of such change was and who caused such change instead of imposing the burden of proof upon the new unit. The labour dispatch company is not the intervening factor for computing the working years.

(10) **Hou Hongjun v Shanghai Longmao Construction Decoration Co., Ltd. (the Case of Labour Contract)**

(Gazette of the Supreme People's Court of the People's Republic of China, Issue 11, 2015).

Gist of Decision:

One-off disability employment grants shall be paid by the employing unit to the labourer suffering from work-related injuries in case of the termination or the cancellation of the labour contract. The employing unit is obliged to pay such grants to the labourer where it offered to terminate the labour contract.

(11) **The People's Procuratorate of Shuangliu, Sichuan v Hu Kejin (the Case of Crime of Refusal to Payment of Labour Remuneration)**

(Gazette of the Supreme People's Court of the People's Republic of China, Issue 6, 2015).

Gist of Decision:

See the abovementioned Guiding Case No. 28.

(12) **Zhang Jianming v Jinglong Technology (Suzhou) Co., Ltd. (the Case of Claim on Compensations)**

(Gazette of the Supreme People's Court of the People's Republic of China, Issue 7, 2014).

Gist of Decision:

The rules and policies of the employing unit are applied within the unit and are about labour organisation and labour management. The validity and reasonableness of the rules and policies shall be probed into where the employing unit terminates the labour contract on the grounds that the labourer breaches such rules and policies and the labourer lodges a lawsuit. The employing unit shall pay compensation to the labourer where it imposes unreasonable obligations on the labourer in such rules and policies and accordingly terminates employment.

(13) **TPS v Shan Jingjing (the Case of Labour Dispute)**

(Gazette of the Supreme People's Court of the People's Republic of China, Issue 12, 2013).

Gist of Decision:

Aticle 82 of the Labour Contract Law of 2012 provides that double wages shall be paid to the labourer where the employing unit fails to sign the written labour contract, which is punitive to the employing unit. The claim on double wages shall be rejected where the following requirements are met: (1) there are other written documents signed between the employing unit and the labourer; (2) the said documents contain the substantive elements of the labour contract, which clearly set out the rights and obligations of the labourer and amount to the labour contracts in essence.

(14) **Shanghai Kedi Paper Packaging Co., Ltd. v Shanghai Human Resources and Social Security Bureau (the Case of Payment of Comprehensive Insurance)**

(Gazette of the Supreme People's Court of the People's Republic of China, Issue 11, 2013).

Gist of Decision:

The unit that provides labour dispatch services shall be duly registered by law. The de facto labour relationship exists between the employing unit and the labourer where the employing unit signs the labour dispatching service agreement with the labour dispatch unit unduly registered, and accordingly, the employing unit is obliged to take out the comprehensive insurance for the benefit of the so-called dispatched labourer. The employing unit is not exempt from taking out comprehensive insurance.

(15) **Liang Jieshu v Nanjing Lefu Catering Management Co., Ltd. (the Case of Labour Dispute)**

(Gazette of the Supreme People's Court of the People's Republic of China, Issue 6, 2013).

Gist of Decision:

The medical period of 24 months shall be granted to the labourer who develops cancers, mental disorders or other diseases that are not curable. The period of the labour contract shall be extended to the expiry of the said medical period where the labour contract expires before the expiry of the said medical period. The termination of the labour contract shall be revoked where the employing unit illegally terminates the labour contract within the medical period and the labourer claims that the employing unit should continue to perform the labour contract.

(16) **Shanghai Guanlong Valves and Machines Co., Ltd. v Tang Maolin (the Case of Labour Contract)**

(Gazette of the Supreme People's Court of the People's Republic of China, Issue 9, 2012).

Gist of Decision:

The labour contract by defraud shall be invalidated where the requirement of education degree is definite listed in the recruitment advertisement and the applicant provides the false certificate of education degree and signs the labour contract with the employing unit. The employing unit may terminate the labour contract in accordance with Article 39 of the Labour Contract Law of 2012.

(17) **Guo Yi v Jiangsu Yifeng Chain Drug Stores Co., Ltd. (the Case of Labour Contract)**

(Gazette of the Supreme People's Court of the People's Republic of China, Issue 6, 2010).

Gist of Decision:

The labour contract shall be validated where with a view of employment, the labourer, who has not graduated from his college, signed the contract with the employing unit, is subject the management of the employing unit and provides labour; and the employing unit knowingly understands that he is not eligible for employment and pays the labour remuneration.

(18) **Wang Yunfei vhanghai Branch Schneider Electric (China) Investment (the Case of Labour Dispute)**

(Gazette of the Supreme People's Court of the People's Republic of China, Issue 11, 2009).

Gist of Decision:

Noncompetition means that the labourer who resigned from his former unit shall not, within the specific period, operate for his own benefit or for the benefit of others the business that directly competes with his unit. The noncompetition clause may be stipulated in the labour contract or the nondisclosure agreement, by which the labourer is entitled to the compensation for noncompetition. The noncompetition clause does not bind the labourer where no compensation is paid, or where the compensation is too low or goes against related regulations.

The First Batch of Typical Cases of Labour Dispute Jointly Issued by the Ministry of Human Resources and Social Security and the Supreme People's Court of the PRC on 10 July 2020[3]

(1) **Can the employing unit suspend the labour contract on the grounds that COVID-19 is force majeure?**

Case Background:

Mr. Zhang was employed by a logistics company. Due to COVID-19, the company shut down on 3 February 2020. At the end of February, Mr. Zhang found his wages unpaid, and the department of human resources responded that due to COVID-19, the labour contract was suspended, he did not work in January and the company was not obliged to pay his wages.

Decision:

The arbitral award was made in favor of Mr. Zhang, by which the company shall pay the wages in February to him. The court of first instance held the same view in the decision of first instance, which came into force.

Case Analysis:

COVID-19 is a public health emergency as well as force majeure. Force majeure is a prescribed clause of exemption from liability. In accordance with Article 1 of the Opinions on properly Handling COVID-19 related Labour Relations, which were issued jointly by the Ministry of Human Resources and Social Security and the Supreme People's Court, the labour contract may not be suspended despite that it cannot be performed due to COVID-19 and the employing units and the labourer may modify the labour contract by consultation. Accordingly, the rules of force majeure in civil law are not applicable to labour disputes.

(2) **What if labourers refuse to provide labour services on the excuse of home-based medical observations during the COVID-19 epidemic?**

Case Background:

On 4 April 2019, Mr. Zhang and a company signed a 2-year labour contract. On the Spring Festival, he went to his hometown to see his parents. On 3 February 2020, Mr. Zhang alleged that there were close contacts in the neighborhoods where his parents lived and that he had to be subject to home-based medical observation for 14 days. On 14 March 2020, he returned to the company, and the labour contract was terminated by agreement. Mr. Zhang thought that it was illegal for the company to pay living expenses for the period from 3 March 2020 to 16 March 2020.

---

[3] The Paper. (2020). *The First Batch of Typical Cases of Labour Dispute*. Retrieved 29 September, 2021, from https://m.thepaper.cn/baijiahao_8591180. Accessed 29 September 2021. The Typical Cases are translated by the author.

Decision:

The arbitral award was made against Mr. Zhang.

Case Analysis:

In accordance with the Opinions on properly Handling COVID-19 related Labour Relations, labour cannot be provided due to the suspension of business or failure to return to the post, the enterprise and the labour may agree the payment of the wages as follows: the standard wages stipulated in the labour contract shall be paid within the period of wage payment and the living expenses, which are determined on the local regulations, shall be paid beyond the period of wage payment. Accordingly, the arbitral award was made against Mr. Zhang, and his claims were rejected.

(3) **How are wages paid to the labourer who was stranded in Hubei Province during the suspension of business?**

Case Background:

Mr. Lee was a software engineer of a company, and on 20 January 2020, he was sent to Hubei to provide maintenance services and was stranded there due to the outbreak of COVID-19. After the Spring Festival of 2020, the company had to suspend the business due to the shortage of raw materials. The company thought that from 14 March 2020 to 13 April 2020, Mr. Lee did not work and only paid living expenses to him. However, Mr. Lee thought that he should have got paid normally.

Decision:

The arbitral award was made in favor of Mr. Lee.

Case Analysis:

In this case, to finish the task designated by the company, Mr. Lee was sent to Hubei and stranded there. Accordingly, Mr. Lee should get paid normally.

(4) **How to pay in case of the suspension of partial business?**

Case Background:

Mr. Zhang was employed by the client club of the car company. The company had car parts production, assembling, and selling businesses. After 3 February 2020, the businesses of car part production, assembly, and selling resumed, but the business of the client club remained suspended. On 10 April 2020, the company paid living expenses for March. Mr. Zhang thought that the company intentionally reduced his wages.

Decision:

The arbitral award was made against Mr. Zhang, and his claim was rejected.

Case Analysis:

The Opinions on properly Handling COVID-19-related Labour Relations are not restricted to the suspension of the whole business. There was no sufficient proof that the business of the client club was suspended intentionally.

(5) **May the employing unit unilaterally arrange the paid annual leave for the labourer during the suspension of the business?**

Case Background:

Mr. Lee was employed by the catering company as a chef. From 2019, he was entitled to the paid annual leave of five days. On February 3, the local government ordered all the enterprises to suspend the business until 17 February 2020. The catering company told him to take the paid annual leave from 3 to 14 February 2020, but he rejected. Mr. Lee thought that it was not legal for the company to make such arrangements and that compensation for unpaid annual leave shall be paid.

Decision:

The claim was rejected.

Case Analysis:

In accordance with the Opinions on Stabilizing Labour Relations and Supporting Resumption of Business during the Prevention of COVID-19, employing units to which working from home is not suitable may, after consultation, first arrange the annual leave or homemade holidays.

(6) **How can the Sharing Employee Agreement be handled if the lending company fails to perform it?**

Case Background:

Mr. Zhang was employed by a catering company. During the Spring Festival, the company suspended its business due to COVID-19. However, an e-commerce company was in great need of employees. The company and the e-commerce company signed the sharing employee agreement, by which Mr. Zhang was sent to the latter company from 3 January to 4 May 2020. On 20 March, the company was declared to be bankrupt, and Mr. Zhang was notified that the labour contract was terminated. Additionally, the e-commerce company was notified that the sharing employee agreement could not be performed.

Decision:

The arbitral award was made in favor of Mr. Zhang, confirming that there was a labour relationship from 3 February 3 to 16 April 2020.

Case Analysis:

Sharing employees are not prohibited by law. In accordance with Article 44 of the Labour Law, the labour contract shall be terminated where the employing unit is declared to be bankrupt. The relationship between Mr. Zhang and the e-commerce company should be judged in accordance with the Notice of Establishment of Labour Relations.

(7) **Are the wages included in the expenses of special training?**

Case Background:

On 1 June 2013, Mr. Zhang signed the open-ended labour contract with a physical examination company. On 3 July 2014, he signed the training agreement with the company, which stipulated (1) that the company paid the training expenses, the travelling expenses and the wages during the training period, (2) that he should work for the company for at least 5 years after the training, and (3) he should pay back all the expenses related to the training and pay the stipulated damages in case of the termination of the labour contract. During the training, the company paid training expenses of 47,000 yuan, travelling expenses of 5600 yuan and wages of 33,000 yuan. After the training, he returned to the company on 3 July 2015. On 1 March 2018, Mr. Zhang presented the written notice to the company, which stated that the labour contract would be terminated on 2 April 2018. The company asked him to pay the stipulated damages of 86,500 yuan, or it would refuse to issue the certificate of termination. Mr. Zhang thought that the sum of stipulated damages was illegal.

Decision:

The arbitral award was made that the company refunded 61,930 yuan to him.

Case Analysis:

The issue in dispute was whether the wages paid in the training were included in the expenses of special training. In accordance with Article 22 of the Labour Contract Law of 2012, the employing unit, which pays the expenses of the special training, may sign the training agreement with the labourer with regard to the service period, and the agreement may stipulate that the labourer in breach shall pay the stipulated damages not more than the expenses of special training paid by the employing unit. Additionally, in accordance with Article 16 of the Regulations of Implementing the Labour Contract Law, the training expenses include the expenses of special training, the travelling expenses and the direct expenses arising from the training. In accordance with Article 50 of the Labour Law, the wages shall not be deducted or defaulted on. Accordingly, the expenses of special training are different from the wages in that (1) the former, by nature, is used as the direct costs for the training, while the latter is paid to the labourer in the performance of the labour contract; (2) the former arises out of the special training while the latter is determined by law or the labour contract; and (3) the former is paid to the training service provider, while the latter the labourer.

(8) **Does the forged certificate of education degree invalidate the labour contract?**

Case Background:

In June 2018, a network company made the recruitment advertisement that the company would recruit one network technician whose education degree was undergraduate in computer engineering or above. Mr. Zhao graduated from a college for professional training and majored in marketing. However, he forged the certificate of education degree and signed the labour contract with the company. Later, the company found that his certificate of education degree was forged and terminated his employment.

Decision:

The arbitral award was made that his claim was rejected.

Case Analysis:

In accordance with Article 8 of the Labour Contract Law of 2012, the employing unit may know about the labourer's basic information directly related to the labour contract, and the labourer shall explain it as it is. Additionally, in accordance with Paragraph 1 of Article 26 of the Labour Contract Law of 2012, the labour contract signed by defraud or duress shall be invalidated wholly or partially. In this case, the requirements of computer engineering and undergraduate education or above are closely connected with the duties of the job and the working performance, and such requirements are within the meanings of the basic information directly related to the labour contract.

(9) **Are double wages appliable when there is no written labour contract even after open-ended labour is deemed to exist?**

Case Background:

On 1 August 2016, Mr. Wan was employed as an inspector by a food company. Mr. Wan was told that the written labour contract would be signed after the expiry of the three-month probation period, but in fact, there was no written labour contract. On 31 July 2018, he terminated the labour relationship with the company and requested it to pay double wages from August 2017 to July 2018, during which the open-ended labour contract was not signed. The request was rejected.

Decision:

The arbitral award was made that his claim was rejected.

Case Analysis:

The issue in dispute is whether the case is subject to Article 82 of the Labour Contract Law of 2012. The double wages shall be paid where an employing unit fails to conclude a written labour contract with a worker for more than a month but less than a year from the date it starts employing him, or where.

An employing unit fails to conclude an open-ended labour contract with a worker in violation of the provisions of the Labour Contract Law of 2012. However, in this case, no conclusion of the written labour contract with Mr. Wan does not fall into the scope of Article 82.

(10) **Will a labourer breach of noncompeting take the liability where an employing unit fails to pay noncompeting compensation?**

Case Background:

In July 2013, Mr. Le was employed as a client manager by a bank. The labour contract for 8 years was signed, which stipulated that his annual wages were 1 million yuan. The contract also contained nondisclosure and noncompeting clauses, by which he could not take a similar job in banks, insurers, securities or other financing companies within two years after his resignation. Otherwise, he had to pay the stipulated damages of 2 million yuan. On 1 March 2018, the bank terminated his employment on the grounds that he violated its rules and policies but failed to pay noncompeting compensation. In February 2019, he was employed as a client manager in the local bank. The former bank claimed that he paid the stipulated damages of 2 million yuan and continued to perform the noncompeting agreement.

Decision:

The arbitral award was made that the claim was rejected.

Case Analysis:

Paragraph 2 of Article 23 provides that with regard to a labourer who has a confidentiality obligation, the employing unit may have stipulated in the labour contract or confidentiality agreement competition restriction and payment of financial compensation to him on a monthly basis during the term of the competition restriction after the labour contract is revoked or terminated. If the labourer breaches the stipulation on competition restriction, he shall pay penalty to the employing unit as agreed upon. Furthermore, Article 8 of the Judicial Interpretations on Application of Law in Hearing Labour Disputes (No. 4) provides that the employing unit fails to pay noncompeting compensation for over three months, and the labourer may terminate the noncompeting agreement. In this case, the bank did not pay noncompeting compensation for 11 months, and it is fair that the labourer terminates the noncompeting agreement.

(11) **Are the irregular working hours system as agreed upon valid?**

Case Background:

On 1 November 2017, Mr. Zhang was employed as a security inspector by a property service company. He and the company agreed that irregular working hours applied to his job. In April 2018, the company applied to the local human resources and social bureau department for irregular working hours, and the irregular working hours were valid from 1 May 2018 to 30 April 2019. On 30 September 2018, he and the company terminated the labour contract by agreement. Both parties agreed that

Mr. Zhang worked for 15 days on holidays from November 2017 to April 2018 and for 10 days on holidays from May 2018 to September 2018. Mr. Zhang requested that the company pay overtime wages, but the company refused to pay on the grounds that he was subject to irregular working hours.

Decision:

The arbitral award was made that the overtime wages from November 2017 to April 2018 shall be paid. The court of first instance held the same view in the decision, which was affirmed by the court of second instance.

Case Analysis:

The issue in dispute is whether Mr. Zhang is subject to irregular working hours without being approved. To be valid, irregular working hours shall be subject to approval by the local human resources and social security department. Irregular working hours are not applicable to the period from November 2017 to April 2018.

(12) **How does an employing unit use its autonomy in management to adjust the job and the place of work?**

Case Background:

In August 2017, Mr. Sun was employed by a mold company, and an open-ended labour contract was signed, which stipulated his job position and place of work. His contents of the job were finance and budget management and other administrational affairs. At the same time, the labour contract stipulated that the company could adjust his job position, the contents of his job and the place of work to satisfy the requirements of the company's business. First, Mr. Sun did some financial and personnel affairs in a development center. On 1 July 2019, to reduce the workload of every development center, the company centralised the financial affairs of every development center in the headquarters. The company suggested another job position for him, but he refused. Finally, the company told him to do personnel affairs in the headquarters, which were adjacent to his former place of work. At the end of July 2019, he expected the company to transfer him to the former job position in the former place of work.

Decision:

The arbitral award was made against Mr. Sun.

Case Analysis:

The issue in dispute is whether the adjustment of his job position and place of the work is within the meanings of autonomy in management, which is provided by the Employment Promotion Law.

Although the proper adjustment of the job position and the place of work is indispensable for business management, it should be made within the boundaries of the laws and regulations. In practice, the following factors are taken into consideration in judging the validity and reasonableness of the adjustment of the job position and the place of work: (1) the requirements of business management; (3) the significant derivation from the stipulations in the labour contract; (3) discrimination and insult; (4) the influence upon labour remuneration and conditions; (5) the affected labourer's suitability for the new position; and (6) necessary assistance or compensation to the affected labourer. In this case, the company shew much respect for Mr. Sun, suggested several choices for him, and did not damage his interests.

The Second Batch of Typical Cases of Labour Dispute of Overtime Jointly Issued by the Ministry of Human Resources and Social Security and the Supreme People's Court of the PRC on 30 June 2021[4]

(1) **May an employing unit terminate the labour contract in case a labourer refuses to work overtime against law?**

Case Background:

In June 2020, Mr. Zhang was employed by an express service company, and the probation period was three months. According to the rules and policies of the company, he should work from 9 a.m. to 9 p.m. on six days for every week. Two months later, he refused to work overtime on the grounds that his working hours exceeded the maximum hours provided by law, while the company terminated the labour contract with him on the grounds that he did not meet the requirements of the recruitment. He applied for the arbitration that the company should pay compensation of 8000 yuan.

Decision:

The arbitral award was made in favor of Mr. Zhang.

Case Analysis:

The issue in dispute is whether an employing unit may terminate the labour contract in case a labourer refuses to work overtime against law. In accordance with Article 41 and Article 43 of the Labour Law, the employing unit may extend working hours as necessitated by its production or business operation after consultation with the trade union and labourers, but the extended working hours per day shall generally not exceed one hour; if such extension is needed for special reasons, under the condition that the health of labourers is guaranteed, the extended hours shall not exceed three hours per day. However, the total extension in a month shall not exceed thirty-six hours, and the employing unit shall not extend the working hours of labourers in violation of the provisions of the Labour Law. Furthermore, in accordance with

[4] MOHRSS. (2021). The Second Batch of Typical Cases of Labour Dispute. Retrieved 28 September, 2021, from http://www.mohrss.gov.cn/SYrlzyhshbzb/laodongguanxi_/zcwj/diaojiezhongcai/202108/t20210825_421600.html. Accessed 28 September 2021. The Typical Cases are translated by the author.

Article 43 of the Labour Contract Law of 2012, a labour contract shall be invalid or partially invalid where it is at variance with the mandatory provisions of laws or administrative regulations. Accordingly, in this case, the 996 working hour system shall be invalid.

(2) **May a labourer claim the overtime wages where he has signed the agreement to waive his right to them?**

Case Background:

In June 2020, Mr. Zhang was employed by a technology company, and his monthly wages were 20,000 yuan. When the labour contract was signed, he was told to sign the agreement to waive his right to the overtime wages, which stated that "I agree to be subject to the Strivers' Plan and waive my right to the overtime wages". Half a year later, he offered to resign from his job and claimed overtime wages. The company refused to pay the overtime wages according to the agreement, even though it conceded that he worked overtime. He claimed that the company shall pay overtime wages of 24,000 yuan for the period from June 2020 to December 2020.

Decision:

The arbitral award was made in favor of Mr. Zhang.

Case Analysis:

In accordance with Article 26 of the Labour Contract Law of 2012, a labour contract shall be invalid or partially invalid where it exempts the employing unit from its statutory responsibility or negates the labourer's rights. The employing unit is obliged to pay overtime wages, which is provided by Article 44 of the Labour Law and Article 31 of the Labour Contract Law of 2012. In this case, it is unconscionable that he waived his right to the overtime wages, and the agreement shall be invalidated.

(3) **Can overtime work be denied where a labourer fails to comply with the approval procedure as stipulated by the rules and policies of the employing unit?**

Case Background:

In December 2019, Mr. Wu was employed by a pharmaceutical company, and his monthly wages were 18,000 yuan. The rules and policies related to overtime work stipulated that "the application sheet for overtime work is necessary for overtime work to be confirmed. Without approval from the company, overtime wages are not paid". Mr. Wu was subject to the 996 working hours system as stipulated by the rules and policies of the company. One day, Mr. Wu submitted the application sheet for overtime work, but the company did not approve his overtime work. In November 2020, Mr. Wu and the company agreed to terminate the labour contract, and he claimed his overtime wages on the basis of his attendance record, WeChat logs and the minute of working meeting. The company refused to pay the overtime wages on the grounds that the overtime work was not approved, although it conceded that the supporting materials of overtime work were true.

Decision:

The arbitral award and the court decision of first instance were made in favor of Mr. Wu.

Case Analysis:

The issue in dispute is whether the company might refuse to pay the overtime wages on the grounds that Mr. Wu worked overtime without approval. In accordance with Article 44 of the Labour Law and Article 13 of the Provisional Regulations on Payment of Wages, an employing unit is obliged to pay overtime wages where the requirements of "arranged by an employing unit" and "work beyond the prescribed working hours" are met. In this case, the company's failure to approve the overtime work does not affect the identification of overtime work arranged by the employing unit.

(4) **Can a labourer claim the overtime wages where the lump-sum payment of the wages is stipulated by the labourer and the employing unit?**

Case Background:

In July 2020, Mr. Zhou was employed by a car service company, and the labour contract was signed, which stipulated that his monthly wages were 4000 yuan, the overtime wages included. In February 2021, he terminated the labour contract and alleged that the company failed to pay the overtime wages in full even if the local minimum wages were deemed to his normal wages for the statutory working hours. The company conceded that he worked overtime but refused to pay the overtime wages on the grounds that they were included in the stipulated monthly wages. Mr. Zhou claimed that the company should pay the balance of 17,000 yuan as the overtime wages.

Decision:

The arbitral award was made in favor of Mr. Zhou.

Case Analysis:

In accordance with Article 47 of the Labour Law, an employing unit may, at its own discretion, determine its modes of wage distribution and wage levels on the basis of the characteristics of its own operation and economic results. Article 48 of the Labour Law provided the minimum-wages system. However, the minimum wages exclude the overtime wages. In this case, after computation, the minimum wages plus the overtime wages exceeded the monthly wages of 4000 yuan.

(5) **May a labourer refuse the workload increased by an employing unit without consultation?**

Case Background:

In September 2018, Mr. Zhang was employed by a newspaper company as a deliveryman. He worked for 6 h every day and for 6 days every week. His monthly wages were 3500 yuan. In June 2020, without consultation, the company allocated the job of another deliveryman who had resigned to him. Mr. Zhang refused because more than 4 h, he thought, were needed to finish the increased task. The company terminated the labour contract with him on the grounds that he did not submit to the management of the company. Mr. Zhang claimed the compensation of 14,000 yuan on the grounds that the company illegally terminated his employment.

Decision:

The final arbitral award was made in favor of Mr. Zhang.

Case Analysis:

The issue in dispute is whether Mr. Zhang might refuse the workload increased by the company without consultation. In accordance with Article 31 of the Labour Contract Law of 2012, an employing unit shall not force a labourer to work overtime. Furthermore, in accordance with the Article of the Labour Contract Law of 2012, after consultation, an employing unit and a labourer may modify the labour contract. In this case, the company should be deemed to modify the labour contract to increase his workload.

(6) **What rule on the allocation of the burden of proof is in handling the dispute over overtime wages?**

Case Background:

In January 2020, Mr. Lin was employed by an education consulting company, and his monthly wages were 6000 yuan. In July 2020, he offered to terminate the labour contract with the company. He alleged that he worked for 6 days for a week and furnished the attendance records on APP and the printed records of wage payment, which showed that the overtime wages were unpaid. However, the company refused to confirm the evidence and alleged that he worked for 5 days for a week without the provision of any evidence. Mr. Lin claimed the overtime wages of 10,000 yuan from the company.

Decision:

The arbitral award was made in favor of Mr. Lin.

Case Analysis:

The issue in dispute is how to allocate the burden of proof between Mr. Lin and the company. In accordance with Article 6 of the Labour Dispute Mediation and Arbitration Law, the parties shall furnish the evidence in favor of their own claims, and an employing unit will be responsible for adverse consequences where it fails to furnish them that were under its control. Similar provisions are also in the Judicial Interpretations on Application of Law in Hearing the Case of Labour Disputes (No. 1). Accordingly, the labourer who claims the overtime wages shall furnish the evidence in his favor, and alternatively, the overtime work may be presumed to exist in case of the company's failure to furnish the evidence. In this case, although the evidence Mr.

Zhang furnished was hard copies, which were negated by the company, the company should bear the bad consequences because it failed to furnish the contrary evidence.

(7) **Shall the labour-user unit and the dispatching unit jointly and severally liable for work-related injuries due to overtime work?**

Case Background:

In August 2017, a dispatching company signed with a media company the labour dispatching service agreement, which stipulated that the dispatching company provided the dispatched labourers for the media company and he worked for 11 h every day, and the minimum working hours per capita per month was 286 h. In September 2017, Mr. Lee was employed by the dispatching company and was sent to the media company. The dispatching company did not take out the work-related injury insurance for him. The total working hours were 319 h, 293 h and 322.5 h for August 2018, September 2018 and November 2018, respectively. His working time was from 8:30 p.m. on 30 November 2018 to 8:30 a.m. on 1 December 2018. Unfortunately, on 5:30 a.m. On 1 December 2018, he fell faint and died of myocardial infarction. In December 2018, the media company and his close relatives signed a compensation agreement, which stipulated that his close relatives were paid 420,000 yuan and waived their rights to any compensation from the media company. His death was identified as a work-related injury by the local department.

Case Analysis:

In the case of labour dispatching, the labour-user unit and the dispatching unit shall be jointly and severally liable for the work-related injury caused to the labourer who works overtime. The compensation agreement between the labourer, the labour-user unit and the dispatching unit shall be invalidated where it is in violation of the mandatory provisions of laws and regulations or where it is signed by fraud or duress. The agreement may be revoked in cases of significant misconception or unconscionability.

(8) **Can the rules and policies of an employing unit negate the fact of overtime work?**

Case Background:

In April 2016, Mr. Chang was employed by a network company and was told that the fingerprint machine was used for the purpose of attendance registration. The employee manual stated that overtime work commenced from 9 p.m. provided that it was subject to the application and approval. From May 2016 to January 2017, he worked overtime for 126 h in total. However, the company refused to pay the overtime wages on the grounds that the working hours before 9 p.m. shall not be included into the overtime work.

Decision:

The court decision of first instance was made in favor of Mr. Chang, and the appeal to the court of second instance was rejected.

Case Analysis:

In this case, on the one hand, there were the rules of overtime work application and approval, which were not in violation of related laws and regulations, and on the other hand, the company argued that the period from 6 p.m. to 9 p.m. was for supper and rest, so the starting time for overtime work was 9 p.m. However, it did not stand to reason that 3 h were too long for supper and rest, and furthermore, the company failed to furnish the evidence in favor of its argument. The rules were invalided by the court.

(9) **May a labourer claim the overtime wages in default where he confirms that they have been paid in the resignation document?**

Case Background:

In July 2017, Mr. Xiao was employed by a technology company with the administrative licence of labour dispatch and was dispatched to an express service company as a deliveryman. He alleged that he was instructed to work on weekends and statutory holidays and furnished the payroll. Both companies confirmed the payroll, which showed that he worked overtime from July 2017 to October 2019. In November 2019, Mr. Xiao offered to resign from the technology company, and they signed the handover document, which stated that wages, overtime wages and economic compensation had been settled. Mr. Xiao argued that he signed the document against his own will and that the company would not go through the resignation procedures unless the document was signed.

Decision:

The court decision of first instance was made against Mr. Xiao, while the court of second instance was made in favor of Mr. Xiao, which held that both companies paid the overtime wages jointly and severally.

Case Analysis:

The issue in dispute is whether the agreement of overtime wages is valid or not. In this case, the technology company failed to furnish the evidence to prove that it paid overtime wages. The statement in the handover document, even though it was signed, was groundless.

(10) **What the limitation of overtime wages in arbitration is?**

Case Background:

In July 2016, Mr. Zhang was employed by a construction company. In February 2019, he resigned. He alleged that he worked overtime, but the company failed to pay the overtime wages. In December 2019, he made the arbitration application that the company should pay the overtime wages to him, and the company defended that the time limitation of overtime wages elapsed.

Decision:

The court decision of first instance was made in favor of Mr. Zhang, which came into force.

Case Analysis:

Overtime wages are within the meanings of labour remuneration. The special limitation of one year shall apply to overtime wages. The special limitation shall commence from the termination of the labour contract.

The Labour Law of the People's Republic of China[5]

(Adopted at the Eighth Meeting of the Standing Committee of the Eighth National People's Congress on 5 July 1994, promulgated by Order No. 28 of the President of the People's Republic of China, and revised by on 27 August 2009 and 29 December 2018).

Chapter 1

General Provisions

Article 1 With a view to protecting the legitimate rights and interests of labourers, regulating labour relations, establishing and safeguarding a labour system to adapt to the socialist market economy, and promoting economic development and social progress, this Law is formulated in accordance with the Constitution of the People's Republic of China.

Article 2 This Law applies to enterprises, individual economic organisations (hereinafter collectively referred to as employing units) and labourers who form a labour relationship with them within the territory of the People's Republic of China.

State organs, public institutions and public organisations as well as labourers who form a labour relationship with them shall be subject to this Law.

Article 3 Labourers shall have equal right to employment and choice of occupation, the right to remuneration for labour, to rest and vacations, to protection of occupational safety and health, to training in vocational skills, to social insurance and welfare, to submission of labour disputes for settlement and other rights relating to labour provided by law.

Labourers shall fulfill their labour tasks, improve their vocational skills, follow rules on occupational safety and health, and observe labour discipline and professional ethics.

Article 4 The employing units shall establish and perfect rules and regulations by law to ensure that labourers enjoy employment rights and fulfill labour obligations.

[5] The Supreme People's Court (2015). *Labour Law of the People's Republic of China*. Retrieved 1 March, 2021, from http://english.court.gov.cn/2015-08/17/content_21624023_2.htm

Article 5 The State shall take various measures to promote employment, develop vocational education, lay down labour standards, regulate social incomes, perfect social insurance systems, coordinate labour relationships, and gradually raise the living standard of labourers.

Article 6 The State shall advocate the participation of labourers in voluntary social labour activities, launch labour emulation and rational proposal campaigns, encourage and protect labourers in conducting scientific research, technical renovation, inventions and creations, and commend and reward model labourers.

Article 7 Labourers shall have the right to participate in and orgaise trade unions by law.

Trade unions shall represent and safeguard the legitimate rights and interests of labourers and independently carry out their activities by law.

Article 8 Labourers shall take part in democratic management or negotiate with the employing units on an equal footing about protection of the legitimate rights and interests of labourers through the assembly or congress of labourers or in other forms as provided by law.

Article 9 The administrative department of labour under the State Council shall be in charge of nationwide labour management.

The administrative departments of labour under the local people's governments at or above the county level shall be in charge of the management of labour in their respective administrative areas.

Chapter 2

Promotion of Employment

Article 10 The State shall create conditions for employment and increase employment opportunities by means of the promotion of socioeconomic development.

The State should encourage enterprises, public institutions and public organisations to initiate industries or expand businesses to increase employment within the boundaries provided by laws and administrative rules and regulations.

The State shall support labourers to seek employment by orgaising themselves on a voluntary basis or by engaging in individual businesses.

Article 11 Local people's governments at various levels shall take measures, by developing employment agencies of various forms, to provide employment services.

Article 12 Labourers, regardless of ethnic group, race, sex, or religious belief, shall not be discriminated against in employment.

Article 13 Women shall have equal employment rights to men. With the exception of the types of work or posts unsuitable to women as prescribed by the State, no units may, in employing staff and workers, refuse to employ women on grounds of sex or raise the employment standards for women.

Article 14 With respect to the employment of the disabled, people of minority ethnic groups, and ex-servicemen or ex-servicewomen, special provisions of laws and administrative regulations, if any, shall apply.

Article 15 No employing units are allowed to recruit minors under the age of 16.

Institutions of literature and art, physical culture, and special arts and crafts that recruit minors under the age of 16 shall go through the formalities of examination and approval in accordance with the relevant provisions of the State and guarantee their right to compulsory education.

Chapter 3

Labour Contracts and Collective Contracts

Article 16 A labour contract is an agreement that establishes the labour relationship between the labourer and employing unit and sets out the rights and obligations of respective parties.

A labour contract shall be concluded in establishing a labour relationship.

Article 17 Conclusion and modification of a labour contract shall follow the principles of equality, voluntariness and agreement through consultation and shall not violate the provisions of laws and administrative regulations.

A labour contract duly concluded by law shall be legally binding. The parties shall fulfill the obligations stipulated therein.

Article 18 A labour contract shall be invalid where it:

(1) violates laws and administrative regulations; or
(2) is concluded by means of fraud or intimidation, etc.

An invalid labour contract shall have no legal binding force ab initio. Where a part of a labour contract is declared invalid and the validity of the remaining part is not prejudiced, the remaining part shall remain valid.

The invalidity of a labour contract shall be declared by a labour dispute arbitration commission or a people's court.

Article 19 A labour contract shall be concluded in writing and contain the following clauses:

(1) term of a labour contract,
(2) job contents,
(3) labour protection and working conditions,
(4) labour remuneration,
(5) labour discipline,
(6) conditions for the termination of employment, and
(7) liabilities for a breach of the labour contract.

Apart from the required clauses specified in the preceding paragraph, a labour contract may contain other clauses agreed upon by the parties through consultation.

Article 20 The term of a labour contract is classified into fixed term, nonfixed term and the term based on the completion of a specific assignment.

A nonfixed term labour contract shall be concluded at his or her request where a labourer has worked in the same employing unit for ten consecutive years or more and both parties agree to extend the term of the labour contract.

Article 21 A probation period may be specified in a labour contract. The probation period shall not exceed six months at most.

Article 22 The parties to a labour contract may stipulate in a labour contract the matters concerning keeping trade secrets of the employing unit in confidentiality.

Article 23 A labour contract shall terminate immediately upon its expiry or the occurrence of its termination conditions as stipulated by the parties.

Article 24 A labour contract may be cancelled by agreement reached between the parties through consultation.

Article 25 An employing unit may cancel the labour contract with a labourer where he or she:

(1) is found not to meet the requirements for recruitment during the probation period,
(2) seriously violates labour discipline or the rules and regulations of the employing unit,
(3) causes great losses to the employing unit through gross negligence of duty or malpractice for personal gain; or
(4) is prosecuted for criminal liabilities by law.

Article 26 An employing unit may terminate a labour contract provided that a written 30-day notice shall be given to a labourer in case of any of the following circumstances:

(1) The labourer is incapable of carrying out his or her original work or any work specially arranged by the employing unit after the expiry of the period of medical treatment in case of illness or nonwork-related injuries,
(2) The labourer is incompetent for his or her work and remains incompetent despite the training or the transfer of the job post, or
(3) There is a material change in the objective circumstances on which the conclusion of labour contract is relied on so that the original labour contract cannot be carried out, and no agreement on modification of the labour contract can be reached through consultation by the parties.

Article 27 Where it is necessary for an employing unit to cut down the workforce in regard to the edge of bankruptcy and undergoes a statutory consolidation or suffers from great difficulty in production and management, the employing unit shall explain the situation of redundancy to the trade union or all the staff 30 days in advance, solicit opinions from them and report it to the competent administrative department of labour before it may cut down the workforce.

Where the employing unit that cut down its workforce in accordance with this Article is to recruit new labourers within six months, it shall give priority in employment to those who have been laid off.

Article 28 An employing unit shall pay economic compensation in accordance with the relevant provisions of the State where it terminates a labour contract in accordance with Articles 24, 26 and 27 hereof.

Article 29 An employing unit may not terminate a labour contract in accordance with Articles 26 and 26 hereof in case of any of the following circumstances:

(1) A labourer is declared to have totally or partially lost the ability to work as a result of occupational diseases or work-related injuries,

(2) A labourer is within the prescribed period of medical treatment for illness or injuries,
(3) A female labourer is during her pregnant, puerperal, or breast-feeding period, or
(4) Other circumstances stipulated by laws and administrative regulations.

Article 30 A trade union may have the right to put forward its opinions where it finds it inappropriate for an employing unit to terminate a labour contract. If the employing unit violates the laws, administrative regulations or a labour contract, the trade union shall have the right to make a request for rectification. Where the labourer applies for arbitration or institutes a lawsuit, the trade union shall render him support and assistance by law.

Article 31 A labourer shall give a written 30-day notice to an employing unit before terminating a labour contract.

Article 32 A labourer may notify at any time an employing unit of his termination of the labour contract in any of the following circumstances:

(1) He or she is within the probation period,
(2) He or she is forced to work by means of violence, intimidation or illegal restriction of personal freedom, or
(3) The employing unit fails to pay labour remuneration or to provide working conditions as stipulated in the labour contract.

Article 33 Labourers of an enterprise as one party may conclude a collective contract with the enterprise for the particulars relating to labour remuneration, working hours, rest and vacations, occupational safety and health, insurance and welfare. The draft collective contract shall be submitted to the congress of labourers or to all the labourers for discussion and adoption.

A collective contract shall be concluded by the trade union on behalf of labourers with an enterprise. Where the trade union has not yet been set up in an enterprise, such a contract shall be concluded by the representatives elected by labourers with the enterprise.

Article 34 Upon conclusion of a collective contract, it shall be submitted to the administrative department of labour. If no objections have been raised by the administrative department of labour within 15 days of the date of receipt of the collective contract, it shall come into force automatically.

Article 35 A collective contract concluded by law shall be binding on both an enterprise and all of its labourers. The standards of working conditions and labour remuneration stipulated in a labour contract concluded between individual labourers and the enterprise shall not be lower than those stipulated in a collective contract.

Chapter 4

Working Hours, Rest and Vacations

Article 36 The State shall put into operation a working hour system wherein labourers shall work for no more than 8 h a day and no more than 44 h a week on average.

Article 37 In the case of labourers working on the basis of piecework, an employing unit shall reasonably fix quotas of work and standards of piecework remuneration in accordance with the working hour system stipulated in Article 36 hereof.

Article 38 An employing unit shall guarantee that its labourers have at least one day off in a week.

Article 39 Where an enterprise cannot follow the stipulations in Article 36 and Article 38 hereof due to the nature of its production, it may, with the approval of the administrative department of labour, adopt other rules on working hours and rest.

Article 40 An employing unit shall, during the following festivals, arrange holidays for its labourers by law:

(1) The New Year's Day,
(2) The Spring Festival,
(3) The International Labour Day,
(4) The National Day, and
(5) Other holidays provided by laws and administrative regulations.

Article 41 An employing unit may extend working hours as necessitated by its production or business operation after consultation with the trade union and its labourers, but the extended working hours per day shall generally not exceed one hour; if such extension is needed for special reasons, the extended hours shall not exceed 3 h per day provided that the health of labourers is guaranteed. However, the total extended hours in a month shall not exceed 36 h.

Article 42 The extension of working hours shall not be subject to Article 41 hereof in any of the following circumstances:

(1) In the event of natural disasters, accidents or other reasons, the life and health of labourers or the safety of property is in peril, and urgent measures are needed,
(2) In the event of the breakdown of production equipment, transportation lines or public facilities, production and public interests are affected, and urgent repair must be done without any delay, or
(3) Other circumstances stipulated by laws and administrative regulations.

Article 43 An employing unit shall not extend the working hours of labourers in violation of the provisions herein.

Article 44 An employing unit shall pay remuneration that is higher than that for normal working hours according to the following standards:

(1) To pay no less than 150% of the normal wages if an extension of working hours is arranged,
(2) To pay no less than 200% of the normal wages if work is arranged on off days and no make-up off days can be arranged, or
(3) Pay no less than 300% of the normal wages if work is arranged on statutory holidays.

Article 45 The State shall put into operation the system of paid annual leave.

Labourers who have worked for one successive year or more shall be entitled to paid annual leave. The specific measures therefore shall be formulated by the State Council.

Chapter 5

Wages

Article 46 The distribution of wages shall follow the principle of distribution according to work and the principle of equal pay for equal work.

The level of wages shall be gradually raised with economic development. The State shall exercise macrocontrol over the total payroll.

Article 47 An employing unit shall, based on the characteristics of its production and business operation as well as economic results, independently determine the form of wage distribution and wage level for its own unit by law.

Article 48 The State shall put in operation a system of minimum wage. The specific standards of minimum wage shall be determined by the people's governments of provinces, autonomous regions or municipalities directly under the Central Government and submitted to the State Council for the record.

Wages to be paid to a labouer by an employing unit shall not be lower than the local standards of minimum wage.

Article 49 The determination and readjustment of the standards of minimum wage shall be made with reference to the following factors in a comprehensive manner:

(1) the lowest living expenses of a labourer plus that of the average number of his or her dependents,
(2) the average wage level of society as a whole,
(3) the labour productivity,
(4) the situation of employment; and
(5) the regional differences in economic development.

Article 50 Wages shall be paid monthly to a labourer in cash. The wages to be paid to a labourer shall not be embezzled, nor shall the payment thereof be delayed without justification.

Article 51 An employing unit shall pay wages by law to a labourer for statutory holidays, marriage or funeral leaves or periods when he or she participates in social activities by law.

Chapter 6

Occupational Safety and Health

Article 52 An employing unit must establish and perfect the system of occupational safety and health, strictly implement the rules and standards of the State with regard to occupational safety and health, carry out education among labourers with regard to occupational safety and health, prevent accidents in the course of employment, and lessen occupational hazards.

Article 53 Facilities of occupational safety and health shall meet the standards set by the State.

Such facilities that are newly constructed, renovated or expanded shall be designed, constructed and put into operation or use simultaneously with the main part of the project.

Article 54 An employing unit shall provide a labourer with occupational safety and health conditions conforming to the provisions of the State and with necessary articles of labour protection and provide regular health examination for a labourer engaged in work with occupational hazards.

Article 55 A labourer to be engaged in specialised operations shall receive special training and acquire qualifications for such special operations.

Article 56 A labourer shall strictly abide by rules on safe operation in the process of employment.

If the managerial personnel of an employing unit give command in violation of the established rules and compel a labourer to operate under unsafe conditions, the labourer shall have the right to refuse such command. A labourer shall have the right to criticise, report or file charges against any acts endangering his or her life or health.

Article 57 The State shall establish a system of statistical reports and dispositions of accidents of injuries or deaths and cases of occupational diseases. The administrative departments of labour and other relevant departments under the people's governments at or above the county level and an employing unit shall, according to law, count, report and handle the accidents of injuries or deaths occurred to a labourer in the process of employment and situations of occupational diseases.

Chapter 7

Special Protection for Female Labourers and Young Workers

Article 58 The State shall provide special protection to female labourers and young workers.

Young workers refer to labourers who have reached the age of 16 but under the age of 18.

Article 59 It is prohibited to arrange for female labourers to engage in work down the pit of mines, work with Grade IV physical labour intensity as prescribed by the State, or other work forbidden to women.

Article 60 It is prohibited to arrange for female labourers during their menstrual periods to engage in work high above the ground, under low temperature, or in cold water or work with Grade III physical labour intensity as prescribed by the State.

Article 61 It is prohibited to arrange for female labourers during their pregnancy to engage in work with Grade III physical labour intensity as stipulated by the State or other work forbidden to pregnant women. It is prohibited to arrange for female labourers who have been pregnant for seven months or more to work in extended working hours or to work night shifts.

Article 62 Female labourers shall be entitled to no less than 90 days of maternity leave for childbirth.

Article 63 It is prohibited to arrange for female labourers during the period of breastfeeding their babies of less than one year old to engage in work with Grade III physical labour intensity as prescribed by the State or other labour forbidden to women during their breastfeeding period, to work in extended working hours or to work night shifts.

Article 64 It is prohibited to arrange for young workers to engage in work that is down the pit of mines, poisonous or harmful, with Grade IV physical labour intensity as prescribed by the State, or other work forbidden to them.

Article 65 An employing unit shall provide regular physical examinations to young workers.

Chapter 8

Vocational Training

Article 66 The State shall take various measures, through various channels, to expand vocational training undertakings to develop professional skills of labourers, improve their qualities, and raise their employment capability and work ability.

Article 67 People's governments at various levels shall incorporate the development of vocational training into their plans of social and economic development and encourage and support enterprises, institutions, public organisations and individuals, if conditions permit, to sponsor vocational training in various forms.

Article 68 An employing unit shall establish a system of vocational training, retain and use vocational training funds in accordance with the provisions of the State, and provide a labourer with vocational training in a planned way and in light of its actual conditions.

A labourer to be engaged in technical work shall receive training before taking up a post.

Article 69 The State shall determine occupational classification, set professional skill standards for the occupations classified, and put into operation a system of vocational qualification certification. The examination and verification organisations approved by the government shall assume the responsibility for conducting examination and verification of the professional skills of labourers.

Chapter 9

Social Insurance and Welfare

Article 70 The State shall develop social insurance undertakings, establish a social insurance system, and set up social insurance funds so that labourers may receive assistance and compensation in case of old age, illness, work-related injuries, unemployment and childbirth.

Article 71 The level of social insurance shall be in proportion to the level of social and economic development and social affordability.

Article 72 The sources of social insurance funds shall be determined according to the branches of insurance, and overall social insurance funds shall be raised step by step. An employing unit and its labourers shall participate in social insurance and pay social insurance contributions in accordance with law.

Article 73 A labourer may enjoy social insurance benefits by law in case of any of the following events:

(1) retirement,
(2) being ill or injured,
(3) being injured or disabled in the course of employment or contracting with occupational diseases,
(4) unemployment, or
(5) childbirth.

After the death of a labourer, the dependents of the deceased shall be entitled to subsidies for such survivors according to law.

The conditions and standards for labourers to enjoy social insurance benefits shall be stipulated by laws and administrative regulations.

The social insurance money that labourers are entitled to shall be paid on schedule and in full.

Article 74 The agencies in charge of social insurance funds shall collect, expend, manage and operate the funds by law and assume the responsibility for preserving and increasing the value of such funds.

The supervisory organisations of social insurance funds shall exercise supervision over the revenue and expenditure, management and operation of social insurance funds by law.

The establishment and functions of the agencies in charge of social insurance funds and the supervisory organisations of social insurance funds shall be prescribed by law.

No organisation or individual is allowed to misappropriate social insurance funds.

Article 75 The State shall encourage an employing unit to set up supplementary insurance for its labourers according to its actual conditions.

The State shall advocate that individual labourers take out endowment insurance.

Article 76 The State shall develop social welfare undertakings, construct public welfare facilities, and provide conditions for labourers to rest, recuperate and convalesce.

An employing unit shall create conditions to improve collective welfare and increase labourers' social benefits.

Chapter 10

Labour Dispute

Article 77 If a labour dispute between employing unit and labourer arises, the parties may apply for mediation or arbitration or take legal proceedings according to law or may seek a settlement through consultation.

The principle of mediation shall be applicable to the procedures of arbitration and litigation.

Article 78 The settlement of a labour dispute shall follow the principle of legality, justness and promptness to safeguard the legitimate rights and interests of the parties in accordance with law.

Article 79 In the case of a labour dispute, the parties may apply to the labour dispute mediation committee of their unit for mediation; if the mediation fails and one of the parties makes a request for arbitration, that party may apply to a labour dispute arbitration commission for arbitration. Either party may also directly apply to a labour dispute arbitration commission for arbitration. If any party is not satisfied with the award of arbitration, the party may bring a lawsuit to the people's court.

Article 80 A labour dispute mediation commission may be established within an employing unit. The commission shall be composed of labourer representatives, an employing unit, and its trade union. The chairmanship of the commission shall be assumed by a representative of the trade union.

If an agreement is reached through mediation in the case of a labour dispute, it shall be implemented by the parties.

Article 81 A labour dispute arbitration commission shall be composed of representatives of the administrative department of labour, representatives from the trade union at the corresponding level, and representatives of employing units. The chairmanship of the commission shall be assumed by a representative of the administrative department of labour.

Article 82 The party that requests arbitration shall file a written application with a labour dispute arbitration commission within 60 days from the date of the occurrence of the labour dispute. The arbitration commission shall generally make an arbitral award within 60 days from the date of receiving the application. If no objections have been raised, the parties must execute the arbitral award.

Article 83 Where a party to a labour dispute is not satisfied with the arbitration decision, the party may bring a lawsuit to the people's court within 15 days from the date of receiving the arbitral award. Where a party has neither brought a lawsuit nor executed the arbitral award within the period prescribed by law, the other party may apply to the people's court for enforcement.

Article 84 Where a dispute arises from the conclusion of a collective contract and no settlement can be reached through consultation by the parties concerned, the administrative department of labour under the local people's government may coordinate with the parties and organisations concerned in settling the dispute.

Where a dispute arises from the fulfillment of a collective contract and no settlement can be reached through consultation by the parties concerned, the parties may apply to a labour dispute arbitration commission for arbitration. If any party is not satisfied with the arbitral award, it may bring a lawsuit to the people's court within 15 days from the date of receiving the arbitral award.

Chapter 11

Supervision and Inspection

Article 85 The administrative departments of labour under the people's governments at or above the county level shall, in accordance with law, supervise and inspect the implementation of laws and administrative regulations on labour by an employing unit and have the power to stop any acts that violate laws and administrative regulations on labour and order the rectification thereof.

Article 86 The inspectors from the administrative department of labour under the people's governments at or above the county level shall, while performing their public duties, have the right to enter into an employing unit to make investigations about the implementation of laws and administrative regulations on labour, consult the necessary data and inspect the premises of employment.

The inspectors from the administrative department of labour under the people's governments at or above the county level must produce their papers while performing public duties, enforce laws impartially, and abide by the relevant regulations.

Article 87 Relevant departments under the people's governments at or above the county level shall, within the scope of their respective functions and responsibilities, supervise the implementation of laws and administrative labour by an employing unit.

Article 88 Trade unions at various levels shall, in accordance with law, safeguard the legitimate rights and interests of labourers and supervise the implementation of laws and administrative regulations on labour by an employing unit.

Any organisation or individual shall have the right to expose and report any acts that violate the law and administrative regulations on labour.

Chapter 12

Legal Responsibility

Article 89 Where the rules and regulations on labour formulated by an employing unit run counter to the provisions of laws and administrative regulations, the administrative department of labour shall give a warning to the unit and order it to make rectification; where any damage have been caused to a labourer, the unit shall be liable for compensation.

Article 90 Where the employing unit, in violation of the stipulations of this Law, extends the working hours of labourers, the administrative department of labour shall give it a warning, order it to make rectification, and may impose a fine thereon.

Article 91 Where an employing unit commits any of the following acts as to infringe upon the legitimate rights and interests of a labourer, the administrative department of labour shall order it to pay a labourer remuneration of wages or to make up for economic losses and may also order it to pay compensation:

(1) To embezzle wages or delay paying wages without reason,
(2) To refuse to pay remuneration of wages for extended working hours,
(3) To pay wages below the local standard of minimum wage; or
(4) Fail to provide economic compensation in accordance with the provisions hereafter after termination of a labour contract.

Article 92 Where the occupational safety facilities and health conditions of an employing unit do not comply with the provisions of the State or the unit fails to provide labourers with necessary labour protection articles and labour protection facilities, the administrative department of labour or other relevant departments shall order it to make rectification and may impose a fine thereon. If the circumstances are serious, such departments shall refer the matter to the people's government at or above the county level for a decision ordering the unit to stop production for consolidation. If the unit fails to take measures against the hidden danger of an accident, which leads to the occurrence of a serious accident, thus causing losses of lives and properties to labourers, persons who are held responsible shall be investigated for criminal liability by criminal law.

Article 93 Where an employing unit compels labourers to operate against the established rules and under unsafe conditions, thus causing major injuries and deaths that give rise to serious consequences, persons who are held responsible shall be investigated for criminal liability by criminal law.

Article 94 Where an employing unit illegally recruits minors under the age of 16, the administrative department of labour shall order it to make rectification and impose a fine thereon. If the circumstances are serious, the administrative department for industry and commerce shall revoke its business licence.

Article 95 Where an employing unit, in violation of the provisions hereof with regard to the protection of female labourers and young workers, infringes upon their legitimate rights and interests, the administrative department of labour shall order it to make rectification, and impose a fine thereon. Where any harm has been done to female labourers and young workers, the unit shall be liable for compensation.

Article 96 Where an employing unit commits one of the following acts, persons who are held responsible shall be punished by the public security organ with a detention of 15 days or less, a fine, or a warning; where the case constitutes a crime, persons who are held responsible shall be investigated for criminal liability according to law:

(1) Compelling labourers to work by means of violence, intimidation or illegal restriction of personal freedom, or
(2) Humiliating, imposing corporal punishment upon, beating, illegally searching, or detaining labourers.

Article 97 Where an invalid contract concluded for reasons of an employing unit has caused damage to a labourer, the employing unit shall be liable for compensation.

Article 98 Where an employing unit, in violation of the conditions specified herein, terminates a labour contract or intentionally delays the conclusion of a labour contract, the administrative department of labour shall order it to make rectification; where any damage has been caused to a labourer, the employing unit shall be liable for compensation according to law.

Article 99 Where an employing unit recruits a labourer whose labour contract has not yet been terminated, thus causing economic losses to his or her former employing unit, the employing unit shall assume joint liabilities for compensation according to law.

Article 100 Where an employing unit fails to pay social insurance contributions without reason, the administrative department of labour shall order it to pay within a fixed period. Where the unit still fails to make the payment at the expiry of the time limit, an overdue fine may be imposed.

Article 101 Where an employing unit unjustifiably obstructs the administrative department of labour and other relevant departments as well as their functionaries from exercising the power of supervision and inspection or retaliates against informers, the administrative department of labour or other relevant departments shall impose a fine upon the unit. Where it constitutes a crime, persons who are held responsible shall be investigated for criminal liability according to law.

Article 102 Where a labourer terminates a labour contract in violation of the conditions specified herein or violates terms of confidentiality agreed upon in the labour contract, thus causing economic losses to his or her employing unit, the labourer shall be liable for compensation in accordance with this Law.

Article 103 Where functionaries of the administrative department of labour or other relevant departments abuse their functions and powers, neglect their duties, and engage in malpractices for private gain, where it constitutes a crime, they shall be investigated for criminal liability according to law; if not, they shall be given administrative sanctions.

Article 104 Where functionaries of the State or personnel of the agencies in charge of social insurance funds misappropriate the social insurance funds, where it constitutes a crime, they shall be investigated for criminal liability according to law.

Article 105 With respect to infringement of the legitimate rights and interests of a labourer committed in violation of the provisions herein, where punishments are provided by other laws or administrative regulations, the provisions thereon in such laws or administrative regulations shall apply.

Chapter 13

Supplementary Provisions

Article 106 People's governments of provinces, autonomous regions or municipalities directly under the Central Government shall, according to this Law and in light of their local conditions, work out the implementing measures for the labour contract system of and report them to the State Council for the record.

Article 107 This Law shall go into effect as of 1 January 1995.

The Labour Contract Law of the People's Republic of China[6]

(Adopted at the 28th Meeting of the Standing Committee of the Tenth National People's Congress on 29 June 2007 and revised on 28 December 2012).

---

[6] The Supreme People's Republic of China. (2015). *Labour Contract Law of the People's Republic of China*. Retrieved 1 March, 2021, from http://english.court.gov.cn/2015-08/17/content_21623832.htm

Chapter 1

General Provisions

Article 1 This Law is enacted to improve the labour contract system, define the rights and obligations of both parties to a labour contract, protect the legitimate rights and interests of labourers, and establish and develop a harmonious and stable labour relationship.

Article 2 This Law is applicable where organisations such as enterprises, self-employed economic orgaisations and private nonenterprise units within the territory of the People's Republic of China (hereinafter collectively referred to as employing units) establish labour relationships with labourers by concluding, performing, modifying, revoking or terminating labour contracts with them.

State organs, public institutions and public organisations and the labourers with whom they are to establish labour relationships shall conclude, perform, modify, revoke or terminate labour contracts in accordance with this Law.

Article 3 The conclusion of a labour contract shall adhere to the principles of legality, fairness, equality, voluntariness, consensus through consultation, and good faith.

A labour contract concluded in accordance with law shall have binding force. Both the employing unit and the labourer shall fulfill the obligations stipulated in the labour contract.

Article 4 An employing unit shall establish and improve labour rules to ensure that a labourer enjoys labour rights and fulfills labour obligations.

When formulating or modifying the labour rules or making decisions on important matters, which have a direct bearing on the immediate interests of labourers, such as labour remuneration, working hours, rest and vacations, occupational safety and health, insurance and welfare, training, labour discipline and labour quota control, an employing unit shall, after discussion by the congress of labourers or all the labourers, put forward plans and suggestions and make decisions after consulting with the trade union or the representatives of the labourers on an equal footing.

If, during the implementation of the rules or the decisions on important matters, the trade union or the labourers hold that such rules or decisions are inappropriate, it or they are entitled to put forward the opinion to the employing unit and have the rules or decisions modified and improved through consultation.

An employing unit shall make public or inform labourers of the rules and the decisions on important matters, which have a direct bearing on the immediate interests of labourers.

Article 5 The administrative department of labour of the people's government at or above the county level shall, together with the representatives of the trade union and the enterprise, establish a sound tripartite mechanism for coordination of labour relationships to jointly discuss and resolve the major issues concerning labour relationships.

Article 6 The trade union shall give assistance and guidance to labourers in lawfully concluding labour contracts with an employing unit and performing the same and establish a collective consultation mechanism with the employing unit to protect the legitimate rights and interests of labourers.

Chapter 2

Conclusion of a Labour Contract

Article 7 A labour relationship is established by an employing unit with a labourer as of the date the former employs the latter. An employing unit shall keep a register of labourers for reference.

Article 8 When an employing unit recruits a labourer, it shall truthfully inform him or her of the job description, the working conditions, the place of work, occupational hazards, conditions for work safety, labour remuneration and other matters that he or she requests to be informed of. An employing unit has the right to acquire the basic information of a labourer, which is directly related to the labour contract, and the labourer shall truthfully provide the same.

Article 9 When recruiting a labourer, an employing unit may not detain the labourer's resident identity card or other certificates, nor may it require him or her to provide guaranty or collect money or things of value from him or her in other names.

Article 10 To establish a labour relationship, a written labour contract shall be concluded.

In the event that no written labour contract is concluded at the time when a labour relationship is established, such a contract shall be concluded within one month as of the date when an employing unit employs a labourer.

Where an employing unit and a labourer conclude a labour contract before the latter starts to work, the labour relationship shall be established as of the date when the latter starts to work.

Article 11 In the event that an employing unit fails to conclude a written labour contract with a labourer at the same time as it employs him or her and that labour remuneration agreed upon with him or her is not definite, the remuneration shall be decided on according to the rate specified in the collective contract; where there is no collective contract or the collective contract is silent on the matter, equal pay for equal work shall apply.

Article 12 A labour contract is classified into a fixed-term labour contract, an open-ended labour contract and a labour contract that terminates upon completion of a given task.

Article 13 A fixed-term labour contract is one the ending date of which is agreed upon between the employing unit and labourer.

An employing unit and a labourer may conclude a fixed-term labour contract upon reaching consensus through consultation.

Article 14 An open-ended labour contract is one where an employing unit and a labourer have agreed not to stipulate a definite ending date.

An employing unit and a labourer may conclude an open-ended labour contract upon reaching consensus through consultation. An open-ended labour contract shall be concluded unless the labourer requests the conclusion of a fixed-term labour contract where a labourer proposes or agrees to renew the labour contract or to conclude a labour contract in any of the following circumstances:

(1) The labourer has been working for the employing unit for a consecutive period of 10 or more years,
(2) The labourer has been working for the employing unit for a consecutive period of 10 or more years but less than 10 years away from the statutory retirement age when the employing unit introduces the labour contract system or when the state-owned enterprise has to conclude a new labour contract with him or her as a result of restructuring, or
(3) The labourer intends to renew the labour contract after he or she has consecutively concluded a fixed-term labour contract with the employing unit twice, and he or she has not been found in any of the circumstances specified in Article 39 or Subparagraph (1) or (2) in Article 40 of this Law.

If an employing unit fails to conclude a written labour contract with a labourer within one year as of the date when it employs the labourer, it shall be deemed to have concluded an open-ended labour contract with the latter.

Article 15 A labour contract that expires upon completion of a given task is one in which the employing unit and the labourer have agreed that the period for completion of the given task is the term of the contract.

An employing unit and a labourer may, upon reaching consensus through consultation, conclude a labour contract that expires upon completion of a given task.

Article 16 A labour contract shall become effective when an employing unit and a labourer reach an agreement through consultation thereon, and both parties sign or affix their seals on the copies of the contract.

The employing unit and the worker shall each keep a copy of the labour contract.

Article 17 A labour contract shall contain the following terms:

(1) name, domicile and legal representative or the principal leading person of the employing unit,
(2) name, address and the number of resident identity card or other valid identity documents of the labourer,
(3) term of the labour contract,
(4) job description and the place of work,
(5) working hours, rest and vacation,
(6) labour remuneration,
(7) social insurance,
(8) occupational protection, working conditions and protection against occupational hazards; and
(9) other terms that are required to be included in a labour contract, as provided for by laws and regulations.

In addition to the requisite terms mentioned above, an employing unit and a labourer may agree to have other matters stipulated in the labour contract, such as probation period, training, confidentiality, supplementary insurance and welfare benefits.

Article 18 If a dispute arises because the labour remuneration rate, the standards for working conditions, etc. are not definitely specified in a labour contract, an employing unit and a labourer may negotiate anew. If the negotiation is unsuccessful, the relevant stipulations of the collective contract shall be applicable. If there is no collective contract or the collective contract is silent on the issue of labour remuneration, equal pay for equal work shall apply. If there is no collective contract or the collective contract is silent on the standards for working conditions, the relevant regulations of the State shall apply.

Article 19 If the term of a labour contract is more than three months but less than one year, the probation period may not exceed one month; if the term is more than one year but less than three years, the probation period may not exceed two months; and if the term is fixed for three or more years or is open-ended, the probation period may not exceed six months.

An employing unit and a labourer may agree upon only one probation period.

No probation period may be stipulated in a labour contract that expires upon completion of a given task or in a labour contract for a term of less than three months.

The probation period shall be included in the term of a labour contract. If a labour contract only provides for a probation period, that period shall not stand, and the period shall be the term of the labour contract.

Article 20 The wages of a labourer on probation shall not be lower than the lowest wage level for the same job of the employing unit or be less than 80% of the wages agreed upon in the labour contract and shall not be lower than the minimum wage rate in the place where the employing unit is located.

Article 21 An employing unit may not revoke a labour contract during the probation period unless a labourer is found in one of the circumstances specified in Article 39 or Subparagraph (1) or (2) in Article 40 of this Law. If an employing unit revokes a labour contract during the probation period, it shall explain the reasons to the labourer.

Article 22 If an employing unit provides special funding for a labourer's training and gives him or her special training, it may conclude an agreement with the labourer specifying the term of service.

Article 23 An employing unit and a labourer may have such terms stipulated in the labour contract as keeping trade secrets of the employing unit and keeping confidential the matters relating to its intellectual property rights.

With regard to a labourer who has a confidentiality obligation, the employing unit may have stipulated in the labour contract or confidentiality agreement competition restriction and payment of economic compensation to him or her on a monthly basis during the term of the competition restriction after the labour contract is revoked or terminated. If the labourer breaches the stipulation on competition restriction, he or she shall pay penalty to the employing unit as agreed upon.

Article 24 The persons subject to competition restriction shall be limited to senior managers, senior technicians and other persons who are under the confidentiality obligation to the employing unit. The scope, geographic area and term of competition restriction shall be agreed upon by employing units and labourers, and such agreement shall not be at variance with the provisions of laws and regulations.

The term competition restriction, calculated from the revocation or termination of the labour contract, for one of the persons, as mentioned in the preceding paragraph, to go to work for a competing employing unit that produces or deals in the same type of products or is engaged in the same type of business as his or her original employing unit, or to establish his or her own business to produce or deal in the same type of products or engage in the same type of business shall not exceed two years.

Article 25 With the exception of the circumstances specified in Articles 22 and 23 of this Law, an employing unit shall not enter into an agreement with a labourer on payment of penalty by the labourer for breach of contract.

Article 26 A labour contract shall be invalid or partially invalid under one of the following circumstances:

(1) The labour contract is concluded or modified against a party's true intention by means of defraud or coercion, or when the party is in precarious situations,
(2) The employing unit disclaims its statutory responsibility or denies the labourer's rights, or
(3) The labour contract is at variance with the mandatory provisions of laws or administrative regulations.

If a dispute arises over the invalidity or partial invalidity of a labour contract, the matter shall be determined by a labour dispute arbitration institution or a people's court.

Article 27 If part of a labour contract is invalid, which does not affect the validity of the rest of the contract, the rest shall remain valid.

Article 28 If a labour contract is declared invalid but the labourer has performed it, the employing unit shall pay the labourer remuneration. The amount of remuneration shall be determined mutatis mutandis according to that for the labourer holding the same or similar posts in the employing unit.

Chapter 3

Performance and Modification of a Labour Contract

Article 29 An employing unit and a labourer shall fully perform their respective obligations in accordance with the labour contract.

Article 30 An employing unit shall pay their labourers remuneration on time and in full in accordance with the labour contract and the regulations of the State.

If an employing unit defaults in payment or underpays labour remuneration, the labourer concerned may, in accordance with law, apply to the local people's court for an order for payment, and the people's court shall issue such an order in accordance with law.

Article 31 An employing unit shall strictly implement the norm set for labour quota and shall not compel a labourer to work overtime or do so in disguised forms.

If an employing unit arranges for a labourer to work overtime, it shall give him or her overtime pay in accordance with the relevant regulations of the State.

Article 32 A labourer shall not be deemed to be breaching the labour contract if he or she refuses to perform hazardous operations under instructions given in violation of rules and regulations or peremptorily given by a manager of the employing unit.

A labourer shall have the right to criticise or report or lodge accusations against an employing unit with respect to the working conditions that endanger his or her life or health.

Article 33 Where an employing unit alters its name, replaces its legal representative, the principal leading person or investor(s), etc., performance of the labour contract shall not be affected.

Article 34 Where an employing unit is merged, divided, etc., the existing labour contract shall remain valid and continue to be performed by the employing unit which succeeds to its rights and obligations.

Article 35 An employing unit and a labourer may modify the provisions of the labour contract if they reach consensus on the matter through consultation. Modification of a labour contract shall be made in writing.

The employing unit and the labourer shall each keep a copy of the modified labour contract.

Chapter 4

Revocation and Termination of a Labour Contract

Article 36 An employing unit and a labourer may revoke the labour contract if they reach consensus on the matter through consultation.

Article 37 A labourer may revoke the labour contract by giving a written 30-day notice to the employing unit. During the probation period, a labourer may revoke the labour contract by notifying the employing unit of his or her intention 3 days in advance.

Article 38 A labourer may revoke the labour contract if the employing unit was found in any of the following circumstances:

(1) failing to provide occupational protection or working conditions as agreed upon in the labour contract,
(2) failing to pay labour remuneration on time and in full,
(3) failing to pay social insurance contributions for the labourer in accordance with law,
(4) having rules and regulations that are at variance with laws or regulations, thereby impairing the labourer's rights and interests,
(5) invalidating the labour contract as a result of one of the circumstances specified in Paragraph 1 of Article 26 of this Law; or
(6) other circumstances in which a labourer may revoke the labour contract as provided for by laws or administrative regulations.

If an employing unit forces a labourer to work by resorting to violence, intimidation or illegal restriction of personal freedom, or if it gives instructions in violation of rules and regulations or gives peremptory orders to the worker to perform hazardous operations, which endanger his or her personal safety, the latter may revoke the labour contract forthwith without notifying the employing unit of the matter in advance.

Article 39 An employing unit may have revoked the labour contract if a labourer is found in any of the following circumstances:

(1) being proved unqualified for recruitment during the probation period,
(2) seriously violating the rules and regulations of the employing unit,
(3) causing major losses to the employing unit due to serious dereliction of duty or engagement in malpractices for personal gain,
(4) concurrently establishing a labour relationship with another employing unit, which seriously affects the accomplishment of the task of the original employing unit, or refusing to rectify after the original employing unit brings the matter to his attention,
(5) invalidating the labour contract as a result of the circumstance specified in Subparagraph (1) of Paragraph 1 of Article 26 of this Law, or
(6) being investigated for criminal liability in accordance with law.

Article 40 In one of the following circumstances, an employing unit may revoke a labour contract if it notifies in writing a labourer of its intention 30 days in advance or after paying him or her an extra one-month salary:

(1) The labourer is unable to take up his or her original work or any other work arranged by the employing unit on the expiry of the specified period of medical treatment for illness or for injury incurred when not at work,
(2) The labourer is incompetent for the post and remains incompetent after receiving training or being transferred to another post, or
(3) The objective conditions taken as the basis for conclusion of the contract have greatly changed, so that the original labour contract cannot be performed and, after consultation between the employing unit and the labourer, no agreement is reached on modification of the contents of the labour contract.

Article 41 If, in any of the following circumstances, an employing unit needs to cut down employment by more than 20 persons, or by less than 20 persons, which, however, accounts for more than 10% of the total number of the enterprise's labourers, it may do so after it explains the situation to the trade union or all of its labourers 30 days in advance, solicits opinions from among them and submit its plan for cutting employment to the administrative department of labour:

(1) The enterprise is to undergo reorganisation pursuant to the provisions of the Law on Enterprise Bankruptcy,
(2) The enterprise is in dire straits in production and management,
(3) The enterprise changes its line of production, introduces a major technological updating or adjusts its business method, and, after modification of the labour contracts, still needs to reduce its personnel, or
(4) The objective economic conditions taken as the basis for the conclusion of the labour contracts have greatly changed so that the original labour contracts cannot be performed.

When cutting employment, the employing unit shall continue to employ the following persons by giving priority to them:

(1) Persons who have concluded fixed-term labuor contracts for a relatively long term with the employing unit;
(2) Persons who have concluded open-ended labour contracts with the employing unit; and
(3) Persons none of whose other family members have a job or who have an elder or minor depending on his or her support.

If an employing unit that has cut its employment pursuant to the provisions in the first paragraph of this Article goes to recruit employees anew within six months, it shall give notification to the laid off persons and, under equal conditions, recruit them before others.

Article 42 An employing unit may not revoke a labour contract concluded with a labourer, who is under one of the following circumstances, by applying the provisions in Articles 40 and 41 of this Law:

(1) Being engaged in operations exposed to occupational disease hazards, the labourer is not given predeparture occupational health examinations, is suspected of an occupational disease, is in the process of being diagnosed or is under medical observation,
(2) Having contracted an occupational disease or being injured at work, the labourer is declared to have totally or partially lost the ability to work,
(3) The labourer is in the prescribed period of medical treatment for illness or for injury incurred when not at work, and
(4) The labourer is during the pregnant, puerperal or breastfeeding period,
(5) The labourer has been working for the employing unit continuously for 15 years in full and is less than 5 years away from the statutory retirement age, or
(6) The labourer is in any other circumstances as provided for by laws or administrative regulations.

Article 43 Where an employing unit intends to revoke a labour contract unilaterally, it shall notify the trade union of the reasons in advance. If the employing unit violates the provisions of laws or administrative regulations or the labour contract, the trade union shall have the right to demand that the employing unit make rectification. The employing unit shall consider the trade union's opinion and notify the trade union in writing of the settlement of the matter.

Article 44 A labour contract shall be terminated under one of the following circumstances:

(1) The term of the contract expires,
(2) The labourer concerned begins to enjoy the benefits of the basic old-age insurance pension in accordance with law,
(3) The labourer concerned dies, is declared dead or missing by the people's court,
(4) The employing unit is declared bankrupt in accordance with law,
(5) The business licence of the employing unit is revoked, the employing unit is ordered to close down or to dissolve, or it decides to dissolve on an earlier date,

(6) Any other circumstances provided for by laws and administrative regulations.

Article 45 At the expiry of a labour contract, under one of the circumstances prescribed in Article 42 of this Law, the term of the labour contract shall be extended until the necessary conditions cease to exist. However, the termination of a labour contract with a labourer who has totally or partially lost the ability to work, as specified in Subparagraph (2) of Article 42 of this Law shall be handled in accordance with the regulations of the State governing insurance for work-related injuries.

Article 46 An employing unit shall pay economic compensation to a labourer under one of the following circumstances:

(1) The labourer revokes the labour contract pursuant to the provisions in Article 38 of this Law;
(2) The employing unit proposes revocation of the labour contract to the labourer pursuant to the provisions in Article 36 of this Law, and the parties reach an agreement thereon through consultation;
(3) The employing unit revokes the labour contract pursuant to the provisions in Article 40 of this Law;
(4) The employing unit revokes the labour contract pursuant to the provisions in the first paragraph of Article 41 of this Law;
(5) The fixed-term labour contract is terminated pursuant to the provisions in Subparagraph (1) of Article 44 of this Law, except that the worker does not agree to renew the contract even though the employing unit maintains the same conditions as, or offers better conditions than, the ones stipulated in the previous contract;
(6) The labour contract is terminated pursuant to the provisions of Subparagraph (4) or (5) of Article 44 of this Law; or
(7) Under any other circumstances provided by laws or administrative regulations.

Article 47 Economic compensation shall be paid on the basis of the number of years a labourer works in an employing unit, the rate being one month's salary for the work of one full year. If he or she has worked for six months or more but less than one year, the time shall be calculated as one year; and if he or she has worked for less than six months, he or she shall be paid half of his or her monthly salary as economic compensation.

If the monthly salary of a labourer is three times the average monthly salary of the labourers of the region for the previous year, which is published by the people's government of the municipality directly under the Central Government or by that of the city divided into districts where the employing unit is located, the rate for his or her economic compensation payable shall be three times the average monthly salary of the labourers, and the number of years involved shall not exceed 12 years.

For the purposes of this Article, the monthly salary means the average of a given labourer's monthly salary for the 12 months prior to the revocation or termination of the labour contract.

Article 48 Where an employing unit revokes or terminates a labour contract in violation of the provisions of this Law and the labourer involved demands continued performance of the contract, the employing unit shall continue performing the same. If the labourer does not demand so or if it becomes impractical for continued performance of the labour contract, the employing unit shall pay compensation pursuant to the provisions in Article 87 of this Law.

Article 49 The State takes measures to establish and improve an interregional system to ensure that a labourer's social insurance account is continued when he is transferred to another region.

Article 50 An employing unit shall issue a certificate of revocation or termination of the labour contract at the time of its revocation or termination and shall, within 15 days, undergo the formalities for the transfer of the labourer's personal file and social insurance account.

The labourer shall hand over the matters related to his or her work as agreed upon by both parties. If the employing unit needs to pay economic compensation to the labourer according to the relevant provisions of this Law, it shall make such payment upon completion of the procedure for handover of the work-related matters.

The employing unit shall keep the copy of a revoked or terminated labour contract for at least two years for reference.

Chapter 5

Special Provisions

Section 1

A Collective Contract

Article 51 The labourers of an enterprise as one party and the employing unit as the other may, through negotiation on an equal basis, conclude a collective contract on matters relating to labour remuneration, working hours, rest and vocations, occupational safety and health, insurance, welfare benefits, etc. The draft collective contract shall be submitted to the labourer's congress or to all the labourers for discussion and adoption.

A collective contract shall be concluded by the trade union on behalf of the labourers of the enterprise with the employing unit. In an enterprise where a trade union has not yet been set up, such a contract shall be concluded with the employing unit by the representatives elected by the labourers under the guidance of the trade union at a higher level.

Article 52 The labourers of an enterprise as one party may conclude special collective contracts with the employing unit with respect to occupational safety and health, protection of the rights and interests of female labourers, wage adjustment mechanisms, etc.

Article 53 In regions at or below the county level, industry-wide or region-wide collective contracts may be concluded between trade unions and the representatives of enterprises engaging in industries such as construction, mining and catering services.

Article 54 After conclusion, a collective contract shall be submitted to the administrative department of labour, and it shall become valid if the department raises no objection within 15 days from the date it receives the text of the labour contract.

A collective contract concluded in accordance with law is binding on the employing unit and the labourer. An industry-wide or region-wide collective contract is binding on the employing units and the labourers engaged in a given local industry or a given region.

Article 55 The rates for labour remuneration and the standards for working conditions, etc. stipulated in a collective contract shall not be lower than the minimum rates and standards prescribed by the local People's government. The rates for labour remuneration and standards for working conditions, etc. stipulated in the labour contract between an employing unit and a labourer shall not be lower than those stipulated in the collective contract.

Article 56 Where an employing unit breaches the collective contract and infringes upon the employment rights and interests of the labourers, the trade union concerned may, in accordance with law, demand that the employing unit assume liability. If a dispute arises over the performance of the collective contract and cannot be resolved through consultation, the trade union may apply for arbitration or bring a lawsuit in accordance with law.

Section 2

Labour Dispatch

Article 57 A labour-dispatching unit shall meet the following requirements:

(1) Its registered capital shall be not less than RMB 2000,000 yuan,
(2) It has fixed premises and facilities for operation, and
(3) It has the management rules of labour dispatching prescribed by laws and administrative regulations.

Any unit that carries out the labour dispatching business shall apply to the administrative department of labour for administrative licence. The unit shall be subject to company registration after the administrative licence is granted. No unit or individual shall not carry out the labour dispatching business without the administrative licence.

Article 58 For the purposes of this Law, a labour-dispatching unit is an employing unit that performs the obligations of an employing unit to the labourers. In the labour contract concluded between the labour-dispatching unit and the labourers to be dispatched shall, in addition to the terms specified in Article 17 of this Law, be specified such terms as the units to which the labourers are to be dispatched, the period of dispatch and the specific jobs.

The labour-dispatching unit shall conclude with the labourers to be dispatched a fixed-term labour contract for a period of not less than two years and shall pay labour remuneration on a monthly basis. During the intervals when there is no work to do, the labuor-dispatching unit shall pay labour remuneration on a monthly basis at the minimum wage rate prescribed by the people's government of the place where the labourers work.

Article 59 When dispatching labourers, the labour-dispatching unit shall conclude an agreement on labour dispatch with the unit that receives the labourers under the dispatch arrangement (hereinafter referred to as the receiving unit). In the agreement on labour dispatch, the jobs dispatched to, the number of persons, the period for dispatch, the amounts and methods of payment of labour remuneration and social insurance contributions, and the liability for breach of the agreement should be stipulated.

A receiving unit shall decide with the labour-dispatching unit on the period of dispatch based on the actual need for jobs and shall not divide a continuous period of employment to conclude a number of short-term agreements.

Article 60 The labour-dispatching unit shall inform the labourers to be dispatched of the content of the agreement on labour dispatch.

The labour-dispatching unit shall not pocket the labour remuneration that the receiving unit pays to the labourers in accordance with the agreement on labour dispatch.

The labour-dispatching unit and the receiving unit may not charge any fees from the labourers dispatched.

Article 61 If a labour-dispatching unit dispatches labourers to a receiving unit located in another place, the labour remuneration and working conditions to be enjoyed by the labourers dispatched shall be provided in conformity with the rates and standards of the place where the receiving unit is located.

Article 62 The receiving unit shall perform the following obligations:

(1) to apply the labour standards of the State and provide the necessary working conditions and occupational protection,
(2) to inform the dispatched labourers of the job requirements and labour remuneration,
(3) to give overtime wages and performance bonuses and provide welfare benefits related to specific posts,
(4) to provide the dispatched labourers training that is necessitated by the job they are on; and
(5) to apply a regular wage adjustment mechanism in case of continued employment.

The receiving unit may not redispatch the labourers to another employing unit.

Article 63 Dispatched labourers shall enjoy the right of equal pay for equal work as the labourers of the receiving unit do. If a receiving unit has no labourers holding the same kind of posts, labour remuneration shall be determined in light of that paid to the labourers holding the same or similar posts at the place where the receiving unit is located.

Article 64 Dispatched labourers shall have the right, in accordance with law, to join the trade union of the labour-dispatching unit or the receiving unit or to organise a trade union to protect their own legitimate rights and interests.

Article 65 Dispatched labourers may have their labour contracts with the labour-dispatching unit revoked pursuant to the provisions in Article 36 or 38 of this Law.

If a dispatched labourer is in any of the circumstances specified in Article 39 and Subparagraph (1) or (2) of Article 40 of this Law, the receiving unit may send him or her back to the labour-dispatching unit, which may have the labour contract with him or her revoked in accordance with the relevant provisions of this Law.

Article 66 The labour contract is the basic mode of employment in China. Labour dispatching is a supplementary mode of employment and only applies to temporary, auxiliary or substitute jobs.

The term temporary in the preceding paragraph means a job position with a duration of no more than 6 months; the term auxiliary means a job position that provides auxiliary service to the core business of a receiving unit; and the term substitute means a job position on which the labourer may be substituted for by another labourer during the period when he or she is absent from work due to off-the-job study or time off.

A receiving unit shall strictly control the number of its dispatched labourers, which shall not exceed the percentage of the staff that shall be determined by the administrative department of labour of the State Council.

Article 67 No employing unit may establish a labour-dispatching unit to dispatch labourers to its own unit or to its subordinate units.

Section 3

Part-Time Employment

Article 68 Part-time employment is a form of employment under which remuneration is chiefly calculated by the hour and the labourers generally work for not more than 4 h per day on average and not more than an aggregate of 24 h per week for the same employing unit.

Article 69 The two parties to part-time employment may conclude an oral agreement.

A labourer in part-time employment may conclude a labour contract with one or more employing units provided that the labour contract concluded later may not prejudice the performance of the one concluded earlier.

Article 70 The two parties to part-time employment may not conclude an agreement on probation period.

Article 71 Either of the two parties to part-time employment may give a notice to the other party at any time to terminate the employment, and in such a case, the employing unit shall not pay any economic compensation.

Article 72 The hourly remuneration rate for part-time employment may not be lower than the minimum hourly wage rate specified by the people's government of the place where the employing unit is located.

Labour remuneration settlement and payment cycle for part-time employment may not exceed 15 days.

Chapter 6

Supervision and Inspection

Article 73 The administrative department of labour under the State Council shall be in charge of supervision over and administration of the implementation of the labour contract system nationwide.

The administrative departments of labour of the local people's governments at or above the county level shall be in charge of supervision over and administration of the implementation of the labour contract system in their own administrative areas.

In supervising and administering the implementation of the labour contract system, the administrative departments of labour of the local people's governments at or above the county level shall listen to the opinions of the trade unions, the enterprise representatives and the departments in charge of the specific industries.

Article 74 The administrative departments of labour of the local people's governments at or above the county level shall, in accordance with law, supervise and inspect the implementation of the labour contract system with respect to the following matters:

(1) the rules formulated by the employing units that have a direct bearing on the immediate interests of the labourers, and the implementation of such rules,
(2) conclusion of labour contracts between employing units and labourers and their revocation,
(3) compliance with the relevant regulations on labour dispatch by the labour-dispatching units and the receiving units,
(4) compliance by the employing units with the State regulations on working hours, rest and vocation of labourers,
(5) payment by the employing units of labour remuneration as stipulated in the labour contracts and their compliance with the minimum wage standards,
(6) purchase of the various types of social insurance by the employing units for the labourers, and payment of social insurance contributions by the same; and
(7) other matters subject to supervision and inspection concerning labour as specified in laws and regulations.

Article 75 When the administrative department of labour of a local people's government at or above the county level conducts supervision and inspection, it shall have the right to check the materials relating to labour contracts and collective contracts and to conduct on-the-spot inspection of the workplaces, and both the employing units and the labourers shall truthfully provide relevant information and materials.

When staff members of an administrative department of labour conduct supervision and inspection, they shall produce their papers, exercise their duties and powers according to law and enforce the law in a polite manner.

Article 76 The departments in charge of supervision over and administration of construction, health, work safety, etc. under the people's governments at or above the county level shall, within the limits of their respective duties, supervise and administer the implementation of the labour contract system by the employing units.

Article 77 A labourer whose legitimate rights and interests are infringed upon shall have the right to request the relevant department to deal with such infringement according to law or to apply for arbitration or bring a lawsuit according to law.

Article 78 The trade union shall protect the legitimate rights and interests of the labourers in accordance with law and supervise the performance of labour contracts and collective contracts by the employing units. Where an employing unit violates the labour laws or regulations or breaches a labour contract or a collective contract, the trade union concerned shall have the right to put forward its opinions or request rectification. Where a labourer applies for arbitration or brings a lawsuit, the trade union concerned shall provide him or her with support and assistance in accordance with law.

Article 79 All organisations and individuals shall have the right to inform against violations of this Law, and the administrative departments of labour of the people's governments at or above the county level shall verify and deal with such violations in a timely manner and reward those that perform meritorious service.

Chapter 7

Legal Responsibility

Article 80 Where the rules of an employing unit that have a direct bearing on the immediate interests of labourers are in contravention with the provisions of laws and regulations, the administrative department of labour shall order it to rectify and shall give it a warning. If harm is done to a labourer, the employing unit shall be liable for compensation.

Article 81 Where the requisite terms provided for by this Law are not clearly stated in the text of a labour contract provided by an employing unit or an employing unit fails to deliver a copy of the labour contract to the labourer, the administrative department of labour shall order it to rectify. If harm is done to the labourer, the unit shall be liable for compensation.

Article 82 Where an employing unit fails to conclude a written labour contract with a labourer for more than a month but less than a year from the date it starts employing him, it shall pay the labourer two times his or her salary for each month.

Where an employing unit fails to conclude an open-ended labour contract with a labourer in violation of the provisions of this Law, it shall pay the labourer two times his or her salary for each month, starting from the date on which an open-ended labour contract should be concluded.

Article 83 Where in violation of the provisions of this Law, an employing unit reaches an agreement with a labourer on a probation period, the administrative department of labour shall order it to rectify. If the illegal agreement on a probation period is executed, the employing unit shall pay compensation to the labourer at the rate of the labourer's monthly salary following the completion of his or her probation for the period of performance by the labourer in excess of the statutory probation period.

Article 84 Where an employing unit, in violation of the provisions of this Law, withholds a labourer's resident identity card or other certificates, the administrative department of labour shall order it to return the same to the labourer within a time limit and impose on it a penalty in accordance with the provisions of relevant laws.

Where an employing unit, in violation of the provisions of this Law, collects money or things of value from the labourers in the name of guaranty or in other names, the administrative department of Labour shall order it to return the same to the labourers within a time limit and impose on it a fine at the rate of not less than 500 yuan but not more than 2000 yuan for each person from whom it has collected money or things of value; if harm is done to the labourers, it shall be liable for compensation.

Where an employing unit withholds a labourer's personal file or other articles when the labourer has his or her labour contract revoked or terminated in accordance with law, it shall be penalised in accordance with the provisions in the preceding paragraph.

Article 85 Where an employing unit commits one of the following acts, the administrative department of labour shall order it to pay the labour remuneration, give overtime pay or make other economic compensation within a time limit; if the labour remuneration is lower than the local minimum wage rate, it shall pay the difference. If it fails to make such payment at the expiry of the time limit, it shall be ordered to pay additional compensation to the labour at a rate of not less than 50% but not more than 100% of the amount payable:

(1) failing to pay a labourer his or her labour remuneration on time and in full as stipulated in the labour contract or as prescribed by the State,
(2) paying labour remuneration at a rate below the local minimum wage rate,
(3) arranging overtime work but giving no overtime pay, or
(4) failing to pay the labourer economic compensation pursuant to the provisions of this Law when revoking or terminating a labour contract.

Article 86 Where a labour contract is declared invalid in accordance with the provisions of Article 26 of this Law, which does harm to the other party, the party in default shall be liable for compensation.

Article 87 Where an employing unit revokes or terminates a labour contract in violation of the provisions of this Law, it shall pay compensation to the labourer two times the rate of economic compensation specified in Article 47 of this Law.

Article 88 Where an employing unit commits one of the following acts, it shall be subjected to an administrative sanction in accordance with law; if a criminal is constituted, it shall be investigated for criminal responsibility according to law; if harm is done to a labourer, the employing unit shall be liable for compensation:

(1) Forcing a person to work by resorting to violence, intimidation or illegal restriction of personal freedom,
(2) Giving instructions in violation of rules and regulations or giving peremptory orders to a labourer to perform hazardous operations, which endanger his or her personal safety,

(3) Humiliating, giving corporal punishment to, beating, illegally searching or detaining a labourer, or
(4) Providing a labourer with hazardous working conditions or a severely polluted environment, thus causing serious harm to the physical or mental health of the labourer.

Article 89 Where in violation of the provisions of this Law, an employing unit fails to issue to a labourer a written statement proving the revocation or termination of the labour contract, the administrative department of Labour shall order it to rectify. If harm is caused to the labourer, the unit shall be liable for compensation.

Article 90 Where a labourer revokes the labour contract in violation of the provisions of this Law or breaches the confidentiality obligation or competition restriction stipulated in the labour contract, thus causing losses to the employing unit, he or she shall be liable for compensation.

Article 91 Where an employing unit recruits a labourer whose labour contract with another employing unit has not yet been revoked or terminated, and thus causing losses to the other employing unit, it shall bear joint and several liability for compensation.

Article 92 Where any employing unit or individual, without the licence from the administrative department of labour, violates the provisions of this Law and provides labour dispatching services, the administrative depart of labour shall order such a unit or individual to stop the illgal acts, confiscates legal earnings and imposes a fine of more than one time but less than five times legal earnings.

Where a labour-dispatching unit and a receiving unit violate the provisions of this Law, the administrative department of labour and other competent departments concerned shall order them to rectify. If they refuse to rectify, a fine shall be imposed on it, with not less than 5000 yuan but not more than 10,000 yuan for each person, and the business licence of the labour dispatching unit shall be revoked by the administrative department for industry and commerce. If harm is caused to the dispatched labourers by a receiving unit, the labour-dispatching unit and the receiving unit shall bear joint and several liability for compensation.

Article 93 An employing unit without lawful business qualifications shall, in accordance with law, be investigated for legal responsibility for its illegal or criminal acts. If the labourers have done their work, the employing unit or its sponsor(s) shall pay them labour remuneration, economic compensation and damages in accordance with the relevant provisions of this Law. If losses are caused to the labourers, the unit shall be liable for compensation.

Article 94 Where an individual who contracts for the operation of a business recruits labourers in violation of the provisions of this Law, thus causing losses to the labourers, the organisation giving out the contract and the individual contractor shall bear joint and several liability for compensation.

Article 95 Where an administrative department of labour or another competent department concerned or its staff member neglects its/his duties and fails to perform the statutory duties, or exercises its/his functions and powers in violation of law, thus causing losses to a labourer or an employing unit, it/he shall be liable for compensation; the person directly in charge and the other persons directly responsible shall be given administrative sanctions according to law; if a crime is constituted, it/he shall be investigated for criminal responsibility according to law.

Chapter 8

Supplementary Provisions

Article 96 Where there are stipulations made in other laws or administrative regulations or by the State Council to govern the conclusion, performance, modification, revocation or termination of labour contracts between public institutions and the persons employed by them under the employment system, the provisions there shall prevail; otherwise, the relevant provisions in this Law shall apply.

Article 97 A labour contract that is concluded in accordance with law prior to implementation of this law and remains valid as of the date this law goes into effect shall continue to be performed. With respect to the number of times for consecutive conclusion of a fixed-term labour contract, as provided for in Subparagraph (3) of the second paragraph in Article 14 of this Law, it shall begin to be calculated from the time the labour contract is renewed after this Law goes into effect.

Where a labour relationship is established prior to the implementation of this Law but no written labour contract is concluded yet, such a contract shall be concluded within one month from the date this Law goes into effect.

Where a labour contract that remains valid as of the date this Law goes into effect is revoked or terminated thereafter, economic compensation shall be paid pursuant to the provisions of Article 46 of this Law, and the number of years for which economic compensation should be paid shall be calculated from the date this Law goes into effect; where the employing unit should pay economic compensation to the labourer concerned according to the relevant regulations at the time before this Law goes into effect, it shall do so in accordance with the relevant provisions then.

Article 98 This Law shall go into effect as of 1 January 2008.

China Interim Provisions on Labour Dispatch

Chapter 1

General Provisions

Article 1 The Interim Provisions on Labour dispatch (hereinafter referred to as the Provisions) are hereby enacted in accordance with the Labour Contract Law of the People's Republic of China (hereinafter the Labour Contract Law), Implementation Regulations for the Labour Contract Law of the People's Republic of China (hereinafter the "Implementation Regulations") and other applicable laws and administrative regulations to regulate labour dispatch practices, safeguard the legitimate rights and interest of labourers and promote the development of a harmonious and stable labour relationship.

Article 2 The provisions apply to the labour dispatch service provided by a labour dispatch unit and the employment of labourers dispatched by an enterprise (hereinafter referred to as a receiving unit).

The provisions also apply to the employment of dispatched labourers by a partnership such as an accounting firm or a law firm incorporated by law, a foundation or a private noenterprise entity.

Chapter 2

Scope and Proportion of Employment

Article 3 A receiving unit may employ dispatched labourers in temporary, auxiliary or substitute job positions only.

For the purpose of the preceding paragraph, a temporary job position refers to a job position that survives for no longer than 6 months, an auxiliary job position refers to a nonmain business job position that provides services for main business, and a substitute job position refers to a job position that can be taken by other labourers instead as a result that a labourer of a receiving unit fails to work due to full-time study, leave and so on over a certain period of time.

Before a receiving unit determines an auxiliary position in which dispatched labourers will be employed, its labourer congress or all labourers shall hold discussions and provide proposals and opinions, the receving unit shall negotiate with the labour union or labourer representatives on an equal basis, and the matters concerned shall be announced internally.

Article 4 A receiving unit shall strictly control the number of dispatched labourers it employed, which shall not exceed 10% of the total number of labourers.

For the purpose of the preceding paragraph, the total number of labourers refers to the sum of the number of labourers under a labour contract with the receiving contract and the number of dispatched labourers it employed.

A receiving unit that calculates the proportion of the dispatched labourers it employed refers to a unit that may conclude a labour contract with its labourers in accordance with the Labour contract Law and its Implementation Regulations.

Chapter 3

Conclusion and Performance of a Labour Contract/Labour Dispatch Agreement

Article 5 A labour dispatch unit shall conclude a written labour contract with the labourers to be dispatched for a fixed period of at least 2 years by law.

Article 6 A labour dispatch unit may agree with the labourers to be dispatched on the probation period by law. However, it may agree on one probation period with the same labourer to be dispatched only.

Article 7 A labour dispatch agreement shall specify the following:

(1) Title and nature of the job position in which the dispatched labourer will be employed,
(2) Job location,
(3) Number of dispatched labourers and the dispatch period,
(4) Amount and payment method of labour remuneration determined in accordance with the principle of equal work for equal pay,
(5) Amount and payment method of the social security insurance contributions,
(6) Working hours, vocation and leave,
(7) Related benefits for the dispatched labourers during work-related injuries, birth-giving or illness;
(8) Occupational safety &health and training,
(9) Expenses such as economic compensation,
(10) The term of the labour dispatch agreement,
(11) Payment method and criteria of the labour dispatch service fee,
(12) Liability for breach of the labour dispatch agreement,
(13) Other matters that shall be included in the labour dispatch agreement are set forth in the laws, regulations and rules.

Article 8 A labour dispatch unit shall perform the following obligations for the labourers it dispatches:

(1) Inform the dispatched labourers of the matters stipulated in Article 8 of the Labour Contract Law, rules of the labour dispatch unit that shall be observed and the contents of the labour dispatch agreement in a truthful manner,
(2) Establish training policies to educate and provide dispatched labourers with pre-employment training and safety education,
(3) Pay to the dispatched labourers the labour remuneration and other benefits in accordance with the requirements of the State and the labour dispatch agreement by law,
(4) Pay the social security insurance contributions and complete the social security insurance related formalities for the dispatched labourers in accordance with the requirements of the State and the labour dispatch agreement by law,
(5) Urge the receiving unit to provide dispatched labourers with labour protection and other occupational safety & health conditions by law,
(6) Provide the certificate of revocation or termination of a labour contract by law,
(7) Provide assistance in resolving a dispute between the dispatched labourers and the receiving unit,
(8) Other matters specified in the laws, regulations and other rules.

Article 9 A receiving unit shall, in accordance with Article 62 of the Labour Contract Law, provide dispatched labourers with position-related welfare benefits without any discrimination against dispatched labourers.

Article 10 In the event that a labourer dispatched by a labour dispatch unit is injured in an incident while working for a receiving unit, the labour dispatch unt shall apply for determination of work-related injuries by law, and the receiving unit shall assist in the investigation/verification for the purpose of determination of work-related injuries. The labour dispatch unit shall bear the liability for work-related injury insurance, but it may negotiate with the receiving unit over the compensatory approach.

In the event that a dispatched labourer applies for the diagnosis and/or assessment of an occupational disease, the receiving unit shall be responsible for dealing with the matters relating to the diagnosis and/or assessment of the occupational disease and providing materials such as the dispatched labourer's occupational history, history of exposure to the occupational disease and test results of hazardous factors at the workplace for the occupational diseases that are necessary for the diagnosis and/or assessment of the occupational disease in a truthful manner. The labour dispatch unit shall provide the dispatched labourer with other materials necessary for the diagnosis and/or assessment of the occupational disease.

Article 11 In the event that the administrative licence of a labour dispatch service provider is not renewed upon expiry or its labour dispatch service licence is rescinded or revoked, the labour contract already concluded with its dispatched labourer shall continue to be performed until the expiry of the labour contract by law. Both parties a labour contract may dissolve the labour contract through negotiation.

Article 12 Under any of the following circumstances, a receiving unit may return a dispatched labourer to the labour dispatch unit concerned:

(1) The receiving unit comes under the circumstances specified in Item 3, Article 40 and Article 41 of the Labour Contract Law;
(2) The receiving unit is declared bankrupt, revoked of its business licence, ordered to close down or cancel registration by law, decides to dissolve in advance or not to continue the business upon expiry of the business period; and
(3) The labour dispatch agreement is terminated upon expiry.

During the period of time when the dispatched labourer has no job after being returned, the labour dispatch unit shall pay remuneration to the dispatched labourer on a monthly basis, at least in accordance with the minimum wage rates set by the local people's government.

Article 13 In the event that a dispatched labourer comes under the circumstances specified in Article 42 of the Labour Contract Law, prior to the expiry of the dispatch period, the receiving unit concerned shall not return the dispatched labourer to the labour dispatch unit in accordance with Item 1, Paragraph 1, Article 12 of the Provisions. The dispatched labourer may be returned only by extending the dispatch period upon its expiry until the disappearance of the circumstances.

Chapter 4

Dissolution and Termination of a Labour Contract

Article 14 A dispatched labourer may dissolve its labour contract with a labour dispatch unit upon a 30-day prior written notice. He/she may dissolve its labour contract with a labour dispatch service provider upon a 3-day written notice during the probation period. The labour dispatch service providers shall inform the receiving unit concerned of the dispatched labourer's notice to dissolve the labour contract in a timely manner.

Article 15 In the event that a dispatched labourer is returned by a receiving unit in accordance with Article 12 of the Provisions, the labour dispatch unit concerned may dissolve the labour contract with the dispatched labourer if the dispatched labourer who is to be redispatched does not agree with the labour dispatch unit to maintain or improve the conditions agreed upon in the labour contract.

In the event that a dispatched labourer is returned by a receiving unit in accordance with Article 12 of the Provisions, the labour dispatch unit concerned may not dissolve the labour contract with the dispatched labourer if the dispatched labourer to be redispatched does not agree with the labour dispatch unit to decrease the conditions specified in the labour contract except where the dispatched labourer makes a request to dissolve the labour contract.

Article 16 The labour contract between a labour dispatch unit and a dispatched labourer is terminated when the labour dispatch unit is declared bankrupt, revoked of its business licence, ordered to close down or cancel registration by law, decides to dissolve in advance or not to continue the business upon expiry of the business period by law. The receiving unit concerned shall negotiate with the labour dispatch unit over the proper placement of the dispatched labourer.

Article 17 In the event that a labour dispatch unit dissolves or terminates its labour contract with a dispatched labourer pursuant to Article 46 of the Labour contract Law or Article 15, 16 of the Provisions, it shall provide the dispatched labourer with economic compensation.

Chapter 5

Social Security Insurance in a Transregional Labour Dispatch

Article 18 In the event that a labour dispatch unit in a region dispatches a labourer to another region, it shall obtain the social security insurance coverage for the dispatched labourer at the place where the receiving unit concerned is located, and pay the social security insurance contributions in accordance with the rules at the place where the receiving unit concerned is located, and the dispatched labourer is entitled to the social security insurance benefits in accordance with the provisions of the State.

Article 19 In the event that a labour dispatch unit dispatching a labourer to receiving unit has set up a branch at the place where the receiving unit is located, the branch shall complete the formalities for obtaining social security insurance coverage and pay the social security insurance contributions for the dispatched labourer.

In the event that a labour dispatch unit dispatching a labourer to a receiving unit does not set up a branch at the place where the receiving unit is located, the receiving unit shall complete the formalities for obtaining social security insurance coverage and pay the social security insurance contributions for the dispatched labourer on behalf of the labour dispatch unit.

Chapter 6

Legal Liability

Article 20 Any violation of the provisions of the Labour contract Law and its Implementation Regulations concerning labour dispatch by a labour dispatch unit or receiving unit shall be dealt with in accordance with Article 92 of the Labour Contract Law.

Article 21 In the event that a labour dispatch unit dissolves or terminates a labour contract with a dispatched labourer in violation of the Provisions, the case shall be subject to Article 48 and Article 87 of the Labour Contract Law.

Article 22 In the event that the receiving unit violates Paragraph 3, Article 3 of the Provisions, the competent department in charge of human resources and social security shall order it to take corrective actions and give it a warning; in the event of any damage caused to the dispatched labourer concerned, the receiving unit shall be liable to make compensation by law.

Article 23 Any violation of Article 6 of the Provisions by a labour dispatch unit shall be dealt with in accordance with Article 83 of the Labour Contract Law.

Article 24 In the event that the receiving unit returns a dispatched labourer in violation of the provisions, the case shall be subject to Paragraph 2, Article 92 of the Labour Contract Law.

Chapter 7

Supplementary Provisions

Article 25 The employment of dispatched labourers by the permanent representative office of a foreign enterprise or by the representative office of a foreign financial institution in China as well as the employment of international oceangoing seamen by a seamen employer in the form of labour dispatch is exempt from the restrictions on the proportion of dispatched labourers employed for temporary, auxiliary or substitutive job positions.

Article 26 Labour dispatch referred to herein does not include the dispatch of labourers of a receiving unit to overseas areas for work or to a family or natural person to provide labour services.

Article 27 The employment of labourers by a receiving unit in the form of labour dispatch in the name of contracting and outsourcing shall be dealt with in accordance with the Provisions.

Article 28 In the event that the number of dispatched labourers employed by a receiving unit exceeds 10% of the total number of its employment prior to the effective date of the Provisions, the receiving unit shall develop a scheme for employment adjustments and reduce the proportion to the specified level within 2 years from the effective date of the Provisions. However, the labour contracts concluded by law prior to the release of the Decision of the Standing Committee of the National People's Congress on Amending the Labour contract Law of the People's Republic of China and the labour dispatch agreements whose expiry date is 2 years from the effective date of the provisions may continue to be performed until expiry by law.

The receiving unit shall file for recording the scheme for employment adjustments it develops with the local competent administrative department in charge of human resources and social security.

The receiving unit shall not employ newly dispatched labourers before reducing the number of dispatched labourers prior to the effective date of the provisions to the specified proportion as required.

Article 29 This Law shall come into effect as of 1 March 2014.

The Social Insurance Law of the People's Republic of China[7]

(Adopted at the Seventeenth Session of the Standing Committee of the 11th National People's Congress on 28 October 2010 and revised on 29 December 2018).

Chapter 1

General Provisions

Article 1 This Law is hereby enacted in accordance with the Constitution for the purposes of regulating social insurance relationships, securing citizens' legitimate rights and interests to participate in a social insurance system and receive social insurance benefits, achieving a fair sharing of benefits of development by citizens, and promoting social harmony and stability.

Article 2 The State shall establish a social insurance system consisting of basic old-age insurance, basic medical insurance, work-related injury insurance, unemployment insurance, and maternity insurance to guarantee citizens' rights to receive material assistance from the State and society according to law against old age, sickness, work-related injuries, unemployment and maternity.

Article 3 The social insurance system follows the principle of wide coverage, modest benefits, multitiered programmes and a sustainable system. The level of the social insurance system shall correspond to that of economic and social development.

Article 4 Each employing unit and individual within the boundary of the People's Republic of China shall, according to law, make social insurance contributions, have the right to access the related contribution records and individual social insurance benefit credits, and request social insurance consultancy and other relevant services from a social insurance agency.

Each individual shall be entitled to social insurance benefits according to law and have the right to exercise oversight over contributions made by the employing unit on his or her behalf.

[7] CECC. (2010). *The Social Insurance Law of the People's Republic of China*. Retrieved 1 March, 2021, from https://www.cecc.gov/resources/legal-provisions/social-insurance-law-of-the-peoples-republic-of-china

Article 5 The People's Governments at and above the county level shall incorporate social insurance into their local economic and social development programmes.

The State shall raise funds for the social insurance system through multiple channels. The People's Governments at and above the county level shall provide financial support as deemed necessary to social insurance programmes.

The State shall support social insurance through tax incentive policies.

Article 6 The State shall subject social insurance funds to vigorous supervision and control.

The State Council and People's Governments of provinces, autonomous regions, and municipalities directly under the Central Government shall establish and improve the supervision and management system for social insurance funds and guarantee safe and effective fund operations.

The People's Governments at and above the county level shall adopt measures to encourage and support all stakeholders to participate in social insurance fund supervision.

Article 7 The social insurance administrative department of the State Council shall take charge of national social insurance administration. Any other relevant department of the State Council shall take charge of social insurance affairs within its jurisdiction of responsibility.

The social insurance administrative department of the local People's Government at or above the county level shall take charge of social insurance administration in its administrative region. Any other relevant department of the local People's Government at or above the county level shall take charge of social insurance affairs within its jurisdiction of responsibility.

Article 8 A social insurance agency provides social insurance services and is responsible for social insurance registration, bookkeeping for the participants, and paying social insurance benefits to the beneficiaries.

Article 9 Trade unions shall defend labourers' legitimate rights and interests according to law, have the right to participate in studies and research on fundamental issues related to social insurance, and act as members of the social insurance supervisory committees to perform supervision over the matters related to labourers' social insurance rights and interests.

Chapter 2

Basic Old-Age Insurance

Article 10 Each labourer shall enroll in the basic old-age insurance system, and an employing unit and a labourer shall jointly make basic old-age insurance contributions.

A proprietor of privately or individually owned business with no hired labour, a part-time labourer who is not covered by the basic old-age insurance system through his or her employing unit, and any other person in employment of flexible forms may elect to enroll in the basic old-age insurance system, and the person in question shall make basic old-age insurance contributions.

The approach to the basic old-age insurance for civil servants and that for working people who are governed likewise by the Civil Service Law shall be regulated by the State Council.

Article 11 Basic old-age insurance shall be a combination of social pooling and individual accounts.

The basic old-age insurance fund shall consist of contributions from employers and employees and government subsidies.

Article 12 An employing unit shall make basic old-age insurance contributions at the State-fixed rate of the labourers' payroll, and the contributions shall be deposited into the basic old-age insurance pooling fund.

A labourer shall make basic old-age insurance contributions at the State-fixed rate for his or her wage, and the contributions shall be deposited into his or her individual account.

A member of the basic old-age insurance as proprietor of privately or individually owned business with no hired labour, part-time labourer who is not covered by the basic old-age insurance system through his or her employing unit, or any other person in employment of flexible forms shall make basic old-age insurance contributions as set by the State; and the contributions shall be divided and deposited separately into the pooling fund and an individual account.

Article 13 The basic old-age insurance contributions due from labourers of state enterprises and institutions for their working years prior to the initiation of the old-age insurance system, which are treated as contributing years, shall be made up by the government.

When there arises a shortfall for the basic old-age insurance fund to cover its obligations, subsidies shall be provided by the government into the fund.

Article 14 Advance withdrawal from an individual account shall not be allowed. The interest rate of an individual account shall be no less than that for a fixed-term bank account, and interests accrued are not subject to taxation. The balances in the individual account are hereditary upon death of the account bearer.

Article 15 Basic old-age insurance benefits consist of pensions from the pooling and from the individual account.

The basic old-age insurance benefit for a member is determined by the following factors: the member's cumulative length of contribution payment and assessed wage for contributions, the average wages of the employees of the district where the member resides, his or her credits in the individual account, and life expectancy of the urban population.

Article 16 A member of the basic old-age insurance shall receive the basic old-age pension on a monthly basis if the member's cumulative length of contribution payment is no less than fifteen years upon reaching the legal retirement age.

If the cumulative length of contribution payment of a member of the basic old-age insurance is less than fifteen years when the member reaches the legal retirement age, the member may receive the basic old-age insurance on a monthly basis once the member makes up the contribution payment to what is required for fifteen years. The member may elect to transfer to the new rural social insurance of the old-age pension or social insurance of the old-age pension for urban residents and receive pensions in accordance with the regulations of the State Council.

Article 17 When a member of the basic old-age insurance dies from illnesses or causes not related to work, the survivors of the member are entitled to receive funeral subsidies and bereavement allowances; when a member becomes completely unfit for work due to illnesses or causes not related to work before reaching the legal retirement age, the member is entitled to illness and disability allowances. The expenses required shall be covered by the basic old-age insurance fund.

Article 18 The State shall set up a mechanism for adjusting basic old-age insurance benefits when necessary and raise the basic old-age insurance benefits at appropriate intervals according to the factors of mean growth of employers' wages and price increases.

Article 19 The basic old-age insurance relationship of a member who has worked across different pooling districts shall transfer together with the member, and the member's lengths of contribution payment shall be cumulative. When the member reaches the legal retirement age, his or her basic old-age pension shall be calculated in segregation corresponding to the phases of contribution payment, yet the pension shall be paid in integration as an aggregate. The concrete approach shall be regulated by the State Council.

Article 20 The State shall establish and improve the new rural social insurance of the old-age pension.

The new rural social insurance of the old-age pension shall be a combination of individual contributions, collective subsidies and government allowances.

Article 21 The benefits of the new rural social insurance of the old-age pension shall consist of base pensions and individual account benefits.

A rural resident who is a member of the new rural social insurance of the old-age pension shall receive benefits of the new rural social insurance of the old-age pension on a monthly basis when the member satisfies the conditions set by the State.

Article 22 The State shall establish and improve the social insurance of the old-age pension for urban residents.

The People's Government of a province, autonomous region or municipality directly under the Central Government may, in accordance with its circumstances, adopt an integrated programme to combine its social insurance of the old-age pension for urban residents with its new rural social insurance of the old-age pension.

Chapter 3

Basic Medical Insurance

Article 23 Each labourer shall enroll in the basic medical insurance system for labourers, and the employing unit and labourers shall jointly make basic medical insurance contributions as set by the State.

A proprietor of privately or individually owned business with no hired labour, a part-time labourer who is not covered by the basic medical insurance system for labourers through his or her employing unit, or any other person in flexible employment may enroll in the basic medical insurance system for labourers, and the individual in question shall make basic medical insurance contributions as set by the State.

Article 24 The State shall establish and improve the new rural cooperative medical system.

The administration of the new rural cooperative medical system shall be regulated by the State Council.

Article 25 The State shall establish and improve the basic medical insurance system for urban residents.

Basic medical insurance for urban residents shall be a combination of individual contributions and government subsidies.

The assessed individual contributions for beneficiaries of minimum living allowances, disabled persons who are unfit for work, senior citizens aged more than 60 years and minors from low-income families shall be covered by government subsidies.

Article 26 The benefits of basic medical insurance for labourers, the new rural cooperative medical system and basic medical insurance for urban residents shall be governed by national provisions.

Article 27 A member of the basic medical insurance for labourers who satisfies the condition set by the State in terms of cumulative length of contribution payment upon reaching the statutory retirement age shall make no more basic medical insurance contributions after retirement and be entitled to basic medical insurance benefits in accordance with national provisions; the member who does not satisfy that condition may make further contributions to reach the length of the years set by the State.

Article 28 Medical expenses for pharmaceuticals listed in the basic medical insurance directory, for diagnosis and treatment services and application of medical care facilities covered by the basic medical insurance, and medical expenses for emergencies and rescue services shall be paid from the basic medical insurance fund in accordance with national provisions.

Article 29 Direct transactions shall be arranged between social insurance agencies and medical institutions and pharmaceutical entities to settle for insured members the proportion of the medical expenses payable by the basic medical insurance fund.

Social insurance administrative departments and health administrative departments shall set up a mechanism to settle medical expenses incurred in different localities, facilitating access of the insured members to their basic medical insurance benefits.

Article 30 Medical expenses listed as follows are not covered by the basic medical insurance fund:

(1) Expenses payable from the work-related injury insurance fund,
(2) Expenses payable by a third party,
(3) Expenses payable by public health, and
(4) Expenses for overseas medical services.

For medical expenses payable by a third party, when the third party refuses to pay or cannot be identified, interim payment shall be arranged from the basic medical insurance fund. The basic medical insurance fund has the right to demand repayment by the third party after providing the interim payment.

Article 31 Social insurance agencies may, for the sake of managing services, sign service agreements with medical institutions and pharmaceutical entities to regulate medical service performance.

Medical institutions shall provide insured members with medical services deemed suitable and necessary.

Article 32 The basic medical insurance relationship of a member who has worked across different pooling districts shall transfer together with the member, and the member's lengths of contribution payment shall be cumulative.

Chapter 4

Work-related Injury Insurance

Article 33 Each labourer shall enroll in the work injury insurance system. An employing unit shall make work injury contributions, and a labourer is not liable for contributions.

Article 34 Differentiated rates of contributions for industries shall be determined by the State with due consideration of the risk levels associated with the industries. The rate for each industry shall be subdivided into stages according to the following factors: expenditures paid by work-related injury funds and frequency of work-related injury occurrences. The differentiated rates of contributions for industries and the rate stages for each industry shall be formulated by the social insurance administrative department of the State Council and published and put into practice after approval by the State Council.

A social insurance agency shall determine the rate of contributions for an employing unit according to the following factors: the employing unit's expenditures paid by the work-related injury fund, frequency of work-related injury occurrences in the business facility, and rate stage for the industry branch of the business.

Article 35 Each employing unit shall make work injury contributions at the rate set by the social insurance agency of its labourers' payroll.

Article 36 A labourer shall be entitled to work-related injury benefits when he or she is injured in an accident arising out of employment or is affected by occupational diseases and has undertaken work-related injury certification. The employee shall be entitled to disability benefits if the person has become unfit for work as assessed in the working fitness assessment.

Work injury certification and working fitness assessment shall be simple and convenient to perform.

Article 37 A labourer who is injured or dies at work due to one of the following factors shall not be certified as a victim of work-related injuries:

(1) Committing a crime intentionally,
(2) Insobriety or drug addiction,

(3) Self-mutilation or suicide, or
(4) Any other circumstance as provided by laws and administrative regulations.

Article 38 The following expenses related to work-related injury are payable from the work-related injury fund in accordance with national provisions:

(1) Medical expenses for work-related injury and rehabilitation expenses,
(2) Food allowances during hospitalization,
(3) Transportation, accommodation and food expenses incurred for medical services outside the pooling district,
(4) Expenses for provision and installation of disability aid equipment,
(5) The expenses of personal care as set by the working fitness assessment committee for people who need personal care in life,
(6) Lump-sum disability subsidies and disability allowances payable on a monthly basis to disabled labourers of degrees one through four,
(7) Lump-sum medical subsidies payable to employees upon termination or rescinding of labour contracts,
(8) Funeral expenses, pension allowances for dependents and subsidies for work-related deaths paid to survivors when labourers die from work-related causes, and
(9) Expenses incurred for working fitness assessments.

Article 39 The following expenses incurred for work injury shall be payable by the employing unit in accordance with national provisions:

(1) Wages and welfare expenses for the duration of work-related injury treatment,
(2) Disability allowances paid each month to disabled labourers of degrees five and six, and
(3) Lump-sum subsidies for disability employment eligible by labourers upon termination or rescinding of labour contracts.

Article 40 When work-injured labourers meet the conditions for receiving basic old-age pensions, payment of disability allowances shall cease, and the labourers shall instead receive basic old-age pensions. If basic old-age pensions are less than disability allowances, the differentials shall be made up of the work injury insurance fund.

Article 41 When a work-related injury occurs while the employing unit does not make work-related injury contributions as required by law, work-related injury benefits shall be paid by the employing unit. If the employing unit refuses to pay, interim payment shall be arranged from the work-related injury insurance fund.

Interim payment for work-related injury benefits paid from the work-related injury fund shall be paid off by the employing unit. When the employing unit refuses to pay off, the social insurance agency may demand repayment in accordance with Article 63 of this law.

Article 42 When a work-related injury is caused by a third party and the third party refuses to pay medical expenses for work-related injury treatment or the third party cannot be identified, interim payment for the expenses shall be arranged from the work-related injury insurance fund. The work-related injury insurance fund has the right to demand repayment from the third party after providing the interim payment.

Article 43 A labourer suffering from work-related injuries shall cease receipt of work injury benefits when one of the following conditions is met:

(1) Losing eligibility for benefits,
(2) Refusing working fitness assessment, or
(3) Refusing medical treatment.

Chapter 5

Unemployment Insurance

Article 44 Each labourer shall enroll in the unemployment insurance system, and the employing unit and labourer shall jointly make unemployment insurance contributions as set by the State.

Article 45 An unemployed person shall receive unemployment benefits from the unemployment insurance fund when the following conditions are met:

(1) The employing unit and the person in question have made unemployment insurance contributions no less than one year prior to unemployment,
(2) Termination of employment is not caused by the intentional actions of the person in question, and
(3) The person in question has registered as unemployed and is a jobseeker.

Article 46 Where the cumulative length of contribution payment of the unemployed person and his or her employing unit prior to unemployment is greater than one year and less than five years, the maximum duration for unemployment benefits shall be twelve months; where the cumulative length is greater than five years but less than ten years, the maximum duration for unemployment benefits shall be eighteen months; where the cumulative length exceeds ten years, the maximum duration for unemployment benefits shall be twenty-four months. Where a person becomes unemployed once again after taking up a new job, the length of contribution payment shall be counted anew, the duration for unemployment benefits shall be counted together with the balances left over from the entitled duration in the previous case, and the maximum shall not exceed twenty-four months.

Article 47 The standard of unemployment benefits shall be determined by the People's Government of a province, autonomous region or municipality under the Central Government and shall be no less than the minimum living allowances for urban residents in the region.

Article 48 For the duration of receiving unemployment benefits, unemployed persons shall be entitled to basic medical insurance benefits if they are members of the basic medical insurance for employees.

Basic medical insurance contributions due from unemployed persons shall be paid from the unemployment insurance fund. Unemployed persons are not liable for basic medical insurance contributions.

Article 49 Where an unemployed person dies while still a beneficiary of unemployment benefits, local regulations on welfare associated with death of an employed person shall serve as a reference with regard to payment to the independents of a lump-sum funeral subsidy and bereavement allowance. The expenditures shall be covered by the unemployment insurance fund.

When a person dies and concurrently qualifies for a funeral subsidy under basic old-age insurance, a funeral subsidy under work-related injury insurance, and a funeral subsidy under unemployment insurance, the dependents can only choose one of the three.

Article 50 An employing unit shall provide documentation on termination or rescinding of labour relationships to unemployed persons in a timely manner and present the list of unemployed persons to the social insurance agency within fifteen days as of termination or rescinding of their labour relationships.

An unemployed person shall take the documentation provided by his or her employer on termination or rescinding of labour relationships and proceed to the designated public employment agency to process unemployment registration in a timely manner.

An unemployed person shall present unemployment registration and personal identity documents to the social insurance agency to process the claim for unemployment benefits. The duration for unemployment benefits shall be counted as of the date of unemployment registration.

Article 51 An unemployed person who is a beneficiary of unemployment benefits shall cease receipt of unemployment benefits and shall cease access to other benefits related to unemployment insurance in case that the person:

(1) takes up a new job,
(2) is enlisted for military service,
(3) migrates overseas,
(4) receives a basic old-age pension, or
(5) declines without justification a suitable job offer referred by or a training programme provided by the department or agency designated by the local People's Government.

Article 52 The unemployment insurance relationship of a member who has worked across different pooling districts shall transfer together with the member, and the member's lengths of contribution payment shall be cumulative.

Chapter 6

Maternity Insurance

Article 53 Each labourer shall enroll in the maternity insurance system. An employing unit shall make maternity insurance contributions as set by the State, and the labourer is not liable for maternity insurance contributions.

Article 54 When the employing unit has made maternity insurance contributions, its labourers shall be eligible for maternity benefits. The unemployed spouse of a labourer shall be eligible for benefits related to maternity medical expenses in accordance with national provisions. The payment shall be made from the maternity insurance fund.

Maternity insurance benefits consist of maternity medical expenses and maternity allowances.

Article 55 Maternity medical expenses cover the following items:

(1) Medical expenses for child-bearing,
(2) Medical expenses for family planning, and
(3) Expenses for other items as prescribed by laws and regulations.

Article 56 A labourer is eligible for maternity allowances in accordance with national provisions in case of any of the following occurrences:

(1) A child-bearing female labourer takes maternal leave,
(2) The labourer takes leave for an operation of family planning; or
(3) Any other circumstance prescribed by laws and regulations.

Maternity allowance shall be calculated and paid at the monthly mean wage of the prior year of the labourers from the unit where the beneficiary works.

Chapter 7

Collection and Payment of Social Insurance Contributions

Article 57 An employing unit shall, within thirty days from the date of its establishment, proceed with the business licence, registration certificate or entity seal to the local social insurance agency to apply for social insurance registration. The social insurance agency shall complete the check and review process and issue a social insurance registration certificate to the employing unit within fifteen days from receipt of the application.

When there are changes in the social insurance registration items of an employing unit or the entity of an employing unit is terminated in accordance with law, the employing unit shall proceed to the social insurance agency to register the changes or cancel social insurance registration within thirty days from occurrence of the changes or cancellation of the entity.

Each administration department for market regulation, department of civil affairs and public sector reform commission shall notify the social insurance agency in a timely manner of entity establishments and terminations; each department for public security shall notify the social insurance agency in a timely manner of citizen births and deaths, and of household registrations, transfers and cancellations.

Article 58 An employing unit shall, within thirty days after employment of a labourer, proceed to the social insurance agency to apply for social insurance registrations on behalf of the labourer. For those whose social insurance registrations are not processed, the assessed scale of social insurance contributions shall be set by the social insurance agency.

A member who enrolls voluntarily in a social insurance system as a proprietor of privately or individually owned business without labourers, a part-time labourer who is not covered by a social insurance system through his or her employing unit, or any other person in flexible employment shall apply for his or her social insurance registration with the social insurance agency.

The State provides each individual with a social security number valid across the whole country. The citizen's identity number serves as his or her social security number.

Article 59 The People's Governments at and above the county level shall devote more effort to collecting social insurance contributions.

Collection of social insurance contributions shall be carried out in a consolidated way. The steps of implementation and the concrete approaches in this regard shall be regulated by the State Council.

Article 60 Each employing unit shall declare on its own and pay on time and in full social insurance contributions. The payment shall not be deferred, lowered in amount or exempted unless due to lawful causes such as force majeure. Social insurance contributions payable by a labourer shall be paid on his or her behalf by the employing unit through transfer from wage deduction. The employing unit shall notify each labourer of details of social insurance contributions to his or her account on a monthly basis.

A member as a proprietor of privately or individually owned business without labourers, a part-time labourer who is not covered by the social insurance system through his or her employing unit, or any other person in flexible employment may pay social insurance contributions directly to a social insurance contribution collecting agency.

Article 61 Each social insurance contribution collecting agency shall collect social insurance contributions on time and in full according to law and notify the employing unit and individuals concerned of their payments at regular intervals.

Article 62 When an employing unit fails to declare social insurance payables as prescribed, the payables by the employing unit shall be set as a 110% multiples of its prior-month payables. When the employing unit has completed a makeup payment declaration, the social insurance contributions collecting agency shall settle the accounts for the employing unit in accordance with relevant regulations.

Article 63 When an employing unit fails to pay on time and in full social insurance contributions, the social insurance contributions collecting agency shall compel the employing unit to pay or replenish the deficiency within the prescribed period.

When social insurance payables by the employing unit remain unpaid or deficient at the expiry of the prescribed period, the social insurance contributions collecting agency has the right to enquire from banks and other financial institutions regarding the employing unit's bank accounts and may apply to the relevant administrative department at or above the county level for a decision on capital transfer for social insurance contributions and notify in writing the banks or other financial institutions where the employing unit has opened accounts to make the transfer for payment of social insurance contributions. When the balances in the employing unit's accounts are less than the social insurance payables, the social insurance contributions collecting agency may require the employing unit to provide a guarantee and sign an agreement on payment deferral.

When an employing unit fails to pay social insurance contributions in full and fails to provide a guarantee, the social insurance contributions collecting agency may request a people's court to seize, seal up and sell at auction properties owned by the employing unit equivalent in value to the social insurance payables and collect the auction earnings as social insurance contributions.

Chapter 8

Social Insurance Funds

Article 64 Social insurance funds consist of the basic old-age insurance fund, basic medical insurance fund, work-related injury insurance fund, unemployment insurance fund, and maternity insurance fund. Each fund shall have its own account, corresponding to its social insurance category, and financial settlement of the accounts shall be kept within the category. The national standard accounting system shall apply to social insurance funds.

Social insurance funds are earmarked for intended purposes. Any organisation or individual shall not be usurped or diverted.

The basic old-age insurance fund shall be progressively put under nationwide pooling, and other social insurance funds shall be progressively put under social pooling at a provincial level. The concrete timeframe and schedules shall be provided by the State Council.

Article 65 Social insurance funds shall maintain a balance of payments through budgeting exercises.

The People's Governments at and above the county level shall provide subsidies when there is a shortfall in social insurance funds to cover obligations.

Article 66 Budget for a social insurance fund shall be set up at the pooling level. Each social insurance fund budget shall correspond to its insurance category and be compiled and formulated in separation from each other.

Article 67 Compilation, review and approval of budget and final account proposals for a social insurance fund shall be governed by laws and by regulations of the State Council.

Article 68 Social insurance funds shall be deposited into dedicated public financial accounts, and the administrative approaches shall be regulated by the State Council.

Article 69 With assured safety as a prerequisite, social insurance funds shall be invested, and managed following rules set by the State Council to achieve maintenance and accrual of capital values of the funds.

Social insurance funds shall be excluded from investments and operations violating the rules, shall not be utilised to offset other government budgets, shall not be spent on building or altering offices, nor shall they be used to cover personnel expenses, operational and administrative costs. The funds shall not be embezzled for other purposes in violation of the laws and administrative regulations.

Article 70 Social insurance agencies shall provide at regular intervals to the public information concerning social insurance coverage and the incomes and expenditures, balances and investment returns of social insurance funds.

Article 71 The State establishes the National Social Security Fund, which is financed by fiscal allocation of the Central Government and other resources approved by the State Council. The fund is used to supplement and adjust social security expenditures. The National Social Security Fund shall be put to the National Social Security Fund administrative and operating agency for management and fund operations. Maintenance and accrual of capital values of the fund shall be realised with assured safety as a prerequisite.

The National Social Security Fund shall provide at regular intervals to the public the information concerning revenues and expenditures, management and investment operations of the Fund. The department of finance, social insurance administrative department and audit office under the State Council discharge supervision of the fund in relation to its revenues and expenditures, management and investment operations.

Chapter 9

Social Insurance Operations

Article 72 Each pooling district shall set up a social insurance agency. A social insurance agency may, given its workload, set up branches and service network points within the pooling district with approval from the local social insurance administrative department and the local public sector reform commission.

Personnel expenses of a social insurance agency, its essential operational costs and administration expenses shall be appropriated from the government at the same administrative level as the agency in accordance with national provisions.

Article 73 Each social insurance agency shall establish and improve the institution for its business operations, finance, safety and risk management.

Social insurance agencies shall pay social insurance benefit obligations on time and in full.

Article 74 Social insurance agencies collect data required for their work on social insurance through business operations, statistics, and surveys. The employing units and individuals concerned shall provide data in a faithful and timely manner.

A social insurance agency shall create files in a timely manner for an employing unit, keep comprehensive and accurate records of the insured members and social insurance contributions, and guard in a safe way original proofs of social insurance registrations and declarations of contributions and accounting invoices of the payments made.

A social insurance agency shall keep an updated, comprehensive and accurate record for each insured member with regard to the contributions paid by the member and by the employing unit on his or her behalf, his or her social insurance benefit credits, and deliver to the member free of charge his or her credit account at fixed intervals.

An employing unit and an individual member may enquire about and verify their records of contributions and social insurance benefit credits with the social insurance agency free of charge and demand from the social insurance agency social insurance consultancy and other services.

Article 75 In line with the overall design of the State, the National Social Insurance Information System shall be jointly constructed by the People's Governments at and above the county level, following the principle of the jurisdiction-based responsibility system.

Chapter 10

Social Insurance Supervision

Article 76 The Standing Committee of the People's Congress at every level shall be briefed by the People's Government at its corresponding level and review its report on income and expenditure accounts, management, investment operations and supervisions of social insurance funds, shall orgaise enforcement inspections on this law and discharge its supervisory functions by law.

Article 77 The social insurance administrative department of the People's Government at or above the county level shall devote more vigorous efforts to supervise and inspect compliance by employing units and individuals with social insurance laws and regulations.

When a social insurance administrative department performs an inspection or supervision, the employing units and individuals concerned shall faithfully provide documents and data related to social insurance and shall not refuse inspection nor provide fraudulent information or practice underreporting.

Article 78 Finance departments and audit offices within their respective jurisdiction shall carry out supervisions on social insurance funds in terms of income and expenditure accounts, management and investment operations.

Article 79 Social insurance administrative departments shall exercise supervisions and inspections over social insurance funds in terms of income and expenditure accounts, management and investment operations. When an administrative department identifies a problem, it shall put forward corrective recommendations and make a punitive decision or recommend a punitive proposal to the relevant authorities according to law. Inspection reports on social insurance funds shall be provided to the public at regular intervals.

A social insurance administrative department shall have the right to adopt the following measures when exercising supervision and inspection over social insurance funds:

(1) Accessing, recording and copying materials related to income and expenditure accounts, management and investment operations of social insurance funds, and sealing materials liable to be transferred, concealed or destroyed for the sake of safekeeping,
(2) Enquiring of the employing units and individuals involved in an investigation and requiring them to explain and provide relevant evidence on the matters under investigation, and
(3) Interdicting and ordering for rectification the acts of concealing, transferring, misappropriating or embezzling social insurance funds.

Article 80 The People's Government in a pooling district shall establish a social insurance supervisory committee composed of representatives of employing units, insured persons and trade unions, and professional experts. The committee shall have full knowledge and conduct an analysis of social insurance funds in terms of income and expenditure accounts, management, and investment operations. The committee can provide consultancies and recommendations on social insurance affairs and perform public oversight.

A social insurance agency shall brief the social insurance supervisory committee at regular intervals on the performance of social insurance funds and report the funds' income and expenditure accounts, management and investment operations. A social insurance supervisory committee can hire an accounting firm to conduct annual audits and specified audits for income and expenditure accounts, management and investment operations of social insurance funds. Auditing reports should be provided to the public at regular intervals.

When a social insurance supervisory committee identifies a problem associated with income and expenditure accounts, management, and investment operations of social insurance funds, it shall have the right to put forward corrective recommendations and shall have the right to recommend a punitive measure stipulated in law to the authoritative department for any unlawful act of a social insurance agency and its labourers.

Article 81 Social insurance administrative departments and other administrative departments concerned, social insurance agencies, social insurance contributions collecting agencies and their labourers shall keep secret the data of the employing units and the individuals according to law, and shall not disclose data in any manner.

Article 82 Any organisation or individual shall have the right to report or complain about any noncompliance of social insurance laws and regulations.

Any social insurance administrative department, health administrative department, social insurance agency, social insurance contributions collecting agency, finance department and audit office shall deal with the complaints or reporting that fall under its jurisdiction according to law; for a case beyond its jurisdiction, a notification in writing together with the documents received shall be passed on to the proper authoritative department or agency to address. The proper authoritative department or agency shall handle the complaints and reporting in a timely manner, and the responsibility shall not be shirked.

Article 83 When an employing unit or individual believes that their legitimate rights have been violated by an act or acts of a social insurance contribution collecting agency, the employing unit or individual in question can apply for an administrative review or initiate administrative proceedings according to law.

For any noncompliance by a social insurance agency with regard to social insurance registration, calculation and determination of social insurance contributions, paying social insurance benefit obligations, processing transfer or renewal of social insurance relationships, or any other act violating social insurance rights, the employing unit or individual concerned can apply for an administrative review or initiate administrative proceedings according to law.

When a dispute on social insurance occurs between an individual and his or her employing unit, the person in question can apply for mediation, arbitration or initiate court proceedings according to law. When an employing unit infringes upon the social insurance rights of an individual, the individual in question may also demand a lawful settlement by the social insurance administrative department or social insurance contributions collecting agency.

Chapter 11

Legal Liabilities

Article 84 When an employing unit fails to apply for social insurance registration, the social insurance administrative department shall deliver to the employing unit concerned an order for rectification within a prescribed period. When rectification does not occur at the expiry of the prescribed period, the employing unit shall be liable for a fine in excess of its assessed social insurance contribution but less than its triple, and the principals who bear direct responsibilities and other persons with direct responsibilities shall be liable for a fine over 500 but less than 3000 Yuan RBM.

Article 85 When an employing unit refuses to provide documentation on termination or rescinding of labour relationships, a sanction shall be given in accordance with the Labour Contract Law of the People's Republic of China.

Article 86 When an employing unit fails to pay social insurance contributions on time and in full, the social insurance contributions collecting agency shall order the employing unit to pay in full within a prescribed period, and an overdue payment fine at the rate of 5 per 10,000 shall be levied as of the date of indebtedness. When the payment is not made at the expiry of the prescribed period, a fine above the overdue amount but less than its triple shall be demanded by the authoritative administrative department.

Article 87 When a social insurance service agency such as a social insurance agency, medical institution, or pharmaceutical entity defrauds payment from social insurance funds by cheating, fake documentation or other means, the social insurance administrative agency shall order the agency to return the defrauded fund and demand a sanction larger than double but lower than quintuple of the amount defrauded. If the agency involved is one with a contract for the provision of social insurance services, such contract shall be terminated; if the principals who bear direct responsibilities and other persons with direct responsibilities are licensed, their licences shall be revoked according to law.

Article 88 For any offence of making fraudulent claims for social insurance benefits through cheating, fake documentation or other means, the social insurance administrative department shall order a return of the social insurance benefits defrauded and levy a fine larger than double but less than quintuple of the amount defrauded.

Article 89 When a social insurance agency and its staff commit an offence included in the following list, the social insurance administrative department shall order it or them to make rectifications. When damage has been done to social insurance funds, an employing unit or an individual, liability for damage shall be assumed by the person(s) responsible according to law. The principals who bear direct responsibilities and other persons with direct responsibilities shall be sanctioned by law.

(1) Not discharging social insurance statutory functions,
(2) Not depositing social insurance funds into dedicated financial accounts,
(3) Underpaying or refusing to pay on time social insurance benefit obligations,
(4) Missing or interpolating social insurance data such as contribution records, payment records of social insurance benefits, and individuals' credit records,
(5) Any other noncompliance of social insurance laws and regulations.

Article 90 When a social insurance contribution collecting agency amends without authorisation the calculating base and rate of social insurance contributions, which leads to under or over collection of social insurance contributions, the authoritative administrative department shall order it to return the overdue or return of the overpayment. The principals who bear direct responsibilities and other persons with direct responsibilities shall be sanctioned by law.

Article 91 For any act in violation of this law involving concealing, transferring, misappropriating or embezzling social insurance funds or engaging in investment operations in defiance of rules, the social insurance administrative department, finance department, audit office shall give an order for repayment of the misappropriated funds. If any illegal gains have been obtained, the gains shall be confiscated. The principals who bear direct responsibilities and other persons with direct responsibilities shall be sanctioned by law.

Article 92 When a social insurance administrative department or any other relevant administrative department, social insurance agency, social insurance contributions collecting agency and its staff disclose information concerning an employing unit or an individual, the principals who bear direct responsibilities and other persons with direct responsibilities shall be sanctioned by law. If damage has been done to the employing unit or individual, liability for damage shall be assumed by the person(s) responsible according to law.

Article 93 Public officials who abuse their power, neglect their duties, or engage in fraudulent acts for personal gains shall be sanctioned according to law.

Article 94 Any offender who violates this Law and commits a crime shall be liable for criminal penalties.

Chapter 12

Supplementary Provisions

Article 95 Rural residents who migrate to work in urban areas shall enroll in the social insurance system in accordance with this Law.

Article 96 When land acquisition is carried out on properties collectively owned by a farming community, a full payment of social insurance expenses shall be arranged for the farmers who lose their land, and the farmers in question shall be covered in relevant social insurance schemes in accordance with the regulations of the State Council.

Article 97 Foreign nationals who are employed in the Chinese territory shall enroll in the social insurance system in accordance with this Law.

Article 98 This law shall enter into force on 1 July 2011.

Rules for the Administration of Employment of Foreigners in China[8]

(Promulgated jointly by the Ministry of Labour, the Ministry of Public Security, the Foreign Ministry and the Ministry of Foreign Trade and Economic Cooperation of the People's Republic of China on 22 January 1996 and revised on 12 November 2010 and on 13 March 2017).

Chapter 1

General Provisions

Article 1 These Rules are formulated in accordance with the provisions of the relevant laws and decrees for the purpose of strengthening the administration of employment of foreigners in China.

Article 2 The term "foreigners" in these Rules refers to persons who, under the Nationality Law of the People's Republic of China, do not have Chinese nationality.

The term "employment of foreigners in China" in these Rules refers to acts of foreigners without permanent residence status to engage in remunerative work within Chinese territory in accordance with its laws.

Article 3 These Rules shall apply to employed foreigners within Chinese territory and their employers.

These Rules shall not apply to foreigners who enjoy diplomatic privileges and immunities employed by foreign embassies or consulates or the offices of the United Nations and other international organisations in China.

Article 4 The labour administrative authorities of the people's government of the provinces, autonomous regions and municipalities directly under the Central Government and those at the prefecture and city level with their authorisation are responsible for the administration of employment of foreigners in China.

Chapter 2

Employment Licence

Article 5 The employer shall apply for the employment permission if it intends to employ foreigners and may do so after obtaining approval and the People's

[8] The State Council of the PRC. (2018). *Rules for the Administration of Employment of Foreigners in China*. Retrieved 5 March, 2021, from http://english.www.gov.cn/services/work_in_china/2018/08/02/content_281476245886934.htm

Republic of China Employment Licence for Foreigners (hereinafter referred to as the "Employment Licence").

Article 6 The post to be filled by the foreigner recruited by the employer shall be the post of special need, a post that cannot be filled by any domestic candidates for the time being but violates no government regulations.

No employer shall employ foreigners to engage in commercialised entertaining performances, except for the persons qualified under Article 9 (3) of these Rules.

Article 7 Any foreigner seeking employment in China shall meet the following conditions:

(1) 18 years of age or older and in good health,
(2) with professional skills and job experience required for the work,
(3) with no criminal record,
(4) a definite employer,
(5) with valid passports or other international travel documents in lieu of the passport (hereinafter referred to as the "travel document").

Article 8 Foreigner seeking employment in China shall hold the Employment Visas of Z for their entry (In case of agreement for mutual exemption of visas, the agreement shall prevail. and may work within Chinese territory only after they obtain the Employment Permit for Foreigner (hereinafter referred to as the "Employment Permit") and the foreigner residence certificate.

Foreigners who have not issued residence certificates (i.e., holders of F, L, C or G type visas), and those who are under study or interim programmes in China and the families of holders of Z Visas shall not work in China. In special cases, employment may be allowed when the foreigner changes his status at the public security organs with the Employment Licence secured by his employer in accordance with the clearance procedures. Under these Rules, the foreigner changes his status at the public security organs with the Employment Licence and receives his Employment Permit and residence certificate.

The employment in China of the spouses of the personnel of foreign embassies, consulates, representative offices of the United Nations System and other international organisations in China shall follow the Provisions of Ministry of Foreign Affairs of the People's Republic of China Concerning the Employment of the Spouses of the Personnel of Foreign Embassies, Consulates and the Representative Offices of the United Nations System in China and be handled in accordance with the clearance procedures provided for in the second paragraph of this Article.

The Employment Licence and the Employment Permit shall be designed and prepared exclusively by the Ministry of Labour.

Article 9 Foreigners may be exempted from the Employment Licence and Employment Permit when they meet any of the following conditions:

(1) Foreign professional technical and managerial personnel employed directly by the Chinese government or those with senior technical titles or credentials of special skills recognised by their home or international technical authorities or professional associations to be employed by Chinese government organs

and institutions and foreigners holding Foreign Expert Certificate issued by China's Bureau of Foreign Expert Affairs,
(2) Foreigner workers with special skills who work in offshore petroleum operations without the need to go ashore for employment and hold "Work Permit for Foreign Personnel Engaged in the Offshore Petroleum Operations in the People's Republic of China", or
(3) Foreigners who conduct commercialised entertainment performance with the approval of the Ministry of Culture and hold "Permit for Temporary Commercialised Performance".

Article 10 Foreigners may be exempted from the Employment Licence and may apply directly for the Employment Permit by presenting their Employment Visas and relevant papers after their entry when they meet any of the following conditions:

(1) Foreigners employed in China under agreements or accords entered into by the Chinese government with foreign governments or international organisations for the implementation of Sino-foreign projects of cooperation and exchange, or
(2) Chief representatives and representatives of the permanent offices of foreign enterprises in China.

Chapter 3

Application and Approval

Article 11 The employer intending to employ a foreigner shall fill out the Application Form for the Employment for Foreigners (hereinafter referred to as the "Application Form") and submit it to its competent trade authorities at the same level as the labour administrative authorities together with the following documentation:

(1) the curriculum vitae of the foreigner to be employed,
(2) the letter of intention for employment,
(3) the report of reasons for employment,
(4) the credentials of the foreigner required for the performance of the job,
(5) the health certificate of the foreigner to be employed, and
(6) other documents required by regulations.

The competent trade authorities shall examine and approve the application in accordance with Articles 6 and 7 of these Rules and relevant laws and decrees.

Article 12 After approval by competent trade authorities, the employer shall take the Application Form to the labour administrative authorities of the province, autonomous region or municipality directly under the Central Government or the labour administrative authorities at the prefecture and city level where the employer is located for examination and clearance. The labour administration authorities described above shall designate a special body (hereinafter referred to as the "Certificate Office") to take up the responsibility of issuing the Employment Licence.

The Certificate Office should take into consideration the opinions of the competent trade authorities and the demand and supply of the labour market and issue the Employment Licence to the employer after examination and clearance.

Article 13 Employers at the central level or those without competent trade authorities may submit their application directly to the Certificate Office of the labour administrative authorities for the Employment Permit.

Examination and approval by competent trade authorities are not required for foreign-funded enterprises to employ foreigners, and such enterprises may submit their applications directly to the Certificate Office of the labour administrative authorities for the Employment Licence, bringing with them the contract, articles of association, certificate of approval, business licence and documentation referred to in Article 11 of these Rules.

Article 14 Foreigners with permission to work in China should apply for the Visas of Z at the Chinese embassies, consulates and visa offices, bringing with them the Employment Licence and the valid passport or other papers in lieu of the valid passport.

The persons referred to in Article 9 (2) should apply for the Employment Visas of Z by presenting their letter or telex of visa notification issued by the China National Offshore Oil Corporation; the persons referred to in Article 9 (3) should apply for the Employment Visas of Z by presenting the approval of the Ministry of Culture. The persons referred to in Article 10 (1) of these Rules should apply for the Employment Visas of Z by presenting the documentation on projects of cooperation and exchange. The persons referred to in Article 10 (2) should apply for the Employment Visas of Z by presenting the registration certification issued by the administrative authorities of industry and commerce.

Article 15 The employer should, within fifteen days after the entry of the employed foreigner, take to the original Certificate Office the Employment Licence, the labour contract with the said foreigner and his passport or other papers in lieu of the passport to receive his Employment Permit while filling out the Foreigner Employment Registration Form.

The Employment Permit shall be effective only within the area specified by the Certificate Office.

Article 16 Foreigners who received their Employment Permit should, within thirty days after their entry, apply for the residence certificate with the public security organs bringing with them their Employment Permit. The term validity of the residence certificate may be determined in accordance with the term validity of the Employment Permit.

Chapter 4

Labour Administration

Article 17 The employer and its foreign employee should, in accordance with law, conclude a labour contract, the term of which shall not exceed five years. Such a contract may be renewed upon expiry after the completion of the clearance process in accordance with Article 19 of these Rules.

Article 18 The Employment Permit of the employed foreigner shall cease to be effective upon the expiry of the term of the labour contract between the foreigner and his employer. If renewal is required, the employer should, within thirty days prior to the expiry of the contract, submit an application to the labour administrative authorities for the extension of term of employment, and after approval is obtained, proceed to go through formalities for the extension of the Employment Permit.

Article 19 The foreign employee should, within ten days after obtaining the approval for extension of his term of employment in China or the change of his employment location or his employer, go through formalities for the extension or change of his residence certificate at the local public security organs.

Article 20 After the termination of the labour contract between the foreign employee and his employer, the employer should promptly report it to the labour and public security authorities, return the Employment Permit and the residence certificate of the said foreigner, and go through formalities for his exit from China.

Article 21 The wage paid to foreign employees by the employer shall not be lower than the minimum wage in the locality.

Article 22 The working hours, rest and vacation, work safety and health and the social security of foreign employees in China shall follow the relevant provisions of the State.

Article 23 The employer of the foreign employee in China shall be the same as specified in his Employment Licence.

When the foreigner switches employers within the area designated by the Certificate Office but stays in a job of the same nature, the change must be approved by the original Certificate Office and recorded in his Employment Permit.

If the foreigner is to be employed outside the area designated by the Certificate Office or switches employer within original designated area while taking up jobs of a different nature, he must go through formalities for a new Employment Licence.

Article 24 For foreigners whose residence status is revoked by public security organs due to his violation of Chinese law, his labour contract should be terminated by his employer, and his Employment Permit should be withdrawn by the labour administrative authorities.

Article 25 Should labour disputes arise between the employer and its foreign employee, they should be handled in accordance with the Labour Law of the People's Republic of China and the Labour Dispute Mediation and Arbitration Law.

Article 26 The Labour administrative authorities shall conduct an annual inspection of the Employment Permit. Within thirty days prior to the end of every year of employment of the foreigner, the employer should go through formalities of the annual inspection at the Certificate Office of the labour administrative authorities. The Employment Permit shall automatically cease to be effective when the deadline is passed.

In case of loss or damage of the Employment Permit during the term of his employment in China, the foreigner should promptly report it to the original Certificate Office and go through formalities for the issuance of the Employment Permit.

Chapter 5

Penalty Provisions

Article 27 Violation of these Rules, i.e., foreigners who work without the Employment Permit or employers who hire foreigners without the Employment Licence, shall be handled by the public security organs in accordance with Article 44 of the Rules Governing the Implementation of the Law of the People's Republic of China on the Entry and Exit of Aliens.

Article 28 For foreigners who refuse to have their Employment Permits inspected by the labour administrative authorities, change their employers and professions at will or extend their term of employment without permission, the labour administrative authorities shall withdraw their Employment Permits and recommend that their residence status be canceled by the public security organs. In the case of deportation, the costs and expenses shall be borne by the foreigners or their employers.

Article 29 For foreigners and employers who forge, alter, falsely use, transfer, buy and sell the Employment Permit and the Employment Licence, the Labour administrative authorities shall take over the Employment Permit and the Employment Licence in question, confiscate the illegal proceeds and impose a fine between ten thousand and one hundred thousand yuan. In serious cases that constitute a crime, they shall be prosecuted for criminal liability by the judicial authorities.

Article 30 In case of abuse of power, illegal collection of fees, and fraudulent practices on the part of official personnel of the Certificate Office or other departments, they shall be investigated in accordance with the law for their criminal responsibility if crimes are committed, or they shall be subject to administrative disciplinary measures if the cases do not constitute a crime.

Chapter 6

Supplementary Provisions

Article 31 Employment in the mainland of the residents of Taiwan, Hong Kong and Macao of China shall follow the Rules for the Administration of the Employment in the Mainland of the Residents of Taiwan, Hong Kong and Macao.

Article 32 These Rules do not apply to the employment of foreigners in China's Taiwan, Hong Kong and Macao.

Article 32 Individual economic organisations and private citizens are prohibited from employing foreigners.

Article 34 The labour administrative authorities of the provinces, autonomous regions and municipalities directly under the Central Government may formulate their own rules for implementation of these Rules in conjunction with the public security and relevant authorities in the locality and report it to the Ministry of Labour, Ministry of Public Security, the Foreign Ministry and the Ministry of Foreign Trade and Economic Cooperation for the record.

Article 35 The Ministry of Labour shall be responsible for the interpretation of these Rules.

Article 36 These Rules shall enter into force as of 1 May 1996. The Provisions Concerning the Employment in China of the Foreigners Who have not yet Obtained Residence Certificate and Foreigners who Study in China jointly promulgated by the former Ministry of Labour and Personnel and the Ministry of Public Security on 5 October 1987 shall be annulled simultaneously.

Interim Measures for Social Insurance System Coverage of Foreigners Working Within the Territory of China[9]

(Deliberated and passed at the 67th Administrative Meeting of the Ministry of Human Resources and Social Security and approved by the State Council and coming into force as of 15 October 2011).

Article 1 These Measures are formulated in accordance with the Law of the People's Republic of China for Social insurance ("Social Insurance Law") for the purpose of protecting the lawful rights and interests of foreign workers employed in China to participate in social insurance and enjoy the benefits of social insurance, as well as for the purpose of strengthening the management of social insurance.

Article 2 "Foreigner employed in China" means a person who is not of Chinese nationality holding employment certificates and foreigner residence permit certificates such as Work Permit for Foreigners, Foreign Expert Certificate, and Permit for Permanent Foreign Journalists, as well as Foreigner Permanent Residence Certificate, and who is employed lawfully with the territory of China.

Article 3 Foreigners employed by organisations duly incorporated or registered in China, such as enterprises, public institutions, social organisations, private nonenterprise entities, foundations, law firms, accounting firms, etc. ("Employer"), shall participate in basic pension insurance for employees, basic medical insurance for employees, work-related injury insurance, unemployment insurance and maternity insurance. The insurance premiums shall be paid by the Employer and the foreigner pursuant to the applicable regulations.

A foreigner who has concluded an employment contract with his overseas employer and then dispatched to any branch or representative office duly incorporated or registered in China ("Domestic Work Unit") shall participate in basic pension insurance for employees, basic medical insurance for employees, work-related injury insurance, unemployment insurance and maternity insurance. The insurance premiums shall be paid by the Domestic Work Unit and the foreigner pursuant to the applicable regulations.

Article 4 An employer who employs any foreigner shall obtain the social insurance registration for the foreigner within 30 days upon issuance of his/her employment certificate.

---

[9] The State Council of the PRC. (2018). *Interim Measures for Social Insurance System Coverage of Foreigners Working within the Territory of China*. Retrieved 5 March, 2021 from http://english.www.gov.cn/services/work_in_china/2018/08/02/content_281476245985894.htm

The Domestic Work Unit shall obtain the social insurance registration for the foreigner who is dispatched to China by his/her overseas employer.

The agencies issuing employment certificates for foreigners shall report the employment-related information of foreigners in China to local social insurance agencies. Social insurance agencies shall regularly enquire about the status of the employment certificates of foreigners with the relevant agencies.

Article 5 Where a foreigner participating in social insurance satisfies the prescribed conditions, he/she may enjoy social insurance benefits.

If a foreigner leaves China before he/she is qualified for enjoying the pension benefits, his/her individual social insurance account shall be maintained, and his/her period of contributions may be accumulated when he/she is employed in China again; upon his/her written application for termination of the social insurance relationship, the balance in his/her private social insurance account may be refunded in a lump sum.

Article 6 The balance in a foreigner's private social insurance account may be inherited according to law in case of his/her death.

Article 7 A foreigner who receives social insurance benefits outside China on a monthly basis shall at least once a year provide the social insurance agency responsible for paying his/her social insurance benefits with an existence certificate issued by China embassy or consulate or an existence certificate notarised by competent authority in the country where he/she lives in and certified by China embassy or consulate.

A foreigner who lawfully enters China may prove his/her existence by personal presence at the relevant social insurance agency and therefore is not required to provide the existence certificate mentioned in the preceding paragraph.

Article 8 Where there is a dispute between a foreigner participating in social insurance and his/her Employer or Domestic Work Unit, either party may apply for mediation, arbitration or file an action according to law. Where an employer or a domestic work unit infringes on the foreigner's lawful rights and interests, he/she may apply with the social insurance administrative authority or social insurance premiums collecting agency for lawful settlement.

Article 9 Social insurance for foreigners employed in China with nationalities of countries who have concluded bilateral or multilateral treaties upon social insurance with China shall be handled in accordance with respective treaties.

Article 10 The agencies responsible for social insurance shall formulate the Social Security Numbering Rules for Foreigners, assign the social security number and distribute the social security cards of the People's Republic of China to foreigners.

Article 11 The social insurance administrative authorities shall supervise and inspect the participation of foreigners in social insurance in accordance with the Social Insurance Law. Where an Employer or a Domestic Work Unit fails to complete the social insurance registration for any employed foreigner or fails to pay the social insurance premium for any foreigner, it shall be handled in accordance with the applicable laws, regulations and rules, including the Social Insurance Law and the Regulations for Supervision over Labour Security.

Where an employer employs any foreign who does not hold a valid employment certificate or the Foreigner Permanent Residence Certificate, it shall be handled in accordance with the Regulations for Administration of Employment of Foreigners in China.

Article 12 These Measures shall come into force as of 15 October 2011.

List of the ILO Conventions Ratified by China

C100-Equal Remuneration Convention, 1951 (no. 100), 2 November 1990, in Force

C111-Discrimination (Employment and Occupation) Convention, 1958 (no. 111), 12 Jan 2006, in Force

C138-Minimum Age Convention, 1973 (no. 138), 28 April 1999, in Force

C182-Worst Forms of Child Labour Convention, 1999 (no. 2), 8 August 2002, in Force

C122-Employment Policy Convention, 1964 (no. 122), 12 December 1997, in Force

C144-Tripartite Consultation (International Labour Standards) Convention, 1976 (no. 144), 2 November 1990, in Force

C011-Right of Association (Agriculture) Convention, 1921 (no. 11), 27 April 1934, in Force

C014-Weekly Rest (Industry) Convention, 1921 (no. 14), 17 May 1934, in Force

C019-Equality of Treatment (Accident Compensation) Convention, 1925 (no. 19), 27 April, 1934, in Force

C026-Minimus Wage-Fixing Machinery Convention, 1928 (no. 26), 5 May 1930, in Force

C027-Marking of Weight (Packages Transported by Vessels) Convention, 1929 (no. 27), 24 June 1931, in Force

C032-Protection Against Accidents (Dockers) Convention (Revised), 1932 (no. 32), 30 November 1935, in Force

C045-Underground Work (Women) Convention, 1935 (no. 45), 2 December 1936, in Force

C080-Final Articles Revision Convention, 1946 (no. 80), 4 August 1947, in Force

C150-Labour Administration Convention, 1978 (no. 150), 7 March 2002, in Force

C155-Occupationaal Safety and Health Convention, 1981 (no. 155), 25 January 2007, in Force

C159-Vocational Rehabilitation and Employment (Disabled Persons) Convention, 1983 (no. 159), 02 February 1988, in Force

C167-Safety and Health in Construction Convention, 1988 (no. 167), 7 March 2002, in Force

C170-Chemicals Convention, 1960 (no. 170), 11 January 1995, in Force

MLC, 2006-Maritime Labour Convention, 2006 (MLC, 2006), 12 Nov 2015, In Force.

Amendments of 2014 to the MLC, 2006, 18 January 2017, Not in Force.

Amendments of 2016 to the MLC, 2006, 8 January 2019, In Force.
Amendments of 2018 to the MLC, 2006, 26 December 2020, In Force.

The manufacturer's authorised representative in the EU is Springer Nature Customer Service Centre GmbH, Europaplatz 3, 69115 Heidelberg, Germany. If you have any concerns regarding our products, please contact ProductSafety@springernature.com

Printed and bound by CPI Group (UK) Ltd, Croydon, CR0 4YY
30/09/2026
02225237-0009